WORK-LIFESTYLE CHOICES IN THE 21ST CENTURY: PREFERENCE THEORY

Work-Lifestyle Choices in the 21st Century

Preference Theory

Catherine Hakim

UNIVERSITY PRESS

OXFORD
UNIVERSITY PRESS

Great Clarendon Street, Oxford OX2 6DP

Oxford University Press is a department of the University of Oxford.
It furthers the University's objective of excellence in research, scholarship,
and education by publishing worldwide in

Oxford New York

Athens Auckland Bangkok Bogotá Buenos Aires Calcutta
Cape Town Chennai Dar es Salaam Delhi Florence Hong Kong Istanbul
Karachi Kuala Lumpur Madrid Melbourne Mexico City Mumbai
Nairobi Paris São Paulo Shanghai Singapore Taipei Tokyo Toronto Warsaw

and associated companies in Berlin Ibadan

Oxford is a registered trade mark of Oxford University Press
in the UK and in certain other countries

Published in the United States
by Oxford University Press Inc., New York

First published 2000

British Library Cataloguing in Publication Data
Data available

Library of Congress Cataloging in Publication Data

Hakim, Catherine.
Work-lifestyle choices in the 21st Century: preference theory/Catherine Hakim.
p. cm.
Includes bibliographical references.
1. Women. 2. Women—Employment. 3. Work and family.
4. Women's studies. I. Title.
HQ1206.H225 2000 305.42—dc21 00–057118

ISBN 0–19–924209–7
ISBN 0–19–924210–0 (pbk)

1 3 5 7 9 10 8 6 4 2

Typeset in Stone Sans and Stone Serif by
Cambrian Typesetters, Frimley, Surrey
Printed in Great Britain
on acid-free paper by
TJ International Ltd, Padstow, Cornwall

For WRH

PREFACE

Individualization has been the driving force for change in late modern societies. Men and women gain not only the freedom to choose their own values and lifestyle, they are also obliged to make their own choices, because there are no universal certainties and no fixed models of the good life. This major study identifies the five separate historical changes in social life and in the labour market which have produced a new scenario of options and opportunities for women. It shows how this new scenario constitutes a fundamental break with the past, giving modern women real choices between a life centred on family work and/or on paid work. This means that we can no longer learn from history when seeking to understand and explain contemporary patterns of women's employment. Building on the most recent empirical research, Catherine Hakim goes further, to identify three preference groups among men and women, each with a distinctive pattern of involvement in careers and family life.

This book offers a genuinely new perspective on women's roles and women's choices. I am sure it will become essential reading for everyone concerned with the new parameters of modern society and those seeking to predict future changes.

Anthony Giddens

ACKNOWLEDGEMENTS

I thank Marianne Sundström in the Demography Unit, Stockholm University, for providing statistics on childlessness from the Swedish Fertility Register. I am indebted to Colin Mills at the LSE for supplying the GHS analyses that formed the basis for Table 7.3. I am indebted to Peter Robert in TARKI, Hungary, for supplying the analyses that formed the basis for Table 7.6. I am indebted to Sophia Alexandraki for her assistance with research on employers' policies for Chapter 8. I am indebted to many people for helpful comments on early chapter drafts and presentations of the theory, in particular Jane Humphries, Nicos Mouzelis, Tony Fahey, John Evans, and George Brown. Table 4.2 is taken from a national survey funded by the Economic and Social Research Council as part of its Research Programme on the Future of Work. Data for Spain quoted in Chapter 4 is taken from an equivalent 1999 national survey in Spain generously carried out for me by Juan Diez-Nicolas, ASEP, Madrid.

The following appear in this book by permission:

Table 3.1 reprinted from Wellings, Wadsworth, Johnson, and Fields, *Teenage Sexuality, Fertility and Life Chances*, 1996, by permission of Kaye Wellings, London School of Hygiene and Tropical Medicine.

Table 3.2 reprinted from Scott, Braun, and Alwin, 'The family way', in R. Jowell (ed.) *International Social Attitudes*, Gower Press, 1993, by permission of Roger Jowell, NCSR.

Table 3.4 reprinted from Hakim, 'A sociological perspective on part-time work', in H-P. Blossfeld and C. Hakim (eds) *Between Equalization and Marginalization*, 1997, by permission of Oxford University Press.

Tables 5.1, 5.2, 5.3, and 5.4 reprinted with minor changes from Dale and Egerton, *Highly Educated Women*, 1997. Crown copyright is reproduced with the permission of the Controller of Her Majesty's Stationery Office.

Table 5.5 reprinted with minor changes from Dex, Joshi, and Macran, 'A widening gulf among Britain's mothers', *Oxford Review of Economic Policy*, 1996, by permission of Oxford University Press.

Table 5.6 reprinted with minor changes from Ward, Dale, and Joshi, 'Income dependency within couples', in L. Morris and E. S. Lyon (eds) *Gender Relations in Public and Private*, 1996, by permission of Macmillan. Copyright © British Sociological Association.

Table 5.7 reprinted from E. Ferri, *Life at 33*, 1993, by permission of the National Children's Bureau.

Table 5.8 reprinted with minor changes from K. Gerson, *Hard Choices: How Women Decide about Career, Work and Motherhood*, 1985, by permission of University of California Press.

Fig. 9.1 reprinted from P. Treadwell, 'Biologic influences on masculinity', in Harry Brod (ed) *The Making of Masculinities*, by permission of Routledge Inc. Copyright © 1987.

CONTENTS

List of Figures xiv
List of Tables xiv
List of Abbreviations xvi

1. Introduction: a Social Science Theory for the 21st Century **1**
A new perspective
The four main tenets of preference theory
Modern society
Reinstating preferences as a causal factor
Britain and the USA as case-studies
Plan of the book
Future changes

2. The Failure to Predict **22**
Prediction versus *post hoc* explanation
The male bias of labour market theory
Feminist contributions
Methodological considerations
Conclusions

3. Causes of the New Scenario **43**
The contraceptive revolution
Voluntary childlessness
The equal opportunities revolution
The expansion of white-collar and service work
The creation of jobs for secondary earners
Lifestyle choices in rich modern societies
Conclusions

4. The Polarization of Preferences and Behaviour **84**
The polarization of sex-role preferences
Does higher education make a difference?
Polarization of attitudes within the workforce
The polarization of women's employment
Continuity and change in income-earning roles
The polarization of household income
Contradictory evidence: rising workrates
Conclusions

5. Things are Different in the Younger Generations: Evidence from Longitudinal Studies 128
The 1958 cohort study—NCDS
Educational attainment
Earnings and the pay gap
Aspirations and sex-role ideology
The financial dependence of wives
Life satisfaction and psychological distress
Younger generations in the USA
Conclusions

6. Heterogeneous Preferences 157
Home-centred women and the marriage career
Work-centred women and the voluntary childfree
Adaptive women: drifters and unplanned careers
Social constraints and contextual influences
Cross-national comparisons
Conflicting interests
Contradictory evidence: female depression
Sources of the three preferences
Conclusions

7. Marriage Markets and Educational Equality 193
Marriage markets
The qualifications gap and educational equality
Educational homogamy of spouses
Role segregation and family relationships
Conclusions

8. Policy Applications 223
The rhetoric and reality of pronatalist policies
Policies for home-centred women
Policies for adaptive women
Policies for work-centred women
Employer and trade union policies
Conclusions

9. Preferences among Men 254
The work-lifestyle preferences of men
Enduring sex differences
The globalization of marriage markets
Male responses to the new scenario
Conclusions

10. Conclusions 273
Work-lifestyle preferences in the 21st century
Beyond sex and gender
Explanations for patriarchy and its success
Methodological implications
Cross-national comparisons
Theorizing social change

References 290
Index 324

LIST OF FIGURES

9.1 Testosterone levels among men and women 259

LIST OF TABLES

1.1 A classification of women's work-lifestyle preferences in the 21st century 6
3.1 Pregnancy and births during teenage years by highest educational qualification among women aged 20–24 in 1991 48
3.2 The increasing acceptability of childlessness 53
3.3 Comparisons of workrates and part-time work in Europe and the USA, 1997 58
3.4 The impact of sex-role ideology on employment rates among women 78
4.1 The diversity of sex-role preferences in Europe 86
4.2 Sex-role preferences in Britain, 1999 93
4.3 Divergent attitudes to the sexual division of labour within the workforce 100
4.4 Patterns of work and inactivity among women of working age by occupational grade 103
4.5 The decline in continuous employment and the marriage career 108
4.6 Young women's workplans and outcomes in the USA 109
4.7 Percentage of total earnings contributed by the husband, on average, in couples with a wife aged 20–60 in 1985 116
4.8 Workrates among mothers of children under school age, Britain 121
5.1 Highest qualifications of men and women: a comparison between 1991 Census data on all 33-year-olds and 1991 NCDS data 132
5.2 Women's earnings as a percentage of men's among full-time employees 136
5.3 Median hourly earnings by highest qualification, hours worked, and sex 137

5.4 Criteria for choosing a new job by highest qualification level 140
5.5 Percentage of potential working life spent employed for two cohorts of young women: NCDS and WES 143
5.6 Income dependency of married and cohabiting women by her employment status and presence of children 145
5.7 Qualifications by number of children at age 33 among NCDS women 146
5.8 Distribution of work-lifeplans of women in their early 30s in the USA 151
6.1 The full classification of women's work-lifestyle preferences in the 21st century 158
7.1 Long-term trends in educationally homogamous marriages and in women marrying up in the USA, 1890–1970 206
7.2 Educational homogamy by highest qualification, Britain, 1949 207
7.3 Educational homogamy in three age cohorts, Britain, 1992 208
7.4 Educational homogamy by highest qualification, Britain, 1996 209
7.5 Long-term trends in educationally homogamous marriages and women marrying up in West Germany, 1900–1978 211
7.6 Trends in educational homogamy at marriage in Hungary, 1950–1992 212
7.7 Trends in educationally homogamous marriages and women marrying up in 23 industrialized nations, 1949–1983 213
8.1 Average tax rate paid by an adult full-time production worker on average earnings in the manufacturing sector, 1994 230
9.1 A classification of men's work-lifestyle preferences in the 21st century 255

ABBREVIATIONS

BHPS	British Household Panel Study
BSAS	British Social Attitudes Survey
EOC	Equal Opportunities Commission
ESRC	Economic and Social Research Council
EU	European Union
GHS	General Household Survey (of Britain)
GSS	General Social Survey (of the USA)
HMSO	Her Majesty's Stationary Office (of Great Britain)
IER	Institute for Employment Research, University of Warwick
ILO	International Labour Office
ISSP	International Social Survey Programme
IUD	Intra-Uterine Device
IVF	*in vitro* fertilization
LFS	Labour Force Survey
NCDS	National Child Development Study (1958 cohort) of Britain
NLS	National Longitudinal Studies (of Labour Market Experience in the USA)
OECD	Organization for Economic Co-operation and Development
ONS	Office of National Statistics
OOPEC	Office for Official Publications of the European Communities
PSID	Panel Study of Income Dynamics (of the USA)
SCELI	Social Change and Economic Life Initiative (of the ESRC in Britain)
WFS	World Fertility Survey
WVS	World Values Surveys

1

Introduction: A Social Science Theory for the 21st Century

This book proposes a new theory for explaining and predicting current and future patterns of women's choices between family work and market work, a theory that is historically-informed, empirically-based, multidisciplinary, prospective rather than retrospective in orientation, and applicable in all rich modern societies. Our aim is a theory that is genuinely universal.

This chapter presents the main tenets of preference theory in summary form. Subsequent chapters elaborate these central themes and present the empirical evidence on which the theory rests. For reasons specified later, we focus on studies carried out from 1965 onwards, and the USA and Britain provide our central case-studies. However, preference theory was developed with reference to all prosperous modern societies, and we draw on research evidence from a wide range of countries in Europe, North America, South America, South-East Asia, Africa, and Australasia.

A New Perspective

Preference theory is concerned primarily with women's choice between family work and market work: a genuine choice in affluent modern societies. This choice does not, yet, arise for men in anything like the same way, although it may do in the future, if men demand equality with women. Throughout the book, the focus is on women and women's work, except for Chapter 9, which briefly considers how the theory might be extended to cover men. The change of perspective proposed here is minor or major, according to taste. In our view, it constitutes a major break with existing economic and sociological theory of labour market participation, for two reasons.

First, preference theory was developed explicitly with reference to women first and foremost. Existing economic and sociological theory has a male bias in that it was developed primarily with reference to *male* labour market participation and the characteristics of *men*'s work-life histories. Modifications and extensions were added later, in an attempt to cover the visibly different patterns of female employment. However it is not satisfactory to explain women's employment as a small deviation from the employment patterns of men, or under the heading of sex discrimination, as so many textbooks do. Far better is a theory that starts from the substantial body of new research evidence on women's work, and that focuses on what is distinctive about the choices women make.

Second, a change of perspective is necessitated by the five historical changes discussed in Chapter 3, which collectively produce a qualitatively new scenario for women in rich modern societies in the 21st century, giving them options that were not previously available to women. True, small élites of women born into wealthy families, or prosperous families with liberal ideas, did sometimes have real choices in the past, just as their brothers did. Today, genuine choices are open to women in the sense that the vast majority of women have choices, not only very particular subgroups in the population.

The usual sociological response to this is to point out that choices are heavily determined by social class of origin. This argument derives from male-centred social stratification theory which, like Goldberg's theory of patriarchy (Goldberg 1993; see also Hakim 1996a: 5–9), takes for granted that all men will seek the best jobs and positions in the public sphere that they can get, commensurate with their abilities, with outcomes influenced by social class of origin and other factors shaping opportunities in the marketplace and in public life (Erikson and Goldthorpe 1993; Marshall *et al.* 1991). However the most important choice for *women* is between a life centred on private, family work, and a life centred on market work or other activities in the public sphere[1] and, in the new scenario, this choice arises equally for women in all social classes (Procter and Padfield 1998: 2–3). Preference theory and social stratification theory address separate, parallel issues. Some scholars go further, to argue that the *relative* importance of social class is declining rapidly in modern societies and that new social values are becoming dominant (Beck, Giddens and Lash 1994; Abramson and Inglehart 1995).

The Four Main Tenets of Preference Theory

There are four central tenets to preference theory (see box).

Tenet 1: Five separate changes in society and in the labour market which started in the late 20th century are producing a qualitatively different and new scenario of

[1] In most of this chapter we refer, for simplicity, to employment as the principal alternative to a life centred on the family. However the conflict is between private, family life—whether or not children are a feature—and activities in the public sphere that usually involve an element of public rivalry, competition for the 'best' positions, highest status, or greater power. Politics, religion, sport, and the arts are the main alternatives to market work as the central life activity.

options and opportunities for women in the 21st century. The five causes of a new scenario are as follows:

1. The contraceptive revolution which, from about 1965 onwards, gave sexually active women reliable and independent control over their own fertility for the first time in history.
2. The equal opportunities revolution, which ensured that for the first time in history, women obtained equal access to all positions, occupations, and careers in the labour market. Sometimes, this was extended to posts in the public sphere more generally. In some countries, legislation prohibiting sex discrimination went much wider than just the labour market, giving women equal access to housing, financial services, and other public services.
3. The expansion of white-collar occupations, which are far more attractive to women than most blue-collar occupations.
4. The creation of jobs for secondary earners, people who do not want to give priority to paid work at the expense of other life interests.
5. The increasing importance of attitudes, values, and personal preferences in the lifestyle choices of prosperous, liberal modern societies.

The five changes are historically-specific developments in any society. They are not automatic, and do not necessarily occur in all modern societies. They may not occur together, at a single point in time in a country. The timing of the five changes varies greatly between countries. The effects of the five changes are cumulative. The two revolutions are essential and constitute the core of the social revolution for women. The five changes collectively are necessary to create a new scenario in which female heterogeneity is revealed to its full extent.

In western Europe, North America, and other modern societies, these five changes only took place from the 1960s onwards. The timing and pace of change has varied, even between countries in Europe. However, the strong social, cultural, economic, and political links between modern countries suggests that no country will lag behind on any of the changes indefinitely. Our discussion focuses on the USA and Britain because the five changes were completed very early in these societies, so that the new scenario was well established by the last two decades of the 20th century. In some young countries, such as Singapore, these five developments seem to be compressed into a relatively short timespan, so that the new scenario seems likely to be broadly in place at the start of the 21st century. In most countries, the new scenario will not be achieved until sometime later in the 21st century. As several examples illustrate, the new scenario is delayed in some modern societies. For example, the contraceptive revolution has not yet been fully implemented in many European countries, and some countries have not yet developed jobs for secondary earners. Government policy can facilitate or impede these social changes.

This study does not pretend to offer a detailed historical account of these five changes in any single country, or more broadly in any particular region of the world. Instead, our aim in Chapter 3 is to identify the central features of the five changes. Examples and illustrative evidence are taken from countries for which information is readily available. This means, inevitably, that our examples come mainly from material written in English, which is now becoming the international language of business, politics, and the sciences.

Tenet 2: Women are heterogeneous in their preferences and priorities on the conflict between family life and employment. In the new scenario, after they have a choice, they are therefore heterogeneous also in their employment patterns and work histories. It seems likely that women have always been heterogeneous in their work-lifestyle preferences, and that this heterogeneity only emerges clearly and manifests itself fully in the new scenario. However, this study looks only at the contemporary situation. Recent research evidence on the heterogeneity and polarization of sex-role preferences and employment patterns is presented in Chapters 4 and 5, first in relation to the adult population as a whole, and then in relation to the youngest age cohorts, using data from cross-sectional surveys, administrative records, and longitudinal studies for modern societies. No one disputes the new polarizing trend in female employment patterns, which was discovered simultaneously in the 1990s by several social scientists working independently in the USA and Europe. Those who seek to sidestep the meaning of this trend argue that things are different in the younger generation, and/or that longitudinal studies do not reveal a polarizing trend. Chapter 5 shows that neither of these arguments are supported by the evidence. Polarization intensifies in each succeeding generation, and heterogeneous preferences are stable across the lifecycle.

The three preference groups are set out, as ideal types, in Table 1.1, with estimates of the variable size of the three groups in advanced modern societies. Chapter 6 describes in detail the characteristics of the three groups of women: home-centred, work-centred and adaptive, and considers the social constraints and contextual influences that help to determine the relative sizes of the three groups in any particular social setting.

The underlying proposition of Tenet 2 is that there is a conflict between a life centred on an employment career and the demands of continuous, full-time jobs, and a life centred on marriage, child-bearing and child-rearing, and the demands of family life. In other words, there is a conflict between production and reproduction as a central life activity and principal source of personal identity and achievement. Economists' usual assumption is that all women give priority to family activities and responsibilities, simply because it is only the female that gives birth. The rise of voluntary childlessness in the new scenario disposes of the faulty assumption—sometimes made by feminists as well—that all women 'naturally' desire to have children, raise, and educate them.

It is sometimes argued that there does not need to be any family–employment conflict, if only governments would organize things so as to allow women to do both simultaneously. The example of Sweden is usually quoted as a successful illustration of such policies. Recent research shows a more equivocal picture. Long-standing egalitarian and family-friendly policies in the Nordic[2] countries have indeed supported rising economic activity rates among women at the same time as stabilizing or even reversing falling birth rates; they allow women to combine child-bearing with a semi-continuous involvement in paid work. But this does not mean that the conflict between a major involvement in child-rearing or, more generally, family work and a major involvement in employment careers has been resolved, as social scientists are now slowly beginning to admit (Moen 1989; Jonung and Persson 1993; Pott-Buter 1993; Hoem 1995). As noted in Chapter 8, the sex-segregation of occupations is much higher in the Nordic countries—notably Sweden, Norway, and Finland—than in other European and North American countries that lack their egalitarian and family-friendly policies (Melkas and Anker, 1997, 1998; Anker 1998). More important, vertical occupational segregation[3] is stronger in Sweden than in liberal and *laissez-faire* economies such as the USA (Rosenfeld and Kalleberg 1990; Melkas and Anker 1997, 1998; see also Hakim 1993b: 310; Sorensen and Trappe 1995). The work histories and work patterns of men and women in Sweden differ qualitatively, even if Swedish women spend more time in market work than do women in some other European countries. The question here is not whether Scandinavian and socialist policies are attractive to women—especially adaptive women—and enable them to combine market work and family work to some degree. Few would doubt that women (and men) can have moderate involvements and moderate achievements in both spheres. The question is whether egalitarian and family-friendly policies can *eliminate* the conflict between two such different, time-consuming, and demanding activities, in the sense that people who do take time out for family work are 'not disadvantaged' in their careers as compared with people of similar ability who do not have a domestic break. This is a practical impossibility. Most women in Sweden combine part-time mothering with part-time employment in careers that are rarely as central for them as they are for men. As a result, men continue to climb higher in all public hierarchies and they dominate in all positions of responsibility,

[2] Scandinavia comprises Sweden, Norway, and Denmark. The Nordic countries are a wider group, including Iceland and Finland as well as the Scandinavian countries.

[3] Vertical occupational segregation occurs when men are concentrated in higher grade occupations and women are employed mainly in lower grade occupations, for example when most surgeons are male and most nurses are female, thus producing an 'authority gap' between men and women as well as a substantial difference in their average earnings. Most studies of occupational segregation look only at horizontal occupational segregation, which exists when men and women generally choose different occupations—for example women are dressmakers and men are tailors, women are cooks and men are carpenters (Hakim 1996a: 149).

TABLE 1.1. *A classification of women's work-lifestyle preferences in the 21st century*

Home-centred	Adaptive	Work-centred
20% of women varies 10%–30%	60% of women varies 40%–80%	20% of women varies 10%–30%
Family life and children are the main priorities throughout life.	This group is most diverse and includes women who want to combine work and family, plus drifters and unplanned careers	Childless women are concentrated here. Main priority in life is employment or equivalent activities in the public arena: politics, sport, art, etc.
Prefer *not* to work.	Want to work, but *not* totally committed to work career.	Committed to work or equivalent activities.
Qualifications obtained for intellectual dowry	Qualifications obtained with the intention of working.	Large investment in qualifications/training for employment or other activities.
Responsive to social and family policy.	*Very responsive* to all policies	Responsive to employment policies.

authority, and leadership in the Nordic countries, especially in the private sector (Wright, Baxter, and Birkelund 1995; Melkas and Anker 1997, 1998; Anker 1998).

Most social science research gives the impression that women form a homogeneous group that seeks to *combine* employment and family work. There are two reasons for this. First, social science methodology tends to focus on measures of central tendency, such as statistical averages. Only rarely do scholars set out to assess the full diversity of women's employment and life histories.[4] Studies that do this have been obliged to devise new methods, measures or indicators, to get beyond the simplistic pictures suggested by measures of central tendency. Second, there is the emphasis on increasingly narrow time-specific measures of labour-force participation. Labour market

[4] Just one example is the convention, in demographic studies, of reporting *average* family size, or *average* fertility rates per woman. Average fertility rates below 2 children per woman usually entail that at least some women are remaining childless while others have children. Demographers regard childlessness as just another quantitative state of parity. But common sense alone tells us that women or couples who remain childless are *qualitatively different* from women and couples who have children. Measures of central tendency are misleading because they fail to identify or report qualitative differences within the so-called 'normal' distribution.

The four central tenets of preference theory.

1. Five separate historical changes in society and in the labour market which started in the late 20th century are producing a qualitatively different and new scenario of options and opportunities for women. The five changes do not necessarily occur in all modern societies, and do not always occur together. Their effects are cumulative. The five causes of a new scenario are:

1. The contraceptive revolution which, from about 1965 onwards, gave sexually active women reliable control over their own fertility for the first time in history.
2. The equal opportunities revolution, which ensured that for the first time in history women had equal access to all positions, occupations, and careers in the labour market. In some countries, legislation prohibiting sex discrimination went further, to give women equal access to housing, financial services, public services, and public posts.
3. The expansion of white-collar occupations, which are far more attractive to women that most blue-collar occupations.
4. The creation of jobs for secondary earners, people who do not want to give priority to paid work at the expense of other life interests.
5. The increasing importance of attitudes, values, and personal preferences in the lifestyle choices of affluent modern societies.

2. Women are heterogeneous in their preferences and priorities on the conflict between family and employment. In the new scenario they are therefore heterogeneous also in their employment patterns and work histories. These preferences are set out, as ideal types, in Table 1.1. The size of the three groups varies in rich modern societies because public policies usually favour one or another group.

3. The heterogeneity of women's preferences and priorities creates conflicting interests between groups of women: sometimes between home-centred women and work-centred women, sometimes between the middle group of adaptive women and women who have one firm priority whether for family work or employment. The conflicting interests of women have given a great advantage to men, whose interests are comparatively homogeneous; this is one cause of patriarchy and its disproportionate success.

4. Women's heterogeneity is the main cause of women's variable responses to social engineering policies in the new scenario of modern societies. This variability of response has been less evident in the past, but it has still impeded attempts to predict women's fertility and employment patterns. Policy research and future predictions of women's choices will be more successful in future if they adopt the preference theory perspective and first establish the distribution of preferences between family work and employment in each society.

research has in the past used the preceding twelve months as a reference period, and some studies still do so (Hakim 1993a: 111, 1996a: 65). But labour market statistics are now usually produced to International Labour Office (ILO) standards, using the preceding week as a reference period, and defining a 'job' as any work for pay or profit done for at least one hour in the preceding week. Unfortunately, the gain in precision is at the expense of relevance and utility, as some national statistical offices are finally admitting—notably in the Netherlands.[5] Measures of central tendency and precise, time-specific measures of labour force participation are probably adequate for studies of male employment. At least they have been adequate until recently. They may become less adequate in the 21st century in affluent modern societies. They are already proving to be seriously inadequate for studies of female employment patterns and work histories (Hakim 1993a: 107–15, 1998a: 142–4, 173–7, 239–40; Jonung and Persson 1993), and there is now a consensus of opinion that new measures are needed.

The introduction of longitudinal studies, always far more expensive and complicated than regular cross-sectional surveys (Hakim 1987a, 2000), allowed the full heterogeneity of female employment patterns to be revealed towards the end of the 20th century. These studies also reveal a *polarizing trend* from about 1970 onwards in rich modern societies. This appears to be a new trend, which is consistent with the idea that female heterogeneity is only fully revealed after social and economic changes have created a new scenario for women. However historical research on women's employment patterns in earlier parts of the 20th century, notably by Goldin (1990, 1997) for the USA, suggests that the polarization of female employment patterns extends a long way back. The reasons for this in the past are probably not the same as in the new scenario. Economic necessity was generally a more important determinant of women's employment decisions in the past than it is in the new scenario. None the less, it is interesting to note that the heterogeneity of women's employment behaviour is not new. It has so far been concealed by statistical methods and measures designed by men for men.

Tenet 3: The heterogeneity of women's preferences and priorities creates conflicting interests between groups of women: sometimes between home-centred women and work-centred women, sometimes between the middle group of adaptive women and women who have one firm priority, whether for family work or employment.

[5] In the 1980s and 1990s European labour statisticians came to agree that the ILO one-hour-a-week definition of a job was inappropriate and should be replaced by some higher minimum hours threshold in order to exclude large numbers of marginal workers on the periphery of the labour market, such as full-time students with small casual jobs. However, they were unable to agree on a common minimum, with proposals ranging from 8 to 16 hours a week as the lower limit for defining a job. From 1987 onwards, Statistics Netherlands has excluded people working less than 12 hours a week from Dutch published employment statistics—so far the only country to make the change. However data on people working under 12 hours a week are still collected, and are available in microdata tapes for research analysis.

The conflicting interests of women have given a great advantage to men, whose interests are comparatively homogeneous, and are one cause of patriarchy and its disproportionate success.

It is important to note that there is no single dividing line between the three preference groups. For example on certain employment issues adaptive women and work-centred women find they have common interests, which may be opposed to the interests of home-centred women, few of whom do paid work after marriage. On other issues, such as childcare, home-centred and work-centred women are likely to find common cause, and be opposed to the interests of adaptive women. These *shifting* lines of disagreement pose major barriers to unified pressure groups representing the interests of all women.

Tenet 3 follows from Tenet 2. It contradicts the currently dominant perspective within feminism, which underlines women's *diversity* without accepting that this produces *conflicting interests* among women. Preference theory presents problems for many feminists because it forces them to confront the problem of women's conflicting interests, and how they interact with the divergent interests of men and women. For example, some feminists are unwilling to accept that there are two groups of women whose interests coincide with and complement the interests of men, albeit for quite different reasons. Home-centred women are not averse to men having priority for jobs and promotion in the workforce, since their own standard of living depends on the economic success of their male partner. Work-centred women have the same interests and priorities as most men in the sense that employment and similar competitive achievements in the public sphere take priority over family work, at least until people reach their 50s, when the achievement ethic often starts to weaken and early retirement begins to look attractive. In most societies, home-centred and work-centred women together constitute almost half of all adult women, and at the minimum they make a sizeable minority (Table 1.1). It is only adaptive women whose interests conflict with men's interests, on most issues most of the time.

As noted in Chapter 9, it is now becoming clear that men do not surpass women in ability and talents (Hyde 1996: 114). In the context of equal talents, patriarchy and male dominance require explanation. Preference theory offers a structural explanation for the disproportionate success of patriarchy in the past, and for its continuation in the new scenario, albeit in more muted and discreet forms. Chapter 9 argues that men appear to be a more homogeneous group than are women. Male heterogeneity exists, but is relatively small compared to female heterogeneity, especially among 'prime-age' men, aged 25–50 years. Compared to women, men chase money, power, and status with greater determination and persistence. The alternative lifestyle of long-term economic dependence and a focus on family work appeals to a tiny minority of men. There have always been women who challenged male dominance in public and private life, but hardly any examples of men who challenged women's dominance in the family and child-rearing. On the contrary, generous paternal leave schemes in the Nordic countries failed to persuade fathers to devote time to family work, even when the leave was fully paid. Given that a substantial proportion of women's lives and energies were taken up by child-bearing and childcare in premodern societies, the emergence of male patriarchy is not surprising. Preference theory helps to explain the enormous, and puzzling *success* of patriarchy, in all known societies and cultures which have positions of power and authority in the public sphere, both pre-industrial (Whyte 1978: 57, 90, 92; Lerner 1986) and modern (Wright, Baxter and Birkelund 1995; Melkas and Anker 1998: 97; Anker 1998). Because women are not only divided but also have *conflicting* interests, men have been exceptionally successful in institutionalizing the social conventions and rules that support, maintain, and extend male dominance in all spheres of life.

Tenet 4: Women's heterogeneity is the main cause of women's variable responses to social engineering policies in the new scenario of modern societies. This variability of response has been less evident in the past, but it has still hindered policy research—often invisibly, because it was not measured—and it has impeded attempts to predict women's fertility and employment patterns. Putting it another way, policy research and predictions of women's choices will be more successful in future if they adopt the preference theory perspective and first establish the distribution of preferences between family work and employment in the populations being studied.

There are two principal interactions between women's preferences and public policy as determinants of behaviour. On the one hand public policies which greatly favour the home-centred group, for example, will encourage this group to expand to its maximum size, will persuade most adaptive women to give priority to family life over other activities, and will probably reduce the size of the work-centred group to its smallest size, in terms of the lifestyles women actually adopt. One example would be the Netherlands in the period when 'pillarization' and religious influence were strong: the vast majority of women gave up work at marriage or soon after, and only a tiny minority of women persisted with continuous careers in the workforce. Similarly, policies which greatly favour the work-centred group will encourage this group to expand to its maximum size and will probably reduce the size of the home-centred group, as reflected in behaviour. Examples would be East Germany prior to 1989, or China before economic liberalization in the 1980s: the vast majority of women were in employment on a fairly continuous basis throughout life, and full-time homemakers shrank to a tiny minority of 10% of the population or less. Sweden provides an example of policies favouring adaptive women, who seek to combine employment and family work, inflating this group to its maximum size.

The other side of the coin is that the three preference groups respond very differently to public policy. For example pronatalist policies will have little effect on work-centred women, many of whom will adopt a childfree lifestyle in the 21st century. But well-designed pronatalist policies can potentially have a large impact on home-centred women, and a smaller impact on adaptive women, raising fertility levels from the average of 1 or 2 births per woman found in most modern societies, to much higher levels.

Modern Society

Thus far, almost all theories of modernity and the modernization process tend towards Eurocentrism. In consequence, the concept of modernity is sometimes rejected as little more than an ideological tool for the promotion of western cultural imperialism. An interesting alternative is offered by Mouzelis (1999) who defines the central features of modernity in such a way as to avoid Eurocentrism and western cultural imperialism. As conceptualized by Mouzelis, a society can be modern without necessarily adopting the characteristic features of western Christian democracies. Modernization is *not* synonymous with westernization and Christian values. Many late-developing countries adopt different routes towards modernity from the route chosen by the west. Mouzelis identifies just two essential defining features of the modernization process:

(1) the creation of large nation-states with an unprecedented level of social mobilization and incorporation of people into the social and political centre;
(2) highly differentiated economic, political, social and cultural spheres (institutions, roles, and organizations) within the larger nation-state, each sphere regulated separately and having a large degree of autonomy.

The economy is organized and regulated by national markets or national planning agencies; political activities are regulated by the nation-state; national systems of population monitoring, management, and welfare provide social integration; and the cultural arena is characterized by mass literacy and nationalistic ideologies. Institutional differentiation means that, in principle, no single sphere has greater weight than the other three. In practice, one sphere often dominates for some period of time, as illustrated by the economic dominance of capitalism in Anglo-Saxon countries up to the oil price shock of the 1970s, the political dominance of the nation-state in the Soviet Union up to the 1980s, and the cultural dominance of religious institutions in the Islamic republic of Iran after 1978.

The modernization process occurred first in western Europe, after the 17th-century scientific revolution produced a kind of knowledge that was built on transcultural and non-moral criteria of validation. This new knowledge base led to the creation of powerful economic, political, social, and cultural technologies which permitted the transformation of society through structural-functional differentiation in combination with greater integration.

In the present global environment, the shift from a command economy to a market economy seems to be a necessary precondition for greater adaptive capacity in a society, and hence seems to be a universal feature of modernity. However, modern societies differ in their dominant values. The economic, political, social, and cultural spheres each have their own values and internal logic: productivity is the dominant value in the economic sphere; democracy or other systems of political mobilization in the political sphere; solidarity in the social sphere; and autonomy, self-realization, and self-fulfilment in the cultural sphere. These values are widely accepted in post-traditional societies. But there may be greater emphasis on one or another of these values in particular societies. For example, social values and solidarity have greater weight than political values and democracy in China and Japan, while Anglo-Saxon societies have given greater weight to economic values over social values.

In sum, Mouzelis (1999) points out that the Anglo-Saxon forms of modernity that are currently globally dominant could potentially be superseded by Chinese, Japanese, or other Asian forms of modernity in the 21st century. All are equally viable and potentially successful variations on the essential form of a modern society. The current global dominance of the West is neither inevitable nor certain in the long term.

Giddens and others offer a very much broader theory of reflexive modernization (Giddens 1991; Beck, Giddens, and Lash 1994; Beck and Beck-Gernsheim 1995), which is arguably Eurocentric in its presentation and detail. They distinguish between the early modernity of industrial society, in which choices and behaviour were dominated by collective organizations such as trade unions and social class, and the late modernity of fully reflexive societies. Individualization is the driving force for change in late modernity. Individualization frees people from the influence of social class, nation, and family. Agency becomes more important than the social structure as a determinant of behaviour, even when 'structure' is understood in Giddens' sense of rules and resources. People do not only gain the freedom to choose their own biography, values, and lifestyle, they are *forced* to make their own decisions because there are no universal certainties or collectively agreed conventions, as in traditional or early modern industrial societies (Giddens 1991: 209–31; Beck, Giddens, and Lash 1994: 12–15, 74–6, 90, 111). The theory of reflexive modernization notes that the feminist revolution was one crucial feature of the social change from early to late modernity, and that the impact of modernity is gender-differentiated: striving instrumentalism has been a characteristic of men's lives in the main, while domesticity has been the main feature of women's lives (Beck, Giddens, and Lash 1994: 26–7, 95). However the full implications for the lives of men and women in the future are not stated.

Preference theory was developed independently of theories of reflexive modernity and the reflexive project of the self, but it is consonant with this other perspective. Preference theory can be seen as an empirically-based statement of the choices women and men actually make in late modernity.

Reinstating Preferences as a Causal Factor

At the extreme, all theories can be shown to be wrong, incomplete, not supported by some piece of evidence, or internally inconsistent or undefined. As Kuhn (1962: 145) pointed out, if every failure to fit were grounds for theory rejection, all theories ought to be rejected at all times. Theories compete on fitting the facts, more or less, better than others. Unfortunately, the emphasis in sociology tends to be on critiques of theory rather than on synthesizing and devising a way forward; on detecting the weaknesses of existing theories rather than on identifying their most useful strengths, on which we can build and develop. We prefer to take the more positive approach.

In line with other sociologists, we believe that sociology should never abandon the effort to explain social phenomena in a holistic manner (Bourdieu and Wacquant 1992: 26–35; Mouzelis 1995: 154). This approach argues against the segmentation of disciplines, and against the fragmented results of variable sociology and multivariate analysis that are currently fashionable in sociological and economic work on the labour market. Further, as Mouzelis (1995: 157–8) notes, a full understanding of social games and social processes requires attention to three dimensions:

(1) roles and positions, some ascribed and some chosen;
(2) dispositions of the actors, who may be individuals, groups, or institutions;
(3) interactions within particular situations, which create their own logic and dynamic.

The importance of each dimension varies from one type of social game to another. The three dimensions all have their own logic and dynamic, which can vary independently, and can therefore never be automatically derived from the other two, *a priori*. One of the reasons why modern societies display such fragmented, discontinuous, fragile social organization is the growing discrepancy between the positional, dispositional, and interactional/situational dimensions of social games. The greater the discrepancies between the three dimensions, the greater the chances that participants distance themselves from the rules that each of the dimensions entail.

Following Bourdieu (1972, 1977; Bourdieu and Wacquant 1992), Mouzelis helps us to reinstate the dispositions of actors as one important dimension of all social processes—that is, what I refer to as attitudes, values, and preferences. At present, the emphasis in research on women's work and gender issues is on the sex-role prescriptions offered to women and on the situational constraints on their behaviour—on what they are *expected* to do and what they are *prevented* from doing, but never on what they *want* to do. One principal contribution of preference theory is to reinstate this third dimension, of women's personal preferences between alternative work-lifestyles.

Bourdieu defines *habitus* as systems of durable dispositions, regulated improvization, history turned into nature, the grammar of social conduct that combines agency and structure, and that homogenizes and catalyses a group or class world-view based on common conditions of existence. His theory was developed in the 1960s, based on research on pre-industrial and industrial society, where dispositions were shaped by the social and cultural environment, and by collective organizations such as class, so that agency and structure combined (Bourdieu 1977: 72–80). By the 1990s, Bourdieu insisted that the theory of *habitus* was not fatalistic, and did not rule out strategic choice or conscious deliberation. Quoting Weber, he pointed out that people obey a rule, or convention, only insofar as their interest in following it outweighs their interest in not following it. He admitted that his theory reflected social processes in stable societies, and that even in stable societies, the theory probably applied to no more than three-quarters of all social actions. Bourdieu accepted that in times of crisis, or in periods of social change, people were obliged to rethink and redesign the rules of social conduct, and would make more deliberate choices (Bourdieu and Wacquant 1992: 115, 131–5). Arguably, the theory can be developed further to apply to the new conditions of modern society, where there is no single prescription for the good life and people have to choose between mutually incompatible values. After the two revolutions and other changes have created a new scenario in affluent modern societies, dispositions become a reflection of heterogeneous personal preferences and individual priorities, in a situation where economic survival is assured and other choices become more important. Dispositions cease to be exclusively marks of social position (Bourdieu 1977: 82) and become more idiosyncratic, personally chosen among the options, roles, models, and styles offered by the local, national, and global cultural environment.

Mouzelis (1995: 10, 175–6) points out that, despite a phenomenal volume of empirical research and debate on women's position in society and the social amplification of any differences between men and women, feminist theory has so far contributed little to sociological theory or to social science theory more broadly.[6] Preference theory is an attempt to do

[6] This may seem a harsh assessment, and the introduction of the feminist concept, and puzzle, of patriarchy is certainly an important contribution to social science. However despite the best efforts of Hartmann and Walby, there is still no compelling feminist explanation for patriarchy which competes successfully with several non-feminist explanations, and which is also consistent

this, on two levels. It is helpful to distinguish between two types of theory:[7]

(1) theory as conceptual framework or paradigm which is useful for the analysis of social situations regardless of time and location; and
(2) theory as a provisional end-product of research, which tells us something new about the social world, usually referring to particular social contexts or time periods.

The appropriate mode of assessment for the first type of theory is its heuristic utility: the usefulness of the concept or paradigm in guiding how we look at, analyse and understand social games and social processes. Empirical verifiability is the appropriate mode of assessment for the second type of theory.

Female heterogeneity, Tenet 2 of preference theory, belongs to the first type of theory and should be assessed by its heuristic utility. Tenets 1, 3, and 4 of preference theory fall into the second category of theory, and should be assessed by empirical research evidence on women's behaviour *after* the new scenario became established in the particular society being studied. There is no single, common date for this: achievement of the new scenario has to be assessed separately for each country. This means that much of the research evidence on women's choices *before* the new scenario is established, or evidence for non-modern societies—especially poor non-modern societies—is not an appropriate test of preference theory. Because the theory refers to *all* adult women, and the choices they make between family work and market work, appropriate research evidence must cover the entire adult female population, not only women who happen to be in the workforce at a particular point in time, nor narrow subgroups in the female workforce. Sample selection bias is one of the most common defects of research on women, not only in case-study research but also in survey analysis (Hakim 1996a: 129–30), and it is often a problem in studies limited to *employed* women.[8]

with and supported by the empirical evidence (Hartmann 1976; Walby 1990; Fine 1992; Hakim 1996a), apart from Firestone's (1974) theory that women's absorption in reproductive activities means that men easily dominate public life. Even this theory does not explain why women fail to organize collectively to ensure that child-bearing is rewarded at an appropriately high level, in social and economic terms. Preference theory provides an explanation for women's failure to organize around a common set of interests, and thus for men's disproportionate success in promoting their more homogeneous interests. Attempts to develop a feminist economics have been no more successful, as yet (Humphries 1998). Of course, some argue that feminist sociology consists primarily of advocacy research, and that feminist theory is shaped by political advocacy for the transformation of gender relations, to such an extent that feminist theory cannot be assessed as just another element within sociological theory, and must be taught by people who are personally committed to the cause (Roseneil 1995).

[7] Following Althusser, Mouzelis (1995: 1) labels them Generalities II and Generalities III.

[8] Selective case studies of women in particular occupations, especially in professional and managerial occupations, are thus not an appropriate test of the utility of preference theory. This is just one of the weaknesses of Crompton and Harris' (1998) early challenge to preference theory. In practice, their small study focused on adaptive women almost exclusively, and displayed the diversity of this group among doctors and bank managers. Home-centred women were excluded completely from the study (Hakim 1998b).

Women's preferences—and hence the heterogeneity of these preferences—will only emerge if we ask them directly and explicitly about their preferences. Preferences cannot be imputed reliably from behaviour, as economists assume. In particular, women's preferences cannot be deduced from the decision to obtain higher education qualifications, in part because educational institutions function increasingly as marriage markets, as noted in Chapter 7. Data on public attitude towards women's role is only a poor proxy for information on personal work-lifestyle preferences. Personal lifestyle choices sometimes differ from, or even contradict, the generalized attitudes studied by opinion polls and social attitude surveys. Paradoxically, the current emphasis on women's right of access to paid work in advanced societies[9] means that it has become rarer, and almost deviant, for women to express a preference for a life centred on marriage and children. The modern equivalent of the courtesy bias in survey research in South-East Asian societies (Jones 1983) is the political correctness bias in western European societies. As noted in Chapter 4, this is leading to a systematic bias in European surveys towards support for the 'egalitarian' model of symmetrical family roles, even in countries such as Spain where the great majority of women do no paid work at all.

There is a remarkable difference between men and women in the way they tell the story of their lives. The masculine life story typically emphasises decisiveness, 'doing it my way', refusing to accept situations that were belittling or boring, overcoming obstacles and enemies, highlighting achievements and the attainment of goals. The feminine life story typically presents a smoothly integrated stream of events in which everything they did was the 'natural' outcome of the situation at the time, the actions of others, chance events. Even women with a will of iron avoid presenting events as the result of their steely determination to achieve their goals—probably because this is seen as 'unfeminine'. If such stories are taken at face value, male life histories are all about agency, while female life histories are all about chance events, situational, and contextual constraints. It appears that many women have difficulty in openly expressing their work-lifestyle preferences. Intentions, plans, motivations, and preferences can disappear into the stories women tell about their lives, like water into sand. Taken-for-granted assumptions are often left unexplored, unstated, implicit. Preferences that go contrary to social norms can be actively concealed or left vague, so as to avoid argument and opprobrium. Thus the desire to have children is rarely stated explicitly because it is natural, obvious and unquestioned. But the desire *not* to have children may also be left unstated because it seems to invite an argument in ordinary social settings. Qualitative research on women's attitudes to childbirth regularly

[9] Women are rarely denied access to productive labour in less-developed societies. On the contrary, they often do most of it (Boserup 1970), and as Whyte (1978: 169–75) has shown, there is no association between women's participation in production or subsistence work and women's status in a society.

encounters difficulties in getting women to talk openly and explicitly about their preferences (Gerson 1985), even though there is nothing deviant or sensitive about the topic, as with criminal activities. But women's reticence about their preferences is not the same as the absence of preferences. It is important for qualitative and quantative studies to ask explicitly about personal preferences. It may also be that willingness to openly discuss their work-lifestyle preferences, as men do, is one indicator of women's emancipation, and of their willingness to take responsibility for their own lives. A sense of personal efficacy seems to be necessary also for high achievement (Duncan and Dunifon, 1998: 140).

In sum, preference theory does two things: it reinstates (heterogeneous) personal preferences as an important determinant of women's behaviour, and it states that attitudes, values, and preferences are becoming *increasingly* important in the lifestyle choices of people in rich modern societies. This does not mean that economic and social structural factors suddenly vanish, or cease to be important. However their *relative* weight declines as the relative importance of lifestyle preferences steadily grows. The change of emphasis may be hidden in survey results, but emerges more clearly in qualitative studies. In surveys, people routinely say they work for the money, for essentials, or from financial necessity. But clothing, a car, leisure activities, or a mobile phone that one person regards as essential will be regarded as a luxury, or even as a waste of money, by someone else, depending on their lifestyle and values. Some lifestyle choices cost nothing—*not* having a TV, or mobile phone—and others cost very little—using a bicycle instead of a car. Women who claim to be working from financial necessity are often lifting their family and lifestyle into a strongly desired higher income-bracket. They are actually making a lifestyle choice, although this will not be clear in routine survey results. As Katona (1975: 153) put it, the needs economy has been replaced by the wants and aspirations economy.

Britain and the USA as Case-Studies

Tenet 1 of preference theory states that two revolutions and three other changes in society and in the labour market produce a new scenario of options and opportunities for women. The USA and Britain provide the main examples of the new scenario in this book, and research on these two countries provides the main source of information on how women's preferences and behaviour develop within the new scenario. Otherwise, we have attempted, as far as possible, to draw on research from a wide range of prosperous modern societies.

Britain and the USA provide the two main case-studies because these liberal societies, *laissez-faire* economies, and relatively unregulated labour markets provide the least restrictive environments for the emergence of new social patterns and innovations in the organization of employment. Despite their differences, the two countries are often classified together in typologies of welfare state systems, gender regimes or labour market regimes as the 'liberal' model (Esping-Anderson 1990; Bosch, Dawkins, and Michon 1994; Mósesdóttir 1995; Hakim 1996a: 17–18; Sainsbury 1996: 9–32; Blanpain and Rojot 1997: 10–12; Cousins 1998). But they can equally well be described as having social, fiscal, and labour policies that are chaotic, confused and contradictory when compared with hegemonic modern societies. In contrast, many European societies impose more coherent, consistent, and unidirectional social, fiscal, and labour market policies based on well-defined models of family life, sex-roles, and the standard job, thus creating an environment in which spontaneous change and innovation are less likely.

It is no accident that the pattern of weekly working hours in Britain is completely different from the pattern of working hours in all other European Union (EU) countries: for both men and women there is a fairly flat distribution across all hours, whereas people typically work standard full-time hours in other EU countries (Hakim 1997: 26–9, 1998a: 106–9) and any deviation from convention provokes strong reactions (Hörning, Gerhard, and Michailow 1995). Similarly, there is relatively greater acceptance of 'eccentric' behaviour and cultural differences in private and family lifestyles, and often in public behaviour. The multicultural, multi-ethnic, 'melting pot' character of the USA is well-known. But Britain also has always been a multicultural and multi-ethnic society,[10] with the same advantages of a higher potential for social innovation and change.[11] Theory attempts to formulate what happens *all other things being equal*. One approximation to this condition is to study societies and situations where there are no major constraints limiting choice or forcing choice in particular directions. The USA and Britain thus provide theoretically important case-studies of developments in the new scenario.

[10] London is probably the most cosmopolitan city in Europe, and even in the world, with the greatest ethnic and cultural diversity of the population. Over 300 languages are spoken in London, and the city has 50 communities of more than 5,000 people who were born outside the UK (London Research Centre 1997; Storkey, Maguire, and Lewis 1997; Baker and Eversley 2000). Just one indicator is the incidence and treatment of mixed-race couples. Mixed-race marriages attract relatively little attention in Britain and the USA, and the attention is rarely negative for purely racial reasons. The ethnocentrism and racism of other northern European countries has so far remained hidden due to the tiny size of their non-native and non-white populations, which have had little impact on the majority culture.

[11] A greater degree of openness to social innovation can be illustrated both historically and in contemporary life. For example when formal, legal divorce, and even formal marriage were too expensive for ordinary people, informal institutions of 'common law' divorce and marriage or cohabitation were established to serve the same purpose at little or no cost, including the institution of public wife sales to establish a *de facto* divorce and remarriage. This informal institution started as early as 1073 and lasted until the 20th century (Menefee 1981). A more recent example is the rapid take-up of new technology in Britain compared with continental European countries. By the 1990s, Britain had higher proportions of homes with a personal computer, of homes with a video recorder, of people with a mobile phone, and of people routinely using credit cards for consumer purchases than in most other western European countries.

Another advantage is that the new scenario emerged very early in these two countries, so there is a longer period in which to study the consequences. Again, this is not an accident, but another indicator of openness, or low barriers to change, in both countries. For example, the equal opportunities revolution was established first in the USA, starting with equal pay legislation in 1963. The emergence of part-time jobs for secondary earners started immediately after World War II in Britain and developed most fully there (Hakim 1993a, 1997, 1998a). The contraceptive revolution took place in the mid-1960s in both the USA and Britain, with immediate consequences for declining fertility rates (Westoff and Ryder 1977; Coleman 1996a). Widespread and free access to modern forms of contraception was delayed in many European countries, especially Catholic countries. The multicultural and multi-ethnic character of the USA and Britain also meant that there was early awareness and acceptance of differences in values and lifestyle choices, although the Netherlands has recently become probably the most tolerant postmaterialist society in the western world.[12]

In sum, there are good reasons for using Britain and the USA as the main illustrative examples of new developments in women's work-lifestyles. By the late 20th century, they already displayed the consequences of the new scenario, with developments that will not emerge until the 21st century in many other modern societies.

Plan of the Book

Chapter 2 explains the need for a new theory, by setting out some of our frustrations with existing economic and sociological theory on the labour market and women's work. Chapter 2 is mainly of interest to theoreticians, and some readers may prefer to proceed straight to Chapter 3.

The four principal tenets of preference theory are elaborated in Chapters 3 to 8. Individual chapters develop particular themes or aspects of the theory, set out the research evidence which contributed to our thinking, and consider apparently contradictory theses. Chapters 4, 5, and 6 describe the polarization of women's preferences, and behaviour, regarding the relative importance of market work and family work. Chapter 4 looks at the polarization of sex-role preferences, work orientations, employment patterns, and household incomes. Chapter 5 looks at the same topics, to see if younger generations display less polarization, as egalitarian ideas take hold. It also considers whether longitudinal studies reveal work-lifestyle preferences to be stable or

[12] Social attitude surveys in the 1990s showed the Netherlands to have the highest percentage of the population espousing postmaterialist values: 36% compared to only 23% in the USA and 20% in Britain (Inglehart, Basañez, and Moreno 1998: 466).

unstable across the life history. Chapter 6 sets out the principal differences between the three preference groups, considers the sources of their differences, explores contextual constraints, and outlines the consequences for differential policy-responsiveness.

Chapter 7 complements Chapters 4, 6 and 9 by showing that even today women often choose to marry men who surpass them in educational qualifications and hence earnings potential, thus creating an inegalitarian basis for many modern marriages, despite the trend towards educational equality in the population as a whole. Chapter 7 looks at the question of 'equality' between men and women from a different perspective from that adopted in most economist and sociological analyses to date: educational equality between spouses instead of earnings equality in the workforce. At the minimum, this analysis underlines the fact that some sociologists have allowed themselves to be overwhelmed by the economic perspective, with its exclusive focus on money, earnings, and income as the sole measures of status and success in life. It also underlines the point that trends in the workforce at the macro-level do not necessarily tell us what is going on within families at the micro-level. Hopefully, it will encourage sociologists to continue the search for a more holistic perspective on women's position in marriage, the labour market, and society.

Chapter 8 first considers governmental fiscal and social policies at the national and international level, identifying policies which support each of the three preference groups. It then looks at the family-friendly policies developed by employers and trade unions to see if they are designed, or could be designed, to offer benefits to all three preference groups.

Chapter 9 offers a first outline of how preference theory might be extended and developed to explain men's choices in the prosperous modern societies of the future. It is necessarily more tentative than previous chapters, because much depends on how quickly men respond to women's new opportunities and choices by demanding similar rights and options.

Chapter 10 summarizes the results, suggests that preference theory offers a new perspective on contemporary theoretical and research puzzles, and argues for a new approach to cross-national comparisons of women's employment.

Future Changes

Social science aims to produce theories with universal applicability as well as more time-specific theories. However, a good theory should be able to reflect on the conditions for its own disconfirmation; theory should never become theology (Galtung 1990: 99–100). In addition, technological change and innovation are speeding up, so that all the basic parameters of social life are also changing, faster than before. In this context, most social science theory will have built-in obsolescence, and a finite utility span. Preference theory is a predictive theory, but we do not expect it to be useful and meaningful in relation to prosperous modern societies for longer than about fifty years after the new scenario is established. By that time the technology for reproducing human life[13] and human life expectancy[14] will have changed so fundamentally that a new theory will be necessary. In addition, robotics, communications, and information technology will have changed the world so much that the conflict between family work and employment will have altered substantially. Preference theory concerns a world in which this conflict is still important, due to the way family life, employment, and public life are organized, and due to the limited mental, emotional, and physical durability of human beings. All this may change in future decades.

[13] In *Sex in the Future*, Baker (1999) predicts that by 2050, IVF technology will have developed to the point where all babies would be born *in vitro*, with reproduction completely separated from sexual activity, living arrangements, and child-rearing. He foresees widespread sexual promiscuity and the disappearance of the co-resident nuclear family as it currently exists, as a result of these developments, plus the elimination of sexually transmitted diseases.

[14] Life expectancy is a crucial variable. Historically, women's lives have been dominated by child-bearing and child-rearing in part because reliable contraception was not available for them to have any real choice in the matter, and in part because women (and men) rarely lived for very long: about 30 years in prehistoric times, rising to between 30 and 40 years from 1540 to 1840 (Drever and Whitehead 1997: 9–10). In the 20th century, life expectancy doubled to about 70–80 years. If life expectancy doubles again, so that people can lead socially active adult lives for up to 150 years, we could expect women (and men) to choose serial lifestyles (as well as serial monogamy): for example 50 years as a home-centred woman followed by 50 years as a work-centred woman, with different partners for each lifestyle phase.

2

The Failure to Predict

Preference theory aims to overcome some important weaknesses in current theorizing in the sociology of work and employment, labour economics, and social psychology. A full critique of these theories is not attempted here. There is already an extensive social science literature devoted to reviews, assessments, and critiques of current theories and debates in all the social sciences that have addressed women's position in society, the family, and labour market (for example Connell 1987; Walby 1990; Blau and Ferber 1992; Delphy and Leonard 1992). Our objective is rather to develop a more satisfactory theory that offers explanations for contemporary trends and also facilitates predictions of future patterns of women's labour market participation. Even so, it seems appropriate to first identify those weaknesses in current theorizing that preference theory resolves or overcomes.

Prediction versus *Post Hoc* Explanation

As economists repeatedly point out, the purpose of social science is not merely to explain what has already happened, but to predict (Blaug 1980: 262). It is the making and testing of predictions that provides the most rigorous test of theories that purport to explain human behaviour—or even the *only* real test, some would say. Without prediction, social science theory remains at the level of historiography and *post hoc* rationalization: ideas and arguments that are more or less consistent with the evidence, more or less plausible but not, ultimately, tested or proven. Prediction is especially important in policy research, sometimes based on a solid knowledge of causal processes, sometimes relying on key indicators of current trends (Hoaglin *et al.* 1982).

It is sometimes argued that the social sciences are unable to predict behaviour, because the social reality they deal with is too complex. However this did not prevent Karl Marx from developing predictive theory. And as Lieberson (1985) points out, prediction remains feasible in the modern world. It may require a different approach from explaining events that have already happened, with attention to asymmetrical causal processes—often the source of social engineering failures—and factors with causal powers—which may not show much variation. Political science and demography are two social sciences where there is a strong emphasis on prediction. They illustrate the potential, and limitations, of predictive social science.

Most social attitude surveys simply document trends up to the present day and offer *post hoc* explanations on the main factors driving change, often with an emphasis on the intellectual and technical puzzle of distinguishing age, cohort, and period effects (for example Scott, Alwin, and Braun 1996). Political opinion polls go much further than this, attempting to predict the future pattern of attitudes and choices. It is true that they only make predictions for a few months, or weeks ahead. But they present precise and public predictions which are publicly tested. On the basis of political opinion polls in the run-up to an election, analysts attempt to predict the voting pattern in the election itself, its distribution across the country, and hence the composition of the new government. In most countries, there are several major opinion poll organizations, with a very public competition between them to achieve the most accurate prediction of election results. This competitive rivalry has been running for decades in the USA, Britain, and many other western European countries, so a substantial volume of experience has been accumulated in making election predictions. The accuracy of pre-election polls has an important effect on public and business perception of the effectiveness of social research and market research. It is a highly visible, public test of ability to deliver. In Britain, the opinion polls have a strong record of correct predictions, apart from the failure to predict the winner in the close election of June 1970. None the less, totally wrong predictions still occur sometimes. They are subjected to close professional scrutiny for the lessons to be learnt. No one predicted the failure of Neil Kinnock and the Labour Party to win the election in 1992 in Britain. In response, the Market Research Society and the Royal Statistical Society carried out *post mortems* to identify the weaknesses in interview survey methods that produced incorrect predictions, with a further review of the successful new methods after the 1997 election (O'Muircheartaigh and Lynn 1997). Good political attitude surveys can usually predict changes of government, with all that implies.

Prediction is also taken seriously in demography, the oldest social science—population censuses were the very first type of systematic social enquiry to be developed. Projections of the population's size and age composition are important inputs to many government service-delivery functions, to social policy, and employment policy. For example schools must expand or contract to match fluctuating birthrates. Despite the substantial investment in the profession, and an even greater investment in the population censuses and demographic statistical databases they analyse, demographers regularly fail completely to predict birthrates correctly, even in the short term. The baby boom of the 1950s came as a nearly total surprise to demographers, and they also failed to predict the severity and duration of the downturn in fertility from the 1960s onwards. There is an expanding academic literature on the causes and correlates of fertility declines in the industrialized countries of the western world—usually labelled the first and second demographic transitions by demographers, following Lesthaeghe and Van de Kaa (1986)—yet few demographers are sufficiently confident of their causal analyses and theories to be prepared to attempt even short-term forecasts of future patterns of fertility and population growth (Cramer 1980; Caldwell 1982; Lesthaeghe and Meekers 1986; Davis, Bernstam, and Ricardo-Campbell 1987; Federici, Mason, and Sogner 1993; Mason and Jensen 1995; Coleman 1996b; Ermisch 1996: 159; Jones *et al.* 1997). Attempts to predict, or shape, fertility patterns in less-developed countries are understandably an even more hazardous undertaking, given the paucity of basic statistical and research information, cultural and other differences, and the rapid pace of social change (Hodgson 1983; Cleland and Hobcraft 1985; Cleland and Scott 1987).

Similarly, the voluminous current literature on changing patterns of women's employment rarely goes beyond description and *post hoc* rationalization. Forecasts of female workrates are simply projections of current trends into the future. Some social scientists are beginning to admit that economic and cultural-structural theories of women's labour market participation are invariably confirmed by research analyses, but only to a limited degree, leaving a great deal unexplained. For example Hendrickx, Bernasco, and de Graaf (2001) conclude that Dutch women are now free to choose whether to work or not, and sociologists are no longer able to predict what their choice will be.

All these examples concern regular and important social activities. Most people vote, and elections can produce profound, if diffuse, changes in the character and direction of societies. Most people have children, and heterosexual activity must be one of the most well-known and extensively examined aspects of human life. Every day, substantial numbers of women enter and leave the workforce. These are not arcane subjects, so any social scientist has access to the psychological, situational, social, and economic factors that may be involved. Furthermore, these topics attract the combined attention of several disciplines: economics, sociology, social statistics, demography and social psychology. So the failure to predict reflects on social science generally, rather than on any single discipline. The failure to predict testifies to the weakness of current social science theory, which is mostly plausible but not proven, partial rather than complete, fragmented into separate disciplines, and backward-looking. The failure to predict constitutes a fundamental weakness for policy research and policy science, which is oriented towards the present and the future even more than towards evaluations of past policies.

The failure to predict is perhaps not surprising given the current orientation and organization of the social sciences. Sociology and other disciplines are 'historical' in that they are often backward-looking rather than forward-looking. They are also not historical enough in that they fail to perceive significant turning points in the constant flow of social events, unless these are overwhelming, such as wars or revolutions. Silent revolutions are rarely detected. Mega-trends are often overlooked. Time is almost always treated as a continuous variable, except in before-and-after policy evaluations. It is remarkable that almost all male demographers failed to see the social and psychological implications of the introduction of modern contraception, which gives control to the woman instead of the man and can, if necessary, be used without male partners' knowledge or agreement—one notable exception is Murphy (1993). Similarly, demographers have been slow to even notice the rise of voluntary childlessness towards the end of the 20th century, let alone to consider its meaning and implications. Some of the best early studies of childlessness were done by journalists, and all the best studies were done by women. An emphasis on the development of theory, especially at the macro-level, within particular social science disciplines may be at the expense of substantive knowledge and sensitivity to new emerging trends. As Kuhn (1962, 1970) pointed out, most scientific careers develop within existing theoretical paradigms, with few or no professional rewards for challenging contemporary dominant theories. Sociology remains peculiar in being multi-paradigmatic, but here too most careers develop within a single paradigm.

A related problem is the history-of-ideas focus in the social sciences, especially in sociology, which encourages purely theoretical, logical, argumentative debates of the sort popular among educated intellectuals, social and political philosophers, instead of a hard-hat emphasis on the real world, data, evidence, the impersonal testing of ideas in order to select those that work and to discard those that are not useful. Some sociological, political, and economic writing appears to be engaged in theological discourse rather than reporting on a scientific enterprise. The history-of-ideas perspective also encourages a backward-looking orientation instead of a future-oriented perspective. Cataloguing the historical origins and antecedents of any idea or theory becomes more important than the empirical validation and testing of theories, and it means that useless or misleading theories are never discarded, as they constitute one link in the chain of ideas.

Of course, social science is harder than the natural sciences because social life is reflexive, and because the best social science knowledge becomes absorbed into the contemporary 'ordinary knowledge' and common sense of everyday life (Lindblom and Cohen 1979). Social scientists' search for general theories also has to take account of non-reversible causal processes, and of selection effects that prevent a 'pure' measure of one social factor in isolation, and even make such an endeavour pointless (Lieberson 1985). Both these difficulties are far more common in the social world than in the physical world. It may be that social scientists have to make do with broad and inexact theories which actually work in the real world instead of seeking to produce precise, tight, and elegant theories which bear no relation to real people and to social life as we know it, but are intellectually attractive—as illustrated by economics.

Within the social sciences, economics has made the strongest claims to being a science in the same mould as the physical sciences, developing universal laws that enable economists to make predictions. But economists are gradually beginning to admit that this approach has not in fact worked; that their predictions are not in fact reliable, and are often worthless; and that the discipline needs to re-orient itself to achieve a better grasp of reality (Lawson 1997; Ormerod 1998). The influential Lucas critique published in 1976 pointed out that econometric models are unstable, and prompted an extended debate on the reasons for predictive failure and possible solutions. Reviewing this debate, Lawson argues that the failure of economics is due to the use of inappropriate methods and techniques, including the ever-increasing complexity of models and simulations that should be rejected in their entirety because they are divorced from reality (Lawson 1997: xiii, 225, 246, 282, 288). Lawson identifies several methodological weaknesses in economics, including atomism, but the chief weakness is the often implicit assumption of *closed* systems, which thus bear little resemblance to the real world, which is an open system (Lawson 1997: 282). Ormerod (1998) also discusses the failures of economics, in particular the failure to predict. He points out that societies consist of complex systems which are poorly modelled by the closed systems embedded in economic theory and methodology, which thus regularly produce results that are wrong or misleading. The solution proposed by Ormerod is to develop the even more complex methods of analysis required by chaos theory—also known as complexity theory—or else to incorporate sociological knowledge into economics, as illustrated by his theory of interacting agents (Ormerod 1998). Lawson's proposed solution is to abandon the reliance on econometric and other modelling in favour of greater use of historical and sociological methods and data (Lawson 1997).[1]

Economics and sociology are the two main disciplines competing for predominance in labour market analysis. Economics offers narrow and precise theories; sociology offers broad and fuzzy theories. Both are incomplete. Labour economics theory, in the shape of human capital theory, competing differentials, the new household economics, sex discrimination theory, and the theoretical framework of the supply and demand for labour, has in practice been adopted by labour sociologists, even though they supplement these theories with discussion of the social structural and institutional factors which also shape behaviour. At the same time, labour economists who

[1] There is of course a long tradition of economists seeking to incorporate social psychological and sociological research knowledge into economics. See for example Katona (1975), Lewis (1982), and Antonides (1991).

address women's position in the labour market usually supplement mainstream labour economics with discussion of occupational segregation in the workforce, sex-role socialization, and the motley collection of references to institutional constraints, social networks, historical change, cross-cultural comparisons, and feminist theories that currently passes for the sociology of work and employment (Grint 1991; Blau and Ferber 1992; Jacobsen 1994; Reskin and Padavic 1994; van Doorne-Huiskes, van Hoof, and Roelofs 1995; Crompton 1997). Attempts to develop a feminist economics reflect a concern to integrate institutional and cultural variables into economic analysis; an insistence that analyses must cover all forms of work, and the broader sexual division of labour; and a challenge to the primacy of agency over structure in causal processes (Humphries 1998). There is no doubt that feminist economics has come 'out of the margins' into mainstream economics and has produced a wealth of new research-based knowledge on women's labour market participation, their contribution to the family, and the economy (Kuiper and Sap 1995). However, many doubt that feminist economics is indeed theoretically different, even if it has contributed a new substantive focus on women (Polachek 1995: 61–4). Some call for a full integration of economics and sociology in the study of women's work, building on the strengths of each discipline (England and McCreary 1987). Others challenge sociology's critical response to labour economics—for example arguments that people are not 'rational', or even that they do not make decisions, or that structural factors are more important than individual characteristics, question whether sociology offers anything of great substance to rival labour economics, for example, for explaining differences in earnings; and propose open acceptance of complementarity instead of open rivalry (Smith 1990; see also rejoinder by Sorensen A B 1990).[2] Some economists argue that unless

[2] There is some evidence that social scientists may be self-selected, to some extent, into disciplines that echo and reflect their own world view and values, and in particular that economists differ in being far less altruistic than others (Marwell and Ames 1981: 306–9). What is certain is that economists tend to focus on the 'free-rider' problem in the provision of public goods, while sociologists and psychologists tend to focus on the development of trust and co-operation, on altruism (Piliavin and Charng 1990). Multidisciplinary research indicates that altruism and individualism are not necessarily in conflict in large and complex human societies where public goods are of benefit to all, including people who do not use them directly. In his *Evolution of Cooperation*, Axelrod (1984) used a series of computer simulations of the effectiveness of various strategies in the Prisoner's Dilemma game. Contrary to expectation, one of the simplest strategies, named TIT FOR TAT, emerged repeatedly as the winner, owing to a combination of being nice, retaliatory, forgiving and clear. Axelrod demonstrated how co-operation can evolve in a society of completely self-interested individuals. However, multidisciplinary theory is as rare as multidisciplinary empirical research. This raises the question of whether economics is male-centred, in the sense of promoting assumptions and theories as universally valid when in reality they apply mainly to male behaviour, while sociology may be more female-centred in relying too heavily on theories and assumptions that apply more often to women's behaviour. The male culture of economics and the female culture of sociology are suggested by the sex-ratios among people holding qualifications in these disciplines. For example, in Britain, the 1991 Census showed that three-quarters of all economics graduates were male and two-thirds of all sociology and psychology graduates were female. Against this evidence is the fact that the most influential theorists in all the social sciences are usually men.

sociological knowledge is integrated into economic analysis, economic theory will become increasingly divorced from reality (Lawson 1997; see also Ormerod 1998).

Whether economic or sociological, all labour market theorising suffers from such a restricted scope that it adds relatively little to common sense and 'ordinary knowledge', leaving the big questions unanswered. As Einstein pointed out over 50 years ago, the whole of science is nothing more than a refinement of everyday thinking (Einstein 1936: 349). Social scientists have to offer something more or better than common sense, or they must adjudicate between equally plausible rival theories, or they must provide the basis for prediction. None of the current theorizing achieves this.

For example human capital theory effectively argues that the higher earnings achieved by men compared to women are fair, because men offer more attributes that are valued and rewarded by employers, such as long years of work experience and formal qualifications. This leaves all the difficult questions unanswered. Why do most, but not all, women give priority to family work over an employment career, and hence invest less in human capital? Why do women who plan careers nonetheless choose subjects and qualifications that lead to less remunerative and less demanding occupations—for example as nurses rather than doctors, cashiers rather than accountants, primary school teachers rather than university professors? Why do able women abandon successful careers to spend time at home bringing up small children? Just what proportion of women anticipate discontinuous employment? Human capital theory offers no ideas at all about how and why women (and men) make the choices they do. It only offers an evaluation of the fairness of the earnings outcome, supporting the *status quo* as efficient and consistent with economic rationality (Humphries 1998: 228).

New theories explicitly developed to answer questions about women's position in the workforce are no more successful. Job queuing theory (Reskin and Roos 1990) states that employers invariably prefer to hire men rather than women, if men are available, so that men get the best jobs and women end up with the worst-paid jobs. As Goldberg (1993) points out, if this were true, there would be no male-dominated occupations that paid substantially less than women's occupations. In fact, in all labour markets, there are numerous male occupations that are just as low status and low paid as women's occupations, both before and after equal pay policies are implemented. There is also substantial evidence that employers do prefer women for certain jobs, such as childcare and the manual assembly of small components. In reality, integrated occupations employing both women and men are now more highly-paid than sex-segregated occupations; integrated occupations also have the largest sex differential in hourly earnings (Hakim 1998a: 41, 73–81). As Goldberg (1993: 108) points out, the evidence offered to support theories that female occupations are socially devalued and hence poorly-paid, or that employers only offer the worst-paid jobs to women, is equally consistent with the opposite theory: that *any* occupation that acquires high status and high earnings will attract men more quickly than women and so will *become* male-dominated as a result of its position in the hierarchy. Men chase money, power, and status harder than women, so are more likely to get them. The question is, why does this happen? And is it possible, or likely to change? Just as human capital theory justifies the higher earnings of men, job queuing theory excuses the lower earnings of women as due to discrimination rather than to women's own choices. But research presenting *correlations* between factors falls a long way short of a *causal* analysis. These and other theories *describe* and justify sex differences in patterns of labour market participation without ever attempting properly causal explanation.

Sociological theory offers almost nothing at all to explain sex differences in labour market participation and outcomes apart from the blanket concept of sex discrimination and facile references to sex-role stereotypes and to cultural or institutional constraints. The theory of differential socialization to roles in the family and the workforce cannot explain why some women (and men) accept, and others reject, role socialization; it does not help to explain the dramatic variations and fluctuations in female workrates over the past century in advanced economies; it is, ultimately, impossible to disprove or refute,[3] and it may even be tautological. Similarly, inequalities within the labour market that are attributed to social class differences are often being described rather than explained. Since sex differences and patriarchy cut across social classes, social stratification theory is not really useful for explaining women's position in society.

In sum, none of the currently available theories provides an adequate framework for understanding the sexual division of labour, women's and men's labour market participation, changes over the past century, and cross-national differences. None of the current theories are much help for predicting future patterns of women's employment, even in the short term.[4] One reason for this is the male bias of most contemporary theory.

[3] Sociological theories on sex-role stereotypes and cultural constraints on what activities, roles and jobs are considered 'suitable' for a woman are unpersuasive because these factors do not have the force of an overwhelming, compelling, or imperative script. They offer no more than recommendations as to what is most appropriate for a woman or man, leaving open the possibility that they will be rejected, revised, or imaginatively transformed. In all societies, a minority of women have successfully rebelled against their allotted position in society, raising the question of why most women (and men) find the sex-role guidelines acceptable.

[4] Economists refer interchangeably to prediction and forecasting. Sociologists tend to differentiate between genuine prediction, which is theoretically based, and forecasting, which simply projects existing patterns, relationships, and trends—for example in female workrates—into the next decade or so, thus assuming that historical time is not a factor.

The Male Bias of Labour Market Theory

Virtually all modern labour market theory rests on research evidence for men, and hence on the employment patterns typical of main breadwinners in full-time continuous employment throughout adult life. Labour economics textbooks typically bring women in only under the heading of sex discrimination (as illustrated by Ashenfelter and Layard 1986; Cain 1986; Adnett 1996), as if there were otherwise no differences between working men and women. Textbooks that explicitly address women's position in the labour market are forced to incorporate sociological and social psychological material on sex-role socialization and the competing priorities of family work and market work (Blau and Ferber 1992; Jacobsen 1994). But even in these texts, theories of labour market participation invariably focus on the male modal pattern as the norm, and all wage-earners are assumed, usually implicitly, to be primary earners.[5]

There are two aspects to this male bias in labour market theory. First, most labour economics assumes, formally, that labour is homogeneous so that, with full information, labour markets are fully competitive and will clear—labour market segmentation theory and insider-outsider analyses provide two deviations from this central theme. Second, there is the empirical reality of virtually all male workers being primary earners and/or being required by social welfare policy to be primary earners,[6] with the homogeneity of labour market behaviour and employment histories that derives from this role. These two features made labour economics a small and unexciting specialism before it started to address women's role in the labour market. Women complicated the picture by behaving differently from men, and in having more complex work histories. Sex differences were sometimes addressed using the concept of primary and secondary earner (Killingsworth 1983), but more often they were swept aside under the anomaly or distortion of sex discrimination, which is inefficient and thus cannot last. Sociologists accepted the labour economics perspective almost unquestioningly, agreeing that labour is homogeneous and that, with the elimination of sex discrimination, women were converging on the employment profiles of men, and that sex differentials in labour force participation were being eliminated (see for example Walby 1990: 9, 56; van Doorne-Huiskes, van Hoof, and Roelefs 1995). The convergence of male and female economic activity rates in modern societies is one of the most

[5] The male modal pattern remains the main focus even in textbooks that do carefully demonstrate how women's labour market participation differs systematically, conforming to the behaviour of secondary earners rather than primary earners, as illustrated by Killingsworth (1983).

[6] In Europe, early retirement followed by a period of part-time and occasional work, and increasing numbers of students with part-time and temporary jobs are gradually changing this picture from the 1990s onwards, but these two groups still remain a tiny fraction of all male earners (Hakim 1998a), and prime-age (25–50 years) men remain primary earners.

commonly misunderstood statistical illusions, the consequence of indicators designed by men to study men (Hakim 1993a, 1998a: 142–4, 239–40; Jonung and Persson 1993). In reality, the employment patterns of men and women continue to be strongly differentiated in every respect (Hakim 1991, 1995, 1996a, 1996c, 1998a), even in socialist countries such as East Germany prior to 1989, and in Sweden after decades of public commitment to egalitarian and family-friendly policies (Einhorn 1993: 114–47; Hoem 1995; Sorensen and Trappe 1995; Melkas and Anker 1998).

The male bias in labour market analysis means that, if sex discrimination is not being discussed, women can disappear from sight completely. One example is a review of labour market trends and policy issues in the second half of the 20th century (Standing 1997). Women are mentioned just once. There is no recognition that they introduce a qualitatively different element into the workforce; that the majority of part-time jobs and other non-standard jobs are taken by women, indeed, were mostly created for women; and that most women are secondary earners whose needs and interests differ from those of primary earners. The policy issues raised by women's growing presence in the workforce are ignored in an analysis that is effectively concerned only with men and the trade union perspective on recent developments.

The new home economics was the first theory to systematically address the sex differential in work orientations and differential investments in market work versus family work (Becker 1965, 1981, 1991; Polachek 1995), and it was largely rejected by sociologists. As formulated to date, it is a static theory that does not easily explain contemporary changes in women's employment and fertility patterns. More important, the theory only specifies that task differentiation and specialization yield efficiency returns in the household as well as in the paid workforce. It does not identify when these efficiency gains will be preferred over other competing values, such as the preference for egalitarian roles in the family rather than role-segregation. In addition, there is evidence that the sexual division of labour is adopted even by childless couples (Hakim 1996a: 91), making it clear that parenthood is not the essential catalyst for role-segregation in the household, as economists assumed. Preference theory builds on this rational action perspective, but incorporates the female heterogeneity so far overlooked by new home economics theory.

Feminist Contributions

At first sight, it appears that new feminist theorizing does incorporate the female heterogeneity overlooked by the new home economics. Postmodern feminist thought includes several core points: a suspicion of generalizations and scientific classifications, which may be the product of patriarchal ideology; a focus on the problem of the subjective standpoint; a concern with subjectivity and personal context as crucial theoretical issues; acceptance that women are not a homogeneous category; and admission that the differences between women can be at least as important as the similarities. By the 1990s, texts regularly included discussions of difference and diversity, and the term 'difference feminism' had emerged (Lovenduski and Randall 1993: 57–92; Evans 1995; Collins *et al.* 1995; West and Fenstermaker 1995). Some comparative studies of women's attitudes and behaviour go no further than commenting on the richly diverse patterns found within Europe (Boh *et al.* 1989; García-Ramon and Monk 1996; Scott, Braun, and Alwin 1998: 36). However, difference and diversity within western feminist theorizing are conceived narrowly as differences arising from class, race or ethnicity, nationality, and sexual orientation.[7] Difference and diversity in feminist thought generally refers narrowly to (the sources of) cultural differences between social groups which produce some variation in work orientations, family values, and labour market participation. Difference and diversity are not theorized in such a way as to constitute *qualitative* differences and *conflicting interests* between groups of women.[8] Preference theory does this, as noted in Chapter 6.

The Swedish concept of the 'gender contract' developed by northern European social policy theorists (Hirdman 1988; Pfau-Effinger 1993, 1998) also appears, at first sight, to recognize genuine diversity in models of the family and sex-roles within the family. The 'gender contract' refers to the model of the family that is recognized and supported by all social institutions in a society: family law, social policy, taxation, and social welfare rules and regulations. Studies adopting this theoretical perspective have so far been limited to northern Europe, and claim to show that the gender contract is important in shaping choices and explaining cross-national differences in women's role in the family and the labour market. There are two main problems with this approach. First, it assumes that every society has a *single* model of the family, and of sex-roles, which is promulgated in a consistent, co-ordinated, systematic, and hegemonic manner. This may well be an accurate description of the small hegemonic Nordic societies, which are characterized by cultural, ethnic, religious, and even political homogeneity. It is not a realistic approach to studies of the larger nation-states, such as Britain and the USA, with populations that are heterogeneous in culture, ethnicity, religious,

[7] Even religion is rarely noticed or mentioned as an important source of cultural differences; apparently everyone is assumed to espouse Christian values (see for example West and Fenstermaker 1995). In Europe, differences between religious groups are more likely to be noticed, but even here the scope is usually restricted to the three linked religions of the Middle East: Judaism, Christianity, and Islam, thus ignoring Buddhism, Hinduism, Shintoism, and Confucianism as distinctive cultural influences.

[8] A partial exception is found among political scientists, who do sometimes notice that varying experiences and identities preclude common political interests among women, and that the women's movement broke down into groups with conflicting interests in the USA, but not in Britain (as illustrated by Lovenduski and Randall 1993: 57–92, 272–9).

and political beliefs.[9] The second problem is that the gender contract perspective assumes that social and political systems are successful in persuading all citizens to accept and aspire to the dominant model of the family. It assumes that conflicting family models and rebellion against the *status quo* never appear to any significant degree in any country, despite the globalization of the mass media which provide everyone with information about the diversity of family models within Europe as a whole, and even more so across the world. Again, the small Scandinavian countries may be successful in achieving cultural hegemony within their frontiers. It is not realistic to expect the same cultural hegemony in the large European countries with heterogeneous populations. Gender contract theory replaces the idea of differences between women with the idea of differences between nations in the ideal model of the family and sex-roles. Foreign cultures become the source of problems and conflicts. The thesis carries xenophobic undertones.

As shown in Chapter 4 (see particularly Tables 4.1 and 4.2), there is in reality no consensus of opinion on the ideal model of the family in any European Union (EU) country. It seems likely that if a single model of the family were consistently endorsed within public opinion, family law, social policy, taxation, and welfare policy of a country, this would boost support for that model against others. But with the possible exception of the homogeneous and hegemonic small Nordic countries, no single model of the family and sex-roles does in fact attract majority support in any European country. We can expect a similar pattern of diversity in other modern societies.

A weaker version of gender contract theory simply states that nation-states have laws and policies that reflect and perpetuate the contemporary ideal-type of family relationships and the sexual division of labour. This thesis is presented by Sainsbury (1996) with substantial supporting evidence for the 1960s for the USA, Britain, Sweden, and the Netherlands. Sainsbury successfully demonstrates that state welfare policies in the four countries reflected and promoted very different conceptions of family roles and responsibilities, and that this was linked to relatively high female workrates in Sweden and relatively low female workrates in the Netherlands—both small countries. However the more complex and contradictory policies of the two large countries, Britain and the USA, meant that they fell in the middle, between the two extremes, on most indicators. In the 1960s, all four countries still endorsed a model of the family with segregated roles. Forty years later, welfare

[9] Large multicultural societies that are not dominated by any single, long-term political tendency, such as Britain and the USA, have no single fixed ideal-type of the family; pragmatic, incremental and short-term policy-making produces a heterogeneous mixture of policies with no single underlying rationale or logic. For example, Britain permitted, and now enforces, the separate taxation of husband and wife, but it also insists on treating cohabiting couples as if they are married and form a single economic unit for the calculation of means-tested welfare benefits. It is easy to give the impression of consistency in family models by omitting to mention the contradictions scattered throughout the fiscal system and public policy.

and other policies have become even more complex and contradictory, if anything, and role prescriptions are becoming even less consistent and hegemonic.[10] It seems unlikely that there will ever be a call for more hegemonic systems in the future.

The thesis that national policies and institutional factors have a large influence on women's behaviour is based, often implicitly, on the assumption that all women have identical goals or utilities, so that country differences in female employment are explained primarily by institutional factors and differences in national policies. If in fact women's (and men's) preferences are *heterogeneous within countries*, as shown in Table 4.1, the results of cross-national comparative studies become much harder to analyse and interpret. Too often, theorizing has been simplified in order to produce hypotheses that are amenable to being tested with a single research method, such as the quantitative analysis of national datasets.

Methodological Considerations

The multivariate methods that are currently fashionable in the social sciences make it more difficult to explain or predict, because they produce fragmented results describing analysis variables rather than integrated results for identifiable social units, such as persons, families, companies, or workers. Multivariate methods fight against holistic explanations and theories.

As Lieberson (1985: 155), Esser (1996), and Hedström and Swedberg (1996) point out, multivariate analysis, and similar methodologies that focus on variables, often use the language of explanation but in reality rarely go beyond description. Esser argues that variable-centred sociology is '*not explanatory*, is *incomplete* and in a specific way is *meaningless*' (Esser 1996: 159, emphasis in the original). He argues further that this type of analysis produces 'facile', 'superficial' and 'mechanistic pseudo-explanations' that 'do not in fact have anything to say about causal processes . . . processual interdependencies or . . . the subjectively sensible decisions taken by actors' (Esser 1996). Lieberson's arguments about (unmeasured) selectivity, asymmetrical causal processes, and the mis-application of controls constitute the most compelling arguments against the now routine use of regression analysis in social science. He points out that the multivariate analyses that have become routine in sociology would never lead to the discovery of gravity or other fundamental causes (Lieberson 1985: 90–103). Multivariate analysis cannot distinguish

[10] For the same reason, Esping-Andersen's (1990) typology of three welfare state regimes is not useful for studies of women's work, even if it is useful for the analysis of social policies at the national level. As Sainsbury (1996: 36–7) and others point out, the typology suffers from a male bias, focusing on main breadwinners as the norm, effectively ignoring (dependent) women. Also the classification of particular countries is challenged on the facts (Sainsbury 1996: 12–32).

between basic and superficial causes, between proximate causes, sensitive indicators, and real driving forces. It frequently clouds the picture with non-essential details about variation in basic causal processes, and the addition of controls can be counterproductive and produce misleading results (Lieberson 1985: 120–51, 185, 189, 194, 207, 211). He points out that the initial zero-order association—found in simple cross-tabulation and correlation—may often be the closest approximation to the true association, and argues for the principle of parsimony in identifying causes and explanations for empirical research results (Lieberson 1985: 42, 196–7).

Multivariate analysis encourages the use of multiple controls, which almost guarantees that research results will bear no relation to the real world. There is a tendency to pile all potentially relevant variables—often, all *available* variables—into a regression analysis, for example, so that results are presented after controlling for everything else. But in the real world, conditions cannot be controlled in this way. All other things do not stand still while a single factor changes, or is changed by a policy-maker. A technique that has its uses for answering particular questions—such as the *relative* impact of two independent causal factors—is also used to try to disentangle the precise impact of closely interlinked factors. Some of the most sophisticated discussions of the substantive meaning, and appropriateness of controlling for social class and other social factors, and imaginative solutions to disentangling the effects of related social variables, are found in epidemiological research, where there is a concern to achieve prediction as well as genuinely causal explanations (Marmot 1996) that can be useful to the health services.

Regression analysis of labour market datasets often produces misleading results because it implies that the impact of each variable can be separated from the impact of all other variables, that the impact of individual economic and social factors can be studied outside the causal process in which they are located. The implicit underlying assumption is that causal sequences and selectivity are irrelevant, that patterns of association are random rather than selective, and that all possible combinations of social and economic variables can be found in the real world, so that we can meaningfully isolate the impact of any factor, such as the age of the youngest child, on women's employment, or wages, net of all other factors. This assumption is false. In the real world, many choices are *connected choices*. Deciding to have large numbers of children or to have a demanding career are connected choices, in that they are seen as mutually exclusive alternatives by most women in most countries.[11]

The fashion for multivariate analysis contributes to the low status of qual-

[11] In countries where it is commonplace to have servants to do all domestic work, childcare and most other tasks as well, such as car-driving and gardening, it is easy to combine a career with numerous children. However the children are raised by other people: their personalities and values shape the children's development, not their parents' values. The contradiction between devoting any substantial time and effort to rearing one's own children and to a career remains, even here.

itative and case-study research as compared with quantitative data analysis, and is responsible for a widespread unwillingness to combine qualitative and quantitative research, to adopt triangulated research designs (Denzin 1978a, 1978b; Hakim 1987a: 119–50, 2000). All too often, quantitative analyses of large datasets are carried out on topics that actually require case-study designs, while sociologists who specialize in qualitative research fail to set their studies in the context of existing survey and statistical data. Multidisciplinary and multi-method research is often treated as an optional extra, or a desirable luxury. At least for research on women's employment, it is a necessity. The failure to adopt multidisciplinary and multi-method research designs has led to the manufacture of misinformation.

The fragmentation of disciplines also impedes the development of social science knowledge. For example labour economists evaluate jobs and occupations by the earnings and income they produce; these are, in practice, the sole measures of utility adopted in relation to employment. Labour sociologists evaluate occupations and jobs by their occupational prestige, social status, authority, terms and conditions of employment, and sometimes also job satisfaction, but they rarely give any special weight to earnings alone.[12] If occupations and jobs offer high earnings or high socio-cultural prestige, but only very rarely both together, as Bourdieu (1984, 1989) claims, then the fragmentation of disciplines ensures that social science research will be manufacturing misinformation as often as advancing knowledge. Similarly, if short and convenient working hours and high earnings are mutually exclusive alternative 'best buys' in the jobs market, then the separation of sociological and economic labour market analysis guarantees one-sided results, with a one-eyed bias that cannot be detected from within any single discipline. Occupations and activities can utilize and enhance a person's economic capital, political capital, cultural capital, or social capital.[13] For example politicians, internationally famous

[12] Equal pay policies have led all social scientists, sociologists as well as economists, to evaluate their success by monitoring trends in the pay gap. But this sort of policy research is distinct from the usual disciplinary concerns. For example, it is notable that the widely respected social class classification developed by Goldthorpe that is utilized in much European sociological research (Erikson and Goldthorpe 1993) does not provide an ordinal scale on earnings (Hakim 1998a: Table 3.5).

[13] The distinction between economic capital, cultural capital, social capital and political capital was originally made by Bourdieu in the 1980s (Bourdieu and Wacquant 1992), but has since been utilized and developed by other sociologists (for example Mouzelis 1995). Economic capital is the sum of the resources and assets that can be used to produce financial gains, including cash in the bank, vocational and educational qualifications. Cultural capital consists of information resources and assets that are socially valued, such as a knowledge of art, literature and music, or scientific knowledge. Social capital is the sum of resources, actual or potential, that accrue to a person or group from access to a network of relationships—who you know as distinct from what you know. Social capital can be used to make money—good social contacts can be crucial to the success of certain business ventures—or to exert power and influence. Political capital is a special form of social capital, and refers to a person's political assets and resources, which may come from family connections or from contacts developed in other contexts. Societies and individuals can accord different weights to the four types of capital. Women and men who have little economic capital can be rich in other types of capital.

professors, and locally important society hostesses can have positions of power and influence that give them access to resources, services and opportunities independently of the monetary economy. In market economies, money and earnings are predominant. But there are also other routes to success and a high standard of living. By focusing exclusively on economic capital and earnings, economists look at only one part of the picture, and some sociologists are now doing the same.

Another example concerns the interpretation placed on one analysis variable in much recent research: higher education qualifications. Economic theory treats qualifications exclusively as investments in human capital with a view to future employment, and their value is measured solely by the earnings generated. Economists must know from personal experience that young people have a multitude of reasons for choosing any particular educational course, but this is ignored. Sociologists do a little better in recognizing this diversity of reasons for attending higher education, and distinguish between qualifications that provide economic capital, such as an MBA or a degree in engineering, and those that provide cultural capital, such as a degree in literature or the history of art. As noted in Chapter 7, we also know that in certain societies where the educational homogamy of spouses is valued, girls attend college or university partly because they provide access to élite marriage markets, partly to obtain the cultural capital that will enhance their quality of life and social status, and partly to obtain a qualification that serves as an insurance policy and safety net in case they become widowed or divorced and are obliged to earn their own living. This third, complex, interpretation of the value of higher education for young women is effectively ignored by human capital theory and is recognized only minimally by sociological theory. In practice, it disappears from sight because it is not 'theorized', or is too complex for existing theories, even though it is the most common reason for young women's attendance at college or university in particular societies and social classes. The segmentation of social science disciplines produces knowledge that is narrow, partial, and fragmented in the perspective it offers on the world. It can also positively blind us to important facts and social processes which remain in a wasteland of real-world knowledge, unless and until they have been built into academic theories which somehow validate them as 'real' or 'important'. What social science theory fails to notice may be just as important as what it does notice.

Another example of the dysfunctional segmentation of the social sciences is the way both labour economics and economic sociology have failed to incorporate social psychological research findings on motivations, preferences, values, attitudes, or satisfaction with work and life. Some economists have insisted that a knowledge of psychology is necessary for economic research to discover the causes, the motive forces behind economic processes (for example Katona 1975: 9; Maital 1982; Antonides 1991: 5). The argument has been accepted most readily in business and marketing economics, but also applies to research on paid and unpaid work. However, with rare exceptions (Oswald 1997), the vast majority of studies by labour economists only use behavioural data on hours worked, earnings, and location within the workforce, and ignore data on motivations and attitudes even it is readily available in a dataset. This is illustrated in Chapter 5 by economic analyses of longitudinal datasets. Labour sociologists do a little better, with studies that look at work orientations, job satisfaction, and work commitment but, as noted in Chapter 3, they rarely collect data on personal preferences and motivations. Furthermore, there is little attempt to relate these to behavioural studies, to synthesize the two elements into a coherent, holistic, picture. Of course, this is exactly what qualitative research and case-studies excel at. But the deep divide between quantitative and qualitative research in sociology means that the two sides are rarely brought together, as we attempt to do here in Chapter 6.

The bias towards quantitative indicators and methods can sometimes seriously distort theorization and the research process. One example is the theory that married women who regard themselves as secondary earners will choose occupations and jobs that are compatible with family work, such as jobs that can be done part-time or intermittently, and occupations that tolerate discontinuous employment. The obvious example of this formalization of everyday knowledge is women's strong preference for school teaching and nursing, occupations where women constitute over half the workforce in most modern societies (Anker 1998: 252–64). Teaching is an ideal mother-friendly occupation because it allows mothers to be at home with their children during school holidays, including the long summer holiday. Nursing has the advantage of offering part-time and temporary jobs, with few or no penalties for taking a career break. However, this thesis, well-grounded in empirical observation, was converted into a quite different thesis when it was operationalized, originally by Polachek, an economist, later by England, a sociologist. They proposed that married women maximise their *earnings*, or minimise the *wage* depreciation resulting from a career break, by choosing jobs which tolerate interrupted employment, or that women in *all* female-dominated occupations experience lower wage depreciation than women in *all* male-dominated occupations. These two reformulations offer the convenience of earnings, or earnings depreciation, being the measure of an occupation's mother-friendly advantages, instead of the more complex, qualitative features described above. Using these reformulations, research results have been mixed, so that the theory is treated as unproven. Polachek's repeated tests using USA census microdata, the Panel Study of Income Dynamics (PSID), and National Longitudinal Survey (NLS) longitudinal datasets, all confirmed the thesis, and he concluded that there would be many more women in professional and managerial jobs if married women were prepared to work continuously throughout life (Polachek 1975, 1979, 1981; Goldin and Polachek 1987). England analysed the PSID and NLS data to show that women in female-dominated occupations do not experience lower rates of wage depreciation than women in male-dominated occupations, and she concluded that the theory was false (England 1982, 1984). Polachek was careful to restrict his analyses to married women, or to study married and single people separately, whereas England grouped all women together, ignoring the point about secondary earners.

Polachek's thesis is essentially that few jobs in professional and managerial occupations, but a larger proportion of jobs in clerical, sales, and unskilled occupations tolerate intermittent or part-time employment. Those that do will attract a large number of women. The thesis requires case-by-case studies of individual occupations, not a small variation in multivariate analyses of earnings, which economists routinely do and sociologists have now also adopted as a standard method. His thesis clearly has some continuing validity, as demonstrated by the continuing high proportion of women in nursery education, in primary and secondary school teaching, in nursing, and in other jobs that tolerate high levels of labour turnover and/or part-time work (Hakim 1998a). Within the professions, pharmacy recently emerged as one of the few to tolerate part-time and intermittent employment, largely due to a continuing labour shortage in the profession. As a result pharmacy attracted increasing numbers of women, as well as men from ethnic minority groups, in the USA, Canada, and Britain. By 1990, the profession was fully desegregated, and women reported that sex (and race) discrimination did not affect job opportunities and careers. None the less, men and women consciously use the profession in very different ways, and choose different types of job in the occupation. Men, including those from ethnic minorities, use it as a route into self-employment, small firm ownership, or management jobs with the large retail chainstores. Women use it as a source of mother-friendly, flexible and part-time employee jobs, with limited responsibilities that do not spill over into their family time (Reskin and Roos 1990: 111–27; Bottero 1992; Hakim 1998a: 221–34; Hassell, Noyce, and Jesson 1998; Tanner *et al.* 1999a, 1999b). The real test of the thesis about mother-friendly jobs will be whether this bifurcation within pharmacy—which is often decried as evidence of resegregation *within* the profession—will persist after the labour shortage in pharmacy comes to an end, as predicted, after the year 2000. In sum, earnings and wage depreciation are poor measures of an occupation's mother-friendly character. The bias towards quantitative methods, in sociology as well as economics, can undermine and invalidate the entire research process.[14]

[14] There are other objections to the thesis as formulated by both Polachek and England. For example it seems unlikely that young women are able to guesss the relative lifetime earnings of jobs or occupations, with or without taking account of wage depreciation from time out of the labour market. Many young women have only the vaguest idea of earnings levels in all the occupations

Finally, a major weakness of much social science research today is a disproportionate emphasis on behavioural data at the expense of information on attitudes, values, and preferences. Many social science research reports read like an action-packed film with the sound cut off. We see what people are doing, but we have no idea *why* they are doing it because the dataset only provides information on behaviour and not on motivations and values, all the dispositional factors that give substance to the concept of agency. Government surveys are most likely to adopt this one-eyed approach, as illustrated by national Labour Force Surveys (LFS), but also by other regular and longitudinal surveys of the workforce. Only rarely does a study admit that the most important explanations for observed behaviour are 'unobserved factors' such as motivation and ability (Ermisch and Wright 1992: 200–2, 209; Blackburn and Bloom 1994). It is equally rare for data analysts to put down their statistical methods of analysis and read survey questionnaire responses as narrative documents, case by case, to set employment decisions in the context of the family's lifestyle goals, social aspirations, and attitudes to the sexual division of labour—an approach used very successfully by Rainwater, Rein, and Schwartz (1986: 92–106). As Lieberson (1985) has pointed out, it is simply not acceptable for researchers to brush aside the problem of unobserved variables, unobserved sample selectivity, and unobserved associations between variables, as if these are minor matters that need not worry us. The 'silent film' version of social science is not very useful any more. Sociologists and social psychologists need to collect better data on motivations and preferences.

Conclusions

The failure of the social sciences to predict seems to be due to several problems of organization, theoretical and methodological orientation. Some social scientists are now rejecting the emphasis on linear causality and variable-centred models in data analysis. For example, Ragin (1987) proposes greater use of case-study logic and methods, and more cross-national comparative research, in order to grasp processes of multiple causation and achieve a holistic perspective. Complexity theory, or chaos theory, also accepts that qualitative studies and a holistic perspective are necessary to grasp complex change

they consider when young, and it is not certain that they give greatest weight to earnings when choosing jobs, as young men do. They are fairly certain to know that occupations such as teaching or pharmacy offer practical advantages for women who anticipate motherhood. In addition, both Polachek and England ignore occupational changes over the lifecycle in their analyses, a factor which could invalidate their results. None the less, the thesis as presented in its original, common sense version remains worthy of serious consideration, in particular to assess the *relative* importance of mother-friendly characteristics in particular jobs versus other causes of occupational segregation.

processes and to identify emergent properties in systems (Byrne 1999; Ormerod 1998).

Preference theory is an empirically-based, predictive theory that tries to avoid and overcome the weaknesses of current theorizing. As will be clear in the following chapters, it has been built up from a synthesis of qualitative, case-study, and quantitative research results on women's work. It synthesizes and builds on what works best in current economic and sociological theory. It offers a new, composite, multidisciplinary theory that:

(1) recognizes the heterogeneity of women;
(2) recognizes the distinction between primary earners and secondary earners; and
(3) provides a holistic account of how women choose between family work and market work.

Preference theory recognizes that occupations and jobs offer a mixed basket of rewards, benefits, and options: not only earnings, but also social status and prestige, work tasks that may be perceived as onerous or attractive according to personal taste, variable opportunities for social contact with colleagues in and out of the workplace, and convenience factors such as flexible hours, short hours, or term-time working. The relative weight placed on any of these varies between women as well as between men and women. While it is reasonable to assume that people seek to maximize rewards from employment, this does not necessarily translate into a goal of earnings maximization, let alone a goal of minimizing wage depreciation. Furthermore, people weight the rewards from employment within the context of all life goals including, for some women, child-rearing and family work as a major life activity. Again, the relative weight placed on different life goals varies between women, as well as between women and men.

Preference theory identifies a new scenario of opportunities for women that is now being established in rich modern societies. Chapter 3 sets out the five causes of the new scenario and shows that, cumulatively, they produce a qualitative change in the options available to women. Chaos theory points out that quite small changes can have major long-term consequences. The five changes identified in Chapter 3 include two fundamental changes and three major changes which, cumulatively, revolutionize life options for women.

The central argument of this book rests on relatively simple data analyses, and the tables mostly present cross-tabulations. Inevitably, some of the literature reviewed in the book has used multivariate methods. However such methods are not essential for demonstrating the case for preference theory. More important, studies based on multivariate analysis are not sufficient, in isolation, to draw conclusions about causal processes. Our interpretation of the results of such studies is informed by the extensive qualitative research and case-studies also reviewed here. The empirical foundation of preference theory is multidisciplinary, multi-method and triangulated, as is necessary for robust, policy-relevant research as well as theoretical research (Hakim 2000).

3

Causes of the New Scenario

The first tenet of preference theory is that a combination of five important social and economic changes create a new scenario. This happened at the end of the 20th century in a few affluent modern societies, but at the start of the 21st century in most countries. The five causes of the new scenario are independent, can proceed at different paces in different societies, and do not necessarily occur simultaneously. The two essential changes are the contraceptive revolution and the equal opportunities revolution, which occurred in the 1960s and 1970s in some, but not all, Western European and North American countries. The expansion of white-collar work throughout the second half of the 20th century, and the workforce restructuring that followed periods of recession in the 1980s and 1990s both produced a labour market with occupations and jobs that are far more attractive to women than was the case in the past, when the emphasis was on full-time manual jobs in manufacturing industries. The fifth change is less visible because it concerns the rising importance of attitudes, values, and lifestyle choices in rich modern societies. The two revolutions constitute the core of the social revolution for women. In those countries where all five changes occur together, a fundamentally different new scenario is created for women, and hence also for men.

These five changes in combination produce a *qualitative* change of sufficient importance that empirical social and economic research on the family, women's role, and women's employment needs to be clearly 'dated' to *before* or *after* the new scenario is established in a particular country. Because social change is a gradual process, there is usually no single date that can be pinpointed, even in a single society. But one can often specify a decade of major changes, so that research reports need to be divided into those with fieldwork dates before or after this period. For Britain and the USA, for example, where the new scenario was established early, the late 1960s and early 1970s seem to be the turning point decade. The options open to women, and the choices women could make, from the late 1970s onwards were of a radically different nature from the situation prior to the 1960s. In other countries, the transitional period comes later and lasts longer, well into the 21st century.

The Contraceptive Revolution

For women, the most important technical innovation of the 20th century is the contraceptive revolution. The equal opportunities revolution is essentially a *social* revolution in customs and values. In contrast, the contraceptive revolution is a technological revolution with massive social consequences.

The technical side of the revolution consists of the development of modern, that is, coitus-independent and reliable methods of contraception that can be controlled, or chosen, by women themselves. Three became widely available in the mid-1960s in North America, Britain, and some other European countries: the contraceptive pill, the IUD or coil, and sterilization (Westoff and Ryder 1977; Murphy 1993; ONS 1997: 144–60). Of these, the pill is the most important and most popular among women, especially young women, because it gives them complete control over their fertility without the co-operation (or even the knowledge) of their partner, while sterilization (of either partner) is more popular among older women. Having children ceased to be an uncontrollable hazard of women's lives, and became voluntary.

The social side of the contraceptive revolution consists of the social and political changes required to deliver free and easy access to modern contraception to all women who want it, plus free and easy access to emergency contraception and abortion if the need should arise.[1] Technically, the contraceptive revolution has already happened, world-wide. But the revolution is not complete in any country until social procedures for delivering the innovation to all women have been implemented. Thus, for example, the contraceptive revolution was not achieved in Eastern European countries prior to 1990 because there was relatively easy access to abortion but not free access to the modern contraception that gives a woman independent control over her fertility, and this situation persisted in Japan well into the 1990s.[2] The use

[1] Emergency contraception consists of the 'morning after pill' and similar procedures for ensuring that no pregnancy ensues from unexpected sexual activity at a time when no other contraception was being used. It is helpful for women who have been raped, for example.

[2] There is nothing inevitable about the contraceptive revolution. Even affluent modern societies can refuse to permit this social change with its consequences for women's autonomy. One example is Japan. Only 5% of Japanese women use the pill and 80% of couples use condoms (Jolivet 1997: 127, 138–40). The Ministry of Health in Japan allows the pill to be used as a treatment, but does not recommend it as a contraceptive because this might encourage the young to become promiscuous, which would lead to the spread of AIDS. Most doctors and other medical advisors in Japan are opposed to widespread use of the pill and other modern forms of contraception, because they would destroy the lucrative business in abortions and condom sales—abortions are paid for privately, as pregnancy is not an illness. Coleman's (1983) analysis points to the patriarchal nature of Japanese society as the explanation for non-modern contraceptive practices. This strongly male-dominated society has a history of powerfully institutionalized male hostility to modern forms of contraception because they give control and sexual autonomy to women. He describes some of the wildly prejudiced information sometimes offered about modern forms of contraception: the pill makes you blind, the IUD produces deformed babies, and sterilization destroys normal hormonal functioning. In addition, wives expect and prefer their husband to take the lead on contraception, or want to

of condoms for contraception leaves control with the male partner and is unreliable. Apart from the many other objections to abortion, it also leaves control in the hands of the medical profession, which is often male-dominated. It is *personal* and *independent* control of her fertility that produces a change of perspective among women, even a psychological change, creating not only contraceptive confidence but also a sense of autonomy and personal freedom. The social and psychological significance for women of the contraceptive revolution has generally been underestimated by male demographers, with rare exceptions (Murphy 1993; see also Cleland 1985).[3]

The contraceptive revolution has three main effects. For the majority of women who choose to become mothers, it enables them to control the timing and spacing of childbirth, and hence improve the fit between employment and family life. For example a woman can delay childbirth until she fulfils the qualifying period for an employer's most generous maternity leave arrangements and benefits. Second, it allows women to avoid unwanted births and restrict family size. The third effect is to allow sexually active women to remain voluntarily childless, an option that is chosen by about one-fifth of women who reach adult life after the two revolutions. There are also wider social consequences.

The contraceptive revolution allows sexual activity to be divorced from reproduction.[4] This has led to the growth and development of recreational and casual sexual activity, and hence to diverse forms of sexual activity as new expressions of identity and lifestyle, such as transvestitism, to informal partnerships and cohabitation, and to the idea of marriage and parenthood for homosexuals as well as for heterosexuals.[5] It probably contributed to the

leave things to 'nature'. Women often exhibit passive personalities and rarely demonstrate autonomy and independence of thought or action, in part because men prefer innocent and sexually passive wives. So although Japanese women, like all women, prefer reliable methods of contraception that they can control themselves, in practice they leave the initiative to their husbands, while husbands do not consider the responsibility to be theirs (Coleman 1983: 89, 92–3,106, 143–4, 152, 166, 172, 173–4, 181). It is estimated that women have an average of two abortions during their married life; but this may be an underestimate, as many Japanese women have three or more abortions during their marriage simply to achieve the timing and spacing of births that is normally obtained by more reliable methods than condoms, with the accompanying emotional distress (Coleman 1983: 4, 195–6; Jolivet 1997).

[3] Reproductive control—free contraception and abortion on demand—was the only issue which attracted the unanimous support of all women during the second wave of the feminist movement in the 1960s and 1970s in Britain and other industrialized countries. Equal opportunities in the workforce tended to be a lower priority and attracted more diffuse support among non-feminist as well as feminist groups (Lovenduski and Randall 1993).

[4] Szreter (1996) shows that the low fertility rates observed in Britain at the beginning of the 20th century were achieved at the price of abstinence from sexual activity: not only the abstinence implied by delayed marriage but also, and more important, abstinence from sexual activity *within marriage*. Similarly, abstinence from sexual activity seems to be the first, and most important contraceptive method known to married women in less-developed countries (Cleland 1985: 229).

[5] Historians and social anthropologists show that antecedents can be found for many of the new expressions of sexual identity and lifestyle. For example there is a tradition of male transvestites and homosexual prostitution in Turkey and in Salvador, Brazil (Cornwall and Lindisfarne 1993), a tradition of male as well as female homosexual lovers and prostitution in Mombasa (Shepherd 1987),

expansion of pornography of various shadings, for women and men, linked to the idea of recreational sex.[6] The contraceptive revolution and the introduction of recreational sex within marriage, as well as with prostitutes and mistresses, has helped to break down the distinction held in many cultures between 'respectable' and 'not respectable' women, 'mothers' and 'whores', which men have long used as an ideological tool to control women (Lerner 1986), as illustrated by the rule that 'respectable' women should not work in mixed-sex workplaces, or should not even leave home unescorted.

The contraceptive revolution took place in the late 1960s in the USA and Britain, resulting in sharp social changes from the 1970s onwards. Therefore it is the USA and Britain that best illustrate the long-term social consequences of the contraceptive revolution. Westoff and Ryder's (1977) report on the USA 1970 National Fertility Study provided an early warning that the contraceptive revolution would produce a sharp and permanent fall in fertility levels. They pointed out that women had adopted the new, reliable forms of contraception with alacrity in the 1960s. In the five years 1965–70, the use of modern forms of contraception—the pill, IUD, and sterilization of either partner—increased from the minority to the majority, 37% to 58%, of all contraceptive practice among ever-married women under 45 years. Most of the increase was due to the rapid acceptance of the oral contraceptive pill. Attitudes also changed: by 1970 half of all wives approved of sterilization as a contraceptive method, and about one in ten couples had already chosen sterilization as their preferred method. Westoff and Ryder concluded that the modern contraceptive era started in the 1960s, enabling most couples, in all social groups, to stop child-bearing at the desired number of children. In this decade, desired fertility fell sharply, and so did unplanned births. After detailed analyses, Westoff and Ryder concluded that all the decline in marital fertility was due to a decline in unplanned births, which previously constituted about 43% of all births (Westoff and Ryder 1977: 304–5). This phenomenon occurred in all social groups, although the decline in unplanned births was greatest among the least educated women. It is notable that this change

and a tradition of male homosexual and transsexual domestic servants, the Xaniths, who formed a 'third gender', in Oman (Archer and Lloyd 1982: 94–100). These are mostly unique cases within each culture. The common element in these practices is that they provide men with wider sexual outlets, through homosexual contacts, prior to the contraceptive revolution, than are available through marriage, which ties sexual activity to responsibility for the reproductive consequences of heterosexual contacts. What the contraceptive revolution made possible in modern societies is alternative lifestyles for women as well as men, and an explosion of diverse forms of sexual activity and identity within a single society and culture, each community supported by clubs, social events, and magazines. The common element in these practices is that sexual activity is divorced from social arrangements for child-bearing and child-rearing, and is thus more of a personal 'lifestyle' choice.

[6] Even the growing demand for plastic surgery can be understood as a consequence of the growth in recreational sexual activity, as well as increasing affluence. As people live longer, and remain sexually active longer, with more turnover in sexual partners, they are more likely to want to retain the features of younger and sexually attractive people, rather than acquiring the features of older, androgenous people who have ceased to be sexually active.

occurred in a period when the majority of women aged under 45 years retained 'traditional' sex-role attitudes: over three-quarters of the survey sample accepted the sexual division of labour in the home and the majority regarded themselves as secondary earners (Westoff and Ryder 1977: 327–8). Large changes in sex-role attitudes came a decade later, in the 1970s (McLaughlin *et al.* 1988: 170–91; Davis 1996). By 1988, only 7% of births in the USA were unwanted (Taeuber 1996: 33–5; see also Davis, Bernstam, and Ricardo-Campbell 1987: 165). In contrast, the high fertility of women in developing countries is due largely to ignorance of contraception and to substantial numbers of unwanted births (Lightbourne 1987; Caldwell and Caldwell 1997). For example, fertility surveys in metropolitan Latin America in 1963–64 showed that, on average, half of all births were unwanted, ranging from a low of 43% in Buenos Aires to 62% in Ecuador (CELADE and CFSC 1972: 107).

A survey of contraceptive practice among women aged 16–49 years in Britain in 1995 (ONS 1997: 144–70) showed that three-quarters of all women and four-fifths of married and cohabiting women were using some form of contraception. Over half (56%) of all women and almost two-thirds (61%) of married and cohabiting women were using one of the modern forms of contraception, including a tiny number who were sterile from another operation. The pill and sterilization were the most popular, with stable levels of use; one-quarter of all women used each of these. This survey also revealed clear indications of voluntary childlessness: 8% of women aged 40–44 and 16% of women aged 45–49 who had no children had chosen sterilization for contraceptive purposes (ONS 1997: 160). After a careful examination of fertility trends in Britain 1963–1980, Murphy (1993: 239) concluded that the introduction of modern contraception in the 1960s caused a substantive change in women's behaviour which eventually caused an increase in female employment. He points out that the contraceptive revolution is an essentially irreversible change. Once women experience the benefits of efficient contraception, they will not revert to the riskier old methods.

As soon as women gain control over their fertility, they choose to have far fewer children than was typical in the past, and some will have none. In the process, they learn to take explicit control of their lives and to make self-conscious choices.[7] This is illustrated by the choices young women are now

[7] From his review of World Fertility Survey results and other evidence, Cleland (1985) concluded that the high fertility levels of the past were not necessarily chosen or intended by women, even if accepted, and were probably due mainly to simple ignorance of contraceptive methods; that the conscious regulation of marital fertility is a very recent innovation, in Europe as well as in Third World societies; and that family size preferences do not seem to have changed greatly over time—rather, the key change was effective modern methods of contraception which allowed preferences to be translated into behaviour. Similarly Caldwell and Caldwell (1997) insist that there was no fertility control in any society prior to the demographic transition of the 20th century which started in the Western world but became a global phenomenon after 1965 due to modern forms of contraception—with the exception of France where the demographic transition started a century earlier, soon after the 1789 Revolution.

TABLE 3.1. *Pregnancy and births during teenage years by highest educational qualification among women aged 20–24 in 1991*

	Degree	Other higher education or A-levels	0-levels	None
Teen birth	0	3	18	42
Abortion only by age 24	16	11	11	6
Neither teen birth nor any abortion by age 24	84	86	71	52
Total N=100%	90	403	541	157

Source: Table 5ii, reporting data from the 1991 Survey of Sexual Attitudes and Lifestyles, in K. Wellings *et al. Teenage Sexuality, Fertility and Life Chances*, London School of Hygiene and Tropical Medicine, 1996, p. 39.

making in modern societies between a life centred around children versus the pursuit of educational qualifications and a career (Table 3.1). Girls who see themselves as having poor prospects of success in the educational system have no reason to delay sexual activity and child-bearing, and see no reason to have an abortion if they have an unplanned pregnancy. Girls who are told, or realize for themselves that they have the potential to get a university degree, have good reason to postpone child-bearing. If they get pregnant accidentally, the solution is an abortion. The choice between a teenage birth and the pursuit of higher education qualifications is a *connected choice* (Hakim 1998a: 241–4) and it makes little sense to ask which came first. Similarly, it makes no sense for highly educated social scientists to impose their own values in classifying teenage mothers as 'deprived' victims. The birth of a baby, and the mother's independent 'ownership' of the child, can give young women as much joy and power as gaining an educational qualification. Since motherhood also gives a young woman priority access to public sector housing and an independent social welfare income in Britain, it can confer as much adult status as a (low-paid) job. Teenage mothers actively choose their lifestyle by choosing *not* to have an abortion, whereas girls who go on to higher education choose an abortion in the same circumstances, and probably switch to more reliable contraception thereafter.[8] The meaning of a

[8] A study based on 59 depth interviews in Toronto, Canada, shows that the two groups have different conceptions of where motherhood fits into their lives (McMahon 1995). Young women with secondary school education took child-bearing for granted as a central feature of their lives, had children earlier, and felt they attained adult status and self-identity through motherhood. Young women with university degrees delayed motherhood until after they had achieved adult status and self-identity through material and personal achievements: a career, home ownership, and the right relationship. Similar results are reported from a national fertility survey in Britain (Dunnell 1979: 24–6).

completed teenage pregnancy after the contraceptive revolution is quite different from its meaning before: it now reflects a real choice in most cases, and one that may be entirely 'rational' for the mothers in question.[9]

The USA and Britain demonstrate that the contraceptive revolution produces a decline in overall fertility and a rise in voluntary childlessness. However this does not mean that all women reject motherhood as a central life activity. Teenage mothers may be an extreme case, but they remind us that some young women still choose to centre their lives on motherhood and family life. Women who start child-bearing early usually go on to have larger than average families.

The evidence for continental Europe shows a very mixed pattern. In countries where male politicians pursue pronatalist policies, often under the ideological cover of religious ideas, the contraceptive revolution has been long delayed. The most obvious example is the Republic of Ireland, a Catholic country where contraception of any sort, and abortion, were still not formally available by the end of the 20th century. But many other countries that claim to honour women, and women's rights, have been almost as slow to change. For example in France, contraception and abortion were legalized only in the 1970s and they did not become free, with costs reimbursed, until the 1980s. Rights to reproductive control are still regarded as sufficiently fragile in France to require pro-active pressure group support, with major public demonstrations to support these rights in the late 1990s. The ban on contraception in Spain was removed only in 1979, and a major decline in fertility occurred in the 1980s.

By the 1990s, around four-fifths of women were using some form of contraception in almost all EU countries. Levels of use only fall below four-fifths in Portugal (66%), Spain (59%), and probably also Greece and Ireland, for which no data are available (European Commission 1997b: 23). However, for our purposes the relevant indicator is the proportion of women using *modern* contraception. A rough measure is whether a good majority of women in any country are using one of the three modern methods instead of other forms. The most recent cross-national comparative study reports survey data for the 1970s and 1980s, which may be dated (Coleman 1996a: 35). The contraceptive revolution had already happened in some countries by the early 1980s. Modern forms of contraception were dominant, providing between 70% and 86% of contraceptive practice in Belgium, the Netherlands, West Germany, Sweden, Norway, Switzerland, and Austria. The contraceptive

[9] A longitudinal study of a nationally representative sample of mothers in Britain suggests that lone mothers have always been a self-selected group who choose motherhood as a main activity due to their failure to obtain any educational qualifications at school. The proportion of women with no qualifications at all declines steadily across age cohorts. In contrast, the proportion is virtually constant among lone mothers: in all age groups almost half have no qualifications at all, giving them access to only the lowest grade, poorest-paid jobs if they did work (Bryson, Ford, and White 1997).

revolution was delayed in Italy (21%), Portugal (35%), Spain (44%), and no doubt Greece and Ireland, for which no data were available. In the late 1970s, Finland, Denmark, and France were still borderline cases, with contraceptive users split fairly evenly between modern and old methods (Coleman 1996a: 35).

What is certain is that, from 1960 onwards, overall fertility fell sharply to new, lower levels in all EU countries (McIntosh 1983; Coleman 1996a: 12–17; European Commission 1997b: 22), a phenomenon which is treated as part of the 'second demographic transition'.[10] Demographers insist they do not know the reasons for the decline in fertility levels, and continue to debate the relative importance of women's employment, relative incomes, attitudinal change, and contraceptive practices (Siegers, de Jong-Gierveld, and van Imhoff 1991). Similarly, few demographers are prepared to forecast fertility in the 21st century (Hall and White 1995: 44–6; Coleman 1996b: 11, 159). Preference theory argues that the contraceptive revolution constitutes a qualitative change in fertility behaviour. However there is no necessary or causal link between the use of modern contraception and overall fertility levels, nor is there any link between the overall fertility level and childlessness rates in any country (Coleman 1996a: 32, 34).

Voluntary Childlessness

Voluntary childlessness is a social change of sufficient importance to merit separate discussion, even though it is just one consequence of the contraceptive revolution. Fortunately, there is substantial evidence on the topic from historical studies, social attitude surveys, surveys of fertility, and case-study research on the childfree.

Rising childlessness is the new trend that many feminists have refused to see, and that many social scientists, including demographers, have been slow to address. Hall and White (1995: 45), Coleman (1996a: 31–40) and McRae (1997: 388–91) are unusual in discussing the steady increase in childlessness in recent years. More often, scholars fail to notice the trend. In Scandinavia, there is a distinct tendency to deny that childlessness exists on any scale at all, that it is rising, and that it is clearly voluntary when it occurs after the

[10] The 'first demographic transition' in Europe began around the 1870s and ran up to the 1930s. It consisted of a transition from high birth rates and high death rates to a new pattern of low birth rates and low death rates. Demographers use the label of 'second demographic transition' to refer to the new decline in fertility, declining mortality, rising divorce, and other demographic changes that developed simultaneously from the 1960s onwards. Van de Kaa (1987) argues that the first demographic transition reflected a change in values, with a new emphasis on altruistic and collectivist concerns for the quality of family life and offspring, whereas the second demographic transition to lower fertility reflects a new emphasis on individualistic values.

contraceptive revolution. For example, Bernhardt (1993) reviews research on fertility and employment without a single mention of voluntary childlessness. In fact, childlessness is rising slowly but steadily in both Norway and Sweden, despite their family-friendly policies, and will soon reach the 20% level that seems to be the stable plateau in most prosperous modern societies. In the 1955–1956 birth cohorts, some 14%–15% of women were childless at age 40 in Norway and Sweden.[11] Rates continue to rise slowly, and are projected to reach 16%–18% in cohorts born in the 1960s (Coleman 1996a: 33).

Hakim (1996a: 125) notes that in Australia, the USA, Britain, and West Germany, about 20% of post-war cohorts are already, or are predicted to remain childless. Coleman (1996a: 33) identifies seven European countries with around 20% of women childless by age 40: Britain, Austria, Finland, West Germany, Switzerland, and Sweden. In Belgium, Denmark, France, Ireland, Italy, and Norway there was a rising trend, sometimes from low levels. In Spain, childlessness was falling. Portugal seems unique in having a low, stable level of about 10% of women aged 40. It is clear that voluntary childlessness can be high in countries with egalitarian and family-friendly social policies, in countries with strong support for role segregation in the family and full-time homemakers, and in countries with contradictory policies such as Britain. Coleman points out that none of the variables usually employed by demographers helps to explain cross-national variations in fertility. He concludes that ideas and values, and hence education and the media, could be far more important than demographers have so far thought (Coleman 1996a: 40).

In the USA, over 20% of women born 1900 to 1914 were still childless at age 35 and beyond that. By the 1935–1939 birth cohort, the rate had fallen to 9% (Gerson 1985: 236). It then started rising again to current levels. By 1994, 19% of all women aged 35–39 were still childless, almost double the 10.5% rate in 1976 (Taeuber 1996: 35). The rate varied with women's qualifications: 34% of women with professional and graduate degrees and 28% of women in professional and managerial occupations were childless. The majority of childless women aged 35–39 do not expect to have any children (Taeuber 1996: 35).

Some argue that high childlessness rates include a large element of involuntary childlessness. This cannot be so. The World Fertility Survey undertaken in the 1970s with the support of the United Nations (Cleland and Hobcraft 1985; Cleland and Scott 1987) shows that primary infertility affects only 2%–3% of women aged 25–50 (Vaessen 1984). Childlessness rates above this level in modern societies are clearly determined by social and economic

[11] Personal communications from demographers in Norway and Sweden, in particular Marianne Sundström.

factors rather than simple infertility.[12] In effect, women are making lifestyle choices when they decide to have children, or not, and when they impose social or economic conditions on their child-bearing. For example, women who are unwilling to have children unless they have a permanent partner to support them, are making a lifestyle choice. Many women of Afro-Caribbean descent are not deterred by potentially unstable relationships, proceed to have children in similar circumstances, and raise them single-handed if necessary.

Childlessness itself is not new. In the past, large proportions of certain cohorts of women have not had any children—for example 20% of women born in 1920 in Britain remained childless. But childlessness in the past has been associated with low marriage rates, shortages of men due to wars, and the poverty and poor nutrition associated with recessions in the 1920s and 1930s. So involuntary and voluntary childlessness were not easily distinguished in the past. The current trend emerges among women who are sexually active from a young age, expect to marry at least once in their reproductive years, and are healthy and prosperous.[13]

Rowland (1999) compares trends in childlessness among the cohorts born between 1840 and 1954 in Britain, France, Finland, West Germany, the Netherlands, Australia, and the USA. He shows that rates rose to between 15% and 32% among cohorts born in the second half of the 19th century. For example in France, one-quarter of the women born in 1900–1904 remained childless by age 45; the rate declined slowly up to the 1945–1949 cohort. From 1900 onwards, childlessness rates fell steadily in all seven countries from around one in four down to one in ten of the cohorts born in 1930–1944, between the two World Wars. From then on they start rising again. Data for other countries show similar trends. Portugal and Hungary also had declining rates among cohorts born in the first half of the 20th century. However, Belgium and Japan had remarkably stable levels of childlessness (Rowland 1999: Table 1).

The causes and circumstances of childlessness in the past meant that it was

[12] Infertility due to ill-health is usually the cause of childlessness in developing countries. Extraordinarily high rates of infertility and childlessness are documented in sub-Saharan Africa, where high levels of fertility are regarded as desirable and advantageous. For example childlessness rates of 20%–40% are recorded for parts of Central Africa, including the Central African Republic, South-Western Sudan, North Zaire, Congo, Gabon, and the United Republic of Cameroon. The main cause is widespread gonorrhoea which remains untreated (Frank 1983). At the same time, childlessness can be desired and preferred even in developing countries. The World Fertility Survey of the late 1970s found that substantial minorities of women aged 15–49 who had not yet had a child wanted to remain childfree, ranging from 0%–3% in African countries, and 2%–9% in South America, to 14% in Portugal. It is not known what proportion of the women who already had children would also have preferred to remain childfree. Overall, in most developing countries, women prefer to have substantially fewer children than they actually have (Lightbourne 1987).

[13] Childlessness in Japan is unusual, in being associated with a refusal to marry among young women (Tanaka 1998; see also Tsuya and Mason 1995). Within marriage, childbirth remains universal.

TABLE 3.2. *The increasing acceptability of childlessness*

Percentage agreeing that a marriage without children is not fully complete

	Total	Men born in –			All men	Women born in –			All women
		1950–1970	1930–1949	pre-1930		1950–1970	1930–1949	pre-1930	
Irish Republic	48	45	59	55	51	39	48	54	45
Britain	45	35	54	73	51	29	40	63	41
USA	44	34	46	64	44	34	46	56	44
West Germany	37	24	45	54	38	25	40	51	36

Source: J. Scott, M. Braun, and D. F. Alwin, 'The family way' in R. Jowell (ed) *International Social Attitudes*, Dartmouth Press, 1993, pp 30–1, reporting 1988 ISSP results.

regarded as an affliction rather than an advantage (Dykstra 1999; Rowland 1999). For example in most societies, children were often important helpers in family farms and businesses, and elderly people had to rely on their children for financial support in old age. Fertility meant survival. Today, pension schemes provide a reliable alternative to support by children. Strong cultural norms in favour of child-bearing as undeniably 'normal' and 'natural' have also led to childless women feeling marginalized and being stigmatized (Goodbody 1977; Boulton 1983: 3–7; McBroom 1986; Morell 1994; Dykstra 1999), and even being accused of witchcraft (May 1995: 28).

This stigma seems to be disappearing now, as childlessness becomes more acceptable, even though an almost unvarying four-fifths of adults reiterate the joys of having children in attitude surveys. Among the cohorts born before 1930 in the USA, Britain, Ireland, and West Germany, half to three-quarters of women and men agreed that a marriage without children is not fully complete. Among the cohorts born in 1950–70, only a minority, around one-third, agreed with this idea (Table 3.2). By 1988, the great majority of women and men in the younger generations felt that a marriage can be complete without children. In all four countries, only a minority, from 15% to 35%, agreed that people who have never had children lead empty lives. Similarly, one-third or less agreed that the main purpose of marriage is to have children: one-third of men and women in the Irish Republic, one-quarter of men and women in West Germany, one-fifth of men and women in Britain, down to one in ten of men and women in the USA (Scott, Braun, and Alwin 1993: 29–32). There is corroborating evidence from other surveys. The spring 1993 Eurobarometer No. 39 found that 15% of Europeans did not regard having a child as personally important to them, while only 17% felt it was 'essential'. Men had the most extreme and polarized views. Overall, children were more important to women than men, in all age groups, but there was notable cross-national variation (European Commission 1993).

In 1962, 84% of a sample of American mothers agreed that 'almost everyone should have children if they can'; by 1980, only 43% still accepted the norm (McLaughlin *et al.* 1988: 188; see also Blake 1979). Surveys of high school seniors in the USA in 1972, 1982, and 1992, and follow-ups in the years after, show that less than half of young Americans now list having children as a major life goal: 39% of boys and 49% of girls (Taeuber 1996: 313). Over the two decades 1972–1992, there was a massive swing towards openly materialist life values among high school seniors. In 1972, only 10% of girls and 26% of boys listed 'having lots of money' as a major life goal. By 1982, the percentages rose to 24% and 41%, and then rose again to 29% and 45% by 1992. Such an upsurge in materialist aspirations must alter the cost-benefit assessment of the rewards of having children.

Children seem to be a lower priority than in the past, but few couples are prepared to say, bluntly, that they want no children at all. Eurobarometer surveys reported by Coleman (1996a: 38–9), Belgian fertility surveys reported in Siegers, de Jong-Gierveld, and van Imhoff (1991: 77, 81) and West German opinion polls reported by Rowland (1999) show that no more than 10% of childless women aged 18–37 years state that they want no children at all, although many others say they are unsure. West Germany had the highest percentages, with 9% in 1979 and 7% in 1989 saying they wanted no children, but even these figures are far lower than the actual proportion remaining childless in recent decades. These results are explained by qualitative studies of childless women, which show that they divide broadly into two groups. Roughly one-third decide explicitly and early, before marriage, that they do not wish to be involved in parental roles. Roughly two-thirds are 'postponers' and the undecided, who repeatedly postpone child-bearing to give priority to other activities, such as careers or the desire to own a home, until the point where they admit explicitly that they are not prepared to give up the advantages of a childfree lifestyle (Veevers 1973; Houseknecht 1979). Only the minority of early deciders would show up in social attitude surveys as explicitly choosing childlessness. The majority, postponers and undecideds, would report the decision as still pending, for years.

There is now a burgeoning research literature on the characteristics, lifestyles and personalities of people who choose to remain childfree—in Canada (Veevers 1972, 1973, 1974, 1979, 1980), the USA (Goodbody 1977; Houseknecht 1979, 1987; Harper 1980; Bloom and Pebley 1982; Gerson 1985; English 1989; Lang 1991; Morgan 1991; Crispell 1993; Somers 1993; Morell 1994; May 1995), Britain (Baum and Cope 1980; Baum 1982, 1983; Campbell 1985; Kiernan 1989; Bartlett 1994; McAllister and Clarke 1998), Australia (Rowland 1982; Callan 1985, 1986; Lewis 1986; Marshall 1993), New Zealand (Cameron 1997), West Germany (Nave-Herz 1989) and Japan (Jolivet 1997), along with more general discussions (Blake 1979; Houseknecht 1982; Brass 1989; Rovi 1994; Chesnais 1995). All this research was done from the 1970s onwards, and reflects the choices women make in the new scenario, after the contraceptive revolution. Only a few studies compare women and men (for example Blake 1979; Kiernan 1989). Dykstra and Call (1999) review the research results on childlessness among older cohorts, in earlier decades. In addition there is a complementary literature on the meaning and value of motherhood for women, women's reasons for choosing to have children, how motherhood changes their sense of identity, and how sex-role attitudes are linked both to child-bearing and employment (Scanzoni 1976; Badinter 1981; Dally 1982; Boulton 1983; Ruddick 1989; Cameron 1990; Carrier 1995; McMahon 1995).

A full review of research findings on people who are childless by choice is beyond the scope of this book, but the main points can be noted briefly. Childless women today are typically sexually active, often married or cohabiting, and not the unmarried spinsters that were so common in earlier decades with low marriage rates. They are found in all social groups, including the most prosperous and well-educated, so childlessness is no longer a misfortune imposed by poverty or ill-health. Childlessness is more common in urban than in rural areas, though it is not clear whether this is due to self-selection into urban residence, or due to the impact of urban crowding and lifestyles—probably both are important. The highest proportions of childless women—up to 50%—are among women with higher education qualifications and women in professional and managerial occupations. Childless women, and couples, are no longer a marginalized or stigmatized deviant group, but people who choose one distinctive lifestyle. There are two groups: those who reject the disadvantages of children—who usually decide early—and those who are not prepared to lose the advantages of a childfree lifestyle—who usually decide late. The paths to childlessness are varied; there is no social homogeneity in the group and no single type of childless woman or man, apart from a greater need for control among the childless as compared with people with children. Childlessness is now a choice that many young women, especially graduate women, consider seriously at some point in their lives, including those who later have children (McMahon 1995: 93). Voluntary childlessness demonstrates that the contraceptive revolution has produced psychological as well as social changes: women have gained control over their lifecourses.

Finally, voluntary childlessness also refutes the idea that all women have a natural or instinctive desire for motherhood. Badinter (1981) has demonstrated that the maternal instinct is a myth, and that women's attitudes towards their children are socially structured, while Boulton (1983) demonstrated the heterogeneity of women's responses to motherhood. The World Values Surveys have shown that the idea that a woman 'has to have children in order to feel fulfilled' is part of the survival-oriented ideology of materialist values but is rejected in postmaterialist ideology (Inglehart 1990: 198–9, 209, 1997: 271, Figure A19; Inglehart, Basañez, and Moreno 1998: Table V215). Active and involved motherhood becomes a lifestyle choice in postmodern society.

The Equal Opportunities Revolution

Some commentators complain that the equal opportunities revolution failed because it did not deliver 'equality for women'. But it was never intended, nor expected, to deliver equality of *outcomes* for women and men (Richards 1994). The intention was, rather, to deliver equality of *opportunity* in society, through equality of access to education and training, the labour market, financial institutions, housing, publicly provided leisure facilities, and so forth. The elimination of systematic, overt, and intentional sex (and race) discrimination from all areas of social life is a major achievement of modern society.

The equal opportunities revolution illustrates the effectiveness and diversity of social engineering. In North America and Western Europe all four of the usual mechanisms of social engineering were employed in various combinations: legislation, fiscal policy, ideological reform and moral exhortation, and institutional change. Like all policy instruments, they sometimes have unforeseen and undesirable effects.

In most countries, legislation prohibiting sex and race discrimination, and promoting equal treatment of men and women in the labour force, and in other areas of public life, has been the principal tool of social engineering. But it is by no means the only one. Lawyers are inclined to forget this, and demand a strengthening of laws so as to give them greater power and authority to mould society and the social roles of men and women (Fredman 1997). In Europe, the main tool of social engineering is legislation prohibiting sex discrimination, especially in pay, and promoting equal treatment of men and women in the labour force. It is the only mechanism common to all member states of the European Union. For this reason, it has attracted a disproportionate amount of attention (Hakim 1996a: 187–201; Hoskyns 1996; Fredman 1997). In practice, other national policies to facilitate women's access to education and to the labour market, or to bring about a change in attitudes on women's role in society, are probably just as important as legislation. These other developments are more dispersed and diverse. They vary between countries and have variable effects, so they remain less visible, less tangible than a catalogue of new laws. They are none the less real in their effects.

In countries where the change in legislation does not reflect a parallel change in the ideological and political climate, equal opportunities laws can have little impact—as illustrated by Japan (Cook and Hayashi 1980; Fujimura-Fanselow and Kameda 1995; Jolivet 1997). In other countries, such as China, ideological reform and moral exhortation were sufficient to achieve major changes in the sexual division of labour and the role of women in society, with legislation playing a secondary, supportive role (Stockman, Bonney, and Sheng 1995: 141–54; Hakim 1996a: 93–8).

In some countries, fiscal policy is actively deployed as a powerful tool of social engineering. Fiscal policy influences the employment decisions of secondary earners and, to a lesser extent, the hours worked by primary earners, by changing income tax rules and social welfare benefit rules to alter the net benefits from different quantities of wage work by one or both persons in a couple (Kay and King 1978: 37; Parker 1995). For example, husband and wife may be taxed separately as individuals or jointly as a couple; tax allowances and benefits may be transferable or not. Eligibility for important welfare benefits, such as pensions, may be dependent on a person's own employment record and contributions, or wives may be allowed to benefit from their husband's work record, or full-time housewives may be credited with pension rights despite not working. For example in Sweden the individualization of taxes and benefits pushed most women, including mothers, into the labour market. In other countries, such as the Netherlands, women acquire rights to maintenance and social welfare through economic dependence on their husband and his taxes, or through their function as mothers and caregivers (Sainsbury 1996). Female employment rates in the Netherlands remain the lowest in Europe as a result, with only 20% of women in full-time work (Pott-Buter 1993; Blossfeld and Hakim 1997). In contrast, Sweden has one of the highest female workrates, both on a headcount basis and on a Full-Time Equivalent (FTE) basis,[14] as shown in Table 3.3.

Institutional change consists of changing the operation of important social institutions, such as elections, the military, the educational system, the legal system, and courts. For women, institutional change often consists of removing barriers to their participation in activities in the public domain. One example is the decision to give all women the vote, which happened before 1950 in most countries. Another example is the decision to allow women to become priests and religious leaders, which is still debated in some religions. Institutional change is the least flexible mechanism of social engineering; it generally produces results only in the long term. For example, introducing military service for all women as well as for men, as did China and Israel, can be one way of breaking down sex-role stereotyping and occupational segregation in the long term. But USA experience with mixed-sex units in the military

[14] Full-Time Equivalent (FTE) employment rates are adjusted to take account of the different hours worked by full-time and part-time workers. At the simplest level, FTE workrates count two part-time workers as equivalent to one full-time worker. In contrast, headcount employment rates give the same weight to full-time and part-time workers.

TABLE 3.3. *Comparisons of workrates and part-time work in Europe and the USA, 1997*

	Working age population 15–64 (millions)	Total employment (millions)	Employment rates (% of working age population)			Part-time workers (% of all employed)		FTE employment rate
			All	Men	Women	Women	Men	Women
USA	165.8	119.4	72	79	65	25	11	57
European Union								
Denmark	3.5	2.7	78	84	71	35	12	60
Finland	3.4	2.2	64	67	61	16	8	57
Sweden	5.6	3.9	70	71	68	41	9	56
Portugal	6.7	4.5	68	77	59	15	6	55
Austria	5.3	3.7	70	80	60	29	4	52
UK	37.6	26.6	71	78	64	45	9	48
France	37.1	22.3	60	68	53	31	5	46
Germany	55.0	33.9	62	70	54	35	4	43
Luxembourg	0.3	0.2	61	76	47	19	1	42
Ireland	2.4	1.4	58	70	45	23	5	40
Belgium	6.7	3.8	57	68	47	31	3	40
Greece	6.8	3.9	57	75	40	8	3	39
Italy	39.1	20.0	51	66	37	14	3	35
Netherlands	10.6	7.0	67	78	55	68	17	35
Spain	26.3	12.8	49	64	34	17	3	31
EU15	246.3	149.0	61	71	51	32	6	42
Other European countries								
Poland	23.9	13.8	58	64	52	13	9	49
Slovenia	1.4	0.9	62	66	58	2	1	57
Hungary	6.8	5.5	81	85	77	2	1	76

Notes: The FTE (full-time equivalent) employment rate assumes that most part-timers work half-time hours, so that two part-time workers are equivalent to one full-time worker. Figures for the USA relate to the population aged 16–64 instead of the population aged 15–64 and part-time jobs are slightly underestimated compared to European countries. USA CPS statistics define part-time workers as people whose weekly hours, in all jobs, total less than 35 hours, rather than people working part-time in their main job. Part-time work is self-defined in the EU Labour Force Survey, with some variation between countries in the upper limit for what are regarded as a part-time hours.

Sources: EU Labour Force Survey data for 1997 and other sources reported in European Commission, *Employment in Europe 1998*, 1998, and estimates from other sources for 1994 for Eastern Europe and for the USA reported in Table 1.1 in H.-P. Blossfeld and C. Hakim, *Between Equalization and Marginalisation*, 1997, Oxford University Press.

is seen as having had undesirable side effects, leading to demands to reintroduce segregation, whereas mixed-race units for men only were more successful.

One of the most universal examples of successful institutional change is the abolition of the marriage bar as a result of laws prohibiting discrimination on grounds of sex or marital status. The *marriage bar* was the prohibition on married women's employment which ensured that jobs, especially white-collar jobs, were reserved for men.[15] In the USA, Britain, and other European countries, the marriage prohibition took the form of strong social norms against wives going out to work, especially in the middle classes; these norms were sometimes institutionalized in company rules and policies, especially for white-collar jobs such as teaching and clerical work (ILO 1962; Oppenheimer 1970: 39–55; Cohn 1985: 99; Walby 1986: 171–2, 180, 247; Grint 1988: 96; Bradley 1989: 211–3; Goldin 1990: 160–79). Throughout history, the non-working wife, or concubine, has been a status symbol, proof of affluence and often essential to achieving high levels of consumption. In the second half of the nineteenth century, formal policies were invented to exclude wives from wage work. Historians and sociologists have shown how the 'bourgeois' ideal of marriage, with the wife devoted full-time to creating a haven of comfort and relaxation for the family, was more often aspired to than achieved by working class families, as it relied on the husband having adequate and regular earnings (Holcombe 1973; Pollert 1981; Roberts 1984). Marriage bars were often strengthened during the Depression (Walby 1986: 180), with social norms sometimes reinforced by law. In the Netherlands, for example, a law introduced in 1935 prohibited wives from holding jobs in the civil service, thus reserving jobs for men during the 1930s recession. However the law was not repealed until 1957, long after the recession, and it encouraged private sector firms to apply similar rules, which lasted until 1979 (Pott-Buter 1993: 246–51; Tijdens 1993: 79, 87). In Britain, the marriage bar was a legally enforceable rule that women left employment upon marriage. It was applied mainly to white-collar occupations and was jointly imposed and policed by employers and trade unions in certain industries. Resignation from work was 'sweetened' by giving the bride a lump sum payment which some scholars understood to be a 'dowry' or bribe to promote turnover (Cohn 1985: 102) but was usually a refund of pension contributions paid so far, as wives were expected to rely on their husband's earnings and pension rights.

[15] To our knowledge there is only one case of a marriage bar that was applied to men instead of women. Up to about 1880–1900, academics at Oxford and Cambridge universities, who were all men, were obliged to resign on marriage, due to the 700-year-old rules of celibacy that were inherited from the two universities' early origins as religious teaching institutions closely tied to the Christian Church, a tradition that also produced the semi-monastic character of many of the oldest colleges. The two women's colleges in Cambridge University, Girton and Newnham, were only established very late, in the period 1870 onwards, at the same time that the celibacy rules were being abolished in all the men's colleges—see Sciama (1984).

There is some debate over the social impact of the marriage bar, its economic efficiency and profitability in the period 1870–1950 in the USA and Britain (Cohn 1985; Walby 1986: 247; Grint 1988; Goldin: 1990: 160–79). It seems clear that its main effect was to support the sexual division of labour, and power, within marriage. The key motive was patriarchy rather than profit, benefiting all men rather than a few employers (Grint 1988: 97). Marriage bars institutionalized the marriage career for women and discouraged young women from investing in qualifications and careers. After World War II, the marriage bar was outlawed through equal opportunities and sex discrimination legislation, from 1971 onwards in Britain, from the 1960s in the USA and other European countries, but not until 1985 in Japan, for example, where the custom of dismissing women on marriage continues regardless (Cook and Hayashi 1980; Jolivet 1997: 46–7, 50–3). Direct and overt discrimination against married women became unlawful throughout Western industrial societies and in many other countries as well by the 1970s.

It is customary to focus on women's recent gains in the labour market as an indicator of the impact of the equal opportunities revolution. Although less easy to measure, the impact on attitudes and expectations may be equally important, and provide the basis for increased achievements in the educational system as well as in employment and public life. For example, psychologists have found that sex differences in mathematical and verbal ability were relatively large before 1973 in the USA, then declined by half after 1973 (Hyde 1996: 112). This suggests that social and cultural factors played an important role in the past in shaping abilities that are sometimes regarded as innate and therefore unalterable. For example boys were expected to be good at mathematics and girls were discouraged from taking such courses, producing self-fulfilling expectations. The change also suggests that sex differences in educational attainment can be virtually eliminated in any society after the equal opportunities revolution.

Opening the educational system to women has dramatic effects. From the 1970s onwards, women flooded into professional and managerial occupations on a scale never seen before in Europe and North America (Blitz 1974; Hakim 1979; Sokoloff 1992; Rubery and Fagan 1993; Hakim 1996a: 152–6). For example in Britain, women's share of top jobs increased sharply after 1971. Between 1971 and 1991, women's share of professional, technical and managerial occupations increased from a trivial amount, in most cases, to a level close to, or above the average 32% female share of full-time jobs (Hakim 1996a: 152–7). For example, the percentage of women in the legal profession—judges, barristers, advocates, and solicitors—jumped from 4% in 1971 to 27% by 1991; the female share of personnel and industrial relations managers, O&M and work study officers rose from 12% to 46% by 1991; the percentage of women doctors and dentists rose from 18% in 1971 to 30% by 1991. A similar influx to professional occupations is found almost everywhere. However, women's entry to management positions was much slower, and was fastest in liberal economies rather than in countries with egalitarian and family-friendly policies. For example only 1.5% of women working full-time have management posts in Sweden, compared to 11% in the USA (Rosenfeld and Kalleberg 1990; see also Wright, Baxter and Birkelund 1995).

By the 1990s, equal pay and comparable worth policies had effectively eliminated sex discrimination in pay at the national level in the USA, Britain, and many western European countries. From the late 1980s onwards, all the pay gap between men and women could be explained by sufficiently detailed information on occupational grade, and the educational and other requirements of the job. In the USA and Britain, there is no longer any evidence that female-dominated occupations pay less than male-dominated occupations purely because women do the work (Macpherson and Hirsch 1995; Hakim 1996a: 149–86, 1998a: 79–81; Tam T. 1997; see also England 1992: 181). As financial institutions are no longer permitted to discriminate against women, access to loans and credit for house purchase and starting a business opened up new opportunities for women. Female self-employment and small firm ownership has in consequence expanded along with male self-employment in the 1980s and 1990s (Hakim 1998a: 200–20). There is increasing acceptance of women in roles carrying power and authority, as senior managers, political representatives, or in senior political posts—such as ambassador. Young women have aspirations and expectations that were inconceivable before the equal opportunities revolution.

A 1998 British court case illustrates the wide impact of laws prohibiting indirect, as well as direct sex discrimination (Barnard and Hepple 1999: 406). Susan Edwards, a single mother train driver found it impossible to care for her child when her employer, London Underground, introduced a new system of seven-day variable shifts, and she was forced to quit her job in 1992. She claimed sex discrimination and won her legal case after several appeals. London Underground pointed out that only 21 train drivers were women, compared with 2023 men, and that all the other 20 women drivers had accepted the new shift system, along with the men. They argued that the change did not disadvantage 'considerably more women than men'; it disadvantaged just one woman while 100% of the men and 95% of the women had accepted the new shift system. None the less, the Employment Appeal Tribunal decided in 1998 that the new shift system discriminated against women, who were more likely to be lone parents, and that the claimant was entitled to substantial damages for loss of earnings.

It seems fair to conclude that the equal opportunities revolution has been achieved in a country where the majority of men and women have been persuaded of the need to rewrite gender roles to allow women to function independently of husbands, if they so wish; where central government legislation exists to promote and enforce equal treatment of women and men in the labour market, education and other main areas of public life; and where there are mechanisms for enforcing rules of non-discrimination even among those workers, trade unions, employers, and service-providers who are inclined to ignore them.[16] On this definition, the equal opportunities revolution took place in the 1960s and 1970s in the USA, in the early 1970s in Britain, from the 1960s up to the end of the century in Italy, in the 1980s and 1990s in Germany, but has not yet taken place in Japan, for example. In many countries, equal opportunities laws were passed some years after the first, basic, equal pay laws. In some countries, it still took many years more for such laws to be implemented in full across all industries and organizations across the whole country. We might also conclude that the equal opportunities revolution is incomplete in countries where there are no mechanisms for enforcing compliance, for example through labour courts.

The Expansion of White-collar and Service Work

The combination of the contraceptive revolution and the equal opportunities revolution gives women a real choice between motherhood and employment as central life activities. Recent changes in the labour market are also important, because they have produced a much more *attractive* range of occupations and jobs for women. The long-term decline of manufacturing industry relative to service industries has changed the *occupational structure*. In addition, recessions and the resulting workforce restructuring in the 1970s, 1980s, and 1990s have changed the type of *jobs* available in the workforce, producing a greater diversity of working hours and contracts. The impact of these two changes together is greater than if they occur singly.

A long-term trend towards services is common to all advanced economies as real income rises and technology advances. In 1996 the service sector accounted for 65% of total employment in the European Union. Since 1980, services are the only area of activity in which there has been net job creation in Europe. Overall, the number employed in services increased by some 19 million between 1980 and 1996, while employment in manufacturing and agriculture fell by around 13 million. However, services account for an even larger share of employment in the USA, at 73% of all jobs (European Commission 1997c: 85). Scientific and technological innovations, notably the introduction of information technology, are reducing the manpower needs of manufacturing industry by making labour more productive. The growth of new service industries, such as financial services, and expanding

[16] The European Commission goes further, arguing for 'gender equality' in all spheres of activity, including political representation (Cockburn 1996; European Commission 1997a).

demand for consumer goods and services, health services, education, and training in affluent modern societies, are all increasing employment in the service sector, where there are often limits to productivity increases and added-value, especially in personal services. A hairdresser can only cut so many heads of hair in a day, no matter how sharp the scissors. Doctors can only see so many patients in a day, no matter how many technical aids they have to facilitate accurate diagnosis and individualized treatment. Labour-use patterns in the service industries are very different from those in the manufacturing industries. Services have a much greater potential for labour-intensive growth, an equal potential for Giffen goods,[17] and they tend to have a high income elasticity of demand (expenditure on services increases more than proportionately as income grows).

However the main effect of the long-term shift from manufacturing to the service industries is the change from a workforce dominated by blue-collar occupations to a workforce consisting mainly of white-collar occupations. Manual occupations often require physical strength and stamina, or productivity is closely related to physical attributes, so that men have a 'natural' advantage, on average. Historically, male manual workers have been paid twice as much as women for doing the same job, a custom that owes something to sex differentials in strength as well as to the principle of paying a family wage to men but not women. For example in Britain, female earnings stood at half male earnings for manual work from 1886 up to 1970 (Hakim 1996a: 175). From the mid-19th century, and long before that (Middleton 1988: 36–9) men were paid twice as much as women, even for identical work.

White-collar occupations do not privilege male physical strength. Most of them require certificated skills, higher education, or professional qualifications, and women have always had a particular facility for passing exams and gaining qualifications. Many service sector occupations include an element of 'caring' or personalized service. This privileges women's skills at interpersonal communication as well as making jobs more attractive to women. It is now well established that, on average, women place more emphasis on relationships and interpersonal communication, while men are more individualistic, competitive, and independent (Gilligan 1982, 1993; McMahon 1995: 268–77; Hakim 1996a: 183). Overall, white-collar occupations and service occupations are more attractive to women than the dirty and physically demanding occupations typical of the manufacturing industries, which are often labelled as 'men's work'. The stereotyping of jobs as 'suitable' for men or women can be more persuasive in relation to manual occupations with a substantial physical element. White-collar occupations, particularly those requiring skills or

[17] Giffen goods are status symbols for which demand remains high because of, rather than despite, their high price, which implies exclusivity. Examples are designer label clothing and champagne. There is equal scope for expensive Giffen services, as illustrated by the celebrity hairdresser, personal trainer, and personal bodyguard.

knowledge, training and education, rarely have any obvious sex-stereotyping. Men and women can both be teachers, accountants, librarians, dentists, lawyers, doctors, musicians, economists, systems analysts, and information engineers. Local, social, economic, and historical factors determine the actual pattern of jobs taken up by men or women at any one time. Work cultures are far more heavily gendered than occupations themselves are (Hakim 1996a: 162–6). Women and children were working in mining in Britain one hundred and fifty years ago, so the masculinity of such work today is socially determined.

In Britain, the occupational structure changed gradually throughout the 20th century, with occupations becoming more skilled, technical, and gender-neutral (Routh 1987: 39, 67). Between 1911 and 1971, the proportion of the workforce employed in professional, managerial, and clerical occupations doubled from 19% to 37% (Routh 1980: 5). Between 1971 and 2001, people in professional, technical, managerial, and clerical occupations will have increased from 40% to 53% of the workforce (IER 1995: 41). Over the century, manual occupations shrank from 81% to 47% of the workforce. Since 1980, the service sector has contributed almost all the growth of employment in the USA, European Union, and Japan. In the USA and the EU, manufacturing jobs were lost over the period, whereas Japan created some new manufacturing jobs as well. In many EU countries, the service sector is the only growth area, and the Commission believes that any significant net job creation in future years is likely to be in services (European Commission 1992a: 77–105, 1996a: 101–25, 1997c: 55–6, 85–98). In 1986, services accounted for just under 60% of total employment in the EU; by 1996, services accounted for two-thirds of all jobs and manufacturing accounted for barely one-quarter. This pattern was repeated across most of the 15 member states. In 1986, Greece and Portugal were exceptions, with less than half their workforce in service industries; by 1996, services had grown sufficiently to employ over half the workforce. In the Netherlands, almost three-quarters of the workforce was in services by 1996. Germany has the largest and strongest manufacturing sector, but here too there was a contraction in the 1990s, in favour of employment in services (European Commission 1996a: 111).

Technological change is also reducing, even eliminating the need for physical strength and risk-taking in many jobs, not just in manufacturing industry. Jobs in construction require far less brute force as machines are now used to lift and place materials. Power steering on buses and other large vehicles allows slender young women to drive and control vehicles that previously required strong male drivers. Even war has become more high-tech and specialized, intellectual rather than physical in many fields of activity. As the entire occupational structure shifts upwards over time, with lower grade jobs shrinking in number and more qualified jobs expanding, the occupational structure is gradually becoming more gender-neutral.

Working class men have the most to lose from the long-term changes in the nature of work. Within the British working class culture, manual labour is valorized as an expression of masculinity through movement, action, and assertion. The physical domination of the world is valorized over the 'effeminate' intellectual domination of the world represented by educational attainment and white-collar jobs. Willis (1977) offers this inverted snobbery as an explanation for working class young men's acceptance of manual occupations at the lower end of the social class structure—although Willis mistakenly equates these attitudes with *machismo*, an entirely different gender ideology with no link to manual labour, valorizing force of personality rather than physical strength. Reliance on a masculine work identity was closely tied to the 'lads' insistence on the sexual division of labour which restricted women to domesticity or to 'effeminate' white-collar work and office jobs. Thus manual labour was associated with the social superiority of masculinity and mental labour with the social inferiority of femininity (Willis 1977: 147–152). Working class men in Britain thus have a strong cultural resistance to taking up 'effeminate' white-collar and service work (Hakim 1996a: 77). This extreme example may not be universal. But in all cultures there are social conventions which create barriers to men taking 'feminine' jobs in the expanding service sector, just like the social barriers that prevented women from taking 'masculine' jobs in the manufacturing industries.

Both men and women have experienced the effects of structural and technological changes in the nature of occupations. As Hakim (1996a: 74–8) points out, occupations have been de-masculinised *and* de-feminised. In 1891 in Britain, one-third of women were employed as indoor domestic servants and one-fifth worked in dressmaking and sewing; over half of all women worked in feminine jobs, often in private households rather than in industry. By 1991, the female-dominated occupation of secretarial work—secretaries, typists, personal assistants, and word processing operators—provided jobs for no more than 7.5% of women, and childcare jobs provided work for only 3%. In 1991, the largest occupations employing women were simply low-skill jobs with no particular association with women's domestic skills, such as sales assistant, sales worker, check-out operator, clerk, and cashier. The most important occupations for women are now gender-neutral rather than typically feminine work. They are often jobs carried out in public locations, involving interaction with a large and diverse clientele. The social seclusion of employment in domestic service has given way to low-skill jobs that are very much in the public eye (Hakim 1994: 445, 1996a: 170–4, 1998a: 68–73, 266–8). These trends are repeated in countries across the world, except in the Middle East (Ankers 1998: 276–93), including the Nordic countries (Melkas and Anker 1998: 54).

The aristocracy of labour used to be in highly skilled craft occupations, and trade unions used to express craft professional identities as well as class interests. Even less-skilled men could take pride in work that was difficult and dangerous, as manual work generally required physical effort, skill, and judgement. Today the aristocracy of labour is in professional and intellectual occupations; many of the most highly paid and risky occupations are in financial services; trade unions are in decline. Women have far less to lose in the decline of manufacturing and they have far more to gain from the expansion of white-collar work, which has only favoured women by being more gender-neutral, without the exclusively masculine character of many manual jobs. White-collar jobs require skills and qualifications plus the social skills required for providing a service to others, as exemplified by the teacher, police officer, and management consultant. Service sector jobs can involve manual work too, albeit combined with social skills, as illustrated by nurses, hairdressers, waiters, and cooks. These jobs are as open to men as they are to women. If women have any advantage in the service industries it is in their greater willingness to service others in contrast with men's more aggressive, self-centred, or 'individualistic' achievement orientation. On the other hand, jobs as cooks, waiters, bartenders, sales, and related work are held equally by men and women in Southern European countries whereas they tend to be female-dominated in Northern European countries (Rubery and Fagan 1993: 46–7). Because it is work cultures that are gendered rather than occupations themselves, the consequences of occupational change are far more open-ended than institutional sociologists admit.

Printing provides an excellent illustration of how technological developments can directly transform male-dominated skilled blue-collar trades into female-dominated white-collar occupations, with radical changes to the associated occupational cultures. Cockburn's (1983) case-study of male newspaper printers in Britain complements the broader, more analytical case-study of printing in the USA by Reskin and Roos (1990: 275–98). Printers are the quintessential craft workers, the aristocracy of the manual workforce, democratic within their élite organisations (Lipset, Trow, and Coleman 1956). Between 1970 and 1990, printing feminized. In Britain, the percentage of compositors who were female rose from 3% in 1971 to 24% by 1991 (13% for printers by 1991). In the USA, the percentage of typesetters and compositors who were female increased from 17% in 1970 to 74% in 1988, as electronic composition and 'desktop publishing' computer programmes changed the labour process, so that relatively dirty, noisy, and heavy skilled blue-collar jobs were transformed into clean, quiet, skilled white-collar jobs—to the dismay of the male-dominated trade unions, who had long opposed women's entry to this well-paid work and did their best to resist the changes. Cockburn's (1983) study of the masculine workplace culture in printing covers the trade unions' long-standing policy of excluding women from the skilled grades of printing work; the links between regular wage work, skill, status, physical strength, endurance, masculinity, and patriarchal attitudes; and men's need to create supportive all-male work groups to bolster fragile sexual egos and to hide from women's gaze their regular failures in the rat-race for success and power. Cockburn describes the many arguments developed by working class men to justify the exclusion of women from skilled work, ranging from natural, physical, intellectual, and temperamental inadequacies which meant women could not do the work, to economic and social reasons why women should not compete with men for skilled work (1983: 132–40, 151–90). Virtually all the arguments and concepts had to do with men's ideology of sexual difference; preserving the sexual division of labour at home and at work; and avoiding competition between men and women in the workplace because this would affect the way they related to women in their private lives. Women were kept out of printing far more successfully in Britain than in the USA due to trade union organization and exclusionary male solidarity rather than anything to do with the nature of the work tasks. Explaining the much faster pace of feminization in the USA, Reskin and Roos point out (1990: 279, 295) that technological change is the most visible factor, but is not in itself the main cause of social and economic change, as proven by contrasting developments in Britain.

In sum, the expansion of white-collar occupations at the expense of blue-collar occupations does not *necessarily* entail the feminization of the workforce. The skill upgrading of occupations is a gender-neutral process, and the new white-collar occupations are gender-neutral in substance and style. Just one example is the new expanding profession of information technology specialist, which is female-dominated in some countries—notably Greece and the Far East—while it is becoming male-dominated in other countries—notably Britain. We can conclude that the occupation is essentially gender-neutral. An analysis of the occupational structure in Britain shows that by 1991 gender-neutral occupations were already a substantial, and growing, minority of one-fifth of all occupations. *Integrated occupations* provide employment for men and women proportionally to their share of the whole workforce—in 1991, this was occupations where women formed between 25% and 55% of the workforce. Almost all this new category of integrated occupations was found to be white-collar work: highly qualified and skilled occupations, most of them in professional, managerial, and technical work. In contrast, the majority of sex-segregated occupations were either in blue-collar work or in the lower grades of white-collar and service-delivery work (Hakim 1998a: 26–73). We can conclude that women's rapid take-up of white-collar work is not due to these occupations being essentially 'feminine' in nature, but to the fact that clean, indoor white-collar work is more attractive to most women than blue-collar work, and because changes in the occupational structure are producing an expanding group of gender-neutral skilled occupations that are equally open to men and women, with recruitment based on certificated skills and expertise rather than stereotyping jobs and skills as 'male' or 'female'. The new occupational structure offers women almost as many opportunities for promotion, for higher grade and well-paid work as are offered to men. At the minimum, women can no longer be actively and overtly excluded from any field of work by the collusion of male trade unionists and employers. Even in printing, women now constitute a substantial part of the workforce in Britain.

The Creation of Jobs for Secondary Earners

Broad changes in occupational structure seem to follow common, long-term trends in advanced economies. In contrast, the diversification of employment contracts was an unexpected development, one response to recession in the last decades of the 20th century. In highly regulated continental European countries, the diversification of working hours and employment contracts was part of a process of deregulating and restructuring the labour market in order to improve flexibility and competitiveness. The deregulation process was hotly debated in the academic community (Rodgers and Rodgers 1989; Pollert 1991; Hakim 1990b, 1997), and was fiercely resisted by trade unionists. It was therefore slow and uneven in timing in continental Europe (Bosch, Dawkins, and Michon 1994; Blanpain and Rojot 1997), producing substantial variation across advanced economies in the incidence of part-time work (Blossfeld and Hakim 1997; O'Reilly and Fagan 1998: 35–76). In the relatively unregulated labour markets of Britain and the USA, the process of flexibilising employment contracts in this period was essentially the continuation of a long-term trend from the Second World War onwards, which accelerated in response to the problems of recession and unpredictable economic cycles and shocks.

The post-war increase in female employment is often interpreted as an indicator of women's rising work attachment. With the exception of the USA, this is questionable, as rising female workrates are due in part to the introduction of part-time jobs, sometimes at the expense of full-time jobs. In Britain, part-time jobs rose from 4% of the workforce in 1951 to 22% in 1991, and 25% by 1997. By the end of the 20th century half of all women worked part-time only, suggesting a decline in work attachment over the past five decades. The increase in part-time jobs was mostly at the expense of full-time jobs, so that the total volume of employment changed little over the century. In the Netherlands, in contrast, there has been a fairly stable 20% full-time workrate among women for at least a century. All the increase in female employment is due to the creation of a new, part-time workforce after changes in legislation made part-time jobs legitimate and legal, so that part-time jobs rose from nothing to two-thirds of all jobs held by women in 1997.

Disparities in female workrates across Europe and North America are due in part to variable levels of part-time work; using Full-Time Equivalent (FTE) workrates (see note 13), the variation shrinks from 34%–71% to 31%–60% (Table 3.3). The growth of part-time jobs is due to the rising workforce participation of groups that have a high propensity to work part-time or not at all, and also to some people in full-time jobs switching permanently to part-time jobs (de Neubourg 1985; Hakim 1993a, 1997, 1998a: 105; Pott-Buter 1993).

Because of a longer period of relatively unrestricted development, the British workforce displays the outcome most clearly: large numbers of part-time jobs; increasing numbers of jobs with variable working hours; smaller numbers of jobs with other non-standard arrangements, such as temporary work, fixed-term contracts, agency temporary workers, subcontracting, homework, freelance work, and self-employment. Some of these were new versions of the 'casual' jobs that trade unions had worked so hard to eliminate. Some were genuinely new re-creations because the nature of work, and employment relationships, had changed so fundamentally in the intervening century. For example the clerical and professional homework that became possible with IT developments and low-cost telephone networks was totally different from manufacturing outwork around 1900 (Hakim 1987b, 1988, 1998a: 179–81). In the flurry of activity to invent new types of job, some major innovations were designed from scratch to suit new flexible labour needs: on-call work, annual hours contracts, and term-time work contracts, for example. To the surprise of trade unionists and academic commentators, these jobs were readily taken up, with interview surveys repeatedly showing even greater unmet interest in such types of job (Hakim 1987c, 1990b, 1997, 1998a). Between 1981 and 1993, full-time permanent jobs declined from 70% to 62% of all jobs in Britain, from 53% to 48% of women's jobs and from 82% to 73% of men's jobs. Part-time and other non-standard jobs now contribute half of women's jobs, one-quarter of men's jobs and one-third of all jobs, with some variation across Europe (Hakim 1996a: 43, 1997: 24).

In 1985 the *Journal of Labor Economics* published a comparative analysis of trends in female employment in twelve countries: Britain, France, Germany, Holland, Sweden, Italy, Spain, the USSR, the USA, Japan, Australia, and Israel. Summarizing the results, Mincer (1985: S5) noted that historically, the shrinkage of farm, family business, and other household-based employment and its eventual replacement by employment outside the home and independent of the spouse, creates a U-shaped trend in aggregate female workforce participation that can take a long time to materialize. What is less well-recognized is that when women returned to the labour market after this temporary absence, they often returned as secondary earners while their husbands remained primary earners throughout.

Historically, women have always worked, with the employment of wives and children dictated by economic necessity for the vast majority of people.

Historically, the non-working wife has been a sign of affluence. When the industrial revolution caused a separation of workplaces and domestic homes, the work done by wives and children was no longer determined automatically by the business or occupation of the male breadwinner. Wives and children who engaged in paid employment could choose an occupation of their own, independently of their husband's trade or their father's. However most wives still regarded their main job as their domestic role. This was ideologically reinforced around the turn of the century in Europe by the trade union campaign for a 'family wage' for men, sufficient to keep a full-time homemaker wife and several children, a strategy that was entirely rational for working class men and their families (Creighton 1996a). The ideology of the breadwinner male was then buttressed by practices such as the marriage bar described above, and higher pay rates for men. When women eventually reintegrated into the workforce in the second half of the 20th century, they came back as secondary earners for the most part, partly because social custom and fiscal policy expected this, but also because rising incomes were reducing financial pressures on families and because affluence creates a locus for the homemaker as consumption manager (Galbraith 1975: 45–53; Hakim 1996a: 46–51).

Secondary earners are not earning a living; they are financially dependent on another person, or on state welfare benefits, for the basic necessities of life such as housing, food, and fuel. Their earnings from employment are *supplementary* or *secondary* to this other, larger source of income. Primary earners must necessarily obtain a *regular* income to cover basic necessities; they will therefore normally work full-time and continuously. Secondary earners may work on an intermittent basis as well as part-time, and they often work closer to home. Secondary earners may take full-time jobs which are relatively low-paid but provide compensating advantages such as convenient hours, an agreeable work environment, and pleasant social relations. Secondary earners may even forego earnings completely in favour of voluntary work, educational courses, or other activities. Their earnings may be an important contribution to the family budget, especially in poorer households, providing some flexibility, clothes, birthday gifts, or the holiday that gives a lift to life. As noted in Chapter 4, a working wife's earnings contribute one-fifth to one-third of household income, on average (see Table 4.7). However the defining factor is not the level of earnings, nor their use. Primary earners are people who may decide to work more or fewer hours, or to vary their work effort in other ways, but for whom the question of whether or not they enter the labour force is not in doubt. Secondary earners are people who may choose to work or not according to a range of considerations, financial and non-financial, and thus have intermittent work histories. Primary earners respond to marginal tax rates, whereas secondary earners are affected by the average rate of tax on the whole of their earnings (Kay and King 1978: 37). Work orientations differ qualitatively between primary and secondary earners (Hakim 1996a: 65–74). Married women have always been the most important group of secondary earners. They are now joined by the growing numbers of students in full-time education and older workers who have taken early retirement, both of whom may supplement their income with a part-time or intermittent job while treating the work as secondary to their other activities (Hakim 1998a: 102–77).

Surveys of employees show that only half of all wives claim that they work to cover 'basic essentials' compared to four-fifths of husbands. Being the primary earner imposes different priorities on men, who value job security and good pay more often than women when choosing a job. Being secondary earners most of the time allows women to prioritize work they like doing, good relations with supervisors, and friendly relations with colleagues (Gallie *et al.* 1998: 196–7). For many wives, a job provides an opportunity to get out of the house and meet people, with the added benefit of earning money. For most husbands, a job is an economic necessity, and they hope to obtain work they like doing, since they *must* work.

The most popular choice of employment for secondary earners is the part-time job: half-time jobs and marginal jobs involving less than 10 hours a week, both of which differ significantly from full-time jobs (Hakim 1998a: 102–44). Part-time workers have the highest turnover rates; they seek jobs rather than careers; their primary identity is as homemaker or student rather than worker; they are highly satisfied with their jobs; and their contribution to household finances is generally too small to have a major impact on their role and power within the family, even though the desire for extra money is often the immediate prompt for getting a job. All of these features are typical of secondary earners rather than specific to part-time jobs (Martin and Hanson 1985; Hakim 1997; Bryson and McKay 1997).

Historically, trade unions have derided part-time jobs as not 'proper' jobs since they were of no interest to men and primary breadwinners. Trade unions' patriarchal and sexist attitudes led unions to give unthinking priority to the interests of male members over the concerns of any female members. Also, the trade unions' long campaign to establish and maintain the 'standard' full-time permanent job as the norm meant that they were always explicitly opposed to other types of employment contract or working hours, seeking to marginalize them and prevent their growth, if they were not able to abolish them altogether. Even today, many trade unions fail to recognize the existence of secondary earners, their distinctive work orientations and job preferences. All the non-standard jobs that are attractive to secondary earners, but not primary breadwinners, are repudiated as 'degraded' jobs (Hakim 1997: 47–52). One consequence is that the part-time workforce has generally developed as a separate, distinctive, segregated workforce (Hakim 1993b, 1998a). But this is not inevitable. It is entirely possible for part-time workers and people in other non-standard contracts and working time arrangements to work alongside people in standard contracts in the same occupation.

One illustration is the occupation of pharmacist, which now employs men and women equally in the USA, Canada, Britain, and many continental European countries, and also recruits large numbers from ethnic minority groups (Hakim 1998a: 221–34; Hassell, Noyce, and Jesson 1998; Tanner *et al.* 1999a, 1999b). Female pharmacists earn less than male pharmacists, even though pay rates are the same for full-time and part-time jobs. In the context of a profession offering relatively unconstrained choice of type of job and a high demand for labour, women consistently choose part-time jobs and employee jobs while men consistently choose full-time jobs and even more demanding self-employment in their own pharmacy business. The marked sex differential in earnings in pharmacy is due to the fact that secondary earners and primary breadwinners both find jobs, of different sorts, in the same occupation (Hakim 1998a: 232). The fact that women have flooded into highly-qualified professional, technical, and managerial occupations does not mean they have all adopted the same career commitment as men. Many women still regard themselves as secondary earners, looking for jobs that can be fitted around their domestic activities, which take priority, ultimately. Today, part-time and temporary jobs give them an attractive alternative to the demands of full-time permanent jobs which leave little time for family life and leisure.

Lifestyle Choices in Rich Modern Societies

The fifth cause of the new scenario is less visible and more difficult to measure. In rich modern societies people have a wider range of lifestyle choices to make than they ever had in the past—assuming of course that they live in societies that are sufficiently liberal to allow the free expression of lifestyle preferences. As Katona (1975: 153) puts it, the needs economy is replaced by a wants or aspirations economy. Marketing and retailing enterprises were the first to recognize this. From the 1970s onwards, market research began to identify qualitatively different 'segments' among consumers, because social class and income alone were less and less useful predictors of lifestyle choices and purchasing patterns. Similarly, computerized match-making agencies found it necessary to introduce questions on lifestyle and recreational preferences as well as on education and occupation. Just one example of the trend is the way food consumption has moved away from a situation where social class and income were the main determinants of consumption choices and presentational styles, such as the garden barbecue versus the formal dinner party. Today, there are new food preference groups that cut across social class and income, ranging from vegans, vegetarians, fishetarians, meat-eaters who do not eat beef, or pork, or who eat all types of meat, to people who will eat anything. A further layer of choices concern the preference for purely local, national cuisines, for wider regional cuisines, or for truly international cuisines. A more arcane lifestyle choice consists of refusing to have a TV in the home. This simple and cheap choice eliminates, at a stroke, a huge volume of media influence on lifestyle choices, ideas, and values. In Britain, only 1% of households still refused to have a TV in 1996. These families do not look any different from families that do have TVs. None the less this lifestyle choice reflects significant differences in attitudes, values, and consumption patterns.

Just one of the lifestyle choices open to people in rich modern societies concerns the relative importance of work, job, or career within life, the relative importance of children and family life, and what kind of sex-roles are preferred in private life. The feminist movement has overturned the idea that everyone prefers the so-called 'traditional'—in fact, modern—sexual division of labour which allocates men to income-earning and women to full-time homemaking and child-rearing. The fact that this model is no longer *imposed* on everyone does not mean it is universally rejected. It has become a matter of personal preference and choice. Similarly, having children, or not, has become a lifestyle choice, rather than an inevitability, for married couples as well as other people. Some people choose to remain childfree while leading a normal sexual life, with or without marriage. Following the contraceptive revolution, this choice is open to people in all social class and income groups, and has a fundamental impact on lifestyle. As noted earlier, studies of the childless failed to identify any particular social characteristics or experiences that distinguish the voluntary childfree. The preference seems to be distributed very widely across populations.[18]

The relative invisibility of lifestyle preferences is one reason why academic social scientists have been slow to recognize their importance. The second reason is an old research literature showing only a weak association between attitudes and behaviour. A review of empirical studies in the 1960s concluded that attitudes were generally 'unrelated or only slightly related to overt behaviours' (Wicker 1969: 65). More recently, Alwin (1973) concluded that it is rarely possible to determine to what extent attitudes cause behaviour or behaviour causes attitudes. A third reason is organizational: research on attitudes is done mostly by social psychologists, while sociologists, economists and demographers usually focus on behaviour. Multidisciplinary research is poorly rewarded in the academic community, so remains unpopular. Another reason is technical. Many methods textbooks are written by statisticians, who typically

[18] Similarly, Davis (1982) found that social class, (as measured by farther's occupation, own occupation, or educational attainment) had little or no association with a wide range of social and political attitudes. Social class seems to be declining in importance with rising economic prosperity.

advise that sets of questions are more reliable than single opinion items and that attitudes should be measured by a series of questions making up a scale or other multi-item measure (for example Oppenheim 1992: 147, 187–259). Researchers are unfortunately discouraged from using their substantive expertise—which statisticians do not have—to identify just two or three key diagnostic questions on values and preferences, which can work better than big scales. And when there is competition for space on a survey questionnaire, large attitude scales can appear to be too expensive, in the space and time they require, and are dropped. Finally, policy-makers and academics alike associate attitude surveys with political opinion polls. It is well known that political attitudes are highly volatile and *responsive* to (media representations of) events, public appearances of politicians, and policy promises. This provides further confirmation that attitudes do not have causal powers, but are themselves moulded by experiences. In the political context, attitudes are important in the run-up to elections, but not otherwise.

However, a new stream of research in the 1990s revealed that attitudes and behaviour are causally connected, and exposed methodological weaknesses in early studies. A recent meta-analysis of 88 attitude-behaviour studies concluded that attitudes predict future behaviour to a substantial degree, but the link is only revealed when data measures specific, rather than general, attitudes (Kraus 1995; see also Ajzen and Fishbein 1977). Two Hungarians, Szekelyi and Tardos, analysed 20 years of microdata for 1968–1988 from the Panel Study of Income Dynamics (PSID) to show that people who plan ahead and express confidence and optimism about their plans subsequently earn significantly higher incomes than those who do not, after controlling for initial levels of income, education, age, sex, race, type of area, and region. The long-term effects of attitudes were stronger than short-term effects. The impact of optimistic planning on earnings was smaller than the impact of education, sex and initial income in 1967, if included, but it was larger than the impact of age, race, and locational variables. Attitudes affected the earnings of both male heads of households and their wives (Szekelyi and Tardos 1993). Similar results are reported by Duncan and Dunifon (1998). At the macro-level, Inglehart analysed the 1970–1994 World Values Survey database to show that economic growth can be better explained by a combination of economic factors and cultural factors, such as the level of achievement motivation in a society, than by economic factors alone (Inglehart 1997: 228–33). Another cross-national comparative study by political scientists confirmed the substantive and analytical primacy of values as an independent variable shaping behaviour; underlined the fragmentation and pluralization of values in the 1990s; and concluded that values now have a larger impact on choice of political party than social differences (Van Deth and Scarbrough 1995: 18, 533–8). Finally, international bodies such as the OECD are beginning to accept that labour market behaviour is strongly shaped by work orientations, in particular women's marked preference for part-time jobs in all advanced economies (OECD 1999: Table 1.13). Attitudes can have important short-term and long-term impacts, even if their influence disappears among social structural factors in many studies, like water in sand. Beliefs and values may be intangible, but people act on them.

Lifestyle preferences are most carefully considered, and stable, in regard to the appropriate roles of men and women, the roles of husband and wife, and family relations. These are deeply held views that change only slowly, quite unlike the highly volatile social and political attitudes that are reported by attitude surveys and opinion polls.[19] In order to reveal lifestyle preferences, we need data on the personal choices and preferences that shape individual behaviour, rather than on public attitude at the aggregate level. Hofstede (1980: 21, 1991) was the first to make the distinction between *choice* and *approval*, between personal goals and public beliefs, between what is desired by the survey respondent for their own life and what is considered desirable in society in general. It is true that there is a relatively weak link between general social attitudes and individual choices and behaviour. But there is a much stronger association between *personal preferences* and individual choices. Even the best opinion polls and social attitude surveys, such as the General Social Survey (GSS) in the USA, the British Social Attitude Survey (BSAS), the World Values Survey, and the International Social Survey Programme (ISSP) internationally, mainly collect data on public approval for selected attitude statements. They rarely, if ever, ask people about their personal preferences for their own life.

Public attitude surveys provide information on a society's collective values, myths and taboos, whereas social research surveys can provide data on the ideas and values that inform individuals' own lives. Most social attitude surveys and opinion polls collect information on public approval for public policies, collective norms, political parties, and representatives. Collective public attitudes and social norms are as much a part of social reality as are behaviour patterns, social conditions or demographic characteristics (Jowell 1984: 3; Inglehart 1997). Public attitudes have a small impact on individual behaviour by establishing a climate of opinion that is favourable or unfavourable to certain behaviours and activities, thus providing varying degrees of social legitimacy, and through their impact on voting choice. However, most academic social scientists are interested in the relationship between behaviour and attitudes, values and preferences at the micro-level, and hence in data on personal preferences and choices. Although they may

[19] Japan provides a rare example of relatively rapid change in sex-role attitudes. In 1972, 83%–84% of women and men agreed that 'the external world is for men and the domestic world is for women', with few differences between age groups. By 1990, only 25% of women and 35% of men agreed with the idea. The decline in support for segregated family roles was repeated across all age groups, but was strongest among young people (Tsuya and Mason 1995: 155). However even in this case, the change in values was spread over two decades.

overlap at the margin, the two types of data can differ hugely, but this is rarely acknowledged in reports and analyses (one exception being Inglehart 1997: 51–2). For example the primary objective of the BSAS is to monitor long-term changes in public attitude and values at the national level (Jowell and Airey 1984; Social and Community Planning Research 1992). The BSAS does sometimes include questions which come closer to asking about personal choices, but these are asked within the context of a public attitude survey and concern speculative situations, so cannot be read as predictions of individual behaviour, as the BSAS research team themselves point out (Jowell and Witherspoon 1985: 58, 124).[20] All these points apply equally to the GSS, World Values Survey, and ISSP data.

Personal choices and preferences can differ fundamentally from the support people offer for generalized abstract values. For example people may approve of women being allowed to become police officers, underground miners, or members of the armed forces, without necessarily choosing themselves to do these jobs or agreeing to their spouse choosing these jobs. Women may approve of mothers of young children having a paid job without necessarily choosing to work themselves while their children are young. A father may approve of working wives and mothers in general, but still remain opposed to his own wife working at all, or while their children are young. Public opinion is concerned with issues of public morality, whereas personal choices have a self-interested focus. In medicine also, the two perspectives can produce apparently conflicting views (Williams and Calnan 1997: 43). Fertility surveys have also established that women distinguish clearly between public norms and personal choice, between what they perceive to be the ideal family size in their society, and their own personal preferences, which more often are for small families or even no children at all (Siegers, de Jong-Gierveld, and van Imhoff 1991: 64; CELADE and CFSC 1972: 102–3).[21] Even in less-developed societies, people distinguish between reporting public opinion—'what most people think'—and personal beliefs (Peil 1982: 118–29).

[20] Most of the BSAS questions ask what people would do in certain hypothetical situations, including the 'lottery win' question on work commitment; questions on how they would respond to the loss of their job; questions on whether they would themselves do something regarded as 'wrong'; and questions on whether people would break a law to which they were strongly opposed (see for example Jowell and Witherspoon 1985: 14–15, 66–8, 122–6). The questions are located in the context of a public attitude survey, and responses are clearly influenced by the desire to conform to socially desirable behaviour. So even the most direct questions about personal choices have to be interpreted as one facet of collective public attitude, as the researchers admit.

[21] Similarly, Newell (1992: 44) established that mothers of young children distinguish clearly between public opinion and their own personal views, on how old a child should be before a mother considers returning to work, given no financial necessity. Only one-quarter of the mothers personally believed mothers should stay at home full-time while children were below school age (that is, up to the age of 5), but three-quarters were aware of public opinion holding this belief, so that mothers were aware of a large discrepancy between personal and public opinion on the question.

Opinion polls ask about people's personal voting intentions and plans in addition to general information on their approval of public policies. Yet social attitude surveys rarely include direct questions on personal preferences, choices, and plans. Public approval for certain ideas or policies can be volatile, change easily and quickly, and have little connection with personal daily life—attitudes to abortion and political parties being just two examples. Quite different questions are required to collect information on the personal choices and preferences which do connect with individual behaviour, and they usually need the context of an interview survey that is clearly focused on the individual respondent's life and activities rather than on current affairs. Surprisingly, social surveys collect public attitude data far more often than data on personal preferences, even when they seek to explain behaviour, leading to the inevitable conclusion that there is only a weak association between social attitudes and behaviour (Bielby and Bielby 1984; Agassi 1979, 1982; Hakim 1991: 111, 1996a: 85).

One example is the British 1980 Women and Employment Survey. All analyses of the data repeatedly showed only weak associations between approval for women's employment and women's own employment choices (Martin and Roberts 1984: 172–176; Dex 1988: 124; Hakim 1991: 105). The same problem appears in the British Household Panel Study (BHPS), which again used generalized public attitude statements as a proxy measure for women's personal work orientations (Corti, Laurie and Dex 1995: 65–69).

The BSAS and the ISSP collect data on approval almost exclusively, quite legitimately, and most analyses address national trends and cross-national differences in public opinion, quite appropriately (Scott 1990; Alwin, Braun, and Scott 1992; Scott, Braun, and Alwin 1993; Braun, Scott, and Alwin 1994; Scott, Alwin, and Braun 1996; Haller, Hollinger, and Gomilschak 1999). Analysts who do seek links between behaviour and attitudes inevitably obtain weak results (Alwin, Braun, and Scott 1992; Braun, Scott, and Alwin 1994). Unfortunately, institutions such as data archives and survey question databanks can encourage researchers to think in terms of the 'best' questions on a subject rather than the appropriate questions for a particular research topic and theoretical perspective. As a result, the distinction between approval and choice is blurred. There is far less data on personal preferences than on public beliefs, and the latter are regularly used as a proxy for the former. Both types of data reveal the increasing importance of attitudes, values,and preferences by the end of the 20th century, but personal preferences are most strongly correlated with behaviour, especially among white women (Dugger 1988: 433, 439). One USA study found that women's responses to general sex-role attitude statements were not associated with employment decisions, whereas their personal preference for and commitment to having a job was a powerful determinant of being in work or not (Geerken and Gove 1983: 64–6).

Surveys show that preferences and values are becoming more important

Table 3.4. *The impact of sex-role ideology on employment rates among women*

Sex-role ideology	Percentage of each group in employment: Highly qualified women	Percentage of each group in employment: Other women	Distribution of sample: Highly qualified women	Distribution of sample: Other women
Modern	92	76	23	14
Ambivalent	84	66	63	67
Traditional	64	54	15	20
All women aged 20–59	82	65	100	100
Base=100%	746	2700	746	2700

Notes: Highly qualified women have tertiary level qualifications, beyond A-level—that is, above the level of the *Baccalaureat* or the *Arbitur*. Other women have no qualifications or only secondary school qualifications, up to A-level.
Sex-role ideology was scored on the basis of nine attitude statements, including the ISSP item 'A husband's job is to earn the money, a wife's job is to look after the home and family'. Of the other eight attitude statements, six concerned the role of a mother and two concerned the role of wives and adult women more generally.
Source: Table 2.3, reporting 1991 data from the British Household Panel Study in Hakim, 'A sociological perspective on part-time work' in H.-P. Blossfeld and C. Hakim, *Between Equalization and Marginalisation*, Oxford University Press, 1997.

than economic necessity and practical considerations as the driving force for employment decisions, as well as for lifestyle choices more generally. This development emerges first among women, and only in the new scenario. For example it has often been argued that the availability of childcare services is the primary determinant of women's employment decisions. By the 1990s, this seems to have changed, if indeed it had been true. Thomson's analysis of the 1994 BSAS indicated that women's employment decisions were informed primarily by their conception of women's role at home and at work, and only secondarily by practical factors such as childcare problems or financial considerations. Careful checks indicated that attitudes to the mother's 'proper' role in the family were not just a form of self-justification or *post hoc* rationalization (Thomson 1995: 80–3). Similarly, Scanzoni (1976: 679, 686) showed that in the USA whether a wife works or not is less important than the couple's *definition* of her employment as subordinate to her husband's employment or as co-equal earner, and that sex-role attitudes determined employment choices. Finally, Agassi (1979, 1982) shows that women's high satisfaction with low-grade jobs can only be understood with reference to their sex-role ideology and the widespread view among women that their own work role is limited to being a secondary earner in support of a breadwinner husband.

The increasing impact of sex-role ideology is revealed by research on women who have obtained higher education qualifications and thus have access to well-paid and interesting jobs and can afford childcare. The 1991 BHPS survey shows that sex-role ideology strongly influences employment decisions among highly-qualified women, who can afford to choose between competing lifestyles, given homogamy (Table 3.4). A two-thirds majority of women, whatever their level of education, hold an ambivalent, or adaptive, sex-role ideology, with minorities firmly accepting or firmly rejecting the sexual division of labour. It is well established that higher education qualifications are associated with higher workrates—an increase of 17 percentage points in Table 3.4: 82% versus 65%. But the impact of sex-role ideology is greater, and it is largest among the highly qualified women, producing an increase of 28 percentage points in employment rates when modern and traditional women are compared: 92% versus 64%. Of course, the influence of traditional attitudes to women's role in the home will only be revealed behaviourally *after* a woman has married and had children. The fulfilment of traditional sex-role aspirations is crucially dependent on achieving marriage to a partner able to support a family, so it can *appear* that socio-economic factors are more important than values and sex-role preferences.

Table 3.4 also shows how small is the impact of higher education on sex-role attitudes, contrary to popular belief. One-quarter of highly educated women hold 'modern' views on women's role in society and the family, a very *small* increase on the proportion among women with only secondary school education or less. In both groups, the majority of women hold ambivalent, mixed, views. It is simply not true that all highly educated women are careerist and put work before family life. Similar results have been reported also for the USA (Ginzberg 1966; Gerson 1985; Sexton and Perlman 1989; Philliber and Vannoy-Hiller 1990).

Recent studies in the USA also find that sex-role identities and preferences have a substantial influence on whether wives translate their educational qualifications into careers, or just jobs, or do no work at all. For example Philliber and Vannoy-Hiller (1990) studied 300 dual-earner couples living in an urban area of the USA, with the sample intentionally biased towards couples in which wives held professional and managerial positions. Wives with a 'traditional' sex-role ideology were far less likely to invest their educational qualifications in a career and thus achieve higher occupational status and prestige. The opposite was true of wives with 'modern' sex-role identities who also espoused competitive values. The authors note that as a result of the marital selection process, wives' attitudes were often reinforced by their husband's attitudes. People seek and marry partners with similar values and sex-role ideology.

There is increasing recognition that attitudes, values, and preferences are becoming more important than previously admitted; that it is possible to study values and preferences directly, through interview surveys; and that preferences do not vary randomly, as economists assume. From the 1950s onwards, Katona argued for the inclusion of data on preferences and attitudes in economic analysis. Studies have periodically shown that attitudes can be just as important as the more commonly measured human capital variables. For example, Filer (1981) found that drive and determination, high aspirations and achievement motivation were strong predictors of earnings after sex, education and occupational grade were controlled. A recent symposium on economics and happiness had economists reiterating the case for the incorporation of data on attitudes and values in economic analysis (Frank 1997; Ng 1997; Oswald 1997). This might eventually have an impact on policy-makers, who have so far proven uninterested in research on attitudes instead of behaviour (Scott and Shore 1979: 233). Studies of the determinants of fertility showed that attitudes became twice as important immediately after the contraceptive revolution (Murphy and Sullivan 1985: Table 10). Within sociology, Giddens (1991, 1992) argues that modern societies allow people the option of choosing self-identity and lifestyle between a variety of options available. Just one of these lifestyle options is the 'conventional' sexual division of labour and role segregation in the family, hence 'traditional' economic dependency of the wife and an instrumental relationship (Giddens 1992: 195), which can still be freely chosen by a couple in the new scenario. Within demography there has been a gradual change of emphasis from theories underlining the economic and social structural determinants of long term trends in fertility, to theories focusing on cultural factors and ideational change. The concept of demographic transition is retained as a useful synoptic description for interlinked changes in demographic variables at the aggregate level, but there has been a marked shift towards treating ideational innovation as an additional causal factor after the contraceptive revolution provided women in advanced and less-developed countries with the idea and the means of controlling their child-bearing, sometimes secretly (Davis, Bernstam, and Ricardo-Campell 1987: 139–200; Mason and Jensen 1995; Jones *et al.* 1997). Some authors, such as Cleland (1985), Lesthaeghe (1995), Lesthaeghe and Meekers (1986) go further to insist that cultural change, ideas, and values, such as familism, are now the driving forces in declining fertility in less-developed countries as well as in Western Europe. Finally, political scientists have belatedly accepted that attitudes and values do have an impact on behaviour and must be treated as significant independent variables (Van Deth and Scarbrough 1995: 538).

Our thesis is that lifestyle preferences and values are becoming more important determinants of behaviour, relative to economic necessity and social structural factors. This thesis is consonant with Inglehart's thesis about the transition from materialist (or modern) values to postmaterialist (or postmodern) values as societies get richer and more stable. Inglehart's thesis is also empirically-based, and also predictive. It has been tested and proven already with analyses of survey data on social, economic, and political attitudes for 1970 (6 countries), 1981 (22 countries), and 1990–93 (43 countries), supplemented by Eurobarometer survey data for all years 1970–1994 and a number of other datasets (Inglehart 1977, 1990, 1997; Abramson and Inglehart 1995; Inglehart, Basañez, and Moreno 1998). His thesis has been refined over three decades of empirical research, and the reference here is to the most recent and complete formulation, presented in *Modernization and Postmodernization* (Inglehart 1997). He too insists that cultural factors—as reflected in social attitude surveys—are cause, as well as effect, of economic growth, and of political and economic systems. But he does not suggest that the relative importance of cultural factors is increasing, only that the substantive content of value-systems is changing. Unprecedented prosperity and the modern welfare state create a sense of existential security in rich societies that is generally absent in poor societies and in societies experiencing wars, recessions or other upheavals, which are dominated by scarcity and survival needs. During the modernization or materialist phase—which characterized the 20th century in Europe—a society's value-system emphasizes economic efficiency, bureaucratic authority, and scientific rationality, values which promote predictability and stability as well as growth. During the postmodernization or postmaterialist phase of the 21st century, a society's value-system emphasizes individual autonomy, diversity, self-expression and individual choice regarding the kind of life one wants to lead. The emphasis changes from survival to well-being, from relatively conformist values to tolerance of diversity in lifestyles, in values, in political, ethnic-cultural, and sexual tastes (Inglehart 1997: 12, 23). The latest World Values Surveys for the 1990s, show that, in almost all societies, rich and poor, modern and premodern, a slightly larger percentage of men than women hold postmodern values. One rare exception is The Netherlands, the most postmodern society of all, where 37% of women and 33% of men held postmodern values in the 1990s (Inglehart, Besañez, and Moreno 1998: 466).

Inglehart's thesis is about changes in values at the macro-level of the nation-state. Our thesis is about the emergence of heterogeneous sex-role and lifestyle preferences among women (and men) within, as well as across, nations. One point of agreement is that this diversity of lifestyle preferences only emerges in affluent modern societies, and is a direct result of economic prosperity, social, and political stability. The second point of agreement is that value-systems in the future will differ from the values that have dominated recent decades in industrial societies. Abramson and Inglehart (1995:

89–96) predict that, with current birthrates and population replacement, postmaterialist values will only become the *majority* value-system in Western Europe well after the year 2020. This prediction does not take account of the impact of immigration—typically from societies with a materialist culture—and other unforeseeable major events, such as wars. In the 1990s, postmaterialist values were dominant only in a minority of social groups in particular countries, such as highly educated left-wing voters in the Netherlands and West Germany. Even in Western Europe, materialist values will remain dominant up to the year 2000 at least (Inglehart, Basañez, and Moreno 1998: 466). The value of Inglehart's theory is in its ability to *predict* emerging trends in the 21st century.

Conclusions

The combination of the equal opportunities revolution and the contraceptive revolution produces the most fundamental change to the material conditions of women's lives in history, giving women real choices as to how to live their lives. The voluntary childlessness that emerged in all countries as soon as women got access to modern contraception shows that there are no absolute or essential characteristics of women that differentiate them from men. Although the majority of women continue to want to bear children, there is a substantial minority of women (and also of men) who have no 'natural' interest at all in motherhood, or an interest so weak that it is overridden by the competing interests of career, job, or leisure interests.[22]

Knowledge-intensive modes of production will be a feature of the 21st century. Given the almost gender-blind, certainly gender-neutral methods of accreditation and qualification for knowledge-based occupations, women suffer far fewer impediments and barriers to access to these better-paid, higher-status, and interesting jobs. Overall, the expanding white-collar and service jobs are more attractive to women than are the blue-collar jobs typical of manufacturing industry. Just as important, the labour market deregula-

[22] Inglehart's World Values Survey contains few items on gender issues and sex-roles, but one is relevant here. In 1981 and 1990, the survey invited responses to the question 'Do you think that a woman needs to have children in order to be fulfilled or is this not necessary?'. The item reveals huge cross-national differences in the percentage agreeing with this essentialist picture of women that presents child-bearing as essential to women's identity and well-being, rather than a lifestyle choice. Further, attitudes are stable, with little or no change across 1981–1990 in most countries. For example, over 90% of adults in Hungary, and over 70% in Japan, South Korea, South Africa, Denmark, and France agree with the statement. The proportion falls to around 50% in Mexico, Argentina, Italy, Spain, Belgium, and Germany. It is below 25% in Ireland, Britain, the USA, Canada, the Netherlands, Norway, Sweden, and Finland. There is no reliable association with Catholicism, with pronatalist public policies, or any other fertility-related values which could explain such large national differences. However, agreement with the statement is clearly associated with people holding materialist, mixed, or postmaterialist values (Inglehart 1990: 198–9, 1997: 271, 380).

tion and workforce restructuring that took place in the late 20th century in Europe especially, but also globally, created a wider range of attractive job options for women. Part-time jobs have increased everywhere, sometimes as a long slow rising trend, sometimes as a sudden upsurge in response to deregulation. In all countries, women have taken the vast majority of part-time jobs, which suit their needs as secondary earners. Prosperity produces secondary earners and part-time jobs. Part-time work is growing fastest, and is most popular, in the most economically successful and prosperous regions of Europe (European Commission 1991b: 79).

The fifth cause of change is the slow, and almost invisible rising impact of values and preferences on employment decisions. Together, these five changes in combination produce a qualitatively new scenario for women at the end of the 20th century and the start of the 21st century. This means that research studies need to be divided into those for the period before, and those for the period after, these changes take place. Using data for 1970 onwards, Chapter 4 shows that the main result of this new scenario is a polarization of women's preferences, employment choices, and outcomes.

4

The Polarization of Preferences and Behaviour

By the 1990s, there was widespread agreement on a new trend towards the polarization of women's employment in Europe and North America. The trend was noticed by numerous social scientists working independently (Bonney 1988; Jenson, Hagen, and Reddy 1988; Power 1988: 145; Jones, Marsden, and Tepperman 1990; Bouffartigue, de Coninck, and Pendariès 1992: 423; Humphries and Rubery 1992; Berger, Steinmüller, and Sopp 1993: 49, 56–7; Coleman and Pencavel 1993: 675; McRae 1993; Burchell and Rubery 1994; Rubery, Horrell, and Burchell 1994: 228–30; Hakim 1996a; Singly 1996: 101–3, 210; Waldfogel 1997, 1998; Davies and Joshi 1998: 52–9; Pencavel 1998). Coleman and Pencavel (1993) concluded that skill differentials have become more important than sex differentials in the workforce. Burchell and Rubery (1994: 109) pointed out that by the 1980s female heterogeneity was already greater than sex differences in employment. Hakim (1996a) noted that female heterogeneity was even greater if all adult women were considered, including those who pursue the marriage career, rather than just working women. Singly (1996: 101–3) concluded that the polarization of women into those centring their lives on family and children, and those who want to combine children and employment, was found at all levels of education.

Other scholars discuss the *diversity* in women's attitudes and behaviour without claiming a growing divergence. However the scale and degree of this diversity are remarkable: some women choose lives centred on full-time homemaking, and hope never to be obliged to do paid work; other women effectively adopt the male lifestyle centred on competitive achievement in the public sphere, and many of them treat child-bearing as an optional extra, or hobby, certainly not the essence of adult life. The evidence of *increasing* diversity is strongest for the USA and Britain, and clearest in employment patterns. Polarization is a long-term trend, and the degree of change over a single decade, for example, may be tiny. However the concept of diversity in women's preferences and behaviour does not point clearly enough to the fact that women are now choosing polar opposite lifestyles.

This chapter begins by examining the evidence on the polarization of lifestyle preferences and work orientations, then summarizes the evidence on the polarization of women's employment. Evidence on sex-role preferences is available for all women. Survey data on work orientations and job preferences are available only for women with jobs, and reveal differences between women working full-time and part-time. We also consider whether highly educated women are invariably committed to careers. We then look at the consequences of the polarization of employment patterns for women's financial dependence on male partners, and for the polarization of household income. Finally, we examine apparently contradictory evidence suggesting that *all* women want paid work, and that women are homogamous rather than heterogeneous.

The Polarization of Sex-role Preferences

The polarization of preferences was first noticed in small-scale qualitative studies, such as Sexton's (1979) study of middle class female graduates of selective colleges in the USA. Despite the narrow selection of interviewees, they divided clearly into those who dreamed of marriage and homemaking as a full-time occupation and those with a strong career orientation. A variety of family backgrounds was found in both groups. The only differentiating factor was that the home-oriented women identified with their mothers, whereas the career-oriented group regarded their father's influence on their lives as greater than their mothers's. Fathers were perceived as successful, interested in their daughters, encouraging them to set high goals and to value independent achievement. Women who identified with their mothers did not necessarily perceive them as being happy with the role of full-time homemaker; sometimes their aim was to succeed where their mother had failed (Sexton 1979). However the study was unable to explain why some daughters develop a stronger relationship with their father than with their mother. It seems likely that an element of self-selection was involved.

By the 1980s, the polarization of sex-role preferences emerged clearly in national survey data. The Eurobarometer question reported in Table 4.1 is unusual in that it asks people about their own personal choice or personal preference regarding family roles. This is a different question from the questions used in public attitude surveys, including the ISSP series of attitude surveys (Jowell *et al.* 1993; Taylor and Thomson 1996). As noted in Chapter 3, there are important distinctions between choice and approval, between personal goals and social beliefs, between what is desired by the survey respondent and what is considered desirable for society in general.

The EU survey shows that one-quarter of European adults still prefer the complete separation of roles in the family, with the wife financially dependent

TABLE 4.1. *The diversity of sex-role preferences in Europe*

Percentage of adults supporting each of three models of the sexual division of labour:

	Egalitarian		Compromise		Separate roles		Total
	1987	1983	1987	1983	1987	1983	
Denmark	58	50	29	33	13	17	100
Spain	50	—	20	—	30	—	100
United Kingdom	49	39	32	37	19	24	100
Portugal	47	—	26	—	27	—	100
Netherlands	46	41	30	27	24	32	100
France	46	42	30	27	24	31	100
Greece	46	53	30	23	24	25	100
Italy	43	42	32	28	26	30	100
Belgium	38	35	33	25	28	40	100
Ireland	37	32	22	26	42	42	100
West Germany	28	29	37	38	35	33	100
Luxembourg	22	27	34	23	44	50	100
Men—all	41	35	31	34	28	31	100
15–24 years	59	49	28	33	13	18	100
25–39	50	40	31	38	19	22	100
40–54	36	28	34	36	30	36	100
55 and over	27	26	30	28	43	46	100
Women—all	44	41	31	31	25	28	100
15–24 years	62	60	26	25	12	15	100
25–39	52	45	29	32	19	23	100
40–54	39	36	33	34	28	30	100
55 and over	28	31	34	29	38	40	100
Total for EC of 12	43	—	31	—	26	—	100
Total for EC of 10	42	38	32	32	26	30	100

Notes: The question asked: People talk about the changing roles of husband and wife in the family. Here are three kinds of family. Which of them corresponds most with your ideas about the family?

1. A family where the two partners each have an equally absorbing job and where housework and the care of the children are shared equally between them.
2. A family where the wife has a less demanding job than her husband and where she does the larger share of housework and caring for the children.
3. A family where only the husband has a job and the wife runs the home.
4. None of these three cases.

Percentages have been adjusted to exclude the 3% not responding to the question and the 2% choosing the last response.

Source: Derived from European Commission, *Eurobarometer* No. 27, Brussels, June 1987. Data for people aged 15 and over, interviewed at home.

on her husband. Rejection of this model does not necessarily mean that people move to acceptance of completely equal sharing of income-earning and family work. One-third of adults only accept a compromise arrangement in which the wife does some paid work as a secondary earner, for example in a part-time job. Less than half of the EU population prefers the completely egalitarian family model.[1] The egalitarian model attracted most support in Denmark, followed by Spain, the UK, and Portugal. This suggests that the so-called 'modern' egalitarian family is really a reversion to a pre-industrial model. As several scholars have pointed out, it is the dual-earner family that is traditional; the single breadwinner model of the family is a *modern* invention, and it remained the popular ideal for a relatively short time (Bernard 1981; Davis 1984; Seccombe 1993: 202–9; Hakim 1996a: 82).[2] However political correctness may also boost support for the 'egalitarian' model of symmetrical roles in the family. For example, Spain has the very lowest female workrate in the EU: only 34% of women of working age have a job, compared to 37% in Italy, 40% in Greece and 59% in Portugal (see Table 3.3). None the less, Spanish people expressed remarkably high levels of support for the 'egalitarian' model of the family, with fully symmetrical roles, one of the highest in the EU in 1987 (Table 4.1). By 1999, support had grown even further, to over two-thirds of people of working age (Hakim forthcoming). It seems likely that these results are influenced by the 'political correctness' bias that affects responses to social attitude surveys in most modern societies to some degree.[3]

The complete separation of roles attracts most support in Luxembourg, Germany, and Ireland, some of the most affluent countries in Europe. But in all countries there is a wide spread of support for all three models of the family, and none receives majority support except in Denmark. Certainly,

[1] The 'egalitarian' symmetrical roles family model attracts disproportionate support in Table 4.1 partly because it was the first response listed in the Eurobarometer surveys, and partly because it is currently the socially acceptable response in western Europe, as indicated by the positive connotations attached to the words 'egalitarian' and 'equal'. Methodological work with this survey question shows that if the order of responses is reversed (with the role-segregated family listed first and the symmetrical roles family listed last), around 10% of respondents transfer their allegiance from the 'egalitarian' model to the role-segregated model, with much larger swings among young women in the 16–24 years age cohort. This would produce a more even distribution of about one-third of respondents supporting each of the three models in 1987. This latter distribution is probably closest to reality, given that we cannot remove the political correctness bias in responses to this question.

[2] European historians are documenting the rise and decline of the male breadwinner family as a popular ideal which was often achieved for at least part of the lifecycle in working class families; showing that it became dominant in Holland, Britain, and the USA, but not in France, for example (Pedersen 1993; Pott-Buter 1993: 285–7; Seccombe 1993: 202–9; Janssens 1998). They have also sought an explanation for it within contemporary historical developments and trade union demands for a family wage for men (Creighton 1996b, 1999). In countries such as Japan, where the transition from an agricultural economy is recent enough for people to remember the heavy labour required of both spouses on family farms, the single breadwinner family is a relatively recent innovation and is regarded as modern and progressive (Tanaka 1998: 95).

[3] There is some evidence that young people are most susceptible to social pressure when reporting their attitudes and values (Hakim forthcoming). This means that responses for people aged under 25 years in Tables 4.1 and 4.2 are the least stable. This age group is also by far the smallest.

there are no sharp differences between Northern and Southern European societies, or by level of prosperity. Overall, a three-quarters majority of European men and women favour the idea of the working wife, but a clear majority *also* favour the wife retaining all or the major part of the homemaker role. Age has a strong influence on attitudes. In part, these results reflect generational differences, and in part the modification of attitudes over the lifecycle, as women often prefer greater role segregation after they have children and confront competing priorities. In some countries, such as Britain, social class is also associated with sex-role ideology, with working class men and women more likely to support the complete separation of roles than do people in professional and managerial classes.

The European Commission's Eurobarometer surveys provide unique evidence on the diversity of sex-role preferences and ideologies[4] *within* European countries, as well as across Western Europe. They show that there is no single, dominant preference among women or men, except among the youngest women, whose views are less fixed. Some women choose to be primary earners throughout life and compete in the labour market on the same basis as men. A substantial minority of women, one in four in the European Union, prefer segregated family roles, which means that wives normally quit the labour market permanently after marriage, if in fact they ever work at all. Finally, one-third of women enter the workforce as secondary earners: they expect or hope to be supported by a husband for most of their adult life, so that they only supplement his earnings rather than being equal co-earners. An appropriate label for this arrangement would be the *modern sexual division of labour* in the family. Equivalent data for the USA in the 1980s reveals a similar pattern of plans and preferences among women of working age who had married in the period 1965–84 (Whyte 1990). Prior to marriage, 30% had aimed to be full-time housewives; 44% wanted to work for some of the time after marriage; and only 25% desired a life-long employment career. In the USA, there was a massive decline in the popularity of the marriage career in the decades up to the 1980s. But it was replaced by the new ideal of the modern sexual division of labour, with the wife as secondary earner, rather than by a swing towards lifelong employment, which was chosen by a minority of wives (Whyte 1990: 48–9).[5]

[4] The term ideology refers to a set of beliefs and theories people construct to make sense of the world and guide their actions in it.

[5] An interesting study by Agassi (1979, 1982) studied sex-role ideology and work attitudes among women and men in the USA, West Germany, and Israel in the late 1970s. She too found that women's role preferences polarized: one-third chose to prioritize the homemaker role without necessarily regarding it as obligatory or traditionally appropriate for all women; one-fifth consistently rejected the homemaker role in favour of a focus on market work in their own lives; and the remaining half of her study sample held more complex or contradictory views, sometimes giving priority to the maternal role over market work (Agassi 1982: 221). Unfortunately, Agassi does not show the distribution of personal choices separately for each of the three countries in her study, although she does say that the three groups all included younger women as well as older women.

Survey data for Australia reveals a similar diversity of preferences in 1991 (Wolcott and Glezer 1995: 79–86). Among married and cohabiting women aged 27–43 years, less than one-third ideally preferred to have a full-time job, over one-third preferred a part-time job, and one-third preferred to be at home full-time. Only 20% of women said they were work-centred; 29% said they were centred on family and relationships; half said they had achieved a balance between work and family. Women who preferred full-time jobs saw themselves as work-centred; they valued independence and freedom in relationships, and were more likely to be in high status occupations. Women who preferred part-time work were less concerned about independence and freedom in relationships, and accepted the sexual division of labour in the family. Many were working full-time involuntarily, had lower job satisfaction and felt themselves to be under financial pressure. Women who preferred to be at home full-time were likely to have a husband in a high status occupation and a preschool child at home.

Table 4.1 results for Europe may be slightly dated, and do not include information for the new EU member states: Sweden, Finland, and Austria.[6] However these three countries are too small, with populations of 9 million, 5 million, and 8 million respectively, to have an appreciable impact on the overall picture for the EU with a total population of 374 million. The addition of East Germany, with a total population of 16 million, could be more important, given continuing substantial differences in work orientations between women in eastern and western Germany.[7] Even so, the pattern of preferences

[6] The European Commission ceased to include this question in the Eurobarometer surveys in the 1990s. We have failed to establish the reason for discontinuing a useful series. Unfortunately, the question does not provide support for the Commission's position on women's employment and the individualization of rights.

[7] Beckmann (1998) and Kreckel and Schenk (1998) report less interest in part-time jobs among women, and less acceptance of the non-working wife, in East Germany than in West Germany in the 1990s. Kreckel and Schenk (1998: 15) show a polarization of opinion on sex-role segregation among wives in particular in the 1990s in West Germany; in contrast, East Germans displayed low, and declining support for role segregation in the family. Beckmann (1998: 7) shows that among West Germans, only a 20% minority prefer the dual-career family with both spouses working full-time; half prefer the compromise arrangement with the wife working part-time only; and another 20% minority prefer complete role-segregation in the family. In contrast, among East Germans, preferences are biased towards the dual-earner family: half prefer the dual-career family with both spouses in full-time work and almost half prefer the compromise arrangement with the wife working part-time only; very few actively prefer complete role segregation. However it is not clear whether these are positive lifestyle preferences, or whether East Germans continue to regard the dual-earner family as an inevitable economic necessity and safeguard against unemployment in a transition economy. Braun, Scott, and Alwin (1994) concluded that East Germans are no less traditionalist than West Germans. Social historians suggest that role segregation in the family continued to attract widespread support in East, as well as in West Germany after 1950 (Oertzen and Rietzschel 1998), and that many women preferred to work part-time hours only, or even become full-time homemakers, if the family could afford it (Einhorn 1993). A series of national social attitude surveys carried out in East and West Germany in the 1990s by the German federal government (Bundesministerium für Familie, Senioren, Frauen und Jugend 1996) suggest that the convergence of attitudes generally takes the form of East German attitudes moving closer to West German attitudes. There is the usual tendency to offer politically correct responses on general topics. For example, the majority of adults in East and West Germany agree that professional success is important

today is probably very close to that shown in Table 4.1. Eurobarometer surveys for the 1990s present a very similar picture of polarized attitudes and preferences, and one recent study shows Sweden to be much closer to the rest of Europe than might have been expected.[8]

The autumn 1990 Eurobarometer No. 34 and the spring 1993 Eurobarometer No. 39 both focused on women and the family. In 1990, women were asked about their ideal preference for working full-time, part-time, or not at all when they had children below school age. The full-time homemakers were the most satisfied group, as three-quarters preferred not to work at this stage of life. Mothers with full-time jobs were the least happy group, with three-quarters or more saying they would ideally prefer not to work at all, or only part-time. Most part-time workers also ideally preferred not to work at all, or only part-time; very few (11%) would have preferred a full-time job. Interestingly, East German women were the least satisfied group (European Commission 1991a: 107). These results suggest that financial motives, rather than personal preference, remains an important reason for mothers' employment. The 1993 survey found a remarkable consensus across Europe on a mother's primary responsibility for young children, and that she should stop working in order to care for her children herself. This view was endorsed by at least 70%—often over 80%—of women and men in all age groups and in all EU countries, with the exception of Belgium and Denmark, where one-quarter or more said she should continue working. In West Germany, 87% of adults held this opinion, compared to a low of 60% in Denmark. Most people had definite opinions; only one in ten gave a Don't Know reply. Not surprisingly, the majority of women and men in all EU countries concluded that having children is an obstacle to women's working life, except for Portugal, Greece, and Belgium (European Commission 1993: 86–9).

The spring 1996 Eurobarometer No. 44.3 shows that women and men in all age groups are divided evenly on whether a woman can combine working and having children (48%) or must choose between the two (48%). Women

for women as well as men, and that economic independence is important for women, even if they are married. Responses to questions about practical and personal topics are more revealing. For example, the majority of West Germans believe a mother should retire permanently from work, or have a long career break after the birth of a child, whereas the majority of East Germans believe a mother should only take parental leave and then return to her job. Among the one-third who express a preference, women prefer a male boss over a female boss by 14 to 1 in East Germany and by 7 to 1 in West Germany; women also prefer male colleagues over female colleagues by 3 to 1 in East Germany and by 2 to 1 in West Germany. Preference for a male boss, or colleague, is stronger among women than among men in both East and West Germany (Bundesministerium für Familie, Senioren, Frauen und Jugend 1996: 33–4, 45–6, 54, 60). A positive preference for a male boss over a female boss is a good indicator of patriarchal attitudes. On this indicator, East German women are twice as patriarchal as West German women, and German women generally are more patriarchal than women in Britain (Hakim 1996a: 115).

[8] In the absence of Eurobarometer data on preferences in the 1990s, we are obliged to rely on opinion poll data to identify trends in this period. As noted in Chapter 3, data on approval is not an exact substitute for data on choice.

and men in all age groups are similarly divided evenly on whether the solution to family–work conflicts is to give financial support to mothers of young children to enable them to stop working (46%), or to provide childcare services to enable them to continue working (49%). Twice as many women as men said they would readily take unpaid leave from their job to bring up a child: 53% of women versus 28% of men. Two-thirds of European women and men think the main reason for women being less likely than men to attain positions of responsibility is because family responsibilities absorb women's time and energy, not because they lack the necessary talents (European Commission 1997d: iv–vi). All these surveys indicate very much smaller, even negligible, differences between age cohorts than are shown in Table 4.1. They confirm that only a minority of women and men are committed to completely symmetrical family roles. The great majority expect and endorse a large degree of role segregation as a result of different parental roles. Moreover, qualitative studies of young women in western Europe show that they prefer and plan the marriage career even when they are advised to pursue employment careers (Chisolm and DuBois-Raymond 1989).

Reports on social attitude surveys, such as the ISSP, usually focus on trends over time, thus giving the impression of substantial change in sex-role ideology in modern society. In fact, the trends are unstable.[9] In the early 1980s in Britain, two-thirds of women and of men agreed that 'A husband's job is to earn the money, a wife's job is to look after the home and family'—a statement that supports the complete separation of roles in the family. By 1988, about half agreed with the statement and about half rejected it, roughly the same proportions as in the USA, whereas a two-thirds majority of men and women in West Germany still endorsed completely separate roles for husband and wife. However attitudes then stabilized in Britain and the USA, with little or no consistent change up to the mid-1990s, although there was a small trend in other European countries (Scott, Alwin, and Braun 1996: 478–80). By the mid-1990s, in all countries except for the Netherlands and Sweden, roughly half of men and women accepted, and roughly half rejected, the idea of a complete separation of roles in the family. In the Netherlands and Sweden, two-thirds rejected complete role-segregation but one-third still preferred it. However, two-thirds of adults in the Netherlands and Sweden also accepted that being a housewife is just as fulfilling as working for pay; only one-third disagreed, the same proportion as in West Germany and Britain. The only value on which the Swedes hold slightly distinctive sex-role orientations is the idea that both man and woman should contribute to household income: four-fifths of Swedes endorse this compared to two-thirds

[9] Similarly, the surveys show that work commitment and work centrality are relatively volatile and vary a lot between countries. There is no evidence of a systematic increase in work commitment and work centrality among women in the 1990s, as would be expected if more women were becoming work-centred and choosing to be primary earners (Bryson and McKay 1997; Russell 1998).

in Britain and West Germany, and only one-quarter in the Netherlands. By the 1990s, it became common for people to reject all collective rules or conventions on sex-roles, and thus to endorse apparently inconsistent ideas. For example most Dutch people now reject the complete role segregation of spouses, yet most Dutch people also reject the idea that both spouses should contribute to household income (Scott, Braun, and Alwin 1998: 30). In sum, the small trend towards 'egalitarian' attitudes in Western Europe and the USA had only achieved a balanced polarization on this question across Europe as a whole by the mid-1990s.

Haller and Höllinger (1994) and Haller, Höllinger and Gomilschak (1999) draw similar conclusions from the same 1988 and 1994 ISSP data. Haller, Höllinger, and Gomilschak (1999) compare 19 nations using the 1994 ISSP data: the USA, Canada, Australia, New Zealand, Norway, Sweden, East and West Germany (analysed separately), Austria, Britain, Ireland, the Netherlands, Italy, Spain, Poland, Hungary, Czechoslovakia, Slovenia, Bulgaria, and Russia. They found that substantial minorities of 30%–40% of adults in most countries still support the complete sexual division of labour in the family, that there are no important differences between men and women in sex-role attitudes, and that attitudes seemed to be independent of people's objective situation, marital status, and employment status.

Some commercial opinion polls also provide relevant information. Comparative opinion polls in France, Germany, Britain, Italy, Spain, and the USA carried out by MORI (1996) suggest that materialistic motivations remain the most important factor driving female employment. If they had enough money to have a real choice, most women in all six countries said they would prefer to work only part-time (33%–46%), or do voluntary work (9%–26%), or be full-time homemakers (12%–25%). In the absence of financial motives, only one in ten women in Europe, and 15% in the USA, would prefer full-time work, compared to one-fifth of men in Europe and one-third in the USA.

Some studies notice that two quite different pictures of attitude change can be found, depending on whether women are asked about their own lives or about the lives of others. Personal commitment to family values is today combined with greater tolerance for the autonomy and choices of other women, including the voluntary childless and feminist minorities (McLaughlin *et al.* 1988: 185–90). This separation of personal familistic values from tolerance for non-conformist family lifestyles among other people is found also at the aggregate, national level across Europe. An analysis of the European Values Survey data for 1981 shows that in some countries, such as France, people are tolerant of non-conformism in marriage and procreation while they continue to attach major importance to parenthood as an element of personal fulfilment. In other countries, such as Denmark, the two sets of values are inversely related: people are tolerant of non-conformism in family

TABLE 4.2. *Sex-role preferences in Britain, 1999*

Percentage of adults supporting each of three models of the sexual division of labour:

		Egalitarian	Compromise	Separate roles	Total	Base =100%
All aged 16 and over						
	Men	45	36	19	100	1540
	Women	41	42	17	100	1813
Men aged	15–24	59	32	9	100	125
	25–44	48	39	13	100	568
	45–64	47	34	19	100	511
	65 and over	31	36	33	100	336
Women aged	15–24 years	63	24	13	100	157
	25–44	43	43	14	100	687
	45–64	37	48	15	100	593
	65 and over	32	41	27	100	376
Married and cohabiting couples of working age (16–64)						
	Men	46	38	16	100	866
	Women	37	49	14	100	1024
	Total	41	44	15	100	1890

Notes: The question asked: People talk about the changing roles of husband and wife in the family. On this card are descriptions of three kinds of family. Which of them corresponds best with **your** ideas about the family?

1. A family where the two partners each have an equally demanding job and where housework and the care of the children are shared equally between them.
2. A family where the wife has a less demanding job than her husband and where she does the larger share of housework and caring for the children.
3. A family where only the husband has a job and the wife runs the home.
4. None of these.

Source: 1999 national survey of work-lifestyle preferences and work orientations reported in Hakim (forthcoming). Data for 3600 people aged 16 and over in Britain interviewed at home, excluding students in full-time education, the 1% not responding to the question and the 2% choosing the last response.

matters and also give low emphasis to parenthood as a central feature of life (Lesthaeghe and Meekers 1986: 241).

The polarization of sex-role preferences remains hidden in part because few studies compare the values and preferences of full-time homemakers and women working full-time: they are treated as living in different worlds. On the rare occasions when comparisons are made, differences emerge. For example the ISSP shows that there are no differences between men and women in attitudes to the importance of children in marriage in the USA, Britain, West Germany, and the Irish Republic. However in all four countries there are differences between homemakers and working women, with full-time homemakers giving greater emphasis to children as an essential part of marriage (Scott, Braun, and Alwin 1993: 32; see also Thomson 1995: 83).

A national survey carried out in 1999 in Britain shows that there is no consistent trend towards 'egalitarian' sex-roles in marriage, and that women's preferences can change markedly after marriage (Hakim forthcoming). Table 4.1 shows a definite swing in preferences in Britain in the 1980s away from complete role segregation towards symmetrical roles in the family. By 1987, half of all adults in Britain preferred the 'egalitarian' model of family roles, and one might have expected this support to grow in the 1990s. In reality, preferences swung back towards the compromise model, away from the 'egalitarian' model (Table 4.2). By 1999, a clear majority of adults preferred some degree of role segregation in the family: about one-fifth preferred complete role segregation, and two-fifths preferred the modern sexual division of labour that identifies wives as secondary earners rather than primary co-earners. It is notable that the swing back to the compromise model was strongest among women, not men, and affected all age groups except the very youngest, who are most idealistic (Table 4.2).

The sharp decline in support for symmetrical family roles which occurs after the mid-20s is in part a reflection of the increased realism that comes after marriage, when the division of labour in the family is confronted in reality rather than in principle. Sex-role preferences among married and cohabiting couples show an even clearer swing towards the compromise model than is observed among all adults (Table 4.2). Again, it is notable that the swing is greater among wives than among husbands. There is no evidence here that it is men who are imposing role segregation on unwilling women. On the contrary, it seems to be women, especially wives, who prefer a secondary earner role rather than fully equal breadwinner roles. At the start of the 21st century, the picture remains one of three quite different work-lifestyles all attracting substantial support, including polar opposite models of the family.

Does Higher Education Make a Difference?

The polarization of preferences is apparent among all groups of women, including the most highly educated. It appears that graduate women, or women of high ability, do not automatically prefer a career over family life. Two early studies of women who graduated from university in the USA (Ginzberg 1966) and Britain (Fogarty, Rapoport, and Rapoport 1971), at a time when this was still sufficiently exceptional for the women in question to be a very selective group, provide a rigorous test of the proposition that higher education makes a difference.

In 1963, Colombia University in the USA carried out a study of what can be regarded as a natural experiment (Hakim 1987a: 109–10). They decided to investigate the work histories and achievements of the men and women who had won scholarships and fellowships to do graduate studies at the university. The results for the women disappointed the university researchers, because they revealed the women to be far less ambitious and career-oriented than the men, many of them 'wasting' their abilities and educational qualifications by becoming full-time homemakers as soon as they married. The survey results for men and women differed so fundamentally that they were presented in separate books, with little attempt at comparison (Ginzberg 1964, 1966). The sample of 311 women represented a 75% response rate to what was effectively a postal census rather than a sample survey. The women surveyed were all of the very highest ability and promise, which was why they were selected for scholarships and fellowships. By the time of the survey, in 1963, two-thirds were aged 37–44 years. One-third had obtained doctorates; 40% were childless; among the ever-married, 14% had only one child. The group had a low marriage rate, low fertility, and high workrates, partly because many of the women had been pulled into the workforce during World War II. What surprised and disappointed the research team was the women's attitudes to work and career.

Only half of the women said they had pursued graduate studies for career reasons, rather than because of an interest in the subject they studied, whereas virtually all the male scholarship holders had career goals of some sort, often ambitious. The sample broke down into three groups:

(1) one-third had a career goal throughout their education;
(2) one-third developed occupational goals during their studies, or else acquired a different occupational goal during their studies;
(3) one-third had never had career goals; their aim was to get a good education and marry well, that is, the marriage career.

In this age cohort, the marriage career was still the expected norm for women in the USA. So it was still acceptable to state this as a life goal, although only a one-third minority of the scholarship graduates did so. In the 1970s, there was a large and rapid swing in attitudes in the USA, toward the *working* wife and mother as the new norm (Mathews and Tiedeman 1964; Komarovsky 1982; McLaughlin *et al.* 1988: 169–91). Today, young women are far more likely to offer socially acceptable answers about jobs and careers than to admit openly to aiming for a marriage career.

When asked how they would or did handle any conflicts between marriage and career, the scholarship graduates again fell into three groups: a minority of about one-fifth gave priority to their career and, if necessary, would forego marriage; a minority of about one-fifth gave priority to marriage and having children, and would possibly stop work permanently once they married or else had done so already; and the majority thought they would try to combine marriage and a career, or had not given any thought to the problem, or did not know how they would resolve the problem (Ginzberg 1966: 40–5). Even in this highly selective group of exceptionally able and highly qualified scholarship winners, there was just as wide a variety of preferences as among all women.

This unique study confirms that women do not automatically become career-oriented just because they are highly qualified, although the possession of such qualifications makes it easier and more rewarding for them to do paid work, if a need arises, as in the case of World War II. It also confirms that intellectually gifted and able women are just as likely to display a range of preferences as less-able groups of women. None the less, there will be some small association between educational qualifications and preferences at the national level because women who are work-centred will generally expend more effort to obtain qualifications than women who are home-centred, unless they use the educational system as a marriage market. Qualifications of some sort have today become a necessary, but not sufficient, condition for a career. However not all women who obtain qualifications will be seeking a career, as distinct from reasonably interesting and well-paid jobs whenever they do decide to work, or are forced to work.

Ginzberg's results from an élite group of graduate women are duplicated in subsequent research. A study of 64 women graduating from college in 1968 who were re-interviewed in 1975, when aged about 29 years, again found that they divided into three distinct groups based on lifestyles and aspirations: *careerists*, *workers*, and *familists* who were mainly oriented towards children and leisure activities and envisaged only occasional paid work after marriage (Almquist, Angrist, and Mickelson 1980). The 1970s was a decade of dramatic change in sex-role attitudes in the USA. But the sudden drop in the proportion of young women anticipating the full-time homemaker role does not mean that they all switched to career plans instead. By 1980, only about one-fifth of college women cited a career as a main life goal and over half chose having children, compared to 5% and 80% respectively in 1952 (McLaughlin *et al.* 1988: 170–8). Well into the 1980s, most American teenage girls continued to focus on romance and marriage as the centrepoint of their lives, with only a minority regarding employment as a major source of meaning in their lives, even though they all knew they might be working for a large part of their lives (Thompson 1989).

Similar results emerge from a 1968 British survey of a nationally representative sample of people who had graduated from university in 1960 (Fogarty, Rapoport, and Rapoport 1971: 186–235). Eight years after graduation, half of all the women and two-thirds of the mothers were full-time homemakers, whereas virtually all the women without children were in full-time employment. Men and single women were career-centred, whereas wives, and more especially mothers, were family-centred. The majority of men and one-third of single women had high career aspirations, compared to less than one-fifth of wives. The men had been more ambitious from secondary school onwards, and their ambitions increased steadily as they got older. In contrast, the women had always been less ambitious, and their ambitions declined steadily over time. In all groups, high ambitions were strongly associated with higher earnings. The married women graduates divided into a one-fifth minority who were career-oriented and a four-fifths majority who were not, with strong correlations between career commitment, work status, and lifetime workplans. Women and men who were still single eight years after graduation—24% and 15% of women and men respectively—emerged as significantly different from the majority of women and men who had married already—the single women being more ambitious and career-centred, the single men being more career-centred but slightly less ambitious than others. Overall, only one-fifth of the sample of female graduates were ambitious and career-committed compared to two-thirds of the male graduates.[10] The largest group, of women with children, was also polarized: one-fifth planned to remain full-time homemakers, one-fifth planned continuous full-time employment, and three-fifths planned some combination of work and family roles (Fogarty, Rapoport, and Rapoport 1971: 557).

There has been a massive expansion in higher education in Britain in the 30 years since this survey, and a wider group of women are now university graduates. However, graduate women appear to be no more career-oriented in the 1990s than they were in the 1960s, when they constituted a small, highly selective, and privileged group. Furthermore, graduate women differ little in sex-role attitudes from non-graduate women, as shown already by Table 3.4. More important, even graduate women with careers in professional and managerial occupations may still regard their husband's career as more important than their own. A study of dual-career couples—as distinct from dual-earner couples—in the 1990s found that two-thirds of couples still gave priority to the husband's career, especially after they had children. The minority of couples treating both careers as having equal weight, or giving priority to the wife's career, were generally childless (Hardill *et al.* 1997). Case-studies of women in well-paid graduate occupations, such as pharmacy and translating, show that most continue to regard themselves as secondary earners who are financially dependent on their partner while their male colleagues regard themselves as main breadwinners. In the mid-1990s, Huws *et al.* (1996)

[10] These proportions had to be calculated from data on career aspirations, which are given for all groups in the study, instead of data on career commitment, which is reported for mothers only, somewhat paradoxically.

surveyed freelance translators across Western and Eastern Europe who worked for Wordbank, a specialist international translation agency. The translators were all homeworkers and teleworkers, receiving and returning their work electronically. Translating is a desegregated occupation, employing men and women equally, and most translators are university graduates. The survey found no differences between the women and men in qualifications, work experience, number of employers, rates of pay, personal characteristics, and personalities. Two-thirds of the sample, and over half the women, had no children under age 18 in the home. However, even in this unisex profession, men and women had different perspectives on their work. Both men and women regarded freelance homework as the ideal work situation, but women liked it because being at home gave them more time flexibility, whereas men liked it for the autonomy of being self-employed. Virtually all the married and cohabiting women said they were secondary earners, whereas most of the men said they were the main breadwinners of their household. Although half the men had been working at home for over five years, there was almost no evidence of role segregation in the family breaking down as a result (Huws *et al*. 1996).

A study of doctor's careers by Allen (1994) showed that women generally chose specialisms with regular work hours that would not interfere with their family life, such as dermatology and radiology, whereas men tended to choose high status and competitive specialisms, such as surgery, with long and irregular work hours, and generally higher rewards. Similarly, Crompton and Harris (1998) use qualitative research on doctors and bank managers in several European countries to demonstrate that women with higher education qualifications and professional/managerial occupations are not necessarily career-centred. On the contrary, most of the women displayed the diverse and ambivalent work orientations typical of adaptive women, with only a tiny number of women being work-centred. As the home-centred group was excluded entirely from the study, their work orientations are not reported. Another study, based on national census microdata, found that female pharmacists in Britain were also mostly adaptive women, choosing a moderate involvement in market work, with very few careerists, whereas male pharmacists were typically careerist and entrepreneurial (Hakim 1998a: 221–34).

In sum, the polarization of women's sex-role preferences dates back to well before the equal opportunities revolution of the 1960s and 1970s in the USA and Britain. The polarization of preferences could possibly be a long standing phenomenon. Certainly, it is not a product of the equal opportunities revolution. Nor does higher education alter the polarization pattern: a minority of career-oriented and work-committed women at one extreme, a minority of home-centred and family-oriented women at the other extreme, and a larger middle group hoping to combine work and family roles in some fashion. The impact of higher education is to give women access to more interesting and well-paid occupations if they do take up paid work, so that workrates are generally higher among highly qualified women than among other women, as noted in Table 3.4.

Polarization of Attitudes Within the Workforce

The most extreme contrasts among women are between the minority of career-oriented women, who plan to work across the lifecycle, and women who aim for the marriage career and hope never to work after marriage or childbirth. However the polarization of women's sex-role preferences is also found *within* the working population, as shown by marked differences between the values of women who work full-time or part-time. Some surveys show part-time workers to be almost identical to non-working women in sex-role attitudes and preferences. Other surveys show women working part-time to fall mid-way between women working full-time and women who are full-time homemakers. This variation is due partly to the precise questions asked, and partly to national differences in the way part-time work is organized (Blossfeld and Hakim 1997; O'Reilly and Fagan 1998). In some countries, such as Britain, Germany, and the Netherlands, part-time work divides into half-time jobs and marginal jobs with very short hours, so that part-time workers are a very mixed group (Hakim 1998a: 102–77).

Table 4.3 shows the percentage of men and women actively or passively accepting separate family roles for men and women. Our focus here is on the first three questions in Table 4.3 that concern a *relative* division of labour rather than a *total* separation of the male breadwinning role and the female homemaking role. Commendably, the questions do not confuse the issue of the domestic division of labour with any reference to childcare tasks, which now constitute a small part of women's domestic work across the extended lifecycle for those who do have children, and a non-existent part for the 20% of women who are now choosing to remain childless, as noted in Chapter 3. The questions concern housekeeping and income-earning roles, both of which are continuous, year-round activities, across the whole lifecycle.

The majority of men and women endorse the modern sexual division of labour. Over half of men and women aged 20–60 think men should retain the *main* breadwinner role and *ultimate* responsibility for income-earning. There is even greater unanimity on women's main role in the home: two-thirds of women and men regard housework and homemaking as the primary responsibility of women. More than half and up to two-thirds of adults in Britain prefer the conventional sexual division of labour to continue even when women have paid jobs in the labour market. Even without any reference to the special demands of childcare, symmetrical sex-roles are a minority taste.

TABLE 4.3. *Divergent attitudes to the sexual division of labour within the workforce*

	Women working			Women not working	All women	All men
	Full-time	Part-time	All			
The female partner should be ultimately responsible for housework						
% agreeing	44	74	59	81	67	65
The male partner should be ultimately responsible for breadwinning						
% agreeing	30	59	44	70	54	59
I'm not against women working but the man should still be the main breadwinner in the family						
% agreeing or indifferent	49	69	58	64	60	56
In times of high unemployment married women should stay at home						
% agreeing or indifferent	27	35	30	48	38	46

Source: Table 3, reporting analyses of 1986 and 1987 SCELI survey data for men and women aged 20–60 years, in C. Hakim and S. Jacobs, *Sex-Role Preferences and Work Histories*, 1997, LSE Sociology Department Working Paper No. 12.

Differences between men and women in sex-role ideology are almost non-existent, as Haller, Höllinger, and Gomilschak (1999) also found. There is no evidence that 'patriarchal' men espouse a more 'traditional' sex-role ideology which they seek to force on women.

Results for men in employment are almost identical to those for all adult men shown in Table 4.3. Among women, there are differences between working and non-working women, and these divisions are repeated within the workforce. On all three questions on sex-role ideology, women working part-time and women out of the labour market hold views that are very similar or almost identical, with a clear majority *supporting* the modern sexual division of labour. In contrast, the majority of women with full-time jobs reject this model for family relationships. The similarity between part-time workers and non-working women is strongest among women aged over 40.

The sex-role preferences of non-working women and women working part-time are closest to those of men generally. Indeed these two groups of women are rather *more* 'traditionalist' than men generally. For example 69% of all female part-time workers, and 81% of those aged 40–60, believe than men should still be the main breadwinner in the family, even if their wife has a job. In effect, a wife's contribution to the household budget is not seen to change the sexual division of labour in any serious way. The majority of part-timers see themselves as secondary earners whose primary role remains in the home and who look to men for financial support. This perspective is not limited to women whose current part-time job places them in the working class, with relatively low earnings. It is also found in the small group of women with part-time jobs in the Service Class,[11] whose jobs are among the most highly paid and who might have been expected to be more career-oriented. Even among women who have Service Class jobs (in professional, technical, and managerial occupations), there are sharp differences in sex-role ideology between those working full-time and those who work part-time: a minority (36%) and a majority (53%) respectively believe that their husbands should still remain the main breadwinner. Like the majority of part-timers who have lower status and less-well-paid jobs, women working part-time in Service Class jobs affirm their primary role as homemakers. However they display greater ambivalence than do other part-timers about the male role as principal breadwinner: close to half accept, and half reject the idea (Hakim and Jacobs 1997), presumably because their earnings constitute a substantial addition to household income. Overall, the impact of sex-role ideology is greater than social class differences.

There is now a substantial body of research showing that women who work part-time differ systematically from women with full-time jobs, in their work orientations and labour market behaviour (Bouffartigue, de Coninck, and Pendariès 1992; Rubery, Morrel, and Burchell 1994; Hakim 1993b, 1995, 1996b, 1996c, 1997; Plantenga 1995: 287; Thomson 1995; Crompton and Le Feuvre 1996; Fagan and Rubery 1996: 245; Harkness 1996: 18–20). It appears that there are important qualitative differences between the two groups in sex-role ideology, and it seems likely that this is the source of continuing differences between full-timers and part-timers in labour turnover and employment stability (Corti, Laurie, and Dex 1995: 50–1; Hakim 1996c, 1998a: 135–8), in patterns of employment and occupational segregation (Hakim 1993b; Jacobs 1995; Hakim 1998a: 134–5), in attitudes to motherhood and childcare (Thomson 1995: 80), and the fact that part-time workers express higher satisfaction with their relatively low grade and low-paid jobs than do full-time workers (Hakim 1991; Curtice 1993; Corti, Laurie and Dex 1995: 54–7; Plantenga 1995: 284). A part-time job does not alter a wife's status and decision-making power within the family (Hakim 1996a: 73).

[11] According to the 1991 Census, only 15% of all women with part-time jobs were in Service Class occupations (Hakim 1998a).

Studies of American women reveal similar differences in sex-role attitudes between full-time homemakers and women with jobs, and that women with part-time jobs hold attitudes closer to those of homemakers than to those of women working full-time (Cassidy and Warren 1996: 312–5). A 1992 survey of married college graduates confirmed that women working part-time, full-time homemakers, and men married to such women, all had markedly more 'traditional' sex-role attitudes than women with full-time jobs and men married to such women. In contrast with other studies, women employed part-time in this sample of graduates were more similar to women with full-time jobs than to full-time homemakers. Compared to the polarization of women's attitudes, relatively few differences were found between the men's groups. The most egalitarian sex-role attitudes were held by educationally homogamous couples, where both spouses held degrees (Cassidy and Warren 1996).

In sum, women working part-time are sufficiently distinctive in their sex-role attitudes, work orientations, and labour market behaviour that they should always be differentiated from women working full-time in research analyses. A large degree of self-selection into full-time jobs, part-time jobs, and full-time homemaking means that these are three qualitatively different groups of women in most modern societies, although there will always be some overlap at the margins.

The Polarization of Women's Employment

As noted at the start of this chapter, social scientists agree that there is a new trend towards the polarization of women's employment in rich modern societies. Some women are achieving the highly paid and interesting work offered by professional and managerial occupations, while others remain in unskilled jobs that offer few fringe benefits and relatively low pay, but are also less demanding and do not intrude upon family life. The polarization of women's employment is reflected in a variety of indicators: women who regard themselves as having careers versus jobs, full-time versus part-time work, continuous employment versus fragmented work histories, highly qualified versus unskilled work, and women who regard themselves as primary earners versus secondary earners. The indicators overlap, mostly, to produce jobs with high earnings versus jobs with low earnings. Whenever the distribution of earnings widens, as it did in the 1980s in Britain and the USA, earnings inequality increases, for women as well as men. But most social scientists conclude that the earnings dispersion for women increased most of all, partly due to the dramatic increase in the numbers of women entering professional and managerial occupations (Humphries and Rubery 1992; Rubery and Fagan

TABLE 4.4. *Patterns of work and inactivity among women of working age by occupational grade*

Socio-Economic Group	Full-time work	Part-time work	Unem-ployed	Economically inactive	Base N=100%	%
Professional & managers/ employers	68	14	3	15	2342	13
Intermediate & junior non-manual	41	32	5	22	9146	51
Skilled manual & own account	39	32	4	24	1409	8
Semi-skilled & personal service	27	31	6	34	3941	22
Unskilled occupations	7	51	5	36	1202	7
All occupations	39	31	5	25	18040	100

Source: Extracted from Table 5.5, reporting General Household Survey, combined data for 1994, 1995 and 1996 for Great Britain, in ONS, *Living in Britain*, 1998, Stationery Office, p.58. The nine SEGs are combined into just five occupational groups in this table. Data are for women of working age (16–59 years) reporting occupation of current or last job. Percentages have been rounded.

1993; Hakim 1992, 1998a). Others insist that the crucial distinction is in women's work orientations, rather than their earnings, which are the outcome of many factors. For some women, employment is an *extension* of their family role: they seek extra income for their family, often in typically-female occupations that pose less of a challenge to the male breadwinner's role as main income-earner. For other women, employment offers an *alternative* to their domestic role, another avenue for self-expression, self-fulfilment, and (competitive) achievement, often in male-dominated occupations, with the expectation of being a financially self-supporting contributor to domestic finances (Matthaei 1982: 278–82; Hakim 1996a: 207). Either way, studies of women's work histories and patterns of employment repeatedly throw up the distribution set out in Table 1.1, with two small(er) extreme groups and a large middle group.

Table 4.4 illustrates the link between occupational grade and employment patterns. Full-time workrates increase sharply from 7% among unskilled women to 68% in the tiny professional and managerial group. Spells out of the workforce and part-time work increase sharply the lower a woman's occupational grade. As noted in Chapter 7, most women marry men of similar educational, occupational, or social status. It seems obvious, therefore, that some women are working purely as a lifestyle preference, especially at the top of the occupational hierarchy, while financial motivations remain important for others, especially at the lower end of the occupational structure. Research analyses that treat women as a single homogeneous group are now unlikely to produce meaningful or worthwhile results, given the enormous and increasing heterogeneity of the female population and the female workforce. Analyses and research methods that rely on averages and other measures of central tendency produce misleading results as regards women's employment patterns.

In the second half of the 20th century, female employment rates have been rising in almost all countries. Initially, this trend was interpreted as demonstrating women's increasing commitment to employment careers. It was assumed that sex differentials in labour market participation would eventually vanish, especially if supported by egalitarian social policies. In the 1980s, some social scientists insisted that sex differentials had already disappeared in the USA and Britain. By the 1990s, it became clear that labour market measures designed by men for men did not work at all well for women, that women's employment patterns were more diverse than had been realized, and that sex differentials were reduced in size but were otherwise persistent and stable (Jonung and Persson 1993; Hakim 1993a, 1995, 1996a, 1996c, 1998a).

In most countries, rising female employment rates have hidden two separate trends: long-term stability in full-time workrates, and the emergence of a new female workforce working part-time and/or with high turnover rates, having a weaker attachment to employment and more fragmented, episodic, or discontinuous employment histories. Pott-Buter (1993) found a remarkable stability in female workrates since 1850 in Britain, France, Belgium, the Netherlands, Germany, Denmark, and Sweden. In Britain, women's full-time workrates remained within the range 30%–38% from 1850—and possibly going back further than that—up to 1998 (Hakim 1993a, 1996a: 63). In France, women's workrates fluctuated within the range 34%–43% for at least a century up to 1970 (Riboud 1985). From the 1970s onwards, full-time workrates fell to a steady level of about 30% in France. All the recent increase in female employment rates is due to the creation of a new part-time workforce after deregulation (Bouffartigue, de Coninck, and Pendaries 1992: 407–10). In West Germany, women's full-time workrates have remained at just over 20% of the working age group throughout the 20th century, and over 40% of women remained in continuous full-time homemaking (Berger, Steinmüller, and Sopp 1993: 55). In the Netherlands, women's full-time workrates remained at a steady level of 20% after World War II; all the increase in employment rates was due to the creation of a huge new part-time workforce after deregulation, including many women with marginal jobs of less than 12 hours a week as well as half-time jobs (De Graaf and Vermeulen 1997: 194). Even in the 1990s, there was no uniform upward trend in female full-time employment rates in OECD countries. Countries which have apparently 'low' female workrates are not in fact very different. Full-time workrates in Greece, Italy, and Portugal, for example, are similar to those in northern

Europe, and these countries have high proportions of women in professional and technical jobs. However southern European countries have not yet developed the substantial workforces of permanent part-time jobs already established in northern Europe (Blossfeld and Hakim 1997; O'Reilly and Fagan 1998: 37, 58–9, 199–213).

The polarization of women's employment did not happen overnight. The pattern only began to be recognized after social scientists obtained access to national data on work histories from retrospective life history surveys and from the new longitudinal studies: the PSID and NLS initiated in the mid-1960s in the USA, the SOEP initiated in 1984 in Germany, the 1946, 1958, and 1970 British birth cohort studies which each took two decades to produce adult samples (Hakim 1987a, 2000). Some scientific discoveries are in practice data-driven. Because longitudinal studies were started very early in the USA, funded by the federal government, there is a larger body of relevant research evidence for America than there is for Europe. The evidence from the somewhat different British birth cohort studies is reviewed in Chapter 5.

An analysis of 1967 NLS data (Stephan and Schroeder 1979; see also Maret 1983: 54) identified three distinct groups among married women aged 30–44 years: one-fifth were permanent housewives who had worked rarely or not at all since marriage; one-fifth were committed career women who had worked virtually all of the time since marriage; and a three-fifths majority were non-career workers with fragmented work histories. There were qualitative differences between career women and non-career women. Career women's employment decisions were not affected by children nor by their husband's earnings. In contrast, the employment decisions of non-career women were strongly affected by childcare responsibilities and their husband's income; they moved in and out of the workforce in response to the short-term 'needs' of the family. Career women tended to be highly educated, to be black, and to have fewer children. They were more likely to be working the higher their husband's education and the higher their own education. In effect, their earnings were not a substitute for or supplement to the husband's earnings, but the outcome of an entirely independent lifestyle choice.

Heckman (1979b) analysed PSID work history data for the seven years 1968–1974 for white married women aged 45–64 in 1968. Using a weak definition of 'employment' as any paid work in a year, he found that the sample split roughly into thirds: housewives, discontinuous workers and those who were continuously employed across the seven years 1968–1974. Four-fifths of the women either worked all the time or did not work at all over the three years 1968–1970. Over the seven years 1968–1974, two-thirds of the women either worked all the time or did not work at all.

Also based on PSID data, another study analysed work histories over the five years 1967–1971 for white married women only (Heckman and Willis 1977). Again, the sample divided roughly into thirds: 35% of wives were permanent housewives who did no paid work at all in the five years 1967–1971; 38% had intermittent employment; 27% were employed to some extent in all five years. A similar analysis of PSID data was later carried out by Moen (1985) focusing on work histories over the five years 1972–1976. Her data was much fuller because wives were interviewed personally in 1976 to obtain detailed work histories, whereas limited data about the wives was supplied by the husband in previous years. She too concluded that there was no modal pattern for female work histories among women aged 18–59. One-quarter of all women (one-fifth of wives and over half the non-married women) stayed in continuous full-time employment over the five year period. One-fifth of women (one-quarter of wives) were permanent homemakers. Continuous part-time work was very rare in the USA, at 5% of the age group. At all educational levels, half of all women had discontinuous work histories, with full-time and/or part-time jobs interspersed with spells out of the work-force. The four groups of women had different characteristics.

Another PSID analysis by Corcoran, Duncan, and Ponza (1984) used work history data for men and women of working age for a slightly longer stretch of thirteen years 1967–1979, with employment in any year classified a little more precisely as full-time (1500 hours or more), part-time (250–1500 hours over the year), or too marginal to count (under 250 hours in any year). They found that only 20%–30% of women aged 23–47 years worked continuously for 13 years. Only 6% of women compared to 64% of men worked continuously full-time over the thirteen year period (Corcoran, Duncan, and Ponza 1984; Treiman 1985: 218).

Ten years later, the picture remained almost identical. Blank (1998) analysed PSID data for the fourteen years 1976–1989, looking at the work histories of family heads and spouses aged 18–50 in 1976, who reached 32–64 years by 1989. She found that only 16% of women (and 13% of wives) compared to 68% of men, worked continuously full-time in all fourteen years. Only one-third of women (and wives) compared to 86% of men, worked in all fourteen years. In addition, 5% of women (and 6% of wives) never did paid work at all: they remained out of the workforce continuously for all fourteen years without ever taking even a part-time job. Further analysis showed that American women divide into three distinct groups: *full-time workers*, who mostly work full-time (about one-third of all women of working age); *non-workers*, who are typically out of the labour market (about one-fifth of women); and *movers*, who move in and out of employment, including many women with part-time jobs (almost half of adult women). Part-time workers were polarized into those who normally worked full-time and those who normally did not work, both types returning to their usual state after a temporary part-time job (Blank 1999).

These studies show that the exact size of the career-women minority depends heavily on whether continuous employment is defined tightly or loosely. In contrast, the large minority group of permanent full-time homemakers is little affected by changes of definition. In the most careful analyses, fragmented work histories of various kinds are found among half to two-thirds of adult women, and they outnumber career women by two to one or three to one. Heckman (1979b) concluded that women's employment histories were shaped by two parallel processes. Female heterogeneity and stable preferences for employment or homemaking meant that labour force participation over the lifecycle was U-shaped, with most women inclined to work all the time, or not at all, after marriage, when a choice becomes available. He also found an investment effect: past work experience increased the rewards from employment and thus increased the chances of continuous employment. Like certain drugs, employment and a personal income can be habit-forming. Or, as Lieberson (1985) points out, some social processes are not easily reversed.

Finally, Goldin's unique analyses of historical and administrative datasets for the USA show that female heterogeneity has an even longer history (Goldin 1990: 30–41). During the early part of the 20th century, when the marriage bar was applied to teaching and other occupations attractive to women, there were women who chose a career in preference to marriage and motherhood. Over half of college women graduating around 1910 either did not marry or, if they did, had no children; most of them had careers in teaching. In the cohorts graduating from college in the period 1966–1979, she found that only one-fifth to one-quarter had achieved a career[12] by the age of 40 among those who became mothers, compared to half of the graduate women who remained childless. Overall, between one-quarter and one-third of all the graduate women achieved a career by the age of 40 years. About half of all the career women were childless, whereas the vast majority of other graduate women had children (Goldin 1997).

Professional women are not a novel product of the equal opportunities revolution (Blitz 1974; see also Mills 1996). Professional women were in fact more common in the first half of the century in the USA than they were in the 1970s. In 1920 and 1930, almost half of all professionals were women, double women's share of the workforce; the proportion then declined to 41% by 1970, close to women's 38% share of the workforce. What has changed is that the removal of the marriage bar means that women who pursue a professional career can now marry, and have children, whereas they were most often single and/or childless in the past. Second, substantial growth of male-dominated professions, such as engineering, from 1900 onwards greatly reduced women's share of professional jobs by 1970 (Blitz 1974).

Studies of women's work histories are a recent development in Europe, but

[12] In her analysis of data for graduate women, Goldin (1997: 25) defined a career as continuous full-time employment for at least two consecutive periods of about 7–10 years.

Table 4.5. The decline in continuous employment and the marriage career

Year of labour market entry	Proportion (%) of each cohort in each category 15 or 20 years after entering workforce:							
	continuous employment		discontinuous employment		homemaker career		Base=100%	
	15	20	15	20	15	20	15	20
1941–1945	20	13	36	51	44	36	511	502
1946–1950	18	13	39	56	43	31	449	433
1951–1955	15	10	47	67	38	23	523	510
1956–1960	11	8	53	73	36	19	609	574
1961–1965	13	—	61	—	26	—	655	—
Total	15	11	48	62	37	27	2747	2019

Notes:—indicates sample too young for results at 20 years stage in 1980 survey. Continuous employment consists of continuous spells of paid work, whether full-time or part-time, without any breaks. The homemaker career is defined as a single employment spell early in adult life that ended in permanent non-work. Discontinuous employment consists of all other work histories combining spells of work and spells of non-work.

Source: 1980 Women and Employment Survey, Great Britain, data for women aged 16–59, as reported in Table 5.2 in C. Hakim, *Key Issues in Women's Work*, Athlone Press, 1996.

all the evidence points to similar levels of female heterogeneity and employment polarization throughout the 20th century (Bouffartigue, de Coninck, and Pendariès 1992; Berger, Steinmuller, and Sopp 1993; Hakim 1996a: 132–9). A national survey of employment patterns among women aged 16–59 years in 1965 in Britain found that one-quarter said they had always worked; one-quarter had retired permanently from employment around marriage or the first birth, or in a few cases, had never worked; and half had fragmented work histories. Among women aged 45–59 years, 15% had always worked, 22% had given up work at marriage, and two-thirds had discontinuous employment histories. Half of the women who were not working in 1965 were permanent homemakers; almost half of the women who were in employment in 1965 had always worked (Hunt 1968a: 74, 1968b: Table D4c), a pattern very similar to that in the USA at this time (Maret 1983: 54). An equivalent national survey of women's employment in 1980 again found one-quarter of women saying they had always worked, and two-thirds had fragmented work histories. Only 10% of women aged 45–59 had worked continuously since leaving full-time education, compared to 15% in 1965 (Martin and Roberts 1984: Table 9.6; Main 1988: 27, 29, 33). Another survey showed that one-fifth of married and widowed women aged 55–69 in 1988

TABLE 4.6. *Young women's workplans and outcomes in the USA*

	Distribution of sample	% working at age 35
Homemaker career:		
consistently indicate no plans for work: aim is marriage, family and homemaking activities	28%	49%
Drifters and unplanned careers:		
(a) highly variable responses over time, no clear pattern in plans for age 35	35% } 47%	
(b) switch to having future work expectations at some point in their twenties	12%	64%
Career planners:		
consistently anticipate working at age 35 throughout their twenties	25%	82%

Source: Derived from Tables 2 and 3, reporting National Longitudinal Surveys data for the cohort of young women first interviewed in 1968, when aged 14–24 years, in L. B. Shaw and D. Shapiro, 'Women's work plans: contrasting expectations and actual work experience', *Monthly Labor Review*, 1987, 110/11: 8–9.

had never worked at all after marriage. Including wives and widows who worked only briefly at some point after age 30, a total of one-third of married and widowed women had followed the marriage career in a period of rising female employment (Ginn and Arber 1996).

In the second half of the 20th century, increasing female workrates were accompanied by more frequent breaks in employment, so that the proportion of women's potential working life spent *out* of the workforce increased across age cohorts (Main 1988: 28–41). The outcome is shown in Table 4.5. There was a dramatic decline, across cohorts, in the proportion of women following the homemaker career: only a quarter of women entering the labour market in the early 1960s gave up work permanently at marriage or when they had children, compared with almost half in the pre-war cohort. However, the proportion of women engaged in continuous employment—a rough indicator of a career—also declined, to one in ten in the 1960s cohort (Table 4.5). Discontinuous employment rose steadily to two-thirds of the cohort entering the workforce in the 1960s. Career women and full-time homemakers became smaller and more selective groups after the equal opportunities revolution. If we focus only on working women, there was a widening gap between those in continuous full-time work and those who moved in and out of the labour market over the lifecycle.

A large scale British survey carried out in 1986 confirms that only a minority of working women, compared to a majority of working men—one-quarter and two-thirds respectively—pursued continuous employment careers with virtually no part-time work, no domestic breaks, and with no influence of domestic factors on employment careers (Burchell and Rubery 1994).

The polarization of women's employment is due to a combination of social structural constraints and personal preferences, or 'tastes', for homemaking versus employment. The long-term importance of preferences is demonstrated by the NLS, one of the earliest national longitudinal studies, as shown in Table 4.6. Young women aged 14–24 years in 1968 were asked in 1968, and at each interview over the next decade, what they planned to be doing at age 35, whether they planned to be working, or keeping house and raising a family. This age was chosen as the peak age for competing work and family roles. The NLS sample divided into one-quarter who aimed for the homemaker career, one-quarter who aimed for an employment career, and half with vague or changing goals. There are several studies of outcomes, all showing that women achieved their employment objectives for the most part, resulting in dramatic 'mark-ups' to career planners in terms of occupational grade and earnings (Mott 1982; Rexroat and Shehan 1984; Shaw and Shapiro 1987). Career planners were more likely to choose male-dominated occupations and to adapt their fertility to their workplans—an option available to women after the contraceptive revolution of the 1960s, as noted in Chapter 3. Many of the women who planned a homemaker career nevertheless were obliged to work by economic factors in half the cases: a husband's low income, divorce, or the opportunity cost of not working. However career planners had higher workrates, better jobs, and earnings 30% higher than those of women who planned not to work. Women who make realistic plans and acquire the necessary skills fare best in the labour market. Those who fare worst are women who aim for an exclusive homemaking career but end up working for economic reasons (Hakim 1991: 111–12, 1996a: 109–13). Overall, the NLS results have repeatedly shown the importance of motivation, values and attitudes as determinants of labour market behaviour, occupational status, and even earnings, an influence that is independent of conventional human capital factors and frequently exceeds the influence of behavioural factors (Hakim 1991: 113).

Continuity and Change in Income-earning Roles

The polarization of women's employment means that wives' financial contribution to household income is increasingly diversified. This slows down the trend towards wives becoming more important, or equal earners within families. The polarization of wives' contribution to family or household income is hidden in studies that analyse averages across all households, or averages within dual-earner households, to look at trends across time. The universal finding is that, despite rising female employment rates, wives' financial contribution to household income has remained fairly stable, and low, in the region of one-fifth to one-third of the total, depending on the definitions used.

There is no doubt that rising female workrates have led to an increase, both absolute and relative, in the number of dual-earner families. By the end of the 20th century, a majority of couples in all social classes in Britain had both partners working (Fry 1984: 56; Bonney 1988: 100; Hogarth, Elias, and Ford 1996: 32; Davies, Joshi, and Peronaci 1998). In the USA, 60% of married couples had two earners by 1997 (Winkler 1998). This led some social scientists to expect economic equality within marriage, a withering of the sexual division of labour in households, and the death of the male breadwinner model of the family. They were surprised to discover that women remained minority contributors to household income, an outcome that was attributed to women's weaker position in the labour market (Rubery *et al.* 1998: 196). This must be a very partial explanation, given that women's earnings in East Germany accounted for only 40% of total household income in 1988, prior to reunification, compared to 18% in West Germany. A government committed to egalitarian social policies, excellent childcare services, reductions in working hours for wives, and continuous full-time employment among women in East Germany, all increased women's contribution to household income, but still left them secondary earners rather than equals, with husbands earning 50% more than wives, on average. Similarly, in the USSR, female full-time earnings remained 65% to 70% of male earnings and most husbands earned substantially more than their wives (Atkinson, Dallin, and Lapidus 1978: 225–39, 391; Lapidus 1988: 95, 100).

The majority of *dual-earner* couples are not *dual-career* couples, who remain a minority of 10% to 20% of all couples in Britain (Bonney 1988; Ferri and Smith 1996: 12–16; Davies, Joshi, and Peronaci 1998) and in the USA (Shelton and Firestone 1989; Winkler 1998). There are two reasons for this. First, the rise in women's employment is due almost entirely to the emergence of a new workforce of secondary earners who engage in intermittent employment, part-time or full-time, and are not committed to long-term careers, as noted in Chapter 3. Second, as noted in Chapter 7, many women (hope to) marry men with higher earnings potential than themselves, with the express intention of being financially supported by their husband, at the minimum throughout the child-rearing phase of their lives. It is thus not surprising that wives contribute on average between one-fifth and one-third of household income, with very little upward movement in their contribution since the 1970s.

A double income does not mean families are twice as well off. Because of additional costs in two-earner families, the net value of a working wife can be far smaller than the initial double income. Lazear and Michael (1980) compared the income and expenditure of childless couples, with and without a working wife. On average, dual-earner couples had gross incomes one-third higher than single-earner couples. This is equivalent to wives contributing one-quarter of total household income if they work. After tax, the 35% gain was halved to 17%. After the additional expenditure on transport, office clothes, and meals out, the net gain of dual-earner couples was reduced to 5% on average. Very often, dual-earner couples are choosing a different lifestyle from single-earner couples. The value of a wife's work in the home is of course higher when there are children to care for, and this may counterbalance the net value of any paid work she foregoes.

In the USA, women who were employed contributed about one-quarter of total household income—40% for wives with full-time jobs—in 1972, and this proportion had not changed since 1950, or even before. Between 1972 and 1982, the mean income of dual-earner families remained about one-quarter higher than in single-earner families, with the gap increasing slowly (McLaughlin *et al.* 1988: 115–16). An analysis of census Public Use Sample (PUS) data for 1940, 1950, 1960, 1970, and 1980 tracked the slow decline in wives' economic dependency in the USA (Sorensen and McLanahan 1987). In 1940, 94% of white wives were largely economically dependent on their husbands, and 84% of them were 100% dependent; only 3% of wives were equal earners and 3% earned more than their husband. By 1980, 85% of white wives were still financially dependent, but only one-third were 100% dependent; 8% were equal earners; another 7% had higher earnings than their husband. Figures for non-white couples differed only in detail from those for white couples. The trend toward dual-earner families has reduced, but not eliminated wives' financial dependency. The main effect is to make couples with secondary earner wives more common than single-earner couples: 54% and 31% respectively among white couples, 49% and 27% respectively among non-white couples by 1980.

Changes in the USA are larger than in most European countries, due to genuine increases in women's full-time workrates over the 20th century in the USA. A replication of Sorensen and McLanahan's analysis using Dutch income data for 1979–1991 shows that wives' economic dependence remains the norm in countries where women's full-time workrates have not changed at all, and all the growth has been in part-time jobs. Van Berkel and De Graaf (1998) defined equal earners a little more broadly than in the USA study as spouses with earnings ±20% of each other instead of ±10%, and they restrict their analysis to couples of working age, excluding pensioners. As a result, a larger proportion of couples are equal earners in the Netherlands: 10% in 1979 and 14% by 1991. However, far fewer wives are the principal earner: 2% in 1979 and 2% in 1991. The vast majority of Dutch wives are financially dependent on their husbands: 88% in 1979 and 84% in 1991. Most of them are 100% dependent: 72% in 1979 and 48% in 1991, compared with 31% of white wives in the USA in 1980. In Dutch society, a wife's economic dependence on her husband is still taken for granted, and is not as risky as it is in the USA, with its higher divorce rates and limited social welfare (Van Berkel and De Graaf 1998: 113–14). Because they expect to be dependent full-time homemakers, Dutch women invest less in education and often marry men with greater education than themselves. Between 1959 and 1991, this tendency for wives to marry 'up' in education was on a rising trend, and educational homogamy declined (Van Berkel and De Graaf 1998: 100), as shown also in Table 7.7. In addition, the Dutch fiscal system and social policy favour dependent wives (Bruyn-Hundt 1992; see also Sainsbury 1996). Although separate taxation of wives was introduced in 1973, single-earner couples continue to benefit from considerable tax privileges and other benefits. In addition, all women get a pension at age 65, irrespective of their work history and contributions record.

The USA and the Netherlands represent two extreme cases as regards the pressure on wives to be financially self-supporting or not. But they differ far less in the actual extent of wives' economic independence, with only 15% and 16% of wives respectively having an income equal to or greater than their husband's in 1980 and 1991 respectively.

Some studies inflate wives' contribution to family income by reporting data for dual-earner families only. As Gustafsson (1995) shows, cross-national differences can be virtually eliminated by presenting figures for the selective subgroup of two-earner families, among whom wives generally contribute about one-third of family income: 30% in the Netherlands, 32% in West Germany, and 38% in Sweden in the 1980s. When figures are reported for *all* couples, large national contrasts emerge, due to the impact of fiscal policies on wives' workrates. Wives' contribution to family income then falls to an average of 12% in the Netherlands, 15% in West Germany, and 29% in Sweden in the 1980s (Gustafsson 1995: 107). In the USA also, wives' contribution to family income is around one-third of the total in dual-earner couples, across all income groups (Winkler 1998). Among *all* married couples, wives' average contribution is much lower, as noted above.

Trends in wives' contribution to household income in Britain have been studied with Family Expenditure Survey (FES) data (Webb 1993: 32; Borooah and McKee 1996; Davies and Joshi 1998) and General Household Survey (GHS) data (Machin and Waldfogel 1994; Harkness, Machin, and Waldfogel 1995). Both datasets yield similar results, with some variation between analyses due to differences in definitions and methods used.

Using data for 1968–1990, Davies and Joshi (1998) showed that dual-earner couples rose from 43% to 64% of all married couples who were both under age 65. Due to rising unemployment in the period, and early retirement, couples with no earner also increased, from 3% in 1968 to 9% by 1990, and the proportion with only the wife working rose from 1% in 1968 to 4% by 1990. The increase in wives' share of net family income over the period was small. In all types of family, including pensioner families, wives' contributions rose from an average of 19% to 28% by 1990; from 12% to 24% in families with children; from 30% to 38% in families without children with spouses under 65 years old. Rising female employment closed the gap between the workrates of the wives of the highest and lowest paid men. Wives' contributions were most important in the poorest families, where they constituted one-third of gross family income compared with less than one-fifth in the most affluent families. Working wives raised some families out of poverty, but they also contributed to widening inequalities between families. The sharpest polarization of family income was between young families where women became mothers in their 20s, or earlier, and those with childless wives (Davies and Joshi 1998: 58).

Borooah and McKee (1996) also address the growing polarization between dual-earner and one-earner or no-earner families. Their FES analysis is restricted to married or cohabiting couples below retirement age. Over the 15 years 1979–1993, the ratio of wives' to husbands' earnings, as an average across *all* couples, rose from 23% in 1979 to 41% in 1993. Over the same period, the contribution of wives' earnings, if any, to total family disposable income rose from 17% to 23%. Among *dual-earner* couples, the ratio of wives' to husbands' earnings rose from 37% in 1979 to 53% in 1993, and the average contribution of working wives to family income rose from 25% in 1979 to 32% by 1993. By the mid-1990s, about one-third of family income in dual-earner couples, and nearly one-quarter in all couples, was contributed by the wife. Borooah and McKee concluded that it is the husband's earnings that make the largest contribution to inequality between couples.

Analyses of GHS data produce similar results. Machin and Waldfogel (1994) used data for married couples aged 24–55 years. Between 1979 and 1991, wives' earnings, if any, rose from 16% to 21% of these married couples' total income. Again, wives' earnings were most important in the poorest families. When the husband had earnings in the lowest decile in 1989–90, wives' earnings contributed 25% of family income among all couples, 35% in dual-earner couples, and 46% if she worked full-time. When the husband had earnings in the highest decile, wives' earnings contributed 10% of family income among all couples, 18% in dual-earner couples, and 28% is she worked full-time. Wives' earnings tended to reduce inequality between families, and over the decade 1980–90, wives' earnings became an increasingly important contribution in the poorest families (Machin and Waldfogel 1994), a conclusion drawn also by Harkness, Machin, and Waldfogel (1995) from a wider analysis of GHS data for 1979–1991. Financial motivations remained an important stimulus to wives' employment in the 1980s and 1990s.

However, it seems mistaken to conclude, as did the British Equal

Opportunities Commission in 1997, that it is now inappropriate to describe women's wages as 'secondary'. Women's wages are an important contribution to family income in the poorest households, but even here they are dwarfed by male wages, which provide three-quarters of family income across all such families. As shown in Table 4.4, very few wives in the lowest occupational grades ever work full-time. In the highest occupational grades, many more wives work full-time, but their earnings still represent only one-quarter of total family income because their husbands also have the highest earnings. An analysis restricted to dual-earner couples with both partners in full-time work showed that by the mid-1990s four-fifths of men still earned more than their wives; 10% of wives were equal earners and 12%–14% earned more than their husband (ONS 1998a: Table 5.12). In this most favourable situation, only one-quarter of wives had earnings equal to, or greater than, their husband's. Wives who work part-time, or not at all, are necessarily even more dependent on their partner's earnings.

Information for other European countries is more patchy, but consistent. In Belgium and Luxembourg, women's earnings constituted 20%, on average, of total household income in 1992. Excluding social benefits, women contributed one-third of total household earnings. In Greece, wives' wage income contributes about 16% of household earned income. Given the importance of wives' contributions to farms and other family businesses in Greece, this figure probably underestimates wives' total contribution to household income. In Spain, women's earnings account for about 25% of total household earnings, with substantial variation across households (Rubery *et al.* 1998: 197). A Eurobarometer No. 38 question asking whether the respondent is the main income-earner in their household found that most men say they are, while few women do. In 1992, three-quarters of all men in the EU said they were the main income-earner of their household, with only small variations across countries, from 87% in the Netherlands to 62% in Italy, where young men live with their parents until they marry, sometimes up to their 30s. Only one-third of women regarded themselves as the main income-earner of their household, with larger variations across countries, from 18% in Spain to 47% in Denmark. Another question asking whether the respondent is the main housekeeper for their household found that four-fifths of women regarded themselves as the housekeeper, with little variation across countries (European Commission 1992b: 84).

The position in the Nordic countries is not, in practice, very different from other modern societies, despite women's more continuous work histories because, apart from Finland, 40% to 50% of women work part-time hours in Sweden, Norway, Denmark, and Iceland (Melkas and Anker 1998: Table 8). Among dual-earner couples, husbands generally earn about two-thirds of total income, or twice as much as wives, on average, and this pattern is found in Sweden and Norway as well as in the Netherlands, West Germany,

TABLE 4.7. *Percentage of total earnings contributed by the husband, on average, in couples with a wife aged 20–60 in 1985*

	All couples	Dual-earner couples
Finland	58	59
Sweden	61	63
Norway	66	67
USA	67	67
Canada	68	66
Australia	68	67
Belgium	74	59
West Germany	74	68
Netherlands	77	68

Source: Calculated from Figure 6.7, p 164 in D. Spain and S. M. Bianchi, *Balancing Act*, Russell Sage Foundation, 1996, based on analyses of Luxembourg Income Study. Percentages have been rounded.

Australia, Canada, and the USA (Table 4.7). In Finland and Belgium, there is a more even balance between the earnings of husband and wife, partly because working wives are a self-selected group of women who are more career-oriented. The only important difference between the Nordic countries and other European countries is that the picture for all couples of working age is similar to the picture for dual-earner couples, because public policy in the Nordic countries pushes most wives into the labour market. For example in Belgium, West Germany, and the Netherlands, husbands generally earn about three-quarters of total income, or three times as much as wives, compared to about 60% of total income in the Nordic countries (Table 4.7).

A tentative conclusion from this research is that wives' decisions to do paid work, full-time or part-time, differ qualitatively across the income distribution. In the poorest households, economic motives can be dominant, and many wives lift the family out of relative poverty. In middle income households, social and economic motives are interlinked: a working wife supports raised lifestyle aspirations, for example for home ownership, ownership of a bigger home, or a more affluent pattern of consumption. In the most affluent households, wives work for essentially non-economic reasons, as a means of self-expression, personal achievement, and sociability. However, in the great majority of households in rich modern societies, the wife remains a secondary earner, supplementing the much larger earnings of a husband who provides the *main* financial support, even in dual-earner households. It is thus not surprising that for women in dual-earner families, social class identity is defined far more by their spouse's occupation than by their own, and in the USA the husband's occupation alone determines the wife's class identity (Wright 1997: 538). One reason for this lack of change is that consumption is becoming just as important as production in defining subjective social class (Wright 1997: 539). Wives define their social class by their spending power, *not* by how they earn it, if they work at all.

The Polarization of Household Income

In the past, wives were less likely to do paid work the higher their husband's income. Today, social class differentials in wives' workrates are shrinking and have effectively disappeared in some countries, such as Sweden, Britain, and the USA (Fry 1984: 55; Rainwater, Rein, and Schwartz 1986: 69). The trend towards dual-earner couples and the polarization of women's earnings are jointly contributing to increasing inequality in family incomes in advanced economies (OECD 1998: 21; European Commission 1999: 21). For example Fry (1984) concluded that in 1968 the interaction between husbands' and wives' earnings reduced family inequality by 8%, whereas by 1981 this interaction increased inequality by 9%. The result is social polarization (Creighton 1999: 528).

A comparative study of family income in the USA, Britain, and Sweden (Rainwater, Rein, and Schwartz 1986) analysed data around 1970 for married couples aged 25–54 years. In all three countries, husbands were the main income-earners, providing four-fifths of family income. In dual-earner couples, wives contributed one-fifth of family income, and their earnings represented 25% to 35% of husbands' earnings. In the USA, wives' contributions appeared to be stable since 1950, or even over the entire 20th century. In all three countries, wives' contributions were broadly the same at all income levels and there was no association between husbands' and wives' earnings. In consequence, wives' earnings lifted many families out of poverty (Rainwater, Rein, and Schwartz 1986: 46, 64–71, 234).

By the 1980s, the picture was changing. Blackburn and Bloom (1994) analysed data for married couples aged 25–64 in the USA, Canada, Australia, Britain, France, Holland, and Sweden. In all countries, wives' earnings still constituted a small part of family income, ranging from a maximum of one-quarter of the total in the USA (1991) and Sweden (1981 and 1987), to a low of 10% in the Netherlands (1983 and 1987). In between were Britain and France with contributions of 15%–18% in the period 1979–1986. However, correlations between husbands' and wives' earnings, although modest, were rising in the USA, Canada, Britain, and Sweden, but not in France, the Netherlands and Australia. In the USA, Canada, and Australia, family income inequality increased, largely due to increases in the inequality of husbands' earnings. The second most important cause of increased income inequality in the USA and Canada was the increasing correlation of husbands' and wives' earnings. This correlation also increased in Sweden and Britain, leading to increased inequality of family income in these countries as well. Further analysis of the data for the USA and Canada suggested that the increasing correlation of husbands' and wives' earnings was not due to increasing marital homogamy but to other, unobservable factors that shape employment patterns (Blackburn and Bloom 1994: 28). In effect, the lifestyle choices of couples were producing a new polarization of family incomes.[13]

This interpretation is supported by a sociological study by Baxter and Kane (1995) analysing surveys in the mid-1980s for the USA, Canada, Australia, Norway, and Sweden. This study was restricted to people in employment, mostly dual-earner couples. In all five countries, wives and husbands had roughly equal wages in fewer than 12% of marriages in the early 1980s (Hobson 1990: Table 1), so the vast majority of wives were financially dependent, to varying degrees, despite substantial differences between the countries in women's position in the labour market, the size of the pay gap, and social and family policies. A measure of wives' relative financial dependence was constructed, with values ranging from –100% to +100% representing single-breadwinner wives and husbands respectively. A measure of approval for role segregation in the family and in public life revealed greater support for role segregation in the USA, at one extreme, and little support in Scandinavia, at the other extreme, with Canada and Australia in between. In all five countries, and especially in the USA, there was greater agreement on appropriate sex-roles among married workers than among non-married workers, and a clear polarization of attitudes between working wives and other women in employment. However the study's main finding is the large and significant association between support for sex-role segregation and the financial dependence of wives. This linkage between sex-role preferences and the actual sexual division of labour within marriages was equally strong across all five countries, among wives as well as husbands. In contrast, having children was not associated with sex-role attitudes, except in the USA, where the association was smaller. Interestingly, sex-role preferences were not associated with income or social class. In sum, the results show that by the mid-1980s, married women and men were choosing family roles according to their tastes, with varying degrees of financial dependence, or independence, for the wife. This pattern emerged in all social classes, and in five countries with substantially different social and family policies, reinforcing our conclusion that the choices were personal rather than imposed by public policy prescriptions or

[13] One consequence is a polarization of the living standards of children. For example in Britain in the 1980s there was an increase in the numbers of children living in relative poverty and in relative luxury (O'Brien and Jones 1999: 600).

by the frequently misused concept of socialization.[14] As Brines (1994) points out, homemaking and income-earning are the expression of (chosen) gendered identities as well as an exchange of services creating mutual interdependence between partners.

One additional factor overlooked by all of these studies is the impact of the overall wage structure and national earnings distribution on the size of the pay gap between men and women, and hence also on the relative earnings of spouses. One reason why the pay gap remained stubbornly higher in the USA, than in European countries that implemented equal pay legislation somewhat later—such as Austria, Norway and Germany—was the relatively high, and rising, wage inequality in the USA in the period 1971–1988 (Blau and Kahn 1994: 107). It follows also, that in countries with relatively high wage inequality, and highly differentiated returns to qualifications and skill, such as the USA, there will be a larger pay gap between *spouses*, as well as in the whole workforce. This inequality of (potential) earnings, which can be enhanced by the tendency for wives to marry 'up' rather than 'down' as noted in Chapter 7, will strengthen any predisposition towards role-segregation within marriage. A cross-national comparative study of the hourly wages of dual-earner spouses around the year 1980 found average husband/wife wage ratios of 2.98 in Canada, 2.44 in the USA, 2.22 in Australia, 1.85 in Czechoslovakia, 1.71 in Germany, 1.64 in Hungary, and 1.50 in the Netherlands (Dirven, Lammers, and Ultee 1990, quoted in Van Berkel and De Graaf 1998: 98, 115). The relative importance of wage inequality for the polarization of household income within countries remains to be studied.

Contradictory Evidence: Rising Workrates

As noted briefly above, the evidence we have reviewed on the polarization of work orientations and employment patterns seems to be contradicted by evidence of rising female workrates and a hidden preference for full-time jobs among part-timers and women at home with their children. Two common themes in research reports and policy documents in the 1990s were that all women want jobs, and that sex differences in workrates are gradually disappearing. We examine this apparently contradictory evidence more fully in this section and show it to be partial or misleading in some cases, or else coloured by a contemporary reporting bias in favour of working women and away from full-time homemakers and the parenting role.

[14] It is puzzling that Baxter and Kane, like many other feminist sociologists, explain support for role segregation in the family in the USA, as due to socialization within the family of origin, but they refuse to explain support for symmetrical family roles in Scandinavia, as also due to socialization within the family of origin, school, and other settings. Socialization is often equated with brainwashing or indoctrination; yet it only refers to a guiding influence, one that can be accepted or rejected.

There is no doubt that female economic activity rates, and employment rates, were rising in most advanced economies from 1950 to the end of the 20th century. However several studies have shown than in many countries there was little or no increase in the volume of women's market work in this period (Tilly and Scott 1978: 70–7; Coleman and Pencavel 1993; Hakim 1980, 1993a, 1995, 1996a; Jonung and Persson 1993; Pott-Buter 1993; Blossfeld and Hakim 1997). In some countries, such as the Netherlands, the increase consisted entirely of the creation of a new female part-time workforce, twice the size of the small full-time workforce. In other countries, such as Britain, the increase was due mainly to a substitution of part-time jobs for declining full-time jobs. In most countries, both processes have been present, to varying degrees, often with no growth in the total volume of women's employment. In effect, the new trend consists of a *redistribution* of the existing volume of paid work across a larger number of people, thus including more women in the workforce. In the European Union, for example, the total volume of employment in 1997, measured by full-time equivalent employment rates, was *below* that in 1986, despite rising female workrates (European Commission 1999: 45). Even the USA witnessed a decline in women's total market hours since 1940 (Coleman and Pencavel 1993). The main point here is that much of the growth in workrates over the past fifty years has been due to part-time jobs, and part-time workers supply few hours of work in total, even when they are numerous. This is especially true in countries with substantial numbers of student jobs, and where the fiscal system promotes marginal jobs with few hours a week by exempting marginal workers from tax and social security contributions (Hakim 1989, 1998a).

A second type of contradictory evidence comes from studies of women's use of the new maternity leave rights and benefits introduced as part of the equal opportunities revolution (Glezer 1988; McRae 1991; Callender *et al.* 1997; Ruhm 1998; Waldfogel 1998, 1999; Ross 1999). Reports on these studies show, for example, that in Britain 'two-thirds of mothers now return to work after childbirth' (Callender *et al.* 1997). In reality, this 1996 survey showed that, in the first year after childbirth, two-thirds of mothers were at home full-time caring for their new baby, a result consistent with other survey data for Britain (Table 4.8). The survey had collected information from all mothers of newborns, but the research report focused exclusively on women who were in employment during pregnancy and fulfilled the eligibility conditions for maternity rights and benefits. This selection process eliminated half of all mothers from the analysis, most of them not in paid work before the birth. Adding them back in totally changes the balance between mothers in employment or not in employment one year after the birth of a child. Mothers' behaviour is consistent with public opinion on a mother's priorities. A 1996 Eurobarometer survey found that the great majority of men and women agree that a mother must give priority to a young child rather than her work.

TABLE 4.8 *Workrates among mothers of children under school age, Britain*

	Mother not employed	Mother works part-time	full-time	N=100%
Age of youngest child				
0	71	16	13	319
1	66	24	10	255
2	62	27	11	252
3	48	41	11	209
4	56	33	11	253
Number of children				
1	55	27	18	469
2	63	29	8	495
3	64	27	9	230
4+	79	18	3	94
Total	62	27	11	1288

Source: Extracted from Tables 2.2 and 2.3 in A. Duncan, C. Giles and S. Webb, *The Impact of Subsidising Childcare*, British Equal Opportunities Commission, 1995, reporting 1991–92 General Household Survey data for mothers with a child under 5 years. Percentages have been rounded.

In Britain, four-fifths of adults held this view, with no difference between men and women. Even in Denmark, two-thirds held this view, with no difference between men and women (Russell and Barbieri 1998: Table 1).

It might be argued that this research was concerned primarily with the operation of maternity rights in the workplace, rather than with a broader, representative view of women's employment patterns before and after a birth. But if the survey results are looked at from the practical perspective of employers administering job-protected maternity leave, the research conclusions are again misleading. Among women who were eligible for job-protected maternity leave, and who notified their employer of their intention to return to work after the birth, the chances of them actually going back to their job with the same employer, or not, were about 50/50, no better than chance, both in 1988 (Hakim 1996a: 127–9) and in 1996 (Callender *et al.* 1997).[15] The proportion only rises to a two-thirds *majority* returning to work

[15] In 1996 in Britain, 58% of mothers in work before the birth returned to work for the same employer, and 47% returned to do the same job for the same employer. In the USA, half of all mothers with a child under 12 months' old were in work even before the 1993 federal legislation giving (some) women the right to 12 weeks' unpaid job-protected maternity leave, and return rates were even higher (Waldfogel 1998: 509). The 1993 legislation mostly covered women who would already

by adding in the women who switched to or were seeking another, less demanding job, often part-time and with a local employer, thus achieving a much shorter journey to work as well as much shorter work hours (Callender *et al.* 1997: 81; Hakim 1998a: 187). The priorities of this group of women clearly changed fundamentally after the birth, to give paid work lower priority to their parenting role. In addition, many of the women who fulfil their obligation to return to their employer after childbirth do not stay in the job very long, especially if they have another child. This is clear from Table 4.8, and it also emerges from longitudinal studies. For example the BHPS shows that only 23% of British first-time mothers were in employment 3 months before *and* 24 months after their first birth (Wetzels 1999: 116). The return to work can be short-lived.

An Australian study produced broadly similar results (Glezer 1988). After taking formal maternity leave, three-quarters of women returned to their job with the same employer within 18 months of the birth; only one-quarter failed to return as promised. But only one-third of all the returning mothers went back to full-time work; one-fifth worked half-time hours (20–34 hours a week) and almost half worked marginal hours (1–19 hours a week). However only half of all Australian women eligible for maternity leave took it; the other half did not take it because they did not intend returning to the same job, or any job, after the birth. Overall, 60% of mothers who had been in employment during pregnancy were back in a job of some sort (usually part-time, often with a new employer) 18 months after the birth, with little difference between those eligible or not eligible for maternity leave. The other 40% were at home full-time with their baby. As in Britain, only half of the mothers had been in employment during their pregnancy. Adding them back into the picture means that three-quarters of mothers were at home full-time after a birth. This study was unusual in collecting data on the women's attitudes towards motherhood versus paid work. It found that these attitudes were the most important single determinant of the decision to return to work, or not, followed by the financial pressures imposed by a husband's low earnings. However, the women themselves typically said that they returned to work because they 'needed the money', a response given across all categories of family income.

Surprisingly, it appears that statutory maternity rights have no causal impact on women's decision to return to work or not, possibly because informal arrangements are so common for valued employees in small firms, while collective bargaining produced company maternity rights schemes in larger

have been covered by state laws and company schemes, but it promoted the idea that maternity leave was legitimate and appropriate for new mothers. The new federal maternity leave right seems to have made little or no difference to the proportion of mothers returning to work, which was already on a rising trend; it seems rather to have increased the incidence and length of maternity leaves, which are generally extremely short in the USA compared to Europe (Waldfogel 1997, 1998, 1999).

organizations. Analyses have looked for, but not found any statistically significant and substantively important impact on women's behaviour, either in Britain (Hakim 1996a: 127), or in the USA (Blau and Ehrenberg 1997: 13; Waldfogel 1998; Ross 1999; see also Fried 1998), or in Australia (Glezer 1988: 5, 25).[16] Small increases in the rate of return to the same employer after childbirth are usually explained by selection effects in the context of the changing composition of the female workforce. As women become more qualified and obtain more attractive and well-paid jobs, especially in professional, semi-professional, and managerial occupations, more women become eligible for, and use, job-protected maternity leave rights and return to their employer. But even in the late 1990s, these returners represented no more than one-quarter to one-third of all mothers of newborns in Britain and Australia. Some women switch to less demanding, part-time, local jobs instead, thus boosting the numbers who 'return to work' after childbirth. The fullest picture is given by national surveys, which show that the majority of mothers of children below school age do not work at all, or work only part-time (as illustrated by Table 4.8 for Britain). Continuous full-time workers constitute between 10% and 20% of mothers with young children. The reality is that *most* mothers give priority to children over paid work while their children are very young. As we have seen, research reports frequently imply the exact opposite. This example is typical of the reporting bias that now affects many studies of women's employment in modern societies.

The third type of contradictory evidence concerns involuntary part-time work: people with part-time jobs—in practice, mostly women—who would prefer a full-time job and are thus underemployed. Data on involuntary part-time work is collected regularly in the EU LFS and the results publicized, with periodic reports of an increase in involuntary part-time work. However the LFS has always shown that the great *majority* of European women prefer their part-time jobs and do not want a full-time job (Hakim 1990a; O'Reilly and Fagan 1998; OECD 1999), even in France (Hakim 1997: 37; OECD 1999: Table 1.13).

More generally, the continuing or even rising importance of materialistic aspirations motivating wives and mothers to take employment, especially in poorer families, and labour market rigidities, warn us against the assumption of many economists that employment behaviour necessarily reflects preferences. There is ample evidence that the two do not coincide completely for

[16] In addition, Waldfogel (1999) looks at the macro-level impact of the 1993 federal maternity leave legislation on women's employment and wages, with equivocal results suggesting no impact, overall. However, she shows an increase in women's leave-taking in the first year after a birth. Because over half of women in the USA returned to work soon after childbirth even before the 1993 federal legislation, evaluation studies in the USA have focused on the impact on women's wages, and on the length of the maternity break, whereas studies in Europe and Australia have focused on any increases in the relatively low proportion of women returning to work soon after childbirth (as illustrated by Ruhm 1998).

women, nor for men, and that we need to collect data on preferences through direct enquiries, among full-timers as well as other groups.

Many surveys reveal a mismatch between the hours ideally preferred and the hours actually worked, especially among full-timers. For example one-third of mothers working full-time in Britain in 1994 would have preferred part-time hours, whereas four-fifths of mothers working part-time actively rejected full-time work. If they had the childcare of their choice, one-quarter of the mothers who were at home full-time would have preferred to have a full-time job, but half preferred to work part-time only (Thomson 1995: 74). Eurobarometer No. 34 found that, across the European Union in 1990, 40% of women with full-time jobs would have preferred part-time jobs with less than 30 hours a week, some of them preferring very short hours. In contrast, less than 20% of women working part-time said they would prefer a full-time job, and another 13% preferred to further reduce their part-time hours. Overall, one-fifth of working women ideally preferred part-time jobs with very short hours (less than 20 hours a week), and women with these smallest jobs were the happiest, with only one-third preferring longer hours (European Commission 1991a). At present, few countries provide such jobs on a large scale, notably the Netherlands, West Germany, and Britain. In Australia, three-quarters of all mothers in employment would prefer part-time work, and half of mothers at home full-time would like to have a part-time job (Glezer 1988: 84–6).

Discrepancies between actual and preferred behaviour seem to be greatest among mothers of pre-school children in the 1990s. A carefully crafted study by Newell (1992) covered working class and middle class mothers. She found that mothers with part-time jobs almost always preferred this option and so, generally, did the full-time homemakers. Most of the mothers working full-time were doing so involuntarily and would have preferred to work part-time or not at all. The mothers were then asked what their *ideal preference* would be if they could ignore all other factors influencing their decision. In this situation, the proportion preferring to stay at home full-time rose from one-fifth to half, and another half saw a part-time job as the ideal. Less than one in ten ideally preferred a full-time job when they had small children (Newell 1992: 42). Similar preferences are found across the EU. Three-quarters of mothers who had worked while their child(ren) were below school age would ideally have preferred to either stay at home full-time in this period (41%), or else to have worked part-time only (36%). Three-quarters of the mothers who had stayed at home full-time when their children were very young reported themselves happy with the arrangement. Less than a quarter would ideally have preferred a part-time job and only 6% would have liked to work full-time instead. Across twelve EU countries, only half of all women had achieved their work preference while they had pre-school children. Satisfaction levels were lowest in East Germany, at 30%; and in all countries the highest satisfaction levels were among the mothers without any paid work when their children were pre-school age (European Commission 1991a: Tables 47 and 51). It appears that statistics of rising workrates among women have sometimes been incorrectly interpreted as expressing career commitment rather than economic necessity or a second-best compromise, a problem underlined by comparisons between women in East and West Germany (Braun, Scott, and Alwin 1994).

One problem is that many occupations are organized exclusively on a full-time basis, so that the option of part-time work is not available in practice. A special survey carried out across the EU in 1994 revealed substantial proportions of involuntary full-time women workers in Belgium (36%), Italy (32%), France (28%), the Netherlands (23%), Denmark (21%), and Spain (14%). Britain was exceptional in having few women working full-time involuntarily, only 9%. In all eleven EU countries except for Britain, for men and women taken together, the number of full-time employees saying they would prefer to work part-time exceeded the number of part-time employees preferring to work full-time (OECD 1999).

The research reports and policy papers of international bodies such as the EC and the International Labour Office (ILO) repeatedly endorse the proposition that *all* women want to work continuously throughout life (Date-Bah 1997: 5, 8, 126; European Commission 1997d: 4) so that this becomes received wisdom. However Tables 4.1 and 4.2 show no consensus on the preferred model of the family in any country in Europe, and Brocas (1997: 171) has pointed out that these conflicting preferences prohibit any simple ILO policy recommendations. Similarly, Gauthier (1996a) has pointed out that the heterogeneity of individual and household employment strategies *within* European countries, as well as across Europe as a whole, makes it impossible to get accurate measures of the impact of family policy measures. Sometimes policy analysts claim that it is only the lack of good childcare services that prevent women from returning to (full-time) work in greater numbers. Studies regularly point to the excellent public childcare system in France which, despite its shortcomings, ensures that French women 'do not have to choose' between gainful employment and family work,[17] unlike the situation in West Germany or Britain, for example, where there are no childcare services on a level with the French system (Blossfeld and Hakim 1997: 44–7, 138). Yet female workrates in France are very similar to workrates in West Germany and Britain. When FTE workrates are used, the three countries have virtually identical female workrates (see Table 3.3). Even among mothers with a child under 36 months old, workrates are broadly similar: 44% in Germany, 49% in Britain, and 50% in France in 1997, although French mothers are more likely

[17] However Plaisance (1986) suggests that the *maternelle* schools for children aged 3–6 years were created primarily within the republican ideology of universalism, and for secularizing purposes, rather than as a service to working mothers.

to be working full-time (Hantrais 1994: Table 2; Moss 1996). Birthrates are also no higher in France than in Britain, although France has the lowest rate of childlessness in western Europe, at around 10% (Hantrais 1994: Table 1; Kaufmann *et al.* 1997: 405–7). In practice, there is little evidence that public childcare in France makes a big difference to women's employment patterns. Similarly the absence of public childcare services in the USA has not prevented a steady increase in women's full-time workrates in the post-war decades, and the fact that childcare costs are tax-deductible, in part, does not really explain higher female workrates in the USA (Hakim 1997: 45). From time to time, there is brief recognition by the EC that childcare services are *not* crucial, in any country (Hakim 1997: 46). But demands for more, better and cheaper childcare have become such a fixed element of policy debates that the research evidence has virtually ceased to be taken seriously in western Europe and North America. Given the exclusive focus on women's (presumed) interests, the potentially conflicting interests of children attract virtually no attention, or are dismissed through claims that collective childcare is invariably of higher quality and more appropriate for all children than family-based care (Blau and Ehrenberg 1997: 277–84), a claim that is, at best, debatable (Dex and Rowthorn 1998).[18] In effect, much recent research on women's employment and women's issues consists of advocacy research rather than dispassionate social scientific research (Gilbert 1997; Hakim 2000)—at least in the Nordic and English-speaking countries. In contrast, West German feminist thought rejected the idea that emancipation meant full-time employment and demanded more support and recognition for women's family work (Lewis 1993: 94–5, 180).

Conclusions

The new trend towards the polarization of women's employment in advanced economies has been widely observed.[19] Our review shows that polarization is found in attitudes, values, and sex-role preferences, in employment patterns

[18] As soon as the focus switches from working mothers to children, it becomes clear that no single, uniform approach to services for children, and hence family policy, is possible. Diversity is accepted as necessary, and positive, in the 1996 concluding report of the EC's Childcare Network. The programme's conclusions included, among others, the need to actively promote choice between employment and caring for children at home, encouraging parents to remain at home until children are three, and extending school hours and services to fill the gaps in current arrangements (European Commission 1996b).

[19] Trends towards polarization, rather than convergence, are also being observed in other fields of enquiry. For example Ormerod, quoting a study by Maddison (1995), shows that there is no long-term convergence in the wealth of nations. On the contrary, late-developing countries were diverging increasingly from the advanced economies of western Europe (Ormerod 1998: 160–2). Ormerod suggests that polarizing trends are inherent in most social processes and in social change.

and work histories, and in household incomes. Some studies reveal the linkages between the three. Most studies find that the polarization trend cuts across social class and income groups, indicating that socio-economic factors are no longer dominant, at least not for the sexual division of labour.

Our first conclusion is that statistical procedures and research methods that rely on measures of central tendency have become misleading, hiding more than they reveal, unless samples are first partitioned into separate work-lifestyle or preference groups. In particular, the well-established economic activity rate is revealed to be inadequate as a *social* indicator of women's changing position in society. There are also doubts about its utility as an indicator of labour market trends, given the huge variations in hours worked that are concealed by the headcount measure of employment. For studies of the family, a more meaningful indicator would be the proportion of the family's or the couple's income earned by the wife (Rainwater, Rein, and Schwartz 1986: 234). However this data is more troublesome to collect.

The second conclusion is that we need more multidisciplinary and multi-method research to draw the separate strands together in triangulated research designs (Hakim 1987a: 144–5, 2000). The study of family income by Rainwater, Rein, and Schwartz (1986) is exceptional in complementing a mainly quantitative economic analysis with a qualitative analysis of sex-role preferences and social attitudes in one chapter of the report. This leads them to conclude that 'a dollar is not a dollar' because its value and meaning depend on where it fits into family income packaging and spouses' employment histories (1986: 101–5).

On their side, sociologists have been slow to recognize that one long-term consequence of more wives working, and of greater marital homogamy, is an increase in household income inequality, although McRae (1997: 399–400) and Engelstad (1998) are two exceptions to this. The polarization of incomes, social networks, and lifestyles between dual-earner and single-earner households is an inevitable consequence of women acquiring real choices between full-time paid work and full-time homemaking. Engelstad concludes that some refinement of theory now becomes necessary. The heterogeneity of family models means that at least two models of decision-making over labour-supply are needed: an equity model for dual-career professional couples, and a complementarity model for couples where the woman has lower education than the man (Engelstad 1998: 8). Our review suggests that at least three models are required to address the different decision-making processes within the three groups of women that have now emerged.

5

Things are Different in the Younger Generations: Evidence from Longitudinal Studies

The evidence reviewed in Chapter 4 suggests that women are heterogeneous in their preferences, and that there is an increasing polarization of the female workforce and the whole adult female population. A frequent objection is that this conclusion rests on cross-sectional evidence, and that a different picture emerges from longitudinal studies. In reality, much of the evidence in Chapter 4 comes from longitudinal studies—such as the NLS and PSID in the USA—or from European studies collecting retrospective life history data. None the less, it is often argued that things are different in the younger generations. Many believe that younger generations of men and women are moving toward more egalitarian relationships in the home, as they recognize the advantages of both partners being able to enjoy paid work and shared activities in the family, including child-rearing.

There is evidence that points in this direction. For example Table 4.1 (and also 4.2) shows a changing pattern of preferences across age cohorts. Among people aged 55 and over, conjugal role segregation is the dominant preference, with 40%–50% of men and women choosing it. This model becomes progressively less attractive to the younger generations. In the cohort aged 15–24 years, the majority preference is for 'egalitarian' symmetrical conjugal roles. Even among people aged 25–39, half prefer this arrangement. Undoubtedly there is a shift in preferences across generations, away from complete role segregation toward symmetrical roles. However, changes across age groups in Tables 4.1 and 4.2 reflect the impact of aging and experiences across the life-course, as well as generational changes in attitudes and preferences. A study of changes in sex-role attitudes in the USA, Britain, and West Germany found that changes *within* age cohorts were broadly just as important as changes *between* cohorts for explaining changes at the aggregate, national level (Scott, Alwin, and Braun 1996). However the trajectories of attitudinal change were very different in the three countries, with periods of 'backlash' reducing support for wives' employment, and the pace of change was slow overall, except in the youngest age groups (Scott, Alwin, and Braun 1996).

The climate of opinion has undoubtedly changed in a more general way as well. There is far less consciousness, or concern, with social class differences, ethnic group differences, religious differences and gender differences among younger people (Chisolm and DuBois-Raymond 1989: 260) particularly in multicultural urban centres. Procter and Padfield (1998: 2–3, 1999) conclude that social class does not, in any event, shape young women's orientations towards work and family life. Young women take sexual freedom for granted, along with attendant responsibility for contraception and sexual health. Magazines for young women express interests, and an outlook on life, that are worlds away from the restricted options offered to unmarried girls before the contraceptive revolution and the equal opportunities revolution. This new spirit is also manifested in women's educational aspirations.

In the USA, there is a long tradition of girls attending college before marriage.[1] Both high schools and colleges function as marriage markets as well as educational establishments. Dating is an integral part of college life, with institutions such as sororities and fraternities underlining heterosexual identities and activities. In the USA, the change in women's aspirations is seen in far fewer female enrolments in courses in humanities, arts, and other subjects that provide cultural capital rather than vocational training, and increasing enrolments in courses which are either vocational—such as business studies, pharmacy, or law—or that have greater practical value in the jobs market, such as the social sciences. Colleges are now treated as having a dual function, as training places as well as marriage markets, by most women as well as men.

In Europe, where there is a long tradition of higher education being male-dominated, female enrolments rose rapidly from the 1960s onwards, and the university with a balanced sex ratio became almost as common as in the USA. By the 1990s, in most countries, female enrolments equalled male enrolments in higher education, and in some countries, such as Finland, Sweden, Norway, Greece, Italy, and Spain, women outnumbered men. The extreme case is Portugal, where women with some type of higher education qualification outnumber men by 70% (Eurostat 1998). Educational institutions in Europe are now acquiring a marriage market function, on top of their basic function as places of learning and vocational training. Equality of educational attainment seems close to being achieved among younger generations everywhere. It seems logical that equality of occupational achievement should follow close behind.

[1] The first girls-only and mixed-sex colleges were established between 1821 and 1870 in the USA. By 1870, women constituted 21% of college and university students. In 1900, women earned 20% of Master's degrees and 6% of Doctorates in the USA; by 1930 these percentages had increased to 40% and 15% (Betz and Fitzgerald 1987: 61–75).

Some social scientists have also underlined the impact of the new maternity rights and benefits introduced from the 1970s onwards in most European countries, and from 1993 onwards in the USA at federal level. Pronatalist policies, including generous maternity rights, were introduced earlier in Sweden and Norway, in order to reverse low and declining birthrates, as noted in Chapter 8. Maternity rights vary across countries and between employers, but they generally provide pregnant women with the right to return to the same job, or an equivalent job, within a specified period after a birth. Schemes vary in the conditions for eligibility, the length of the permitted absence at home after a birth, and how much of the maternity absence is paid for, by the employer or by social insurance. Individual employers sometimes offer more generous rights than the statutory minimum. Maternity rights do make it easier for women to keep their jobs and continue working during the child-bearing years (McRae 1991; Joshi, Macran, and Dex 1996; Callender *et al.* 1997; Waldfogel 1997; Ross 1999). However these point-in-time studies of women's employment immediately before and after a birth are too narrow in scope to be used as an indicator of trends and patterns in the whole female labour force. And as noted in Chapter 4, there is little or no evidence that the new rights changed women's behaviour.

We can expect younger generations to be different simply because social change takes time. All the changes reviewed in Chapter 3, which produced a new scenario in certain countries by the late 20th century, take some time to impact on expectations and attitudes, so that women's patterns of employment and equality in marriage change progressively across generations rather than suddenly. We must look at the younger generations to read the future. Fortunately, a major longitudinal study in Britain provides an excellent opportunity to examine closely the achievements and changes in the younger generation. A very different, qualitative study of the life histories of a similar age cohort of young women in the USA provides equivalent data on younger generations in the USA (Gerson 1985). This study also illuminates the decision-making process, values, and preferences that underlie large-scale survey results. Overall, despite the changes observed in younger generations, these longitudinal data tell the same basic story as the cross-sectional and longitudinal data reviewed in Chapter 4.

The 1958 Cohort Study—NCDS

The National Child Development Study (NCDS) is a longitudinal study of all children born in Great Britain in one week in March 1958. About 17,000 babies were born in this week and data have been collected on their development and life events at seven points in time, at birth, age 7, 11, 16, 23, 33, and 42. At ages 11 and 16, immigrants to Britain who had been born in the relevant week in 1958 were identified from school registers and added to the sample. Some of the original sample died or emigrated, and others did not respond to every survey of the cohort. At the fifth interview survey, in 1991, 86% of the target sample of 15,666 were traced to their current address, and response rates of over 80% were achieved on the personal interview, self-completion questionnaire, and other data collection instruments for the traced sample, resulting in data for a sample of 11,400 people aged 33 years. A sixth sweep, in 2000, has yet to report.

When a longitudinal study has been running as long as 42 years, sample attrition is always an issue. Studies have been carried out comparing the NCDS-5 sample in 1991 with 33-year-olds in the 1991 Census, with people aged 30–33 years in the General Household Survey (GHS), and with NCDS respondents at younger ages. Overall, it appears that non-response has been slightly larger at the bottom of the income scale. Comparisons with earlier NCDS surveys show that there was a greater loss of respondents among ethnic minorities and low-achievement groups than among other groups. Comparisons with people of the same age in the GHS show that the NCDS sample is biased towards higher earners at age 33, and even more so for respondents at age 23 (Waldfogel 1993: 12). Comparisons with the 1991 Census show a small shortage of people not in the labour force and a small excess of people in work. Overall, the NCDS-5 sample is representative of the age cohort, with a small bias towards high achievers.[2] This can be seen by the comparison between the 1991 Census and NCDS-5 in Table 5.1.

The NCDS cohort reached adulthood after the contraceptive revolution of the 1960s and just after the equal opportunities revolution of the early 1970s. They were in compulsory schooling until age 16 in 1974, at which point about half obtained O-levels—equivalent to the French *BEPC*. After 16, they could leave school and get a job, obtaining vocational and other qualifications through an apprenticeship or night-school, or else continue their full-time education through to A-levels—equivalent to the *Baccalaureat* or the *Arbitur*—and on to some form of higher education, as one-quarter of them did. Only 11% of the men and 14% of the women had no qualifications at all by age 33. The NCDS studies the first cohort of people who had the full benefit of equal opportunities policies, as is reflected in the absence of any major sex differential in their educational qualifications. There are now numerous analyses of the NCDS database, especially data from NCDS-5 in 1991, which

[2] One factor that helps the NCDS retain its representativeness is the fact that sample attrition is not consistently one-way. Some people come back into the study when they are adults even if they or their parents dropped out of earlier surveys. The research team goes to some trouble to maintain contact with everyone in the sample, whether or not they were respondents at the last survey.

TABLE 5.1. *Highest qualifications of men and women: a comparison between 1991 Census data on all 33-year-olds and 1991 NCDS data*

	1991 NCDS-5			1991 Census		
	Men	Women	All	Men	Women	All
Higher degrees of UK standard	2	1	2	2	1	2
First degrees and equivalent qualifications of UK first degree standard	12	10	11	12	9	10
Higher education below university degree standard	11	12	11	7	9	8
Total with no higher education qualifications	75	77	76	79	81	80
of which:						
A-level and equivalent	21	11	16			
O-level and equivalent	25	35	30			
other qualifications	17	18	17			
none	11	14	13			
Total=100%	5,485	5,708	11,193	7,551	7,668	15,219

Note: the 1991 Census did not collect information on qualifications below tertiary level. English A-levels are the equivalent of the German *Arbitur* and the French *Baccalaureat.* English O-levels correspond to the BEPC in France and correspond roughly to a high school diploma in the USA.

Sources: Tables 1.1 and 2.1 in A. Dale and M. Egerton, *Highly Educated Women: Evidence from the NCDS*, 1997, London: Stationery Office for the Department for Education and Employment, and author's analyses of 1991 Census SARs microdata.

specifically address the question of how this generation of young people used these new opportunities (Pilling 1990; Ward and Dale 1992; Ferri 1993; Wiggins and Bynner 1993; Dex, Joshi, and Macran 1996; Ferri and Smith 1996; Joshi 1996; Joshi and Davies 1996; Joshi, Macran, and Dex 1996; Macran, Joshi, and Dex 1996; Paci and Joshi 1996; Paci, Joshi, and Makepeace 1996; Ward, Dale, and Joshi 1996*a*, 1996*b;* Blundell *et al.* 1997; Dale and Egerton 1997; Ermisch and Di Salvo 1997; Saunders 1997; Waldfogel 1993, 1998; Joshi and Paci 1998; Buckingham 1999; Breen and Goldthorpe 1999; Gregg and Machin 1999). There are also studies comparing outcomes in the 1990s for the 1958 birth cohort with results for an earlier 1946 cohort (Joshi and Paci 1998) and a subsequent 1970 birth cohort study (Bynner, Ferri, and Shepherd

1997).[3] The huge body of research evidence from the NCDS-5 is supplemented here by unpublished information on 33-year-olds from the 1991 Census, which allows us to compare this age group with the entire workforce aged 16–64 years.

Educational Attainment

Opening up the educational system to young women had dramatic effects in Britain, as elsewhere in Europe. There is little difference between NCDS men and women in level of educational attainment: they are equally likely to have no qualifications at all (11% and 14% respectively), basic school-leaving qualifications (43% and 52%), completed secondary school qualifications (21% and 11% respectively) or higher education qualifications: 25% of men and 23% of women have some form of higher education qualification. It is only at higher degree level, Masters and Doctorates, that men still outnumber women by two to one (Table 5.1).

What has not changed is horizontal segregation by subject (Dale and Egerton 1997), although it is declining slowly (Harkness and Machin 1999). Young women still choose nursing and teaching qualifications below university degree level, or arts, humanities and social science subjects at degree level. Men still choose engineering and other technical subjects below degree level and they predominate in business studies, mathematics, and the natural and physical sciences at degree level. Finer grain studies also reveal that men outnumber women in all degree-level qualifications and in all the subjects with the highest earnings potential—economics rather than sociology, for example. When women do have a degree, it is more likely to have been obtained at a less prestigious institution, a college or polytechnic rather than a university. Even finer grain analysis reveals that men outnumber women two to one in the vocational academic subjects which provide training for specific professional occupations: medicine, dentistry, law, accounting and finance, architecture, and veterinary studies. By age 33, these qualifications led to jobs with the highest status, earnings, and quality of worklife, including the autonomy of self-employment (Dale and Egerton 1997). They also generally require full-time employment, often with very long hours. So important sex differences in educational attainment still remain, but they are now concentrated at the higher education level. As a result they are invisible in ordinary interview surveys, which group together all forms of higher

[3] There are three major birth cohort studies in Britain, covering people born in 1946, 1958, and 1970. All are carried out by the Centre for Longitudinal Studies at the Institute of Education in London.

education,[4] and are often overlooked by researchers (Smith 1990: 831; Harkness 1996: 2, 18–20), and even by NCDS-5 analysts (Paci and Joshi 1996; Joshi and Paci 1998: 45, 93).

Earnings and the Pay Gap

Qualifications have an enormous impact on the kind of job people can get, therefore on earnings, and hence on the pay gap between men and women. Surprisingly, the 1991 Census shows that the pattern of occupational segregation among 33-year-olds is virtually identical to the pattern in the whole workforce in 1991. It appears that each younger generation reproduces the pattern observed among older generations rather than changing it (Hakim 1998a: 8, 47). Similarly, the RG social class distribution for the NCDS-5 sample is very close to the national picture for all people aged 33 years in the 1991 Census, and it is also very close to the class composition of the whole workforce in 1991 (Hakim 1998a: 69–71). By age 33, women have already divided into childless women pursuing the 'male' employment career, and women with children. Among those who left full-time education at age 16, who could have spent a maximum of 16 years in employment, 71% of men had at least 15 years in full-time work, compared to 64% of childless women and 10% of mothers. The mean number of years worked was 14 for men, 13 for childless women, and 8.5 for mothers (Bynner, Morphy, and Parsons 1997: 70). As a result, some researchers have switched attention from the pay gap between men and women—which is slowly shrinking—to the widening pay gap between mothers and childless women, sometimes labelled the 'family gap'. By 1991, young mothers in employment earned three-quarters of the average earnings of childless women of the same age, and the gap was widening, in the USA as well as in Britain (Waldfogel 1998).

The pay gap is normally taken as the difference between average female full-time hourly earnings in *all* occupations and average male full-time hourly earnings in *all* occupations. It thus takes no account of the large degree of occupational segregation by sex found in all modern societies, including

[4] As Hakim (1998a: 33–9) shows, this is now a more general problem. Except in very large surveys such as the GHS (ONS 1998), higher education qualifications are almost invariably grouped together in sample survey datasets, even though this group contains very significant differences of level, quality of degree, subject, and awarding institution. Hakim also shows that sex differences in qualifications are found *within* each occupational grade. For example male managers are generally more highly qualified than female managers (Hakim 1998a: 35; see also Wyatt and Langridge 1996: 242). Research in the 1990s has found that men invest in qualifications even more than do women, to gain access to careers and promotion up career ladders. After entering the workforce, men are more likely than women to study for and obtain additional professional qualifications that assist careers within particular industries, such as Institute of Banking qualifications (Halford, Savage, and Witz 1997; see also Halford and Savage 1995).

those with egalitarian policies, such as Sweden and China (Hakim 1996a: 145–86, 1998a: 7–64; Melkas and Anker 1997, 1998; Anker 1998). Restricting analyses to full-time workers and hourly pay eliminates one of the most important sources of the pay gap, which is the huge sex differential in hours worked, among full-time as well as part-time workers (Hakim 1998a: 102–44). An earlier cohort study of people born in 1946 revealed a 36% pay gap among full-time workers in 1978, at age 32. By 1991, the pay gap had almost halved, falling to 19% among full-timers at age 33. The NCDS-5 sample thus displays the effects of the broad equalization of educational qualifications achieved by the 1990s (Paci and Joshi 1996; Joshi and Paci 1998).

A study by Blundell and others (1997), which unfortunately does not differentiate between full-time and part-time workers, shows that the impact of education on women's wages is considerably larger than its impact on men's wages, probably due to selection effects. (Women who pursue higher education seem to be a more committed, self-selected group than is true of men.) Compared to women who obtained A-levels but had not continued into higher education, working women with vocational higher education qualifications below degree level had hourly wages 26% higher on average; for women with first degrees, hourly earnings were 39% higher on average; and women with higher degrees had wages 43% higher than the group with only A-levels. The equivalent figures for men were much lower: 15%, 21%, and 16%. After adding controls for a variety of family characteristics, scores on ability tests at school, school type at age 16, and employer characteristics at age 33 (but, puzzlingly, not for hours worked, occupation, industry, and subject of degree) the mark-ups for a higher education qualification for people in work were reduced only slightly: 14%, 12%, and 8% among men, and 22%, 34%, and 32% among women for a vocational sub-degree qualification, a first degree, and a higher university degree respectively (Blundell *et al.* 1997: v; see also Harkness 1996: Table 5a; Harkness and Machin 1999). Similarly, T. Tam (1997: 1682) shows that by the late 1980s returns to vocational training and education in the USA are consistently *higher* for women than for men, among whites and blacks.

Surprisingly, Blundell *et al.* (1997) found no important wage differences between people taking different subjects at higher education level, and a sizeable pay gap between men and women. A more carefully detailed analysis of the NCDS-5 data (Dale and Egerton 1997: 12–13, 60–1, 67–73) shows substantial earnings differences across subjects, and a small pay gap after controlling for level of qualification and hours worked (Tables 5.2 and 5.3). Among employees working full-time, the hourly pay gap was only 10% for people with a university degree or better, rising to 15% among people with no qualifications at all or with qualifications below O-level, usually obtained by age 15 or 16. Of course, weekly earnings vary a lot more, due to the very different hours worked by men and women, even in full-time jobs (Hakim 1998a:

TABLE 5.2. *Women's earnings as a percentage of men's among full-time employees*

Highest qualifications	Weekly earnings	Hourly earnings
Academic higher education	82	90
Vocational higher education	78	87
A-levels and equivalent	77	87
O-levels and equivalent	71	83
Below O-level and no qualifications	68	85
All full-time employees	75	87

Source: Table 8.3 in A. Dale and M. Egerton, *Highly Educated Women*, 1997, London: Stationary Office for the Department for Education and Employment.

121–5, 211), so the pay gap for weekly earnings is 18% among the most highly qualified rising to 32% among the unqualified. Having a child does not generally lead to a fall in hourly earnings, unless the woman transfers to part-time work (Table 5.3), with associated changes in occupation, location, and primary focus in life.

The pay gap between women in full-time and part-time jobs is larger than the pay gap between men and women in full-time work, but it is also readily explained (Paci and Joshi 1996: 69; Joshi and Paci 1998). Part-time workers are in very different occupations, often working in small establishments close to residential neighbourhoods that offer much shorter trips to work, and they are concentrated in particular service sector jobs in the public and private industries (Hakim 1998a). By the 1990s, part-time workers were significantly less well qualified, and had the most discontinuous employment histories (Harkness 1996: 20; Paci and Joshi 1996; Joshi and Paci 1998; Hakim 1998a: 102–77). In terms of the wages offered, there is no evidence that employers discriminate against young mothers with childcare responsibilities (Paci and Joshi 1996: 93; Joshi and Paci 1998). Thus the pay gap between full-time and part-time workers is easily explained (Harkness 1996: 35; Paci and Joshi 1996: 101; Joshi and Paci 1998: 93, 133–6). Similarly, in the USA, T. Tam (1997: 1676–7) shows that by the late 1980s women working part-time actually had a *wage advantage* over women working full-time.

Following the recent equalization of qualifications, the hourly pay gap for full-time workers at age 33 is explained primarily by the different types of work, occupations, and industries chosen by men and women, plus differences in work experience and tenure with the current employer. Collectively, these factors explain over one-third of the gross pay gap, leaving only 12% of hourly earnings not explained by the variables selected by the researchers

TABLE 5.3. *Median hourly earnings by highest qualification, hours worked and sex*

	Men	Women working FT	Women working PT
Academic higher education	6.93	6.20	6.47
Vocational higher education	5.94	5.17	5.29
A-levels and equivalent	5.29	4.62	3.51
O-levels and equivalent	4.80	4.00	3.33
Below O-level and no qualifications	4.08	3.45	3.00
All employees	5.13	4.45	3.33
Base	3,597	1,678	1,363

	Women working FT			Women working PT		
	No child	Child under 5 years	Youngest child 5+	No child	Child under 5 years	Youngest child 5+
Academic higher education	6.24	6.33	5.22	6.72	6.74	4.17
Vocational higher education	5.49	5.14	4.81	3.63	5.73	5.13
A-levels and equivalent	4.81	4.89	4.19	3.88	3.54	3.37
O-levels and equivalent	4.26	4.10	3.48	3.13	3.68	3.14
Below O-level and no qualifications	3.63	3.51	3.26	2.93	3.12	3.00
All employees	4.85	4.74	3.65	3.50	3.90	3.10
Base	974	283	421	77	581	705

Source: Tables 8.2, 8.5 and 8.6 in A. Dale and M. Egerton, *Highly Educated Women*, 1997, London: Stationary Office for the Department for Education and Employment.

(Paci and Joshi 1996: 60–1; Joshi and Paci 1998: 133).[5] Given the large number of directly relevant variables omitted from pay gap studies, this final portion could easily be explained also (Tam, T. 1997).

Interestingly, occupational segregation, as measured in the 1991 Census, was of no significance in explaining the pay gap at age 33 in 1991 (Paci and

[5] There are two other studies of the pay gap based on the NCDS-5 apart from the Paci and Joshi (1996) study summarized here. Blundell *et al.* (1997) studied the pay gap among *all* workers, grouping together women in part-time and full-time jobs. Joshi contributed a short section to Dale and Egerton's (1997) report, analyzing the pay gap in *weekly* earnings. Inevitably, these studies find larger gaps between average male and female earnings and have more difficulty explaining them through multivariate analysis.

Joshi 1996: 59; Joshi and Paci 1998: 85). This result is consistent with other research showing the absence of any link between occupational segregation and pay from 1991 onwards in Britain (Hakim 1998a: 41, 66–85). Similarly, in the USA, T. Tam (1997) found that by the late 1980s there was no evidence at all of the devaluation of women's occupations; occupational sex ratios contributed nothing to the pay gap. In East Germany also, at the end of 1989, the sex segregation of occupations and industries added almost nothing to explanations for the pay gap between women and men (Sorensen and Trappe 1995: 402), and substantial occupational segregation in the Nordic countries coexists with an apparently small pay gap (Melkas and Anker 1998).[6]

In sum, the NCDS-5 shows that by age 33, working women obtained very substantial gains in earnings from any higher education qualifications they obtained, greater than men's gains. The pay gap had virtually been eliminated, especially among the most qualified, or could effectively be explained by differences in job choice, industry, hours, and other factors. This is *not* to say that sex discrimination had been eliminated in the workforce, either for this young cohort, or for workers generally. But it does appear that conscious, overt, explicit, and visible sex discrimination had been eliminated by making it unlawful. What remains is the unconscious, covert, and invisible sex discrimination that is hard to detect and eliminate but limits women's promotion into senior grades (Hakim 1996a: 184). In addition, men are more ambitious than women.

Aspirations and Sex-role Ideology

One of the remarkable things about the NCDS analyses summarized above is that, with the exception of Dale and Egerton (1997: 47–54), the wealth of information in the longitudinal NCDS was not utilized. Despite being aware of the many variables in the NCDS tapping aspirations, motivations, and work orientations, most researchers eschewed these 'subjective' variables to focus exclusively on 'objective' behavioural data. Most of these studies reflect the disciplinary and methodological bias of economics noted in Chapter 2.[7] The few sociological analyses of the NCDS database have incorporated the data on aspirations and motivation, and have invariably found them to be important. For example Pilling (1990) found that aspirations were not simply a reflection of ability, and that adolescent aspirations and motivation had a powerful influence on achievements in adult life. She found that many

[6] This anomalous finding in the ILO report is questioned in Chapter 8.

[7] In the model attempting to control for selection bias, Joshi and Paci, both economists, included high/low ambition at age 16 as one variable in analyses of the 1946 cohort study data but not, unfortunately, in the equivalent analyses of the 1958 cohort study (Joshi and Paci 1998: 153).

people from socially disadvantaged families were none the less high achievers by their mid-20s, and all of them explained their success by their own determination and hard work.[8] Dale and Egerton (1997) show that parents had equally high aspirations for their sons and daughters in this age cohort. Despite this family support, boys were twice as ambitious as girls at age 16, with higher occupational aspirations. Those few girls with high aspirations at age 16 were even *more successful* than boys in achieving the necessary qualifications to realize their aims.

It seems clear that from the mid-1970s onwards, the educational system in Britain and in most other prosperous modern societies, was equally open to women and men. Educational systems are universally perceived as offering equal opportunities, unlike the labour market and the political system (Sorensen, J. B. 1990: 158; Tokyo Metropolitan Government 1994: 17–32). It does not follow that there is no sex differential in aspirations, workplans, motivation, and work orientations. And there is plenty of evidence that high aspirations are a necessary, if not sufficient, condition for higher achievement in the workforce. One reason for lower, or just different aspirations among women is that many—particularly those classified as adaptives in Chapter 6—seek a different family-work balance from men, and thus have different priorities, when choosing a job, from men's customary emphasis on maximum pay, promotion, and other benefits. This is a *qualitative* difference which does not readily translate into the economists' preference for quantitative indicators of good jobs.

The NCDS-5 shows continuing sex differences in job preferences and ambition. In 1991, people who had recently changed jobs were asked their reasons for choosing the new job. Differences between men and women are relatively small but important. A substantial minority of *working* women—part-time and full-time together—have different priorities from men (Table 5.4). Women who are not in the workforce will have yet further differences in priorities. Men give greater emphasis than do women to good career prospects and pay, as already observed in the USA (England 1992: 35). At the age of 33, career prospects matter most to university graduates and good earnings matter most to people with few or no qualifications. People are fairly evenly divided on whether the new job is expected to be interesting, with university graduates most likely to anticipate this. Conversely, people in lower-grade jobs that require few or no qualifications place greater emphasis on good employment conditions. These four criteria are more important to men than to women, by greater or smaller amounts.

The factors which are more important to women than to men are invariably convenience factors, such as a less stressful job or an easier journey to

[8] A study with the opposite focus concluded that work orientations and other attitudes were important correlates, possibly predictors, of membership of the underclass at age 33 among young men (Buckingham 1999).

TABLE 5.4. *Criteria for choosing a new job by highest qualification level*

	Academic higher	Vocational higher	A-level & equiv.	O-level & equiv.	lower & none	Total
MEN						
Better career prospects	72	75	64	56	45	61
Well paid	49	51	55	60	64	56
Interesting work	66	60	53	48	40	52
Good employment conditions	27	37	38	40	34	36
Easy to travel to	13	18	17	20	24	18
Less stressful	9	9	12	10	12	10
WOMEN						
Better career prospects	56	53	50	43	25	43
Well paid	32	31	49	50	52	45
Interesting work	58	56	45	47	38	48
Good employment conditions	21	25	30	35	29	29
Easy to travel to	17	19	25	26	27	23
Less stressful	12	12	10	11	13	12
Base(men)=100%	406	290	472	515	468	2151
Base(women)=100%	258	249	193	546	364	1610

Note: Criteria on which men and women did not differ are not shown here. Base is people changing jobs to get a better one

Source: Extracted from Table 4.7 in A. Dale and M. Egerton, *Highly Educated Women*, 1997, London: Stationary Office for the Department for Education and Employment.

work (Table 5.4). The convenience of a part-time job might be added to the list—It was not included in the survey question.

Differences between men and women are relatively small, but they are cumulative and point to *qualitatively* different priorities for a large part of the female workforce. The fact that the *majority* of men and a *minority* of women were concerned about good career prospects is significant, even if the precise gap is 'only' 18 percentage points. After all, the total pay gap in Britain is 'only' 20 percentage points, and the unexplained pay gap in this NCDS-5 cohort is 'only' 12 percentage points, as noted earlier. If one-fifth of men give greater priority to career development and pay, this could potentially explain the small pay gap in the age group.

The persistence of a small but important sex differential in career orientation is all the more notable because sex differences have shrunk to low levels among 33-year-olds on some work attitudes. Only a minority of women and men (31% and 41%) agreed that a job is less important for a woman than a man. A majority agreed life can be satisfying without a job, but rather more women felt this, 69% compared to 56% among men. A majority of men compared to a minority of women agreed a job is necessary to feel a full member of society (55% and 35%). Half of women compared to one-third of men think being a housewife is just as fulfilling as working for pay (48% and 35%). Most tellingly, a two-thirds majority of men compared to a minority of women agreed that being single provided fewer worries or responsibilities than being married: 66% versus 43% (Wiggins and Bynner 1993). For men, it is marriage that imposes extra responsibilities and worries, no doubt due to the breadwinner role. For women, it is being single, and hence financially self-supporting, that imposes extra responsibilities and worries. It is clear that the majority of young men and women still have work orientations that are heavily coloured by assumptions about the sexual division of labour in marriage, with the income-earning role falling primarily to men.

Surveys show persistent differences between men and women in the *relative* importance attached to career and family as life goals, even in societies with a long tradition of wives working full-time in long-term careers. A 1994 national survey of people aged 25–35 years in France posed the question: 'What are the two most important things in your life?'. Women were most likely to choose 'Having children and sufficient time to look after them': 71% compared to 58% among men. In contrast, men gave greater emphasis to 'Success in your career', chosen by 41% compared to only 26% of the young women (Singly 1996: 8–9).

Even among young people who enjoy all the benefits of the new equal opportunities scenario, it is clear that men still chase money, power, and status harder than women. One explanation may be the breadwinner role that is still imposed on men by at least two-thirds of the women in this age cohort. The alternative explanation offered by Goldberg is that psycho-physiological differences between men and women, for example in testosterone levels, produce sex differences in motivation, ambition, and competitiveness (Goldberg 1993; see also Hakim 1996a: 5–9). Sexual differentiation in motivation to attain the high status positions in any society is statistical and probabilistic rather than an absolute difference, so it would show up in attitude surveys as a difference of *degree* in ambition, aggression, and competitiveness. Whichever explanation is preferred, and the evidence is consistent with both, it seems likely that the sex differential in competitiveness in the workforce may shrink yet further, but will never disappear completely. In effect, it is not sex and gender *per se* that are significant in this generation, and in the generations that follow it, but motivation, ability, and work-lifestyle preferences.

This conclusion is supported by an imaginative analysis of the NCDS data by another sociologist. Saunders (1997) was interested in the impact of social class, rather than sex differences, on upward social mobility, defined as obtaining an occupation of substantially higher status than the father's occupation. This analysis was restricted to people in full-time work at age 33, thus excluding the one-third of women who were full-time homemakers and the one-third of women in part-time work at age 33. Saunders found that ability and motivation as measured in school at age 16—in 1974, just prior to labour market entry for many of the sample—plus work commitment measured at age 33, outweighed social class of origin in predicting outcomes in terms of social class or occupational prestige at age 33.[9] Sex was not a factor in this process. It seems self-evident that work orientations and motivation were factors predicting outcomes for the two-thirds of women in part-time work or in full-time homemaking at age 33.

In the USA, the educational system has been less of a barrier to women's achievement of high-grade and well-paid jobs in the labour market because there has long been a convention of girls as well as boys obtaining a college education, if at all possible. It was only after women's sex-role ideology and occupational aspirations changed that American women started to enter the attractive professional and managerial occupations previously dominated by men. There is no doubt that, in the absence of equal opportunities laws, male exclusionary practices were important in keeping women out of such jobs, and they continue to be important in certain specialisms such as surgery and police management. But women's previous lack of work commitment and career ambition was also important, and it remains important today after the equal opportunities revolution.

European social scientists have tended to overlook this evidence for the USA to argue that it was lack of access to higher education that held women back from equal achievements in the workforce. The NCDS cohort study shows that, at a broad level, there is now virtually total equality between men and women in educational attainment but that, in terms of subjects chosen, a large measure of segregation remains, leading to very different employment profiles and careers later on, if any. The pay gap is reduced to a small level, and can effectively be explained. Does this mean that sex equality has now been achieved within the family? The NCDS study shows that there is virtually no change at all in the sexual division of labour in the family among younger generations, despite women's gains in the labour market. The main trend is that the polarization of working women, and of adult women generally, that is observed in older generations, and in the workforce as a whole (Hakim 1996a) is intensifying in each successive generation (Dex, Joshi, and Macran 1996), and can even be seen in changes within a decade (Table 5.5).

[9] A re-analysis of the NCDS data by Breen and Goldthorpe (1999) confirmed that ability and effort were important predictors of social mobility, but underlined that social class of origin remained important as well. In addition, they found (1999: 25) a higher degree of fluidity in women's social mobility—comparing father's occupation at age 16 with the woman's current or last occupation at age 33—and that ability and effort had a greater impact than among men.

TABLE 5.5. *Percentage of potential working life spent employed for two cohorts of young women: NCDS and WES*

% employed	1958 cohort aged 33 in 1991		WES sample aged 30–34 in 1980	
	All women	All mothers	All women	All mothers
under 10%	5	4	1	1
10–49%	22	28	27	29
50–89%	54	55	53	60
90% or more	17	13	19	10
Base=100%	5,685	3,894	746	644

Source: Table 4 in S. Dex, H. Joshi, and S. Macran, 'A widening gulf among Britain's mothers', *Oxford Review of Economic Policy*, 1996, 12: 65–75, reporting special analyses of 1980 Women and Employment Survey (WES) and NCDS-5.

The Financial Dependence of Wives

The financial dependence of wives has been studied at age 23, when half of NCDS couples had no children (Ward and Dale 1992), and at age 33 in 1991, when four-fifths of couples had children (Joshi and Davies 1996; Ward, Dale, and Joshi 1996*a*).[10]

At age 23, a working wife contributed 39% of a couples' joint earnings, 27% when they had children living with them in the household and 40% when they had no children. In about half of couples the wife worked full-time and in 42% she did no paid work; only 10% of wives did part-time work at this age. On average, wives contributed 39% of family income when they worked full-time, 24% when they worked part-time, and were totally dependent when they were full-time homemakers. Across all couples, wives contributed an average of 21% of family income. Even in this group of very young couples, half of them childless, with almost half of the wives in full-time employment, four-fifths of family income was contributed by the male partner. The pattern in this younger generation was no different from the pattern in the adult population as a whole in 1991. There are several reasons for this. Even the childless wives sometimes worked part-time (7%) or not at all (15%), while cohabitees were more likely to preserve their financial independence, with or without children. As noted in Chapter 7, women usually marry men who are slightly older, and who thus have greater work experience

[10] All these analyses group together married couples with a small number of cohabiting couples.

and higher earnings. Even at age 23, women work significantly shorter hours than men: 38 on average instead of 43 hours a week among those in full-time employment. Furthermore, many women marry men of higher occupational status than themselves, with the conscious aim of being dependent, in whole or in part, on a high-earning partner (Ward and Dale 1992: 520). Finally, case-studies of young couples in the 1980s show that they still anticipate a high degree of sexual division of labour, with the wife assumed to be a secondary earner even before they have children (Mansfield and Collard 1988).

By age 33, three-quarters of all wives contributed less than 45% of family income (on average this was 22% of the total), only 14% were equal earners with their spouse (contributing 45%–55% of family income), and another 11% contributed over 55% of joint income (72% on average), either because husbands were temporarily unemployed or low earners. Overall, wives contributed 31% of family income, or 28% when the husband was in employment. At this age, there was a fairly even three-way split among wives between full-time work (36%), part-time work (34%), and full-time home-makers (30%). There was a weak correlation between the incomes of spouses: 0.09 over the whole NCDS-5 sample and 0.22 in couples where both worked full-time (Joshi and Davies 1996: 39). Between 10% and 20% of the NCDS couples were dual-career couples (as distinct from dual-earner couples) at age 33.

The 14% of wives who contributed an equal half share of family income were generally full-time workers continuously employed in higher grade occupations, half of them still childless at age 33 (Joshi and Davies 1996: 45, 48, 50). With welfare state benefits included, and with Child Benefit treated as the wife's income rather than the child's income, only 12% of couples were equal earners, with another 10% of wives earning over 55% of joint income (Ward, Dale, and Joshi 1996*a*: 109). At this age, it becomes clear that full-time work is a necessary, but not sufficient, condition for wives to be equal contributors or the principal earner, among both childless couples and those with children. However when children precipitate a transfer to part-time work, or to full-time homemaking, wives invariably become partially or totally dependent on their husband (Table 5.6). As the base totals in Table 5.6 indicate, only 16% of wives choose to work part-time or not at all when they are childless, but four-fifths do so after they have children. As a result, the great majority of wives (75% or more) are either totally dependent, or else secondary earners contributing a minor share of family income, even in this younger generation. This is perhaps not surprising. Yet virtually all these NCDS reports express astonishment at the absence of any major changes in this equal opportunities cohort, possibly because of the idea that sex discrimination had been the *main* or *only* barrier to women's equality and that women could not benefit from financial dependence on a husband.

TABLE 5.6. *Income dependency of married and cohabiting women by her employment status and presence of children*

	No children			With children		
	FT	PT	home	FT	PT	home
	employment		maker	employment		maker
Dependent male	23	9	0	19	5	4
Equal contributors	31	9	0	30	5	2
Total not dependent	54	18	0	49	10	6
Partial dependence	46	80	54	51	90	89
Complete dependence	*	2	46	*	*	5
Total dependent	46	82	100	51	90	94
Base=100%	477	54	24	580	1,081	951

Note: * less than 0.5%

Source: Extracted from Table 6.5 in C. Ward, A. Dale, and H. Joshi, 'Income dependency within couples' in L. Morris and E. S. Lyon (eds) *Gender Relations in Public and Private*, 1996, Macmillan.

The conclusion drawn by all these NCDS reports is that the dominant trend is, once again, the polarization of patterns of employment and of household income. The gains made by the 10%–15% of women who retain the male work pattern of continuous full-time work by age 33 are balanced by the substantial minority of women who have no paid work at all. Indeed, between 1980 and 1991, the only visible change in work histories for women in their early 30s was the five-fold increase (from 1% to 5%) in women who had spent virtually none of their adult life in employment, plus a small increase (from 10% to 13%) in mothers in continuous employment (Table 5.5). In the middle are the vast majority of women, who regard themselves as secondary earners even if they work full-time, and who transfer quickly to part-time jobs after they have children.

The polarization of young women's lifestyles can also be illustrated without reference to employment profiles. Table 5.7 indicates that early marriage and child-bearing substitute to a certain extent for educational goals, and for the career opportunities education opens up in a meritocratic society, providing an alternative source of adult identity. Among women with five or more children by age 33, a two-thirds majority have no qualifications at all or only minimal qualifications. Although only 11% of women in the NCDS cohort achieved a university degree, or better, this doubles to 19% among the women who remained childless by age 33. In this cohort of women who have

TABLE 5.7. *Qualifications by number of children at age 33 among NCDS women*

Qualification level	Number of children 0	1	2	3	4	5+
University degree or higher	19	13	9	7	3	0
Other higher education	15	14	14	11	7	6
A-levels or equivalent*	15	13	14	11	10	3
O-levels or equivalent	27	32	33	32	33	22
Lower qualifications	15	16	19	22	19	27
None	10	12	12	18	25	38
Base=100%	3,376	1,998	3,869	1,370	325	76

Note: * equivalent to *Arbitur* or *Baccalaureat*

Source: Table 3.6 in E. Ferri (ed) *Life at 33*, London: National Children's Bureau, 1993.

the advantage of equal opportunities and fertility control, the choices they make are even more polarized than they have been in the past.[11]

Life Satisfaction and Psychological Distress

The attitudinal data collected by the NCDS at age 33 included measures of overall life satisfaction, marital satisfaction, and psychological distress. Together they provide indicators of the impact of parental roles, jobs, and the sexual division of labour in the family on the happiness of young couples, the majority of whom had young children (Ferri and Smith 1996). As usual, the great majority of people expressed satisfaction with the way their lives had turned out so far (85%), and with their marital relationship (over 80%). Only 10% of mothers and 5% of fathers gave responses that suggested they were suffering from depression on a 24-item checklist of symptoms including anxiety, irritability, and depressed mood. Because a minority of young mothers and fathers expressed dissatisfaction or depression, comparisons between subgroups necessarily concern variations in these small percentages.[12]

[11] An analysis of NCDS data by Gregg and Machin (1999) suggests that early child-bearing provides an alternative route to adult status for young women who do not do well at school, whereas the main alternative for young men seems to be a career in crime. However, those who upgraded their educational qualifications later on, between ages 23 and 33, achieved wage gains, with larger gains for women.

[12] National survey data on satisfaction with jobs, or with life in general, are sometimes criticized as simplistic or misleading, and researchers such as Agassi (1979, 1982) have tried to 'go behind'

Contrary to expectation, couples with a wife at home full-time and a breadwinner husband were the happiest with life in general, followed by dual-earner couples with a wife working full-time or part-time. The most dissatisfied group was couples with no earner at all, followed by those where the wife worked while the husband was unemployed. Clearly the financial stress of being out of work is an important cause of unhappiness, but role-reversal couples, with only the wife working, express almost as much unhappiness.

There were some differences between wives and husbands in patterns of marital satisfaction. Not surprisingly, breadwinner husbands with a wife at home full-time emerged as the happiest group, certainly happier than men in dual-earner couples with a wife working full-time or part-time. Indeed role reversal in the family caused the highest levels of marital dissatisfaction among men, followed by having no earner in the household. A husband's unemployment clearly put a lot of stress on the marital relationship; but the psychological stress was even greater if the wife was working while the husband had no job, despite the reduction in financial problems.

Among wives, the happiest group was those with a part-time job, and the tiny group of wives who were the sole breadwinner in the family. Wives with a full-time job were more likely to express dissatisfaction with the marital relationship, followed by wives at home full-time caring for young children, irrespective of whether their husband had a job or not. Marital dissatisfaction was prompted in part by the burden of childcare when children were young, especially if combined with a paid job, and was reflected in mothers' dissatisfaction with their husband's involvement in the care and social education of their children. The most dissatisfied wives were those with full-time jobs (35 hours or more a week) whose husbands were not much involved in their children's upbringing. Among women, children and childcare were crucial factors shaping marital and life satisfaction. In contrast, involvement with their children was of little importance to men, and it had no impact on their satisfaction with their marriage and with life in general. If anything, the opposite was

broad job satisfaction responses to reveal lower 'real' levels of satisfaction with jobs. But the methods adopted for these small scale studies are just as open to doubts about validity as the national survey data they claim to outshine. For example Agassi asked whether a woman would recommend her current job to a daughter, and to a son. Those who would not, were classified as dissatisfied with their jobs. However there are many good reasons for not recommending one's own occupation to a younger person, who may be far better educated, have different talents and abilities, and so on. The occupation itself may be technologically dated or be in a declining industry. Agassi also failed to consider the sample selection bias in her study, which was limited to working women and thus to women who are generally happier with their jobs, as dissatisfied women can often leave the workforce. Finally, these critiques fail to distinguish between the very different purposes of macro-level analyses of national data and micro-level studies of particular groups and situations (Hakim 1987a, 2000). Sophisticated analyses of national data on job and life satisfaction yield important findings on enduring differences between groups of workers, or between men and women (Hakim 1991, 1997; Curtice 1993) whereas case-study research is more appropriately used to study causal processes.

sometimes observed: men who were closely involved in the care and social development of their children were most unhappy with their marriage, and with life generally, especially if they also put in long hours on their job, 60 hours or more a week in some cases. It appears that few men are interested in caring for and training babies and young children. At the age of 33 years, many men are heavily invested in their careers. The NCDS showed that fathers in professional and managerial occupations were the *least* involved with their children: only one-third played an equal part with their wives compared to well over half of semi-skilled and unskilled manual workers. This social class difference was not limited to the care of small babies and persisted among those with older children, up to the age of 11 years (Ferri and Smith 1996: 27–8).

Fathers' lack of interest in very small children seems to be a fairly widespread characteristic, rather than being due to circumstance. As noted in Chapter 8, huge investments in parental leave schemes for fathers in Nordic countries have produced meagre results, with take-up rates so close to zero as to be almost invisible, even in Sweden. The argument that paternal leave schemes would facilitate more equal parenting roles has little support in the research evidence on parenting roles among young couples in the 1990s, at least as regards children up to the age of 11 years. This leaves open the possibility that fathers would be more inclined to become involved with their children during the teenage years, when children are moving beyond the home environment to fully explore the public world that fathers spend much of their time in.

The NCDS also suggests that there has been a general *decline* in fathers' involvement with their children since the 1960s (Ferri and Smith 1996: 30–1). This could be due to the growth of professional and managerial jobs in the workforce, at the expense of unskilled jobs, over the past three decades. What is certain is that the majority of young men in professional and managerial occupations today find their work more interesting and absorbing than their children, and that young men's happiness owes nothing to a close involvement with their family. Young women do most of the childcare work, whether they have paid jobs or not, and are resentful if their partner does not get involved, even if he has a full workload in his job. Attitudes and expectations concerning the sexual division of labour in the family are also important, but it appears that people generally choose partners with compatible attitudes, making this less of a problem. This conclusion is supported by the NCDS results on the psychological distress scale. Among men and women, levels of psychological distress were consistently low in dual-earner couples and in single-earner couples with a wife at home full-time. Distress levels only rose sharply among couples with no earner, that is, with an unemployed husband. Distress levels were also somewhat higher for men in role-reversal couples, with the wife only in work. Presumably, a husband's social embarrassment at being unemployed is underlined by a wife who keeps or gets a job—even if this reduces the financial pressures.

In sum, the happiest young women are the full-time homemakers and those with part-time jobs. This suggests that many young women doing full-time jobs are still prompted by materialistic motivations rather than by personal lifestyle choice. And there is no evidence that young fathers are becoming more involved with their children.

Younger Generations in the USA

A very different USA study of a broadly similar cohort of women reports similar results (Gerson 1985, 1986). The study is of special interest because it is one of the few to ask women about their work-lifestyle preferences. Gerson carried out long and detailed structured interviews with 63 women in their early 30s in California, who were selected randomly from the records of a community college offering vocational training for high school graduates and a four-year college offering university degrees.

The interviews were held in 1979, at the end of a decade of major changes in sex-role attitudes in the USA (McLaughlin *et al.* 1988: 170–8; Davis 1996), and a massive influx of women into professional occupations.[13] Equal pay was introduced and enforced in 1963 in the USA, much earlier than in most European countries. Gerson's sample of well-educated young women represented the first cohort of women in the USA to reach adulthood after the contraceptive and equal opportunities revolutions. All the women were successfully using contraception to control and plan fertility, and half were still childless: double the national average for women aged 25–34 years.[14] The sample was chosen to represent women from working class as well as middle class backgrounds. Among those in employment, half were in clerical, sales, and similar relatively low level white-collar occupations, and half were in professional and managerial occupations.

[13] From 1970 to 1979, the percentage of women earning degrees in law increased from 5% to 28%; the increase in medicine was from 8% to 23%. Women's share of BSc degrees in business management rose from 9% in 1971 to 30% in 1979, and in engineering from under 1% to 8% by 1979 (Betz and Fitzgerald 1987: 64).

[14] A tiny minority of 5 women—8% of Gerson's sample—reported an 'unplanned' pregnancy. As Gerson notes, when male partners are reluctant to embark on having children some women still resort to the old gamble of getting pregnant 'accidentally' in the hope that this will force the issue. Access to reliable contraception now exposes these women as really wanting to get pregnant and have a child. Similarly, research on fertility control has shown that people who desire (more) children appear to be more haphazard, less determined, in their use of contraceptives, although publicly they claim that contraceptives are not reliable, no matter what type they use (Scanzoni 1976: 685, 688). Dunnell also found that women who choose to centre their lives on child-bearing do not plan ahead, like women choosing employment careers; they rely on 'just letting things happen', which typically results in a greater number of children being born (Dunnell 1979: 24–6).

Gerson's sample was well-educated by national standards in the USA in the late 1970s: one-quarter had finished high school, one-fifth had some college education, one-third had finished college with a university degree and/or teaching qualification, and one-fifth had other qualifications. The sample was also biased towards middle and upper income groups, with few poor women. A two-thirds majority of the women were in full-time year-round work—above the national average of about half for women aged 25–34; 27% were full-time homemakers—fewer than the national average of 32%; and very few were in part-time jobs, 8% compared with the national average in 1977 of 17% (Gerson 1985: 251). The interviews covered women's life since childhood, including employment decisions, without collecting work histories as such. The focus of the study was to explore and understand the diversity of women's preferences and choices between being a full-time mother and homemaker, being a working mother, and being childless and working full-time.

Like many social scientists, Gerson dichotomizes her subjects into those giving priority to and preferring domestic life, and those preferring and giving priority to non-domestic activities, in practice employment careers. However she provides sufficient information on her subjects, their preferences and outcomes for the data to be recast in terms of the preference theory trichotomy set out in Table 1.1. The analysis which follows thus departs substantively from Gerson's presentation, but it relies entirely on the information she provides on her research results.

The sample of 63 women divides into 11 (17%) who were consistently home-centred from childhood up to interview, all of whom had married, had children, and were at home full-time; 19 (30%) who were consistently work-centred from childhood up to interview, all of whom were working; and 33 (52%) adaptives, whose preferences and priorities had changed in response to experiences and events, most of whom were already combining motherhood and employment, some of whom were working but planned to start child-bearing soon. The future plans of the women display even more sharply the three-fold grouping identified by the preference theory framework. One-quarter of the women planned full-time homemaking; half were adaptives planning some combination of family life and employment; one-quarter planned to remain childless and continue their lifelong career (Table 5.8). It is notable that the three groups emerge with similar proportions in both the university sample and the community college sample. Gerson confirms that the diversity of preferences also cuts across social class divisions, which were unimportant (Gerson 1985: 212).

About half of the sample of 63 young women had modified their preferences and plans since childhood and planned some combination of motherhood and employment in the longer term—the adaptive group. Gerson devotes most of her attention to this group, and to the events and experiences

TABLE 5.8. *Distribution of work-lifeplans of women in their early 30s in the USA*

	University graduate sample	Community college sample	Total
Childlessness and work-centred life	23	21	22
Combination of work and motherhood	28	32	30
Motherhood with erratic work	26	19	22
Full-time homemaker with children	23	28	25
Base=100%	35	28	63

Source: Table C22 in K. Gerson, *Hard Choices*, Berkeley: University of California Press, 1985.

to which they were responding. In contrast with the dynamic stories of change and adaptation in this group, the life stories of the women who remained consistently focused on either family or career, and achieved their aims, seem dull and uninteresting by comparison. Gerson concluded that most women have changing or variable preferences.[15] This illustrates a more general problem of selective perception and selective interest among social scientists, and people generally. Dynamic stories of change, unforseen opportunities, unexpected difficulties, accidents, change events, and reversals are more interesting to write about and to analyse, and are more likely to be remembered, than the plain accounts of apparently uneventful lives in which aspirations were achieved, whether for a career or for marriage and full-time motherhood. So it is not surprising that research reports seem to discover change more often than stability, thwarted ambition and unexpected success more often than contented achievement of early goals.

Gerson's report is especially useful in identifying the events that adaptives respond to: divorce, often initiated by the woman herself; financial constraints in the family of origin; failure to achieve the qualifications aimed for; failure to advance in employment; failure to marry a man with high earnings so that the wife felt obliged to work as well; unexpected promotion at work, often due to new equal opportunities policies; the post-natal discovery

[15] This is not strictly correct, as her sample was evenly split between the two stable groups and the adaptive group. However Gerson is still right to conclude that adaptive women with unstable and changing goals are generally more numerous than women with well-defined goals.

that caring for small babies is boring; the post-natal discovery that rearing a child is far more enjoyable, creative, and challenging than expected. It should be obvious that some of these events were genuinely external events that impacted on the women—such as new promotion opportunities opened up by equal opportunities policies. But many events were subjectively defined, such as the women's diverse reactions to a new baby, or were even instigated by the woman herself, such as divorce, or deciding that the family 'needed' more money to be comfortable. Gerson collected enough information about her subjects' lifestyle and financial position to be clear that the 'need' for extra income was invariably the woman's subjective definition of the situation, possibly a *post-hoc* rationalization of her decision to take a job for other reasons (Gerson 1985: 76). Similarly, the 'blocked work opportunities' which led some women to transfer to full-time motherhood never occurred to women who reported themselves as committed to a career, who changed jobs rather than quitting work. It is in the nature of studies like this, that accept women's accounts unquestioningly, that most accounts consist of rationalizations after the event, with a tendency to identify 'external' events as the catalysts for an inevitable train of events (Semin and Manstead 1983). An alternative conclusion from this interesting and rich study is that adaptive women are, in practice, self-made women just as much as the women who consistently give priority to career or to family. Women who achieve their stable preferences appear to be more single-minded, focused and, sometimes, self-conscious about their aims. In contrast, adaptive women can appear confused, undecided, unfocused, lacking in self knowledge, leading some studies to describe them as 'drifters' and women who achieved 'unplanned careers' (Shaw 1983; Rexroat and Shehan 1984; Shaw and Shapiro 1987). Gerson's study suggests that adaptive women are just as determined to achieve their goals as other women. They simply have multiple goals.

All of these young women saw a major distinction between a *career* and having a *job*.[16] A career implied long-term, full-time employment with the expectation, or at least the hope, of advancement over time or some degree of progression in the activity. A career did not necessarily imply a professional job, but rather a major investment in paid work and a coherent pattern of employment. Jobs were viewed in a short-term perspective. It was recognized that full-time, closely supervised working class jobs could be even more

[16] The distinction between careers and jobs is found in the 'ordinary knowledge' of the general public and in the academic literature (for example, Fogarty, Rapoport, and Rapoport 1971: 189). So it is surprising that it no longer appears today in research reports, especially in quantitative studies, which now treat all women in employment as a homogenous group, and divide couples crudely into dual-earner and single-breadwinner couples (for example, Rubery *et al.* 1998). The rare survey that does collect the information, such as the 1986 SCELI survey in Britain, invariably finds that *most* working men regard themselves as having a career while *most* working women regard themselves as having jobs (Burchell and Rubery 1994; 91–2) but the implications of this difference were ignored.

inflexible and arduous than prestigious professional and managerial jobs, and thus imposed clear-cut choices between family and work (Gerson 1985: 126). It is notable that in the 1980s in North America and Europe, in professions experiencing a labour shortage, such as pharmacy, it became possible for graduate women to choose to work in a series of (well-paid) part-time and temporary jobs rather than being obliged to adopt the commitment and constraints of a career (Hakim 1998a: 232–3). Graduate women are not necessarily career-oriented, as Table 5.8 indicates.

Gerson's study is especially useful in demonstrating that even the most modern, educated career women still expect to have a husband with equal or higher earnings. None of the women were prepared to support a dependent househusband, that is, role reversal (Gerson 1985: 113, 143, 174–5). Self-evidently, women who accepted the sexual division of labour and chose to be full-time homemakers looked for a good provider within their social milieu. Despite the bias towards well-educated, high-earning women and high-income households in Gerson's sample—as compared with all earners and all households aged 25–34 years in 1977—most of the women had husbands who earned more than themselves. A two-thirds majority (69%) of husbands earned more than their wives; only 22% of wives were equal contributors; and 9% of wives earned more than their husbands; with little difference between the university sample and the community college sample (Gerson 1985: 253). Although the case-study sample is small, the results are an astonishingly close parallel to the NCDS-5 results on wives' financial dependence. Gerson's study provides an explanation for this result, namely that even the most educated, modern, high-earning women actively seek, even insist on, a husband with at least equal and preferably higher occupational status and earnings. This pattern of modern women rejecting role reversal, or even equality, and insisting upon a male partner who is 'superior' in terms of money, power or status was noted by Goldberg (1993: 152, 192) as an important piece of evidence supporting his theory of male dominance in personal and sexual relationships, and patriarchy in the public arena.

Gerson's USA sample was relatively well-educated. However the polarization of preferences emerges also among working class women. This is illustrated by a similar study carried out in the 1980s, of 50 young women, all with children under 12 years old and living in Flin Flon, a mining town in Canada (Luxton 1987). This research was also unusual in asking the young women about their ideal-world preferences regarding family roles. Again, three groups emerged. One group advocated a strict gender-based division of labour, with women taking responsibility for the home and child-rearing while husbands were responsible for breadwinning. Some of these mothers found themselves obliged to work, full-time, but they insisted they would stop as soon as the 'emergency' was over. A second group believed women could work if they wanted to, regardless of economic necessity, and that both spouses should share responsibility for domestic work and income-earning. The third group fell between these two extremes, and had the most ambivalent views and the most flexible behaviour. On the one hand, they insisted that men and women were different, and thus had different roles in the family. On the other hand, they saw marriage as requiring co-operation, with both partners helping the other as necessary. Some of the women had full-time jobs; some were full-time homemakers; but all were consciously adaptable in their attitudes and behaviour, with 'financial necessity' regularly invoked as a justification for a mother's employment. The three groups had quite different approaches to domestic work, child-rearing practices, and marital relationships. For example the women who preferred strict role-segregation also accepted hierarchical relations between spouses, with the wife deferring to her husband in his role as family head. In contrast, the women who preferred symmetrical and shared family roles expected an egalitarian marital relationship (Luxton 1987). These particular attitudes may reflect the working class culture of a mining town in the 1980s, rather than being universal features of the three preference groups.[17] But they remind us that some women welcome a relationship of acquiescence to a dominant male who can be expected to provide all their needs, while others do not.

Conclusions

Gerson's USA study is methodologically different from the British NCDS cohort study. The two data sources are otherwise broadly similar in describing outcomes in a sample of young women who entered adulthood in the equal opportunities era of the USA and Britain respectively, had the benefit of full control of their fertility and of access to higher education, and the professional and managerial jobs it leads to. The results contradict the proposition that younger generations are choosing substantively different work-lifestyles. The main trend is polarization, both in the USA (Gerson 1985: 210, note 12) and Britain (Ferri 1993: 46; Ferri and Smith 1996: 12–16; Dex, Joshi, and

[17] Although cross-national comparisons of gender roles are hazardous, several conclusions can be drawn from contemporary exercises (Adler 1993). Almost all societies promote differentiated gender stereotypes and ideal-type models of female and male behaviour to children and adolescents, in the family, school, and other settings. For example boys are expected and allowed to be active, while girls are expected and allowed to be passive. But it does not automatically follow that one gender is seen as 'superior' to the other. Some cultures present the differences as complementary and equal in value, while others present them as justifying male superiority within a hierarchy. However, even societies with strongly egalitarian gender role ideologies and collective childcare arrangements, such as Finland and the Israeli *kibbutz*, do not eradicate differentiated behaviour, which typically arises from differentiated involvement in child-rearing versus other activities. Occupational segregation is extremely high in Scandinavian societies and in the Israeli *kibbutzim*, higher than in liberal polities (Melkas and Anker 1998; Anker 1998; Agassi 1989).

Macran 1996: 66, 73; Macran, Joshi, and Dex 1996: 290–2; Paci and Joshi 1996: 38; Bynner, Morphy, and Parsons 1997: 70, 96). The undoubted achievements of young career-oriented women who are taking advantage of new job opportunities in the new scenario and are producing a massive inflow to professional and managerial top jobs (Rubery and Fagan 1993: 19; Hakim 1996a: 155; Thair and Risdon 1999) are balanced by the substantial numbers of young women who still choose a life centred around home and family. These contrasting preferences cut across social class, ethnic group, education, and ability differences.

In addition, even the most qualified and high-earning women reject role reversal in favour of a partner who is at least equal, preferably superior, in earnings, status, or power. So the sexual division of labour is maintained, most wives remain financially dependent on their husbands for much of their lives, and the younger generations do not differ significantly from the adult workforce as a whole. Indeed, the evidence is that polarization intensifies in each succeeding generation. This is apparent in Table 5.5, which shows increasing polarization over just a decade. It is also emerging from comparative analyses of the NCDS 1958 birth cohort and the 1970 birth cohort study when surveyed in 1996 at age 26. Bynner, Ferri, and Shepherd (1997) found that the polarization of young women's and men's work-lifestyles in 1996 was even greater in the younger cohort than in the NCDS at a similar age in 1981, fifteen years earlier. Childless women were ten times more likely than mothers to have gained a degree or an equivalent qualification by age 26. Whether married or cohabiting, childless women and men were also more likely to have bought their own home, to be in a professional or managerial occupation, and to have been in continuous full-time employment since leaving full-time education. The better qualified tended to be in couples with two full-time earners, and the least qualified were over-represented in partnerships with no earner, because he was unemployed and she was at home full-time caring for young children. The polarization of material circumstances and family situations was echoed in a polarization of political orientations, in feelings of efficacy and being in control of their lives, in satisfaction with life generally, and in depression. Although there was strong support for sex equality among 26-year-olds, role segregation in the family remained a strong feature of young parents' lives, in contrast with the childless couples. Bynner, Ferri, and Shepherd (1997: 126) concluded that the 1970 birth cohort represented a more polarized generation than their predecessors in the 1958 cohort, with signs that the gap was widening, especially for women.

Similar results are found in a qualitative study that, like Gerson's study, claimed that young women are unable to prioritize careers or family life consistently, and focused on the events and experiences that produce animated life histories. Procter and Padfield repeatedly interviewed 79 young women aged 18–27 years over the period 1992–1996 in England. All the young women were chosen within the middle range of household incomes, excluding the least affluent and the wealthy, so they represented just half of all young women aged 18–27 in the 1990s. Within this admittedly non-representative sample, only 8 women (about 10%) were career-oriented, most of them planning to remain childless. Another 12 (about 15%) planned a marriage career, and most of them had already embarked on early marriage and child-bearing, with no investment in qualifications. The remaining 59 (about 75%) were adaptives, some of whom had invested early on in qualifications and work experience and delayed child-bearing, some of whom had entered marriage and motherhood early in life but thought they would return to employment later on (Procter and Padfield 1999). Within this small sample, the two extreme groups of work-centred and family-centred women are smaller than might be expected, but the polarization of preferences and priorities remains clear, even among young women born around 1970, well after the two revolutions.[18] Like Gerson, Procter and Padfield's main report focuses on the twists and turns of life to which the adaptive women constantly responded, giving the impression that all young women are buffeted by their social context (Procter and Padfield 1998).

It appears that cross-sectional results are not misleading, as some enthusiasts of longitudinal studies would have us believe. Longitudinal studies confirm that polarization is a trend that cuts across all sectors of society, all age groups, classes, and sub-cultures. Given real choices in how to live their lives, women now differ radically in the choices they make, and sharp differences emerge at the very start of adult life. Longitudinal studies do, however, add substantially to our knowledge. They show that the two 'extreme' groups, of home-centred and work-centred women, are consistent and persistent in goals and priorities across the lifecycle. It is only in the middle group of adaptive women that priorities and activities change across the lifecycle, in response to experiences and events, opportunities and constraints. Instead of demolishing the picture from Chapter 4, longitudinal studies extend and reinforce it, whether they are based on large-scale quantitative data-collections or small-scale qualitative research. However analyses that seek to identify the 'average' or 'typical' woman's life history will tend to obscure the very real and growing process of diversification.

[18] Unfortunately, Procter and Padfield never asked their interviewees explicitly about their long-term preferences and priorities. The classification of these 79 cases is thus based on the elegant summary presented in Procter and Padfield (1999) rather than their full report (Procter and Padfield 1998). The 8 career-oriented women consist of 7 single workers who intended to remain childless *and* were career-oriented, plus 1 who planned to work continuously across the child-bearing years *and* was career-oriented. The 12 home-centred women consist of 9 early mothers who planned the marriage career, plus 3 single workers who also planned to give up work permanently after marriage, even though they currently enjoyed their jobs. All other women in the study would be classified as adaptives, most of them planning to work only part-time after having children. Procter and Padfield (1999) claim that their results challenge preference theory, whereas in fact they fully support it.

6

Heterogeneous Preferences

The central tenet of preference theory is that women are not a homogeneous group but divide into three groups that are not only qualitatively different but also have *conflicting* interests. Table 6.1 summarizes the key features of the three groups more fully than in Table 1.1, and gives our best estimate of the relative sizes of the three groups in societies where government policy does not actively *force* women into accepting only one model of women's role. That is, Table 6.1 shows the relative size of the three groups in liberal and *laissez faire* societies. In Britain and the USA, by the end of the 20th century, the female population of working age divided very roughly into one-fifth in each of the two extreme groups: home-centred and work-centred, and over half in the adaptive group, which is generally the largest and most vocal in most countries. Within the minority group of university graduates in these two countries, the distribution was approximately one-quarter in each of the two extreme groups, and half in the adaptive group. In western Europe as a whole, the female population of working age divided very roughly into one-third in each of the three groups, because public policy favoured the role-segregated family in some EU countries but promoted the symmetrical roles family in other EU countries, as noted in Chapter 8. Irrespective of national policies, all three preference groups are found in all countries, as indicated by several Eurobarometer surveys, including Table 4.1.

The distribution of women across the three groups corresponds to a 'normal' distribution of responses to the family–work conflict.[1] The largest, middle group is labelled adaptive but could also be seen as ambivalent, torn between the conflicting pulls of family life, especially children, and employment. The two extreme groups are smaller, being the tails of the distribution, and represent more decisive choices in favour of one or the other priority in life.

Descriptions of the three groups of women which follow take the form of sociological *ideal-types* that are based on empirical research results. Few women have lives that conform exactly to these three ideal-types. The descriptions highlight the central tendencies and essential features of the

[1] I am indebted to Tony Fahey for this idea.

TABLE 6.1. *The full classification of women's work-lifestyle preferences in the 21st century*

Home-centred	Adaptive	Work-centred
20% of women varies 10%–30%	60% of women varies 40%–80%	20% of women varies 10%–30%
Children and family are the main priorities throughout life.	This group is most diverse and includes women who want to combine work and family, plus drifters and unplanned careers.	Childless women are concentrated here. Main priority in life is employment or equivalent activities such as politics, sport, art, etc.
Prefer **not** to work.	Want to work, but **not** totally committed to work career	Committed to work or equivalent activities.
Qualifications obtained for intellectual dowry	Qualfications obtained with the intention of working.	Large investment in qualifications for employment or other activities.
Number of children is affected by government social policy, family wealth, etc. Not reponsive to employment policy.	This group is **very responsive** to government social policy, employment policy, equal opportunities policy/propaganda, economic cycle/recession/growth, etc. Such as: income tax and social welfare benefits educational policies school timetables childcare services public attitudes towards working women legislation promoting female employment trade union attitudes to working women availability of part-time work and similar work flexibility economic growth and prosperity and institutional factors generally.	Responsive to economic opportunity political opportunity artistic opportunity etc. Not responsive to social/family policy.

three groups, hence their differences and the contrasts between them. Reality is of course more variable and untidy, and there are overlaps between the groups at the margins.

Home-centred Women and the Marriage Career

Home-centred women accept the sexual division of labour in the home, prefer not to work, and give priority to children and family life throughout their life. Once married, they prefer to be full-time homemakers, and child-rearing activities are of central importance to them. The term 'homemaker' is preferable to 'housewife' for two reasons. First, the term housewife has acquired pejorative connotations. Second, the full-time homemaker may employ servants to do virtually all domestic work and basic childcare. The homemaker's role goes beyond housework to include family work: the education and social development of children and grandchildren; creating a home that all members of the family are pleased to return to at the end of the working day; the maintenance of family relationships; entertaining family and friends; organizing leisure activities, holidays and festival celebrations; general household management and the management of consumption.

Some home-centred women never do paid work at all. Others have a job until marriage or childbirth. Those who plan to work until marriage or childbirth may invest in qualifications and a short-term career with the aim of maximizing the short-term rewards—which may be financial, social, or something else entirely. For example, many young women regarded the job of air hostess as ideal, prior to marriage, both for the opportunities to travel around the world and for meeting people. Home-centred women may return to work after marriage, but normally only in extreme circumstances—for example if they become widows, if they get divorced, or if their husband is unable, due to ill-health or for other reasons, to support the family. Occasionally, home-centred women with no caring responsibilities will take a job if it fits in completely with their family-centred lifestyle: if it involves few hours a week, pleasant social contacts, and is located close to home. Such jobs are treated almost as a hobby or as an alternative to voluntary work, and do not involve competing commitments.[2]

The full-time homemaker is not necessarily someone with few or no qualifications, as economists have assumed. Some women attend college and university with a view to meeting and marrying a man of at least equal education and social status. Colleges and universities function as élite marriage

[2] A small study of female part-time workers in Australia found that one-quarter were women with no dependent children, who regarded themselves as secondary earners, and had no plans ever to do a full-time job (Walsh 1999: 190).

markets as well as educational institutions. Similarly, workplaces function to some extent as marriage markets, and one ideal job for a home-centred woman is to work, whether as a secretary or in a professional post, in a large company in a city centre where there are many opportunities for meeting young men with good career prospects in professional and managerial occupations. Women with educational qualifications bring an 'intellectual dowry' to a marriage, enabling wives to be an intellectual partner and equal to their husband as well as helping to educate their own children. The cultural capital represented by educational qualifications, especially in non-vocational subjects in the arts and humanities, contribute to, and shape, the style of consumption in the home and in leisure activities, and help to define the family's position within the cultural hierarchy (Bourdieu 1984). Similarly, a wife's social capital may extend and complement her husband's economic capital.[3]

The current emphasis on employment careers for women, and women's disadvantage in the labour market, overlooks the fact that the marriage career provided the principal avenue for upward social mobility from social class of origin for women throughout the 20th century, and it still offers the potential for greater upward mobility than women can achieve through their own employment, especially for working class women who are not intellectually or academically gifted but are attractive and ambitious (Elder 1969). The picture of consistent disadvantage for women produced by comparisons of the employment successes of men and women is replaced by a picture of equality when women's marital mobility is compared with men's employment career mobility. Research in the USA and Europe consistently shows that women's chances of achieving an upper class lifestyle through marriage are at least equal, and often better than men's chances of getting there through occupational ladders, and certainly far better than women's chances of upward social mobility through employment careers (Glenn, Ross, and Tully 1974; Tyree and Treas 1974; Chase 1975; Girod 1977; Thelot 1982; Dunton and Featherman 1985; Portocarero 1985, 1987; Goldthorpe 1987; Erikson and Goldthorpe 1993: 231–77). These conclusions are based on research evidence covering the 20th century up to the 1980s, so they take no account of women's increasing share of professional and managerial occupations towards the end of the century, after the introduction of equal opportunities policies (Rubery and Fagan 1993; Hakim 1992, 1996a: 155, 1998a: 42). Employment careers are now open to women as well as men, and provide a genuine alternative to the marriage career. However these research findings on marital mobility remain valid into the 21st century, for the home-centred women who continue to rely on the marriage market as their main avenue for

[3] The terms social capital, economic capital, cultural capital, and political capital are defined in note 13 to Chapter 2.

'doing well' in life, and who do not expect to work to any serious extent after marriage. While they are young, such women may choose to work as fashion models, secretaries, receptionists, in public relations and other occupations that valorize youthful attractiveness and do not always offer long-term careers, because they do not anticipate continuing in employment in the long term anyway, and these occupations allow them to meet a large number of potential marriage partners. But they can be found in all occupations, including professional and managerial occupations as well as blue-collar work.

The marriage market continues to offer women equal or better chances of success than the labour market, even though very few marry a multimillionaire or a prince. In the past, women were often forced to adopt the marriage career, given their poor opportunities in the labour market, where male workers were preferred automatically, due to their obligation to be family breadwinners. Single women could be financially independent, but they rarely achieved affluence (Cargan and Melko 1982; Simon 1987; Gordon 1994). The fact remains that women can do as well from marriage careers as do men from employment careers. More important, women today have a choice between using the marriage market or the labour market to achieve social status, self-expression, and material well-being. The two options are not open to men because, as noted in Chapters 5 and 9, women and men rarely accept the idea of role reversal in the family.

The marriage career option remains permanently open to women, even in the new scenario. Women who work hard at an interesting job when young, can at any time switch to the marriage career instead if the right opportunity, that is man, comes up. The classic examples are the young model who marries a wealthy man and drops out of a career that would have been short-lived anyway, however successful, and the professional woman who realizes she does not have the talents or determination to rise very far and drops out of the labour market to become the model wife in a two-person career.

The *two-person career* is a useful term developed to identify those occupations and careers that can in practice involve the spouse in a junior partner support role. Examples are the wives of diplomats, politicians, and clergymen (Papanek 1973, 1979; Taylor and Hartley 1975; Finch 1983; Maret 1983: 112, 115; see also Fowlkes 1980). Upwardly mobile men in professional and managerial careers also find it advantageous to have the full support services and status-production work of a wife who has no competing career or job (Papanek 1979).

The fact that the marriage career option is permanently open to all women, does not guarantee that they have the necessary talents to be a success in this sphere. The productivity and quality of work done by full-time homemakers will of course vary, but its essentially private nature means that there are no public, fixed standards by which it can be assessed. There are four separate roles or functions that such a woman can offer in exchange for a man's financial support. Baby-making and child-rearing are the first and most enduring functions of wives, and require mothering skills. The prominence of this role has diminished over time as families have become smaller in modern societies and as women live longer. Housekeeping and domestic work is the second function and, like childcare, can be delegated to others, but must be organized and supervised. Budgetary control cannot be delegated, and can be crucial in affluent as well as poor households. The third function played by the dependent wife is the specialist manager of consumption, leisure, and social relations. The expensive non-working wife is herself a status symbol, and her conspicuous consumption advertises her husband's wealth and success. This function is increasingly important in rich consumer-oriented societies (Veblen, 1899/1953; Galbraith 1975) where leisure and consumption styles define a family's social status (Bourdieu 1984).[4] This role often requires superior social skills, for entertaining a husband's business or political contacts and clients at home, or for maintaining good social relations in public social gatherings or other social events at which status and wealth are displayed. The fourth role or function is the wife as a luxury consumption good herself: the doll, the beauty, the skilled sexual partner, the decorative and charming companion, the 'trophy wife'. Youth and beauty are at a premium in this area. Upwardly mobile and ambitious men are most likely to value physical attractiveness in a spouse (Elder 1969: 520). In countries where serial monogamy is the rule, rich men can change their wives for a younger model at regular intervals, just as they exchange their cars for younger models. In countries where polygamy is the rule, rich men add younger wives to their existing collection. Most full-time homemaker wives combine all four functions, to a greater or lesser extent, with varying degrees of skill, at different times. But in particular occupations, classes, cultures or countries, one or another function may carry most weight in determining the success and longevity of a marriage contract. For the senior diplomat, the third function may be the most important, and form the basis of a two-person career. For the working class man, the first two functions are often crucial. In some cultures, a marriage was not confirmed until children were born, or a man could divorce a woman who failed to produce children: child-bearing was the essence of marriage.[5] The key point here is that the services supplied by a dependent wife may be of four quite different types, mothering being only one of them. In the future, these four roles may become more sharply differentiated, especially in the context of serial monogamy.

The successful marriage career requires that a woman first catch, then keep

[4] Veblen (1899/1953: 74) predicted that, with economic development, conspicuous leisure would be replaced by the conspicuous consumption of goods. Thus the non-working wife today is just as busy as a woman in paid employment, devoting all her time to consumption work, as Galbraith (1975) pointed out.

[5] This is one reason for the custom of young women giving birth prior to any formal marriage to the father. Such births are socially acceptable in many cultures.

her husband, unless she can 'trade up' to an even better catch. In periods when there is a shortage of males, due to wars for example, many aspirants to the full-time homemaker role may fail to marry and are obliged to work all their lives. If a woman marries, but the services she provides are considered inadequate in a competitive field, she may lose the post of full-time homemaker and be forced to seek another position. Alternatively, a husband may be less successful than his wife expected, or be deficient in other ways, and she may be forced to leave him and find another partner and/or work herself. Much depends on a good choice of partner right from the start; errors are costly, on both sides. In contrast, the labour market offers a wider range of opportunities, although redundancy can be equally disastrous for workers who have spent their entire career with one employer, and have such employer-specific skills that they cannot regain an equivalent grade job elsewhere.

Modern societies usually provide some form of financial assistance administered by the state to individuals and families that are temporarily suffering extreme hardship, assistance that is variously termed welfare, social security, family assistance, income support, and so forth. (In some societies, such as Singapore, the family has this welfare role.)[6] For home-centred women, public welfare can be regarded as an acceptable alternative to the financial support of a male breadwinner, for example during economic recessions, when unskilled young men are often unemployed and make unattractive marriage partners. Mothers who accept the sexual division of labour in the home and do not work after marriage, or only work part-time or occasionally, are most likely to become welfare dependents if their marriage ends (Rainwater, Rein, and Schwartz 1986: 237). Some young women embark on a motherhood career as solo mothers, without marriage, because they know they can rely on state welfare to house and support them and their children. In some countries, lone mothers have priority for access to public sector housing. The key point here is that the home-centred woman who sees her role in life in terms of reproductive work rather than productive work may not take up employment even in a situation of relative poverty that would prompt an adaptive woman to take a job (Rainwater, Rein, and Schwartz 1986: 95–103, 237). There are diverse responses to the same situation in the same society depending on a person's aspirations, values, and preferences.

Home-centred women are not responsive to employment policy and to other policies that open or close opportunities in the public sphere. They are responsive to family policies and social policies that facilitate or reward—financially, or in public recognition and status—child-bearing and child-rearing. Similarly, the wealthier their husband, the larger the number of children they will usually have, although some pursue a more hedonistic lifestyle.

[6] In Europe, access to welfare state benefits became one of the defining features and consequences of citizenship. In Singapore, other mechanisms were utilized to define and develop national identity and citizenship (Hill and Fee 1995).

Work-centred Women and the Voluntary Childfree

The polar group consists of *work-centred* women, who can also be described as careerist or career-centred women. Strictly speaking, these labels are incorrect. The defining characteristic of this group is that their main priority in life is some activity other than motherhood and family life. At present in capitalist society *economic* activity is the principal channel for self-actualization, so employment is by far the most common type of central life activity in this group. But it might equally well be political activity, religious activity, intellectual activity, sporting activity, or artistic activity, all of which provide channels for competitive achievement and self-expression. Whatever line of activity is chosen, it is pursued with single-minded determination throughout life. This is the stereotypical 'male' career and work history, which became accessible to women as a result of the contraceptive revolution and the equal opportunities revolution. Childless women are concentrated in this group, but are not exclusive to it. About half of all women in the top professional and managerial grades remain childless (as illustrated by Wyatt and Langridge 1996: 243). Some work-centred women have children, but motherhood never provides their core self-identity and principal activity in life. Their priorities do not change suddenly after childbirth, as with some adaptive women. Work-centred women have children in the same way as men do: as an expression of normality, and as a weekend hobby. Childcare is mostly delegated to others, either purchased privately or left to public sector day care nurseries and schools.

Whether they choose it or not, this work profile is at present imposed on the vast majority of men. Men only stop working when they are unemployed, temporarily or permanently sick, in prison, or retired. In effect, men cannot voluntarily leave the labour market, as women do. In the new scenario, a minority of women also adopt this lifestyle. All the evidence suggests that it will remain a minority, probably no more than one-third in any industrial society and more commonly closer to 10% to 20% depending on local social constraints and opportunities.[7] There is also some evidence that the proportion of work-centred women can remain as low as 20% even among exceptionally able and highly qualified university graduate women (Ginzberg 1966: 45). The vast majority of women who claim to be career-oriented discover that their priorities change after they have children. The minority of work-centred women effectively adopt the male role and gender, even if their presentational style remains resolutely feminine.

Work-centred women do not fall into careers by accident. Their commitment

[7] Recent studies show that around 20% of women are in continuous full-time work across the lifecycle, with a maximum of about 30% in France (for example Hakim 1996a; Blank 1998; Marry *et al.* 1998; Tanaka 1998: 93–5).

to employment or equivalent activities in preference to motherhood as a central activity, emerges early in life and normally leads to a serious investment in educational qualifications or other equivalent training for their chosen main activity. For those choosing politics, religion, sport, or art, formal educational institutions may not provide the most directly relevant training.

The term 'career' is often associated with high status or professional occupations, and the term 'career-centred' is often used to imply a workaholic obsession with a job to the exclusion of all else. But these distortions do not have to be accepted. A career is a sequence of jobs or activities that offer some kind of progression or personal development within the chosen sphere of activity. In countries such as Germany, where private life and worklife are kept separate, a career-centred man may work regular 9 am to 5 pm hours, and reserve weekends and summer holidays for family life. In France, a shop assistant can regard herself as having a career, and can take pride in the development of her specialist knowledge of the products sold and her ability to advise customers. A career-centred person does not cease to have a private life, but fits family life around the career—for example relocating the family to a new city, or country, in order to take up attractive career or business opportunities, instead of choosing a career in teaching because it provides longer holidays and more time for family life than office jobs.

This group of people is responsive to policies that shape opportunities in the labour market, politics, business, sport, or the arts. For example, it is this group that responds first, and most energetically, to the new options opened up by equal opportunities policies. But this group is generally not responsive to social policy, in particular family policy. For example, work-centred women, especially those who choose to remain childless, are not affected by incentives to have more or fewer children, or by schemes permitting them to stay at home to care for children full-time.

Adaptive Women: Drifters and Unplanned Careers

Adaptive women form the largest and most diverse group among women, potentially encompassing 80% of all adult females, as indicated by the research reviewed in Chapters 4 and 5. It is often assumed that they are the *only* group, and hence representative of *all* women. However this group excludes the two minorities of women who have a clear primary commitment to one main activity—either work in the public sphere, or motherhood and a domestic role.

The adaptive group consists of women who want to *combine* employment and family without either taking priority, as illustrated by women who choose to become schoolteachers because it allows them to be at home with their children during the summer months and other school holidays. It includes women with *unplanned careers* who develop successful employment or political careers more by accident than by design or because the economic or political environment created special opportunities for them. The adaptive group includes large numbers of *drifters*, women with no definite ideas about the life they want, who respond to opportunities as they arise or not, and who modify their goals quickly and repeatedly in response to the changing social and economic environment. For example, they will take advantage of opportunities for higher education, but they may drop out before completing their course if they meet an attractive marriage partner.[8] They will enter the labour market during economic booms, but will not actively seek work during recessions. Adaptive women who do not actively seek employment may still take a job if it is offered to them. The ambivalent attitudes and mixed objectives of the adaptive group are reflected in their approach to education and other training, which they will take if it is offered to them, or is readily accessible, or becomes fashionable, but will never pursue against the odds. Some adaptive women acquire good educational qualifications more as an insurance policy than in the expectation of using them, in case their marriage ends in divorce or widowhood and the woman is obliged to earn her own living for a while. In addition, higher education, and the professional and managerial occupations that ensue, can in practice function in part as élite marriage markets.

The adaptive group includes women whose plans and behaviour depend very heavily on who they marry, whether they marry, and whether they stay married. In effect, their plans can be determined largely by their husbands. If they marry a wealthy businessman, an ambitious politician or a dedicated academic, they may engage in a two-person career, actively supporting and assisting their husband in all his endeavours rather than developing a business or career of their own. If they marry someone with only moderate earnings, they may work themselves to boost family income to a higher level. They return quickly to work after divorce even if they never worked while married, unlike home-centred women (Rainwater, Rein, and Schwartz 1986: 95–103, 237). If they do not marry, or marry late in life, they may work throughout life, and thus appear, in behaviour, to be work-centred women. However they differ from work-centred women in not being committed to a career from the start. There were large numbers of women in Europe and the USA who remained single, or were widowed very early, and worked throughout life in the 20th century due primarily to the shortage of marriageable men

[8] This may be one contributory factor in women's higher drop-out rates from educational courses that are demanding but lead eventually to remunerative careers (Fiorentine 1987; Cole and Fiorentine 1991: 220). It may be easier to marry a man who will complete the course, especially if one's own academic performance has been only moderate or poor.

after two World Wars. These women appeared to have 'male' careers, but by accident rather than by design, and most of them would have stopped working if they had married young. Many of them attained the very highest levels in their profession, in part because they never had the competing demands of a family.

Gerson's (1985) study of young American women shows that the adaptive group divides into two halves, suggesting two dominant approaches to solving the work-family conflict. Some adaptive women give a slight priority to motherhood over employment. They transfer to part-time jobs or to intermittent work, often in less demanding jobs in the local labour market, which offer convenience factors attractive to women, instead of the pay and promotion characteristics attractive to men. One example would be the women who have part-time jobs in local shops, supermarkets or offices.[9] Another example would be the woman pharmacist who does regular part-time or *locum* work in a local pharmacy while she is bringing up her children, or even permanently (Hakim 1998a: 221–34). Teaching and nursing are often chosen by women who want to fit paid work around their domestic role, rather than vice versa.

Adaptive women in professional, managerial, and other occupations that do not offer plentiful opportunities for part-time or intermittent work adopt other strategies to combine continuous full-time work with family life. Perhaps the most common strategy is to have only one child.[10] Substitute childcare is purchased, and husbands are invited to contribute to the child-rearing and domestic workload. It is the rise of the one-child family, rather than childlessness, that has had most impact on national fertility rates and that testifies to the absence of policies and structures enabling women to combine family life with paid work.

The adaptive group is very responsive to all government policies, just as they are responsive to all accidents and opportunities in their social and economic environment. Because this group is the largest single group in any society, and because it is so responsive to government policy, social scientists have often concluded that women 'generally' can readily be manipulated into working or not working, as the government wants, or as the economic cycle

[9] Part-time jobs exhibit even more diversity than full-time jobs, and are taken by widely varying groups of worker (Hakim 1998a: 102–77). However, in all advanced economies, only a minority of part-time workers would prefer to be working full-time (Hakim 1990a, 1997; OECD 1999), so they are clearly a distinctive group. A small 1996 study of women working part-time in banking in Australia suggested that the vast majority were adaptive women: four-fifths were working part-time voluntarily, with no interest in a full-time job; four-fifths regarded themselves as secondary earners, being married women or students; almost half had been out of the labour market before they took their part-time job, being full-time homemakers or students; and well over half had no intention of ever returning to full-time employment (Walsh 1999). It seems clear that market work had a low priority in the lives of these women working part-time.

[10] In countries where full-time jobs are the norm for women as well as men, and there are relatively few opportunities for part-time work, such as the USA and France, there is a higher incidence of one-child families than in countries where part-time work is plentiful, such as Britain and Holland.

dictates. However the responsiveness of women 'generally' will decline if the adaptive group declines in size relative to the two groups of committed women, both of whom are far less responsive to prompts and constraints in their social environment.

Social Constraints and Contextual Influences

Even the most liberal society and *laissez-faire* polity still has social institutions, laws, customs, national policies, and cultural constraints that shape and structure behaviour.[11] Preferences do not express themselves in a vacuum, but within the context of local social and cultural institutions. Most societies and cultures have models of the ideal man and woman, the ideal family and the ideal lifestyle, which are respected or given substance by government policy, the educational system, the arts, and mass media advertising, and are offered to young people as models to emulate and reproduce. In some societies, these models are defined tightly; in others they are drawn loosely and permit substantial variation. In addition, the choices people make are moulded by an unpredictable circus of events: economic recessions and booms, wars, the creation of new states or mergers of old ones, the rise and demise of socialism or dictatorships, revolutions, the rise or demise of religious fundamentalism, earthquakes and drought, simple changes of government with dramatic consequences. The vast majority of people accept the destiny offered to them by the country they are born in. Others design their own destiny by migrating to another country they like better—from an old nation to a new nation, or from a new nation to an old one. On top of these social, economic, and political influences on the shape of people's lives, there are the micro-level constraints and influences. The ambitious young man or woman may discover at some point in their education that they do *not* have the talents and abilities required for a particular career. The unambitious young man or woman may discover talents and abilities 'on the job', in the real world, that never blossomed in the sterile learning environment of the educational system. Accidents and ill-health, 'disastrous' marriages and 'brilliant' marriages, the luck of being accepted or rejected for a particular post, a particular company or trainee scheme—all these and many other accidents of fate shape individual lives.

[11] One illustration of this was the case of an immigrant Moslem man with four wives who claimed welfare benefits for all four dependent wives and their children when he was unemployed in England. He was informed that although his choice of religion, and hence polygamous marriages, were respected, so he would not be prosecuted for polygamy under English law, the benefit system would only recognize one wife and her children as being entitled to financial support. He was thus asked to decide which wife was to be his 'official' wife for the purposes of the English social welfare system.

Preferences do not predict outcomes with complete certainty because of the innumerable intervening factors in the social, political, and economic environment. But in the prosperous modern societies that permit a much greater variety of lifestyle choices than in the past, preferences become a much more important determinant of outcomes than in the past, when economic necessity or relative affluence was generally the dominant force shaping women's employment decisions. In particular, the combination of the contraceptive revolution, the equal opportunities revolution, and changes in the workforce discussed in Chapter 3, mean that in the new scenario women have genuine choices in how to shape their lives. The full-time homemaker role is no longer forced on women as the 'natural' choice for all, some modern Arab societies of the Gulf being exceptions; none the less a minority of women continue to choose it. The full-time work role is also not forced on women as a social obligation, Sweden and China being exceptions; yet a minority of women take up this option anyway. The majority of women fall between the two extremes and want the 'best of both worlds', in the sense of some combination of paid work and a family role. In practice, this choice often means lesser achievements in one or both spheres, compared to women and men who decide on one main priority.[12] The ambivalence of adaptive women also makes them highly responsive to external social, political, and economic influences and to cultural prescriptions about what is 'proper' or 'best'.

Table 6.1 presents estimates of the size of the three groups in the absence of systematic social structural influences, as evidenced by countries such as Britain and the USA, where contradictory policies are in force simultaneously, due to constant changes of government; where a *laissez faire* approach produces a relatively unregulated labour market and a great variety of jobs; and where a population that is richly diverse in terms of ethnic groups, religious groups, and political groups means that there is no single dominant ideology or intellectual perspective. Most societies are less 'open' than this, with social pressures which inflate, or squeeze the size of the three groups. With pronatalist policies offering strong public policy support for large families and stay-at-home mothers—as illustrated in the 1990s by France—the home-centred group can increase to one-third of all women. With strong fiscal and public welfare policies that push virtually all women into wage work—as illustrated by Sweden—the home-centred group shrinks to about 10% of women. In a society that offers no ideological, social, or economic

[12] Very few women have the talents and good luck to achieve significant success in public life and have a rich family life, notwithstanding appearances to the contrary. The fact that this is not possible routinely for *all* women is sometimes presented as evidence of sex discrimination and regarded as unfair. In reality, it is due to the fact that no one can be in two places at the same time and hard choices have to be made as to where one's priorities lie. Men understand this better than women, as noted in Chapter 9.

support for the full-time homemaker, there will be few women who develop, and retain, an open preference for this lifestyle. Similarly in societies that offer no ideological, social, or economic support for work-centred women, this group shrinks to one in ten of all women. With more encouragement, one-third of women can openly express this as their preferred lifestyle.[13] The adaptive group also shrinks or expands as social structural constraints and contextual influences encourage or discourage more decisive choices. Women appear to be more malleable than men, though this may change in the future.

None the less, social structural and cultural influences are no more than that: influences, not coercive powers. As theorists often point out, social structures create *variable* degrees of constraint and opportunity with which individual actors construct their choices (Giddens 1984; Mouzelis 1989). People can choose to reproduce or transform social structures. Women can and do reject even the most dominant patriarchal definitions of their proper role in society to do something else instead (Rosen and Aneshensel 1976).

Japan provides one example. Japan has a low and declining birthrate, despite constant moral exhortation for women to conform to their primary social duty and role in life, which is to have and raise children. By 1993, the fertility rate had fallen to an average of 1.46 children per woman, and continued falling in the 1990s. Young Japanese women find it increasingly difficult to accept the terms and conditions of motherhood, in the context of alternative options opening up to them. When they do succumb to social pressures, it is often at the most minimal, reluctant level, by having just one child (Jolivet 1997). Socialization processes and social pressure do not have guaranteed results in modern society.

Among social psychologists, there is renewed interest in self-concept and identity as central determinants of behaviour in affluent modern societies. As Breakwell puts it, identity directs action. Situational constraints remain important, but they gain meaning in the individual's definition of the situation. Situational constraints are mediated by identity (Breakwell 1986: 43). For example, one young woman simultaneously pursues a full-time job, studies for a postgraduate degree on a part-time basis, and gives birth to two children in quick succession. Another young woman regards the three activities as sufficiently demanding to be mutually exclusive. A situation that presents an impossible stumbling block to one person may be perceived as a stepping stone by someone else.

[13] An important feature of rich modern societies is that they permit all three work-lifestyle preferences to be openly expressed and implemented, even if only one type attracts the greatest social approval and support.

Cross-national Comparisons

Preference theory offers a substantially different perspective on cross-national comparative studies of women's role in society.

At present the usual approach is to seek to identify typologies of societies that have similar institutional profiles, similar economic, political and social histories, or apparently similar patterns of female employment. This approach builds on a well-established tradition in political science, sociology, and social policy analysis. Esping-Andersen's (1990) classification of the three types of welfare state is currently one of the most influential European contributions to this field. Adopting Kohn's (1989) classification of cross-national research, comparative analyses of women's employment treat nation as context, or unit of analysis, in order to develop and test the generality of findings and interpretations about the position of women in the family and in the labour market, and the relationship between the two. This approach is adopted in several unsuccessful recent attempts to explain the very variable levels of part-time work among women (Rosenfeld and Birkelund 1995; Fagan and Rubery 1996; Blossfeld and Hakim 1997; O'Reilly and Fagan 1998). Similarly, specialist analyses of the Eurobarometer surveys have tried to identify meaningful clusters of countries. For example the European Commission (1991a) tried to identify a typology of EU countries based on patterns of women's employment, especially around childbirth. Analysing a list of indicators taken from Eurobarometer No. 34, they concluded that East Germany and Denmark were each single isolated types, that southern European countries were similar, northern European countries were similar, with France and Belgium forming a separate special type. This typology was compared with those of other researchers, none having any obvious advantage, and none improving greatly on common sense classification. Studies usually conclude that the national societal context has some impact on patterns of women's employment at the national level because, of course, differences between countries have been observed.

It has to be asked whether any of these societal typologies do any more than offer *post hoc* rationalizations for cross-national differences or research findings that are already perceived as 'important' in some sense. Do they stand up to rigorous testing?[14] For example, can they explain why it is that two very different countries in Europe, Finland and Portugal, both have the highest and most stable *full-time* workrates for women, whereas high workrates include substantial amounts of part-time work in other countries,

[14] To be fair to Esping-Andersen's classification, it virtually ignored women, and was never intended to provide an explanatory framework for patterns of female employment, but has been adopted as a general classification of European societies.

such as Denmark and Sweden?[15] So far no one has been able to fully explain women's employment in Portugal, why it differs from the pattern in the other three southern European countries (see Table 3.3), and why full-time workrates are so high in the absence of any of the institutional supports and childcare services that are considered essential elsewhere in Europe. Portugal is often sidelined as 'peculiar', or even excluded altogether from comparative studies to avoid confronting the problem. Attempts to explain female employment in Finland, as compared with West Germany and the Netherlands, or in comparison with other Scandinavian countries, are little more successful (Pfau-Effinger 1993, 1998; Melkas and Anker 1998). Typologies of countries that focus on institutional factors do not have real predictive value, in practice, when tested properly. For example, Evans (1996) tested Esping-Andersen's thesis using ISSP data for 25 countries and several points in time. He found that awareness of social inequality was not related to support for redistributive policies across the 25 countries, and that attitudes in Britain were closer to attitudes in other European countries, such as West Germany, Sweden, and the Netherlands, than to the USA, New Zealand, Australia, and Canada. Overall, Esping-Andersen's typology of the three types of welfare state failed to predict country differences in support for redistributive policies. Competing theories proved no better at predicting actual national differences in support for redistributive policies (Evans 1996).

Most typologies of societies refer to institutional differences in the main, and assume that these institutional and social structural factors mould choices and behaviour. This assumption seems indisputable as regard political systems. It is less obvious as regard social institutions. They can mould choices and behaviour, if they are coercive enough, in the short term. But there must be some doubt as to whether they mould sex-role ideologies and preferences in the long term. First, as shown in Chapter 4, there are major differences *within* countries in sex-role ideologies and preferences, and the broad pattern of preferences is relatively constant across countries that seem to have little in common. Both Denmark and Spain have the highest proportion of adults preferring egalitarian family roles (see Table 4.1). This leads us to question whether country differences really are more significant than differences in lifestyle preference in shaping behaviour, unless societies are coercive. Second, the case of East Germany, and other socialist countries of eastern Europe, suggests that institutional factors can have just as tenuous a hold on behaviour today as attitudes and values were perceived to have in earlier decades.

In the former East Germany, the socialist government's policy of forcing all

[15] Sweden appears to have high workrates, but only because statistics are not comparable with those for other countries. Swedish statistics on the workforce include large numbers of mothers who are at home on long parental leave but retain the right to return to their jobs in due course. See also note 17.

non-disabled citizens to do paid work, in part because of labour shortages, meant that some 90% of women were in employment prior to unification (Braun, Scott, and Alwin 1994: 30). Some scholars have interpreted these high workrates as implying high levels of commitment to work. In reality, women's commitment to work was driven primarily by economic necessity, rather than by an intrinsic interest in paid work, because two incomes were necessary for a family, especially a family with children, and remained necessary in the transition period after unification. Otherwise, Braun, Scott, and Alwin (1994) found little difference between East and West Germany in sex-role attitudes in 1991, despite 44 years of very different social, economic, and political organization. Differences between East and West Germany in female workrates did not reflect substantial differences in sex-role ideologies. Women were equally likely to regard themselves as secondary earners in both East and West Germany.[16] This helps to explain why the pay gap between men and women was just as large in East Germany prior to unification as it is in most other western European countries, with occupational and industrial segregation contributing nothing to the pay gap (Sorensen and Trappe 1995). Braun, Scott, and Alwin (1994) conclude that egalitarian socialist states were more effective in changing behaviour than in changing sex-role attitudes. Similarly, other eastern European societies retained their sex-role attitudes virtually unaltered by 45 years of egalitarian socialist policies and high female workrates. For example, Hungarians still endorse role segregation in the family and believe that what most women want is a home and children, rather than a career. In effect, egalitarian socialist societies were able to alter women's behaviour in the short term, without changing sex-role ideologies and preferences in the long term (Braun, Scott, and Alwin 1994).

Similarly, China was successful in promoting egalitarian attitudes in many areas of family life, for example in eradicating centuries-old perceptions of sex differences in ability and in the practice of male dominance in the household. There was also substantial success in eradicating the sexual division of labour: a low-wage full-employment policy made it necessary for all adults to work and for couples to share domestic work. However in 1988, after the economic reform programme had introduced a new climate of opinion, there was a

[16] For example, there were similar patterns of agreement with the statement 'For a woman, it is more important to help her husband with his career than to get ahead herself'. As expected, West Germans were more likely than East Germans to agree that 'It is much better for everyone involved if the man is the achiever outside the home and the woman takes care of the home and family' (Braun, Scott, and Alwin 1994: Table 3). But the difference was surprisingly small, given that this statement proposes complete role segregation in the family, and given 44 years of separate ideological and institutional development in East and West Germany.

By 1996, East/West German attitudes had polarized again on this question. In West Germany, 65% of non-working wives compared to 30% of wives with jobs, endorsed the idea of complete role segregation in the family. In East Germany, the proportions were 30% of non-working wives and 18% of wives with jobs (Kurz 1997: Table 1). So the principal difference of opinion was between non-working wives in East and West Germany. In all four groups of women about one-quarter (or more) still endorse complete role segregation in the family.

major public debate over a new trend for women to withdraw from wage work. A survey carried out in 1993 in Beijing showed that one-quarter of women, one-third of wives, and two-fifths of men regarded role segregation in the home as the ideal to aim for (Hakim 1996a: 96). These results come from a survey of residents in Beijing, thus including the most educated groups in Chinese society, almost half of them professionals and senior administrators. Half the wives had earnings similar to or higher than their husbands. The one-child policy and excellent childcare services meant childcare was not a problem for these families. None the less, a substantial minority of women and men would still have preferred role segregation in the family, if this option were financially and politically feasible (Hakim 1996a: 95–8).

Treating nations as the unit of analysis, or context, for analyses of women's employment choices does not seem to have been fruitful, theoretically or empirically, even if it is convenient. We should in future identify the relative sizes of the three preference groups within each country, their relative visibility, and how preferences are translated into choices and behaviour, given the varying amounts of institutional support for each one. In effect, preference theory argues that work-lifestyle preferences are at least as important as social and economic factors in determining women's employment patterns in the new scenario. This perspective will of course only work well if all the countries being compared have achieved the new scenario for women. As the discussion in Chapter 3 indicates, this has not necessarily happened in all modern societies, not even in western Europe. Many countries are currently in a transition phase. Even so, cross-national comparisons should in future pay attention to work-lifestyle preferences as one main factor explaining cross-national differences, a factor of growing importance.

Other social scientists are drawing similar conclusions. An enormously detailed historical and comparative analysis of women's employment in the Netherlands, Belgium, France, Germany, Denmark, Sweden, and Britain led Pott-Buter (1993) to conclude that preferences offer the only explanation for the continuing exceptionally low female workrates in the Netherlands when compared with the other six neighbouring countries. She reached this conclusion only after replacing the misleading conventional headcount employment rates with more comparable full-time equivalent (FTE) workrates, although she was unable to adjust statistics for Sweden to take account of the practice of recording women as in employment when they are in fact at home full-time on extended maternity leave (Pott-Buter 1993: 203–8, 321–2).[17]

[17] For example, while the labour force participation rate of women with children under seven years was 86% according to Swedish labour force surveys, only 55% of the group were actually going to work, with the remaining 31% at home full-time (Jonung and Persson 1993; Pott-Buter 1993: 208).

Conflicting Interests

There are substantive differences between the priorities and values of home-centred women, adaptive women, and work-centred women that produce conflicting interests between the three groups, especially on family policy and employment policy. This phenomenon goes well beyond the current emphasis on 'diversity' in feminist theory.

The feminist idea of the diversity of women refers to cultural variations due to ethnic group or nationality, religion, sexual orientation—heterosexual versus homosexual—affluence, or social class. There is no suggestion that these variations are sufficiently important to break up the essential homogeneity of women as a social group and as an interest group. This means that the principal conflict of interests remains the conflict between men and women, and women's groups can continue to represent all women, more or less effectively. Feminist theorists are likely to overlook, trivialize or ignore conflicting interests *between women* because this heterogeneity of values and preferences weakens political demands for policy changes in favour of 'women generally'.[18]

Dependent wives, secondary earners, and career women who behave consistently like primary earners, whether they are married or not, form three interest groups with conflicting interests, which will vary in significance and intensity between countries or cultures, depending on local conventions and the local policy framework. However there is no single dividing line between the groups.

The childfree and couples with children might be expected to form two groups with conflicting interests. In practice, this does not always happen, because the childfree are often the first to recognize the serious burden of dependent children (Gerson 1985: 123–57), and to accept the need for state subsidies or other assistance for families with children. However the childfree may demand some public involvement, monitoring or control over parenting couples, on the grounds that if they are paid or subsidized for providing a public good and a public service, they must also be accountable for the quality of their work.

In some cases, the main conflict of interests is between women pursuing the marriage career and the two other groups, between women who prefer not to work after marriage, and women who want to work throughout life. In

[18] Most writers discuss women's diversity as a source of *variation* in attitudes, without concluding that this destroys women's common experience of male oppression. However, Lovenduski and Randall (1993: 89–91) state that women's diverse *experience* and cultural *identities* preclude common political *interests*; and they conclude that the increasing emphasis on women's diversity has divided the women's movement and eroded its political influence. Skocpol showed that a universalist maternalist movement was successful in the USA even before women got the vote. She concluded that the women's movement today would be more successful if it addressed the concerns of home-centred women as well as the concerns of career women (Skocpol 1992: 525–39, 1995).

other policy areas, it is adaptive women whose interests conflict with the other two groups. Demands for subsidized or public childcare services provide an example of the second type. Home-centred women do not need childcare services because they prefer to look after their children themselves, full-time. Indeed they are likely to resent public subsidies for childcare for 'irresponsible' and 'selfish' working mothers. Work-centred women do not hesitate to pay the cost of childcare services, whether full-cost private services or subsidized public services, partly because they are far more interested in their own activities than in child-rearing, and partly because they often have better-paid jobs and can afford to pay for good quality substitute childcare services. Paying for childcare is accepted by work-centred women, along with paying for other domestic services, work clothes, and transport to work. It is adaptive women, who are torn between the desire to work and the desire to be full-time homemakers, who are most likely to demand affordable high quality childcare services provided by the state, in order to improve their flexibility of choice and assuage their guilt. They claim their interests are common to all women, but they are simply one interest group among three.

In employment policy, the main conflict of interests is between home-centred women and the other two groups, as working women stand together to defend their right of access to the labour market and the need to safeguard equal opportunities policies. Home-centred women who look to the male breadwinner to support them can be deeply ambivalent, at best, about policies that give equal chances to men and women in the labour market, as illustrated by the Equal Rights Amendment (ERA) debate in the USA (Ehrenreich 1984; Marshall 1987). They do not forget that the long-standing convention of male advantage in the workplace was based on the assumption that, sooner or later, all men would have a family to support and therefore needed a breadwinner wage—and for them this still holds true. The old 'marriage bar' rule that forced women to resign from their (white-collar) jobs at marriage has been eliminated by sex discrimination laws. But the weaker idea that male breadwinners should have priority when jobs are scarce continues to attract widespread support. For example, the idea is still endorsed by half of all men and half of all full-time homemakers in Britain. Across all social classes, half of all homemaker women and half of adult men agree that 'in times of high unemployment married women should stay at home', whereas a two-thirds majority of working women reject the idea (see Table 4.3), with little difference between women working full-time or part-time, or between social classes. In Germany, immediately after World War II, widows and male workers waged a bitter war against married women who took scarce paid jobs, denouncing them as 'double income earners'. The idea that main breadwinners should have priority in getting jobs persisted well into the 1980s in both Germanies, along with the idea that main breadwinners were entitled to higher wages and to preferential tax treatment (Braun, Scott, and Alwin 1994:

37–8; Oertzen and Rietzschel 1998: 178–9, 182–3, 186). There are similar historical antecedents for the conflicting interests of working wives and dependent wives in Britain (Kessler-Harris 1990: 64–80).

A cross-national comparative study of women's support for policies to reduce gender inequality in the labour market produced similar conclusions. Davis and Robinson (1991) used the ISSP to compare women in the USA, Britain, West Germany, and Austria in the mid-1980s. They found that hours worked had no impact at all, confirming that women working full-time and part-time hours stand together on employment policy issues in all four countries. The main division within the female population was between those women who were dependent on a male breadwinner and those who were not. The wives of a sole breadwinner were significantly less supportive of policies to reduce sex inequalities in the labour market. As one of the attitude questions proposed positive discrimination in favour of women in the workforce,[19] the study revealed differences more clearly than studies using more anodyne questions. The USA was also different from European countries in that women's own employment experience significantly increased support for equality policies compared to women who had never worked. Overall, there was far more variation in the level of women's support for policies to eradicate gender inequalities in the labour market than in awareness of these inequalities, with no association between the two. Support for interventionist policies was greatest among less-educated women (Davis and Robinson 1991).

The conflicting interests of women are illustrated by debates over women's access to education in Europe and by the abortion debate and conflict over the ERA in the USA. Women's colleges were established in Cambridge University only in the late 19th century, creating new teaching staff positions for women as well as giving girls access to higher education. This stimulated hostility and conflict between the wives of male academics, many of whom were not well-educated and/or openly rejected any professional ambition for themselves, and the women academics who taught in the women's colleges who did, often, espouse feminist causes. Women academics and university students were ridiculed as unfeminine, unattractive, and even immoral. Men exploited the conflict between the two groups, using it to discourage too many girls from obtaining a university education and competing with men for jobs (Sciama 1984: 53).

[19] Positive discrimination is currently unlawful in the European Union, although it is often confused with affirmative action, which is permissible, as noted in Chapter 9. In the USA, there is no national policy or federal law on the matter, and 'affirmative action' policies often combine positive discrimination in employment hirings with affirmative action, especially to boost access to the educational system among blacks and Hispanics. Some states, institutions, and employers have implemented 'affirmative action' policies that include positive discrimination, but the fairness and legality of such policies became disputed by the end of the 1990s. For example in 1996 the State of California voted to end policies allowing any form of preference, or discrimination, in favour of or against ethnic or social groups, men or women, in state-funded education and employment.

In the USA, the abortion debate was turned into a debate on the place and meaning of motherhood in women's lives (Luker 1984; Gerson 1987; Skocpol 1987). On both sides, over 80% of activists were women, of similar age, family status, and education. The two groups were divided primarily by lifestyle choices and associated values, one group having a primary commitment to family life, and the pro-choice group having a primary commitment to full-time, lifelong employment outside the home. The real issue is, of course, women's access to reliable contraception, which enables them to manage and control their fertility so as to pursue lifetime employment careers or other roles in public life. In the USA, the debate about changing sex-roles, and the implications for family life, focused on abortion instead. It developed into a deep and bitter conflict between women, which over-rode social class and ethnic cleavages, a conflict about what type of family the state should support, and about women's 'proper' place in society (Luker 1984; Gerson 1987; Skocpol 1987; see also Marshall 1987).[20]

Gerson (1987) describes the battle as profoundly and inescapably ideological, with both sides viewing their disagreement as a zero-sum game, where one group's victory is defined as another group's loss. Her understanding of this very public conflict of interests between what has been described as the two women's movements in the USA was based on her research on young women's preferences and choices between full-time motherhood, combined employment and motherhood, or a career combined with childlessness discussed in Chapter 5. That study also revealed the conflicting interests, ideologies, and political positions of home-centred and work-centred women (Gerson 1985: 132, 186–90, 223). Home-centred women resented social pressures on them to go out to work, the devaluation of the homemaker role and of full-time mothering, and the withdrawal of public support for single breadwinner families. They were often ambivalent about equal opportunities policies that created a more competitive labour market, because this might impact on their husband's opportunities for obtaining good jobs or promotion. For career women who were considering remaining childless as a permanent option, full-time homemakers represented everything they had rejected and left behind. Gerson sees polarization between the two groups of women as growing slowly over time, so that women's political views are likely to diverge further in the USA in the future (Gerson 1987).

A more optimistic view is that the heterogeneity of women's preferences opens up opportunities which can be exploited to the mutual advantage of all. For example full-time homemakers might be the ideal childminders for

[20] Beck (1986/1992) went a lot further to argue that in some societies, particularly Germany, but not yet France or Britain, social class has ceased *generally* to be the main determinant of lifestyles and biographies, which are becoming individualized. Although he admitted that there is a possibility of polarization of lifestyles within younger generations of women along the lines of the educational hierarchy (Beck 1992: 120), he did not foresee the emergence of conflicting interests.

work-centred and adaptive women. However, it is important for public policy, especially family policy, to recognize that there is a diversity of lifestyle choices, and to offer *all* of them equal levels of moral and financial support. Bitter disputes over public policy are caused in effect by the 'one policy fits all' approach, which necessarily treats one lifestyle group more advantageously than the others, an issue discussed further in Chapter 8.

The problem of conflicting interests helps to explain why opinion polls and attitude surveys regularly show women collectively to have apparently contradictory or inconsistent views. With women divided into three groups—rather than the common assumption of a single dividing line between career women and homemakers—there are cross-cutting views and interests on, say, childcare policy and employment policy. Similarly perspectives are too complex to be fitted onto a continuum from 'pro-feminist' to 'anti-feminist', or from 'modern' to 'traditional'. Cross-national comparative studies that differentiate between the many aspects of attitudes to women's role in society discover that there is little or no correlation between the separate aspects (Haller, Höllinger, and Gomilschak 1999). People can favour separate roles for men and women but also support women's right to work and the case for equal opportunities. People can favour the dual-earner family and also recognize that children suffer detriment from a working mother. It seems that social scientists' thinking has so far been less sophisticated than that of the people we observe.

Contradictory Evidence: Female Depression

The heterogeneity of women's preferences and the idea of conflicting interests between groups of women are sometimes challenged. The strongest piece of conflicting evidence currently available is research showing that full-time housewives are more often depressed than women with jobs. The usual interpretation of this finding is that women generally prefer to have paid jobs and that being a housewife depresses self-esteem and mental health. However, the reasons for this research result are somewhat more complex than is usually recognized. There are three generally observed patterns in mental health that contribute to this.

First, there is the 'healthy worker effect'. In general, employers select the healthiest people for jobs, so that people not in employment are physically and mentally less healthy than people in employment, due to selection effects. The healthy worker effect is a well established and undisputed phenomenon. Because women leave and re-enter the workforce more frequently than men, even after the equal opportunities revolution (Hakim 1996a, 1996c), and because the female workforce is generally smaller than the male workforce, selection effects will be even stronger among women than among men. So the healthy worker effect is stronger among women than among men.

Second, it is well established that women as a group have much higher rates of mental illness than men as a group. Women are twice as likely to experience clinical depression, that is, major depression that may require treatment. Women outnumber men two to one among psychiatric patients in the western world. Women are more than twice as likely as men to attempt suicide.[21] As noted in Chapter 5, young women in the NCDS sample were twice as likely as young men to report depression, with a similar imbalance in the 1970 cohort when interviewed in the 1990s (Bynner, Ferri, and Shepherd 1997: 79). It appears that women invest more of their identities in personal relationships, especially in their children, and they are more often distressed, even destroyed, when these primary relationships go wrong or fail in some way. What is less well understood is the steady increase in rates of depression and mental illness during the 20th century, among both men and women, at a time of increasing prosperity. James (1997) provides a detailed discussion of the possible explanations for rising rates of mental illness and rising demand for counselling and psychotherapy of all kinds in prosperous modern societies, and he also considers reasons for the continuing large sex differential. One possible explanation is that women have lower levels of serotonin than men. Many textbooks on sex differences discuss the sex differential in rates of mental illness (for example Archer and Lloyd 1982). Looking at the issue from a sociological perspective, Mirowsky and Ross (1995) note that there are also sex differences in rates of psychological distress, as distinct from clinical depression. After controlling for all likely causes and explanations, including sex differences in emotional expressiveness and 'feminine' rather than 'masculine' emotional responses to problems, they found that women still experience distress about 30% more often than men. Similarly, Warr and Yearta (1995) found a persistent 50% sex differential in sickness absence from work, even after all possible causes were added as controls to their analysis of LFS data for employed people of working age (16–59/64 years) in Britain in 1991. In general, women with full-time jobs had the highest rates of sickness absence. Contrary to expectation, the sex differential is largest in the highest grade, professional and managerial occupations, and almost disappears in the lower grade occupations. They concluded that motivational factors must contribute to these patterns of sickness absence.

Third, it is well-established that general happiness and satisfaction with life displays a U-shaped trend among people who have children. Contrary to the popular stereotype, children seriously depress satisfaction levels in the

[21] However some argue that sex differences in mental health disappear if alcoholism and drug use are added into the picture.

middle years of marriage. Spouses are most satisfied with their marriage, and with life in general, at the two extremes of the lifecycle, prior to having children and after the children have left home. Marital satisfaction declines from the time children are born up to the teenage years, then rises again to former levels after children leave home and after retirement. These patterns were established from the 1970s onwards in societies such as the USA and western Europe, but are believed to have wider validity (Burr 1970; Luckey and Bain 1970; Rollins and Feldman 1970; Boulton 1983: 18–19; Whyte 1990: 140–1). Consistent results are reported by other studies. Divorcing couples have more children than couples who remain married, and their children are born closely spaced in a short period of time, so that the impact of child-rearing work is concentrated in a narrow time frame (Gibson 1980). In the past, psychotherapists, psychiatrists, counsellors and social workers have regarded voluntary childlessness as emotionally unhealthy or immature, and they have routinely insisted that parenthood would provide a solution to personal or marital problems. This belief that children help to forge a stronger bond between spouses has now been quietly dropped, with increasing recognition that childless marriages are happier than those with children (Goodbody 1977: 428; Boulton 1983: 3–7). This conclusion coincides with small group theory which has long stated that a dyad is the most satisfactory of human relationships. It also explains why couples with children often react with envy or resentment to couples who avoid the burdens and costs of child-rearing. Overall, studies have always found that happiness, however measured, is lower, on average, and depression and mental health problems are more common among women with children than among women without children, despite the fact that marriage is generally associated with higher levels of physical and mental health than among non-married people.

Almost all these studies were carried out on people whose adult lives started before the contraceptive revolution gave women (and men) real control over child-bearing. That is, these studies must include the women (and men) who had children because it was a woman's unavoidable destiny and the price of marriage rather than because they chose to, women who today would be childfree by choice. The problem of unwanted or resented motherhood would thus be added to the financial burden of children and the negative impact of children on lifestyle and careers. In the new scenario after the contraceptive revolution, when motherhood becomes an active choice rather than an imposition, we might expect smaller differences in the marital satisfaction and life satisfaction of couples with and without children. There is some evidence of this already. A study of highly educated women in Australia in the 1980s found that women had become consciously calculating in their well-defined preferences for childlessness, one child only, or two or more children. Women explicitly weighed up the advantages and disadvantages of a career and/or children, but the three groups drew quite different conclusions in support of their preferences (Callan 1986; see also Callan 1985). The negative consequences of a child upon lifestyles and careers are discounted by women who do want children, who perceive the costs as outweighed by the benefits.

Healthy worker selection effects alone ensure that women and men with jobs will always be a group displaying higher rates of physical and mental well-being than women and men without jobs.[22] The persistent sex difference in mental health means that wives collectively are more likely to suffer depression than husbands collectively. These two fairly universal factors in combination automatically predict that women at home full-time will have the highest rates of clinical depression while men in full-time employment will have the highest levels of psychological well-being and the lowest rates of ill health. If we add in the negative impact of child-rearing on marital satisfaction and general happiness, mothers of young children without jobs will undoubtedly be the most depressed. This last factor may possibly decline in importance after the contraceptive revolution, but it was still observed among 33-year-olds in the 1990s, as shown in Chapter 5.

All of these patterns are reflected in a series of studies by George Brown and his colleagues, which provide perhaps the most detailed and careful research on the aetiology of clinical depression currently available (Brown 1993; Brown and Harris 1978; Brown, Harris, and Hepworth 1995; Brown and Bifulco 1990; Nazroo, Edwards, and Brown 1997). The *Social Origins of Depression* concluded that the lack of employment outside the home was not in itself a cause of clinical depression in women but a contextual factor defining a woman's vulnerability to mental illness. A job outside the home usually increased a woman's friendship network, and good personal relationships generally helped women to cope with the pressures imposed by stressful life-events, such as divorce or a husband losing his job, and ongoing difficulties, such as living in poor quality housing or persistent poverty. The study confirmed that depression was far more common among women with children at home, especially those in the less affluent working class, who were more likely to experience severely stressful life events and major ongoing difficulties (Brown and Harris 1978).

This first report, showing clinical depression to be an understandable response to adversity, especially life events involving rejection, loss, and disappointment, was regarded as controversial, and provoked a lively debate over its methods and conclusions. Useful summaries of this debate are provided by Marshall (1990: 205–33) and Brown (1993). The timing of the study is also

[22] Solo mothers seem to contradict this rule, as those with full-time jobs have much higher rates of depression than those with part-time jobs or no jobs (Brown and Bifulco 1990: 173; Brown and Moran 1997: 27). However solo mothers have many distinctive characteristics that cloud the picture, notably higher levels of financial hardship and social isolation, and their decision to work full-time is often driven by financial hardship rather than personal preference.

important. This early report was based on interviews over the period 1969–1975 with women aged 18–65 years, the great majority of whom would thus have reached adulthood before the contraceptive revolution of the mid-1960s in Britain, and before women had genuine lifestyle choices to make.

A subsequent study carried out in the early 1980s, of low-income mothers aged 18–50 with one or more children under 18 years at home is thus of even greater interest (Brown and Bifulco 1990). This sample of mothers is young enough for half the sample to have reached adult life after the contraceptive revolution. This study compared women with full-time jobs, women with part-time jobs, and non-working women, all of whom had recently experienced a severe crisis. It found that women working part-time had the very lowest risk of clinical depression, among solo mothers as well as among wives. Wives with full-time jobs and wives at home full-time had equally high rates of depression. Solo mothers only developed depression if they were working full-time. This suggests that part-timers really do have 'the best of both worlds' and that the working/not-working dichotomy is too simplistic for studies of female depression. For example, negative self-evaluation—which is related to depression—did not differ between working and non-working women. Once again, Brown found that the presence of a child under five years old at home was associated with higher rates of clinical depression among mothers without jobs. Among women with full-time jobs, family crises and problems with family relationships were the main catalysts for depression, whether they were personally committed to work or were working for purely financial reasons. Among the non-working women, long-term financial problems seemed to be just as important a catalyst as the presence of a young child at home and problems in relationships with partners. In effect, family problems of one sort or another were the main causes of depression, among both working and non-working women. The study concluded that depression was least likely if women were able to pursue their preferred activity and role, whether as full-time mother or as a worker in the market economy, and that women should be helped to achieve their desired role (Brown and Bifulco 1990: 178; Brown 1993: 33–5).

Reasons for sex differences in depression were explored more fully in an elegantly designed study of 100 married couples who had recently suffered a common stressful life event in the 1990s (Nazroo, Edwards, and Brown 1997). Wives were five times more likely than their husbands to suffer depression as a result of a crisis concerning the couple's children, reproduction, or housing, especially if they identified strongly with the homemaker role. No doubt, fathers were just as upset as mothers at a son becoming delinquent or criminal; however they did not become clinically depressed as often as the mothers. Wives were also more likely to get depressed at other events that affected both partners, such as a husband's arrest. Husbands were most likely to suffer depression when they failed in their role as financial provider for the family, but wives also became depressive in these cases, although less often. So the disproportionately high rates of female depression—23% compared to 13% for husbands in this sample—were connected primarily with problems in family relationships, especially problems with children, as found in the previous study, but were not limited to this. In sum, the research of Brown and his colleagues shows that it is problems with children and relationships with partners that are the most important catalysts of female depression, among both working and non-working women. The homemaker role does not, of itself, carry higher risks. Problems that produce feelings of loss, humiliation, and entrapment have the highest risk of causing depression, and these occur to (full-time) working women as well as to full-time mothers.[23]

Complementary results emerge from a longitudinal study of 292 mothers who were interviewed on four occasions before their baby reached three and a half years (Hock *et al.* 1988, reported in James 1997: 187–8). The mothers were asked about their preference between continuing with paid work or staying at home full-time with their child. As Table 4.8 shows, most mothers do stay at home with young children, or else they work part-time hours only. Few mothers work full-time when their children are very young. Significant psychological differences were found between the women whose identity was heavily invested in the role of mother and who worked primarily for financial reasons, if at all, after the birth, and women who were committed to their careers, who worked for personal reasons as much as for the money, and who regarded motherhood as just one of their many interests in life. The two groups differed in their feelings about leaving their child. The home-centred women who did work were very anxious about having to leave their child, and were distressed by doing so. The work-centred women were happy to leave their children in a daycare centre so they could continue with their job.[24] In effect, it was the *consistency*, or lack of it, between role preferences and actual activities that determined women's psychological well-being, not the decision to return to work or to stay at home of itself.

Finally, life events and the social environment may produce the catalysts for depression, but they cannot provide a complete explanation. All studies show that only a minority of about one in five women experiencing a stressful life event goes on to develop depression (Brown 1993: 30). Four-fifths are able to cope with crises. Clearly, many other factors, including psychological and biological factors, play a part in resistance or vulnerability to depression, as Brown himself recognizes (1993: 38–9, 45).

[23] George Brown's research on female depression was done in Britain, where social support for full-time homemakers caring for children dwindled rapidly after the equal opportunities revolution. It thus provides a strong test of the thesis that being a homemaker, of itself, carries a higher risk of depression. Any risk would of course be lower in countries with high social support for full-time mothers and homemakers, such as West Germany, Italy, and Japan.

[24] This study dichotomized participants into just two groups, those centred on motherhood and the family role, and those centred on the work role outside the home.

Sources of the Three Preferences

There is no single factor that determines or explains why women differ so significantly in their preferences. Ability, however measured, is certainly not a principal determinant, nor is educational level, although work-centred women are generally the most highly educated group. Economists have overstated the importance of educational qualifications as a predictor of employment decisions. It appears that qualifications attained have often been acting as a proxy variable for the effects of work-lifestyle goals, status aspirations, and motivation (Rainwater, Rein, and Schwartz 1986: 99). As shown in Chapter 3, sex-role attitudes become more important the more highly educated and affluent a woman is (see Table 3.4). And as shown in Chapters 4 and 5, the polarization of preferences is found among all groups of women, including the most highly educated and most able.

So why do women develop different work-lifestyle preferences? What determines their belonging to one or another of the three groups? An enormous array of factors in combination, the significance of each varying from one person to another. Socialization within family, school, and peer group is not a sufficient explanation for the choices people make. In *all* societies, girls are taught to be girls, and boys are taught to be boys, with hugely variable results (Adler 1993). A woman who rejects motherhood and prefers the employment career is frequently rejecting her mother as a role model, yet her sisters may respond to the same experiences by emulating the mother in question. Responses differ. Psycho-physiological factors of the sort described by Goldberg (1993) under the general label of 'testosterone' may make a small contribution. Testosterone levels vary little across women, whereas the variation across men is huge (see Figure 9.1), especially over the lifecycle (Treadwell 1987: 269, 279). Only a tiny minority of women approach the range for men, potentially leading to 'masculine' levels of aggression, determination to succeed, and achievement orientation. Social factors must contribute the greater part of explanations for women's achievement orientation expressing itself within the public sphere rather than in the private sphere of the family.

Social psychologists, especially career counsellors, have an interest in *predictive* theory, and have expended more effort than sociologists in trying to explain why women form such very different work-lifestyle preferences. They have so far failed to identify any single family characteristic, experience, or personal characteristic that is sufficiently important to predict a woman's preference as between home and work, or to predict career-orientation and career-achievement (Faver 1984; Betz and Fitzgerald 1987; Farmer and Associates 1997). Sociologists are unlikely to be more successful. Gerson explains the differences between women as the result of 'uneven exposure to social change and differing reactions to that exposure' (Gerson 1985: 214). Which amounts to no more than saying that people's reactions vary.

A massive compendium and synthesis of the USA research literature on this subject was compiled by Betz and Fitzgerald (1987). They found that personality and sex-role ideology are strongly associated with career-orientation and career-achievement for women, and might even be treated as predictors, as they seem to develop early in childhood and adolescence. However from our perspective, sex-role ideology and career-orientation are two aspects of a single over-arching work-lifestyle preference. Psychologists measure them separately, with different scales, but conceptually they are connected, describing the role(s) one wants to play in life. Personality is a conceptually separate factor.

Women who are career-oriented tend to have high self-esteem and self-confidence, and this factor is predictive of women's career achievements, especially in male-dominated occupations such as scientist or politician. Women generally tend to underestimate themselves, whereas men usually overestimate their abilities and performance. This pattern is linked to women's tendency to attribute success to external factors, such as luck, whereas men attribute their success to their own abilities, as noted in Chapter 1. Women tend to attribute their failures to internal sources, such as lack of ability or effort, whereas men excuse failure by external factors, such as bad luck. A higher level of what psychologists call *instrumentality* or *independence*—essentially self-assertion and an emphasis on competence—among women is related to the choice of 'male' subjects in school and male-dominated occupations and greater career achievement. Women following high status professional careers such as medicine are more independent, individualistic, autonomous, and significantly less suggestible and submissive than women in general. Career-oriented women are more similar in personality to career-oriented men than to women in general. Career-oriented women generally obtain higher scores on aptitude, ability, and achievement tests than do home-centred women. Several studies found that women who persist and succeed in science courses, have the very highest ability scores whereas science courses attract men with variable levels of ability. Interestingly, career-oriented women score as high on tests of 'feminine' expressiveness as they do on tests of 'masculine' instrumentality/independence. What distinguishes home-centred women is that they score high on the 'feminine' expressiveness scale only (Betz and Fitzgerald 1987: 123; Farmer and Associates 1997: 299–300).

An interesting study of 200 professional couples found significant personality differences between full-time homemakers and working wives, and between their husbands. Burke and Weir (1976) studied 200 couples in Ontario, Canada, all with a husband who was an engineer or an accountant. The occupational grade of the working wives varied substantially, so they can be described as dual-*earner* couples, thus understating differences between dual-*career* couples and single-career couples. Full-time homemakers were more passive, and were more concerned with relationships and with belonging. The husbands of housewives were most concerned with authority, and were most dominant and assertive in relationships. The personality structure of working wives resembled that of working husbands rather than that of housewives, except for a low desire to control other people. The results indicate personality differences between the two types of marriage, with dual-earner couples operating a collegial partnership, while single-earner couples had well-matched complementary personality structures. Burke and Weir (1976: 453–4) note that several other USA studies also found personality differences between working and non-working college-educated women. Given that women had access to a college education in the USA long before educational equality was achieved in Europe (see Chapter 7), these early North American studies indicate the likely pattern of developments in Europe in the 21st century.

Psychologists have devoted substantial effort to devising attitude scales that explore and measure all aspects of sex-role ideology, going well beyond the question of preferences regarding sex-roles in the family (Beere 1979; Betz and Fitzgerald 1987: 124–8). The main findings are fairly consistent across studies: women are more 'liberal' than men;[25] younger women are more 'liberal' than older women, with some evidence of (generational) change over time; 'liberal' sex-role attitudes are associated with stronger career motivation, higher educational aspirations, higher career aspirations, a tendency to remain single, a tendency to remain childless if married, perceived self-competence, higher intelligence on several measures, and stronger career development. A 'liberal' sex-role ideology has been found to be a powerful predictor of women's career involvement, in virtually any field of work, including skilled crafts and technical fields as well as male-dominated professional and managerial occupations. There is no evidence of any sex differential in achievement motivation, but men and women do seem to 'apply' it differently.

Finally, almost all these variables are interlinked, more or less strongly. Self-esteem and instrumentality are associated. Instrumentality is linked to competitiveness. And competitiveness, which is stronger among men, is strongly related to a preference for extrinsic rewards from work: pay, promotion, and advancement up the hierarchy. One important finding is that the *expression* of high intellectual ability is linked to the rejection of 'traditional' sex-role ideology. It seems that home-centred women are just as able as career-oriented women, but they eschew the overt display of high competence, especially in competitive contexts (Betz and Fitzgerald 1987: 124).

One problem with all these studies is that the differences they report, even

[25] In these studies, a 'liberal' sex-role ideology is more career-oriented whereas a 'traditional' sex-role ideology is more home-centred.

when statistically significant, are often *substantively small*. It appears that there is no single personality type or psychological factor which strongly distinguishes the work-centred woman from the home-centred woman. Cumulatively, all these factors may be important and predictive. But the fragmented approach of variable sociology and psychology means that researchers do not look at the collective impact of clusters of linked variables.

The social background factors that are associated with a career-orientation in women are: a working mother; access to female role models; a supportive father; highly educated parents; work experience as an adolescent; a relatively androgenous upbringing; and attendance at girls-only schools and colleges (Betz and Fitzgerald 1987: 143). Other studies have found that young women are more likely to develop a close relationship with a supportive father, who then introduces them to the possibilities of male-dominated professional and managerial careers, if there are no brothers in the family, especially if the girl is an only child (Fogarty, Rapoport, and Rapoport 1971: 300–33). Smaller families make this family situation far more common today than it was in the past. So this could be an important factor contributing to the inter-generational trend toward a more work-centred outlook among women. Attendance at all-women schools and colleges also regularly emerges as a crucial factor that allows women's talents to develop unconstrained by the presence of men. Education in all-women schools and colleges, plus a strong bond with their father, are the only common characteristics that emerge from comparative studies of women who became political leaders: Golda Meir, Margaret Thatcher, Isabel Peron, Corazon Aquino, Violetta Chamorro, Indira Gandhi, and Benazir Bhutto (Genovese 1993: 214–7; see also Sunder Rajan 1994). Similarly, single-sex education regularly emerges as a characteristic of women who reach the highest levels in management and the professions (for example, Wyatt and Langridge 1996: 241). Virtually all studies show that the husband's attitude toward his wife working is a crucial intervening factor.

It appears that a large number of factors in combination produce the 'normal' distribution of women's responses to the conflict between family and employment. The distribution simply reflects the usual variation in women's experiences and responses to them, and the three preference groups constitute three identifiably different ideal-types within it. There is no single factor, or experience, that stands out as especially important, and responses vary anyway.

As Nuttin (1984) points out, *all* people have a need to exercise agency, to act upon the world, to demonstrate competence and efficacy. The only difference between women and men is that women can exercise agency through two extra social roles in the private sphere: parenting and homemaking. These two roles have so far generally been less accessible to men, and women's attitudes to them have been the subject of some debate among feminists. Research suggests that, even in the new scenario, these roles will continue to be attractive to many women as avenues for exercising agency and getting 'causal pleasure', as Nuttin (1984: 93–7) puts it.

Conclusions

Preference theory identifies three distinct 'packages' of predispositions and work-lifestyle preferences which lead people to respond in different ways to the social, economic, and political environment they are born into, or migrate into. Preference theory states that women are not a homogenous group but divide into three distinctive groups, with different patterns of behaviour, and different responses to policies. Women are heterogeneous and so also are men, to a lesser extent. These differences are becoming increasingly important in affluent modern societies in the 21st century. The presentation here has focused on women because they were already exhibiting heterogeneous behaviour by the end of the 20th century in some societies—notably the USA and Britain—and are thus the pioneers of the new scenario. As we move into the 21st century, it is likely that men will begin to reveal variations in their work-lifestyle preferences, a topic discussed further in Chapter 9.

Neither socialization processes nor biological programming are so uniformly successful and complete as to have guaranteed results. Public policies and social institutions may encourage and promote certain choices and behaviours, but they too cannot guarantee acceptance and conformity. A minority of women have no interest in employment, careers, or economic independence and do not plan to work long term unless things go seriously wrong for them. Their aim is to marry as well as they can and give up paid employment to become full-time homemakers and mothers. The group includes highly educated women as well as those who do not get any qualifications. As shown in Chapter 7, universities provide an élite marriage market as well as a springboard for employment careers. In contrast, other women actively reject the sexual division of labour in the home, expect to work full-time and continuously throughout life, and prefer symmetrical roles for husband and wife rather than separate roles. The third group is numerically dominant: women who are determined to combine employment and family work, so become secondary earners. They may work full-time early in life, but later switch to part-time jobs on a semi-permanent basis, and/or to intermittent employment (Hakim 1996a: 132–9; 1997). The characteristics and size of the three groups are revealed most fully in *laissez-faire*, liberal societies.

In the past, employment has almost always been driven by financial considerations, and it still is, for wives in poor families (Davies and Joshi 1998). After the new scenario is achieved in affluent modern societies of the

21st century, women's employment decisions, and, eventually, those of men also, will be driven primarily by their personal preferences for one of three qualitatively different work-lifestyles. Differences between men and women will become less important than the *conflicting* interests of people with three work-lifestyle preferences, who create three types of family. Preference theory throws new light on existing social and economic theories, restricting them to particular contexts, rather than replacing them wholesale. And female heterogeneity explains the often contradictory results of research in recent decades.

The three work-lifestyle preferences are presented here as ideal-types, that is, simplifications of reality. It is to be expected that case studies will reveal a more complex reality in particular situations, particularly as regards adaptive women, the largest group, whose priorities are the least stable on a day-to-day or year-to-year basis. The test of the classification is whether it proves useful as a heuristic tool, as a framework to guide new research and to make sense of research results for societies that have achieved the new scenario. The classification cannot be falsified by case-studies revealing a more complex reality. This is true of any abstraction.

Economists assume that preferences and tastes are stable, permanent. Preference theory states that there are indeed two groups with stable preferences, but these are contrasting preferences, for the marriage career or for the employment career. In contrast, the third group does not *appear* to have stable tastes, because adaptive women readily modify their outlook and behaviour to take advantage of special opportunities or to comply with constraints. The heterogeneity of women's preferences requires a reassessment of theories that worked reasonably well before the two revolutions. The problem is not that women are different from men, but rather that some women are not at all different, while others are seriously different in their orientations to home, children, and employment. In addition, the new scenario for women entails that some previously useful theories are now becoming dated.

Preference theory clarifies that certain theories apply only to particular groups of women, not to *all* women, because women are heterogeneous. For example Becker's (1991) theory that the sexual division of labour in the home is adopted and maintained because it is more efficient remains useful after women acquire genuine choices, but it only applies to two groups of women. The theory is contingent on women having a preference for a home-centred life, with a complete sexual division of labour, or for the combination of work and family life that still leaves women with a primary responsibility for domestic affairs. Work-centred women will insist on 'egalitarian' symmetrical conjugal roles or will forego the pleasures of child-rearing for the pleasures of a rewarding career. Childlessness of itself alters the domestic bargain in fundamental ways. And dual-career couples in professional and managerial occupations can often well afford to purchase childcare, housekeeping, and gardening services that leave them free to pursue their main interests outside the home. Becker's efficiency explanation is particularly relevant to couples where the wife has 'married up', to a husband who is superior in education, occupation, and earnings. As noted in Chapter 7, trends in homogamy and wives marrying up vary a good deal in the post-war decades, even within Europe (see Table 7.7). We cannot assume that this practice is dying out as a result of women's greater education. It is not clear that Becker's theory has any applicability at all to couples who are equal in education, occupation, and earnings; who remain childless; and who are agreed that both are career-oriented. Any slight advantage the wife might have in cooking will be balanced by the husband's slight advantage in Do-It-Yourself and odd jobs, or vice versa. Both will be equally inefficient at domestic activities and equally productive in paid work, so a symmetrical, balanced sharing of tasks can emerge if it is preferred.[26] It is puzzling that no economic theory predicts dual-career symmetrical role partnerships, as distinct from dual-earner couples with adaptive wives. The mutual benefits of dual-career partnerships were of course invisible to male theorists living in single-breadwinner marriages. The only sociological theory to predict this arrangement went too far, arguing that all couples would eventually choose this arrangement (Young and Willmott 1973), whereas others have seen dual-career couples as restricted uniquely to higher grade professional and managerial occupations (Fogarty, Rapoport, and Rapoport 1971).

Recent research shows that there are additional mutual advantages to spouses within dual-career couples, which may outweigh the practical inconvenience of having no full-time homemaker, especially as many of these couples have no children, or none living at home (Philliber and Vannoy-Hiller 1990; Robert and Bukodi 1998). Shared social capital, intellectual, and work interests can allow spouses greater achievements and upward mobility than they would achieve alone. Husbands can afford to develop risky businesses or to pick and choose work they find most interesting, cushioned by their wife's steady income. Some degree of similarity in spouses' occupations has strong positive effects on a woman's professional career (Ginzberg 1966; Philliber and Vannoy-Hiller 1990; Robert and Bukodi 1998) and more generally on both spouses' careers (Bernasco, De Graaf, and Ultee 1998; Engelstad 1998: 13–15). Such couples can then afford to purchase services to compensate for the fact that neither have the time or skill for domestic activities.

[26] Becker argues that even a slight comparative advantage of one party in domestic work is sufficient to produce conjugal role segregation, even among basically identical persons (Becker 1991: 77). However he overlooks the fact that men also have a slight advantage in certain domestic tasks, such as car maintenance, putting up shelves, gardening, and house repairs. In practice, Becker's theory rests heavily on the idea that women have an advantage in the care of babies and small children, which sets in motion a separation of roles that was already anticipated anyway. This factor is eliminated completely among voluntarily childless couples and among older couples with no children at home (Atkinson and Boles 1984).

Most obviously, they can afford to purchase substitute childcare, but also catering services for special social events, cleaning and housekeeping services, gardening services and so on. These couples do not benefit from the efficiencies of the sexual division of labour, but they benefit from another form of task specialization, with alternative efficiencies.

Human capital theory assumes homogeneity of the workforce and fails to cope with female heterogeneity. Human capital theory assumes that qualifications are obtained primarily and exclusively as an investment in economic capital, and it treats the humanities degree as undistinguishable from the accountancy degree. The theory cannot cope with people who obtain qualifications as an investment in cultural capital and/or because higher education, and the jobs it leads to, provide access to élite marriage markets. It is discouraging that many sociologists have adopted this economic theory and applied it unquestioningly, without seeking to modify it to incorporate sociological knowledge and research findings. Preference theory offers a new integration of economic and sociological theorizing about involvement in paid and unpaid work. Unlike most earlier top-down theorizing, it is grounded theory, built up from empirical research evidence. Because of this, it is open to development by contributions from other social scientists with relevant research findings.

One promising development is the renewed emphasis on self-concept and identity in social psychology. Social and personal identity combine past experiences, the present and anticipated futures. Aspirations and life goals are an important part of self-concept and identity. Goals and plans for the future regulate and motivate behaviour through conceptions of 'possible selves' (Markus and Nurius 1987: 166) or ideal selves represented in 'the dream' (Levinson 1978, 1996). Thus a woman is home-centred if she looks ahead to a time when she will marry and become a full-time mother, even if she is currently happy in a full-time professional job. Social psychologists also recognize that there is a large element of choice in the particular identities adopted by people, and even in the choice of primary sexual identity (Breakwell 1992; Goodman 1999).

Chapter 8 looks at the policy implications of the theory. However the most important consequence for policy is that preferences are *not* converging on a single sex-role model for women, and there is no convergence on a single model of the family in western Europe, as many scholars have been anticipating, as if this were a logical consequence of agreement to a common European currency and common European labour laws. It seems even less likely that there would be convergence on a single model of sex-roles, or the family, across *all* modern societies, given cultural diversity. Policy-making for a heterogeneous society will be more difficult than in a society where there is a broad consensus backing a single model of the family, as illustrated by Sweden.

7

Marriage Markets and Educational Equality

Preference theory underlines the fact that marriage markets continue to be just as important as labour markets for women's status achievements, and hence for understanding women's position in society as a whole. For some women, marriage markets are more important than labour markets and have provided an equally effective ladder for upward social mobility, as noted in Chapters 6 and 9. Unfortunately, there is comparatively little research on marriage markets, especially when compared with the enormous volume of recent research and information on women's changing position within labour markets (for example, Hakim 1996a; Rubery *et al.* 1998). Becker's (1965, 1981, 1991) work on the economics of marriage and the family provides an important theoretical foundation for the analysis of marriage markets within economics, but there is no equivalent theory which serves to focus research in sociology. Becker argues that even if a husband and wife are identical, they achieve efficiency and productivity gains from a division of labour between employment and household work. The sexual division of labour in the family is mutually advantageous. Parsons' functionalist view of marriage was broadly consistent: he argued that the sexual division of labour in the family was functional and even essential. The family performed essential functions for society, in particular the socialization of children and the stabilization of adult personalities. Men were oriented to the public sphere and performed an instrumental role as main breadwinner in the family. Women performed an expressive role, concentrating on relationships and the internal dynamics of the family. The separation of parental roles was presented as beneficial: it helped to avoid competition between spouses, and between the universalistic and competitive values of the labour market and the particularistic values of kinship relations (Parsons and Bales 1955). The Parsonian view of the family is now rejected by many sociologists. However there are several recent sociological theories that offer similar justifications for the sexual division of labour in the family. Resource theory and exchange theory also present role segregation in the family as rational and efficient (Pleck 1985: 12–15), along lines similar to Becker's thesis.

Preference theory shows that the model of marriage based on comparative and complementary advantage, and differentiated but complementary roles, is only one of three possible models for people living in modern societies of the 21st century. Seeking to develop and extend Becker's theory, Lam (1988) has already pointed out that there are at least two models of marital choices: if all household goods are purchased on the market, then there is no advantage in the marriage of complementary unequals; on the contrary, there is every incentive for assortive mating, in wages, tastes, and education. This is effectively the usual logic of dual-career partnerships, especially those that remain childfree. However, preference theory identifies an intermediate, third model as well. Adaptive women seek to combine employment with a major role in the family, so they are likely to choose some compromise between a husband able to fulfil the 'good provider' role and a partner with similar status and tastes, effectively using *both* the marriage market and the labour market to achieve their goals.

The separation of marriage markets and labour markets is itself notable, and is one of the many consequences of the separation of home and workplace in modern societies. When the vast majority of people worked in family enterprises, such as a family farm, shop, or business, a woman's choice of spouse effectively determined her choice of employment and work role as well as her social status. This constituted one entirely practical reason for class homogamy: a farmer's daughter would generally make the more accomplished and experienced farmer's wife, as she would already be trained for her responsibilities on a farm. The separation of home and workplace means that marriage partners can now be chosen with little or no concern for their work skills; spouses can today engage in totally unconnected occupations, in different industries. Even so, endogamy remains the custom in most societies. Most people marry within their own social group, defined by social class of origin, religion, geographical region, ethnic group, clan, or tribe. In some societies, spouses are often similar in personal characteristics as well, such as age, height, IQ, and education.

This chapter reviews the research evidence on marriage markets, looking especially at the way women use them as avenues for marital mobility and as an alternative 'career ladder' to labour markets. As far as possible, the focus is on the most recent research, and on recent decades, to look at marital selection within the new scenario. However, as noted already, there is far less research on marriage markets than on labour markets, so the information available is somewhat limited.

It is sometimes argued that women have only used marriage as an avenue for upward mobility and status achievement because they were denied full access to career ladders in the labour market, in competition with men. In the new scenario, employment careers are open to women as well as to men. We might therefore expect a decline in women's use of the marriage market, rather than the labour market, to achieve their desired status and economic well-being. In practice, our review suggests increasing use of marriage markets to achieve upward social mobility.

The role of education in women's status achievement process is important but equivocal. Economists treat education as an investment in human capital, which is then exploited in the labour market to generate higher occupational status and earnings. Because of the almost exclusive focus on earnings and income in economics, research reports focus on trends in women's earnings, the pay gap, the earnings gap between spouses, and wives' financial contribution to household income, as shown in Chapters 4 and 5. Sociologists have often supported this focus by showing that money is the basis of power and control in the family, that women only gain an equal role in decision-making if they are full-time workers making substantial contributions to family income (Kiernan 1992: 103; Vogler 1994: 246). From the economic perspective, there has been very little change in recent years in women's status as dependents within marriage, as noted in Chapters 4 and 5.

However there are many sources of power in personal relationships. Money is only one of them. Education is another. An alternative thesis is that education provides cultural capital and an intellectual dowry that women can 'invest' in the marriage market to achieve marriage to a man of similar or greater education and earnings potential. Qualifications and occupations score high on cultural capital, or on economic capital, but rarely on both together (Bourdieu 1984; Kalmijn 1994). Women who have little economic capital to bargain with may none the less have substantial cultural and/or social capital, quite apart from any other advantages, such as physical attractiveness, sexuality,[1] and erotic power.[2] It can be argued that women's increased access to the educational system, and to educational equality with men, now provides the basis for a new culture of sex equality within marriage. In effect, the emphasis on occupational and earnings equality in marriage is mistaken, and it is educational equality that is now the source of a new egalitarian culture among younger generations. This emphasis on the *social* value of education, as distinct from the *economic* value of educational qualifications, is supported by recent research on marriage patterns. Uunk (1996: 134, 141–3) found that in the 20th century, in industrial societies, educational

[1] Some wives use sexual access as a power asset and bargaining resource in marriage, especially after the second or third child, when they themselves lose interest in sexual activity (Dallos and Dallos 1997).

[2] A little-known paper by Zetterberg (1966) identifies erotic power as a separate dimension from sexuality and physical attractiveness. He defines it as a person's privately known probability of being able to induce a state of emotional surrender in persons of the opposite sex or, for homosexuals, the same sex. However he points out that men and women are equally likely to have erotic power, so that it is not a resource that gives women an advantage when bargaining with men. Zetterberg considered erotic power to be relatively invisible, secret, and interactional, making it virtually impossible to do research on the phenomenon, even if it is recognized in common sense knowledge.

homogamy replaced social class homogamy as the main factor in marital selection, and Singly (1996: 39–41) effectively draws the same conclusion for France. In other words, achievement values replaced ascriptive values in marriage markets as well as in labour markets. At the minimum, this thesis suggests that the conventional emphasis on women's economic contribution in marriage is partial and therefore biased. A wider, multidisciplinary approach would consider the value of women's social and cultural contributions as well. This is precisely the new perspective proposed by preference theory.

This chapter addresses several topics that have attracted little research attention as yet. It is necessarily more exploratory than other chapters. It helps to point to areas where further research is needed and in the process identifies substantial gaps, even biases, in social science research.

Marriage Markets

The research literature on marriage patterns always emphasizes the large degree of homogamy observed in all societies. The main conclusion is that people usually marry people like themselves. Most people marry within their own racial, religious, nationality, or ethnic group, and within the same social class (Whyte 1990: 99–118). However a second theme is the preference for particular differences in a spouse. On average, women prefer husbands who are three years older and up to three inches (7.5cm) taller (Mullan 1984: 78–85; Buss 1989; Bourdieu 1998: 41–3). In some societies and classes the age gap is much larger, and this has been taken as an indicator of patriarchal relations between spouses (Cain 1993; Bourdieu 1998: 43). In the USA and Europe, spouses are often closely matched on education (Uunk 1996), but this still leaves up to half of all couples who are heterogamous, which generally means that the wife has married a husband with higher education qualifications. The exceptions to the rule of homogamy are of substantive interest, because they generally consist of wives marrying up.

Social anthropologists have identified a variety of social mechanisms which ensure that wives have less power and status in marriage, such as: the husband is substantially older; the husband has more education or training, and thus higher earnings capacity; the husband is taller and bigger than the wife; the husband alone is sexually experienced at marriage; the husband is from a higher class, higher status or more affluent family; or the couple live with the husband's parents, or in his village, so that the wife is separated from her family and becomes isolated (Federici, Mason, and Sogner 1993: 268–9). The last factor is less important in modern societies, where good transportation services reduce the social significance of geographical separation. Otherwise, these social mechanisms operate just as effectively in prosperous modern societies as they do in poorer or less developed societies. A small but consistent male advantage in all these domains can add up to a definitive power imbalance in a marriage. More important, all the research evidence on mate selection preferences indicates that women actively seek, and prefer, a husband who is 'superior' on all these dimensions. It appears that class homogamy, marrying on the same socio-economic level instead of marrying up, may be a second-best option for women, even if it is the most frequent outcome, and marrying up is the preferred ideal, even if it is attained by only a minority of women. Marriage to someone of lower status can cause significant marital stress, especially for those who have high social aspirations (Pearlin 1975).

All the available research evidence shows that most women prefer to marry up the social ladder, if they can. Marriage and dating agencies are aware that women generally seek upward mobility through marriage, while men seek impossibly beautiful partners. In practice, most agencies try to match people on essential factors, such as social class—as indicated today by people's own occupation or education rather than social class of origin—and other important cultural criteria—such as caste or religion—and then to match people on lifestyle, as indicated by leisure interests and sporting activities (Mullan 1984: 60, 77–84; see also Godwin 1973). However agencies nearly always observe the two virtually universal rules of marital selection: that the male partner should be older and taller than the woman (Mullan 1984: 83–4), thus ensuring a minimum degree of male 'superiority' that is publicly visible, not only a private reality (Bourdieu 1998: 42).

The preference for an age gap, of about 3–4 years on average, in favour of men is noteworthy and emerges in all studies. This seems to be a universal preference, found in all cultures, in societies at very different levels of prosperity, and across all generations and age groups (Buss 1989: 8–9, 1994: 27–30, 51–2; Kenrick and Keefe 1992; Kenrick, Frost, and Sheets 1996: 35–45). This alone ensures that most husbands will already have an economic advantage over most wives, in terms of work experience and earnings, at the time of marriage, well before child-bearing interrupts the wife's economic activity (if any).[3] However most women go beyond this to actively prefer mates who have good financial prospects or good career prospects, who are already wealthy, or display the ambition and industriousness that promise economic prosperity. Marriages which experience the husband's unemployment are much more likely to break up than those where the man is continuously

[3] An age gap of three years does not imply a substantial difference in work experience for spouses in their 40s and 50s. But most people first marry in their 20s, and at this age three extra years of work experience for the husband can produce a significant increment in actual earnings and in the value of accumulated job tenure, so that spouses would typically be significantly unequal in economic terms at this age, even if equally qualified.

employed. Men generally assign far less importance to a female partner's economic potential. The nearly universal male preference is for youth and beauty in a partner. This trading of physical attractiveness for money intensifies when relationships are of relatively short duration (Buss 1994: 86–7). One example is the practice of offering gifts or money to women during sexual encounters of relatively short duration, as illustrated by prostitution and mistresses.

The most commonly cited evidence for this exchange of physical attractiveness for economic power is a cross-national comparative study organized by Buss in the late 1980s (Buss 1989). Although it covered 37 countries and cultures in five continents, the project obtained small and unrepresentative samples in most countries, with a clear bias towards the urban, affluent, and educated sectors of society. For our purposes, this bias is advantageous, because it ensures that the results report preferences that are typical of rich, modern societies. The project found that even the most educated modern women prefer male partners who are economically strong, and that men seek physical attractiveness in return, or the close approximation achieved by good grooming and attractive dress. In this trade, youth seems to function as a proxy for physical attractiveness, offering the equivalent advantages of smooth skin, lustrous hair, and an athletic physique.

Buss and others explain these results by evolutionist—or Darwinian—theories, and often extend the argument to explanations for the pay gap as well (see for example Browne 1995, 1997, 1998; James 1997; Badcock 2000). The main problem with evolutionary theories is that they are difficult, even impossible to test and disprove, so they remain at the level of plausible idea rather than tested and proven scientific theory.[4] Female social scientists generally dismiss the idea that physical attractiveness and sexuality are power assets for women *vis à vis* men. For example Lipman-Blumen (1984: 89–90) lists this as just one in a series of 'control myths' adopted by men to justify the *status quo*; she rejects the idea on the grounds that male vested interests must necessarily bias any argument offered by men, even if they are disinterested social scientists. Walby (1990: 109–27) discusses sexuality exclusively in terms of male control over women, never the reverse.

Webster and Driskell (1983) offer an alternative, simple, and elegant sociological explanation for these results. They state that physical attractiveness,

[4] Strictly speaking, evolutionary theorists argue that *youth* is valued, because it offers the promise of higher fertility, hence survival of the father's and mother's genes. However contemporary evidence for human societies is that *beauty* is now valued, for itself, and irrespective of any connection with youth and fertility. For example men prefer attractive women even for casual affairs, when procreation is ruled out. Beauty, unlike youth, has no special value for survival. If it did, after billions of years of evolution, we should *all* be beautiful by now, as ugly people would have died out millions of years ago. The argument that beauty is valued as a luxury good is consistent with the huge variations in concepts of beauty across societies, cultures, and historical periods. Evolutionary explanations seem also to be contradicted by the fact that high status and highly educated couples generally have the lowest fertility rates in modern society.

or beauty for short, confers status.[5] It is a valued commodity which is in short supply in any society, and therefore is a luxury good.[6] They review a large body of empirical research evidence showing that beauty confers substantial concrete benefits on individuals, and even on their spouses, by association. For example, attractiveness is an important determinant of popularity, of persuasiveness in a disagreement, of attributions of ability and competence, of marital success and happiness, and of influence over other people. Attractiveness affects not only perceived abilities but also actual interaction, so that attractive people are more successful at wielding influence to get what they want, in the workplace and in business as well as in private relationships. Webster and Driskell demonstrate that attractiveness effects are substantial, function equally for men and women, and are not dependent on the sex of the observer or respondent.[7] They note that what counts as beauty is culturally-specific and hard to define, but is real in its consequences.

From adolescence onwards, young people learn the social value of physical attractiveness for attracting mates, and also the generalized status value of beauty. This process is exposed in the ruthlessly competitive culture of high schools and colleges in the USA, most of which are mixed-sex, so that they function as marriage markets as well as training centres (Elder 1969; Whyte 1990: 33–4, 74–7). Coleman's classic study of *The Adolescent Society* was carried out in the 1950s, and the results do not necessarily depict social relationships in high schools and colleges at the start of the 21st century. But it remains a useful case-study showing how the cultures of mixed-sex schools reinforce sex-role differentiation, can devalue academic ability and scholastic success relative to social popularity, and disadvantage girl scholars in particular. Girls in mixed high schools, even more than boys, learnt not to seek or to display academic achievement. They learnt that popularity and social success were most often tied to physical attractiveness, good grooming, and popularity with boys. The constant message was that, for girls, beauty was more effective than brains as a path to success (Coleman 1961: 30–1, 39, 41–51, 164–72, 245–7, 251, 257, 262–5). It seems likely that women today perceive beauty

[5] The natural asset of beauty is rare, and concentrated among the young. Physical attractiveness is broader, and can be achieved through skilful presentation and dress, as illustrated by the concept of the *belle laide*, the woman who is technically ugly but achieves attractiveness through presentational skills. Webster and Driskell treat beauty and attractiveness as synonymous in practice.

[6] In rich modern societies, women have access to innumerable aids to enhancing their physical attractiveness and grooming: cosmetics, hairdressers, wigs, tanning beds, cosmetic surgery, diets, gyms, advice manuals on how to dress, and so on. This suggests that a much higher proportion of the female and male population will be able to present a physically attractive persona. On the other hand, constant exposure to exceptionally attractive female and male models in the media, films, and advertising raises beauty standards and contributes to inflated expectations of a partner's attributes. The overall effect must be for exceptional beauty to remain a minority characteristic, and thus retain the high value of a luxury good and a characteristic of high status.

[7] Zetterberg (1966) argued that erotic power has similar, concrete, and positive effects in the mixed-sex workplace as well as in private life, but he left others to test the thesis. See also Note 2 above.

and brains as *equally* effective paths to success. But there is no reason to believe that women have completely rejected beauty as a source of generalized status and an asset in marriage markets. The constant growth of the cosmetics industry suggests otherwise.

Physical attractiveness is far less easy to measure in social science research than variables such as education or earnings. Beauty is normally one of the many variables that remain unmeasured in studies of marriage and mating, along with sexuality. By definition, it is a commodity or status characteristic held by a small minority of the population, so the *relative* impact of beauty compared to other characteristics may be small at the aggregate level, even if it can be of conclusive importance in specific cases. The few studies that manage to measure physical attractiveness show that attractiveness and intelligence are not associated; that women with high social aspirations actively deploy good grooming to maximize the value of their physical assets; and that women exchange beauty for male economic status (Elder 1969; Glenn, Ross, and Tully 1974; Taylor and Glenn 1976; Udry 1977, 1984; Townsend 1987; Stevens, Owens, and Schaefer 1990; see also Whyte 1990: 169; James 1997: 222–37). For example, girls who were attractive when in high school were more likely to marry; were more likely to marry young; and had higher household income 15 years later (Udry 1984). Because white women and men are equally likely to attend college in the USA, and colleges function as marriage markets, *inter alia*, educational homogamy is far more likely to be identified by studies than the additional process of women trading attractiveness for a man's earnings potential.

It is also possible that beauty carries greater weight in societies with an egalitarian ethos, such as the USA, and less weight in European societies, where social class distinctions continue to colour social relationships. For example Singly (1996: 42–6) claims that in France beauty is only an asset if it is combined with social status, for middle class women, or with a good education, for women of working class origin.

The relative importance of beauty and education for women is identified more clearly in studies of black women in the USA, among whom college education is less common. A study carried out in the early 1970s showed that among black women attractiveness and education were *equally* important and significant as predictors of a husband's occupational status, whereas among white women attractiveness was important only if a woman did not go to college (Udry 1977). The 1980 National Survey of Black Americans also found that attractiveness—as indicated by a paler skin tone—was more important for women than men because of its value in marital selection. More generally, the study found that skin tone was a strong predictor of occupation and income, for men and women, and was more consequential than background characteristics such as social class of origin (Keith and Herring 1991). Among black Americans light skin tone became an important criterion for attaining prestige in the black community, and it eventually became a status indicator in the same way that physical attractiveness operates as a status characteristic for women generally (Keith and Herring 1991). Thus, this study confirms the value of Webster and Driskell's theoretical framework treating beauty as a status characteristic in its own right.

In sum, endogamy and homogamy constitute only part of the picture in marriage patterns. The other part of the picture consists of women marrying up, whenever they can. Research on marital *preferences* shows that, in general, men and women seek different qualities in a partner. Men seek beauty, and/or youth as a proxy for physical attractiveness. Women seek men who already have money, status, and power, or whose careers promise these rewards. The important research finding is that these preferences remain even among women who themselves have achieved careers, status, and high income, whereas similar men choose trophy wives who offer youth and attractiveness instead (Buss 1994: 46; Kenrick, Frost, and Sheets 1996: 32, 37–41, 46; James 1997: 227, 237). The demand for toyboys among successful women is still tiny, unlike the demand for attractive young women among successful men. So it is not lack of access to the education system, and to rewarding jobs, that explains women's preference for successful and powerful men. As Goldberg (1993) points out, the lack of interest in role reversal tells us something important about relationships between men and women. For our purposes, the key conclusion is that many women continue to prefer some degree of male dominance in marital relationships, even when they have their own career.

Another test of the thesis that women seek equality in marriage is whether expanded access to education for women has led to an increase in educational homogamy, to which we now turn.

The Qualifications Gap and Educational Equality

In most countries, the educational equality of men and women is a very recent development. Educational equality is a powerful force. It allows a wife to answer back, to have self-confidence in her own abilities and competence, to develop her own view of things instead of adopting her husband's position on everything. It seems likely that an important source of egalitarian relationships between men and women, husbands and wives, in the younger generations could be the fact that young women are now as well educated as young men.

A recent analysis of changing patterns of educational attainment in 13 countries provides information on how and when the sex differential in education, or the 'qualifications gap', was closed in the USA, Germany, the

Netherlands, Sweden, Italy, Switzerland, Poland, Czechoslovakia, and Israel (Shavit and Blossfeld 1993). The study also covered Britain, Taiwan, and Japan, but unfortunately the datasets for these countries excluded women. Another study provides comparative data on France and Germany (Marry *et al.* 1998).

In the USA, the qualifications gap was always small, even invisible, for most of the 20th century. Enrolments of young women parallel those of young men, at all educational levels. Sex differences in attainment are small and can be difficult to detect except in close analyses. In particular, college education has been as common for young women as for young men. In the cohorts born before 1905, over 60% of the young men and women who completed secondary schooling went on to higher education of some sort, and around 50% of them completed college. Entry to college, and completion, declined in younger cohorts, but without any large or consistent qualifications gap emerging between men and women. By the 1980s, sex differences had been completely eliminated, reversing male advantage into female advantage at the lower levels of education and producing near equity in higher education (Shavit and Blossfeld 1993). Even in 1930, American women earned some 40% of Bachelors and Masters university degrees and 15% of Doctorates (Betz and Fitzgerald 1987: 61–75). However most of them did not work after marriage. In 1940, even college graduates were typically not in employment after the age of 25. The strong association between qualifications and workrates is a new phenomenon among women in the USA (McLaughlin *et al.* 1988: 37, 106–15). This long tradition of educational equality for men and women, and for spouses, may help explain why the second wave of the feminist movement started in the USA rather than in Europe, with equal pay laws passed in the 1960s in the USA, well before most European countries did this.

The picture in Europe is varied (Shavit and Blossfeld 1993; Marry *et al.* 1998: 361–3). Some countries, such as France, Sweden, and Hungary, had small sex differences in education which were shrinking even in the first half of the century. Other countries, such as Germany, Austria, and Holland, had a large qualifications gap between men and women which was only reduced and eventually eliminated in the second half of the century.

In Hungary and Sweden, access to education was determined primarily by social class, with very small sex differences *within* classes. In Sweden, for example, upper class families regarded a good education as necessary for a girl's success in the marriage market. Similarly in Italy, an open educational system meant fewer barriers for women as well as for working class men. Sex differences within classes were relatively small, even before 1950. In all these countries, however, full sex equality in education was only achieved after the Second World War.

In contrast, countries such as Germany, Austria, the Netherlands, Britain, and Denmark had substantial sex differences in educational attainment which were only eliminated after 1950. In the Netherlands, for example, men were two to four times more likely to obtain higher education qualifications throughout the century, a qualifications gap that was only eliminated in the cohorts born after 1950. A very similar pattern was found in the former West Germany, with the qualifications gap disappearing at the same time as the rapid rise in educational attainments in the post-war decades (Shavit and Blossfeld 1993). By 1992, the qualifications gap among people aged 25–34 years was eliminated or negligible in all EU countries except Austria, Germany, the UK, and the Netherlands where a small gap remained (Rubery, Smith, and Fagan 1996).[8]

Educational Homogamy of Spouses

The educational homogamy of spouses does not automatically follow from educational equality for men and women at the aggregate level, although it certainly becomes more probable if there is no qualifications gap. Even in a society where there were no major differences in the educational attainments of men and women at the national level, it would still be possible for men to systematically choose brides with less education than themselves, leaving the most highly educated women unmarried or obliged to seek a spouse from another, more egalitarian society, as Singly (1996: 175) observed in France. Thus the educational inequality of spouses at the micro-level could be maintained even in a society with educational equality at the macro-level. It is notable that educational homogamy tends to decline with economic development, and is lower in democratic countries (Smits, Ultee, and Lammers 1998). Our thesis is that educational homogamy is just as likely to provide the basis for a relationship of mutual respect as a marriage in which both partners contribute equally to family finances. The current emphasis on paid work as the sole source of 'equality' in marriage (Greenhalgh 1980; Singly 1996) has perhaps overlooked the equally important role of educational homogamy. A wife's educational equality with her husband may be more important than her occupational equality. Whether she works or not, a wife's educational level shapes the nature of conversations over dinner every evening, provides a basis for an equal say in family affairs, can be crucial in her contacts with her husband's work colleagues or social network, and contributes enormously

[8] The qualifications gap disappears only when qualifications are grouped into 3–5 broad bands, for example when all higher education qualifications and equivalent professional qualifications are treated as a single category. As noted in Chapter 5, substantial sex differences remain *within* the higher education band, as regards subject, level of degree, prestige of awarding institution, and the vocational-professional nature of qualifications.

to her role in the socialization and education of children. For most of the 20th century, and in most societies, men, and hence husbands, were far better educated than women, or their wives. Arguably, it was this, rather than the fact that wives did not work and were financially dependent, that allowed men to be dominant in marriage at all social levels except the very poorest, where equality is a structural inevitability (Pahl and Pahl 1971; Edgell 1980). In modern societies, educational equality within couples is greater than any matching on their social class of origin (Blau and Duncan 1967: 354; Berent 1954: 336–7; Kalmijn 1991: 499, 513, 520; Uunk 1996: 72). Another advantage of looking at education rather than occupations is that the information is more inclusive: occupational data is only available for the selective group of wives who are in work, whereas education allows all couples and individuals to be studied and compared. Furthermore, we can study educational homogamy in countries where social class may be a disputed concept.

Societies, cultures, and social classes differ in regarding a less-educated wife, or an equally-educated wife, as the ideal. In many Moslem societies there is a bias in favour of less educated wives, thus giving the husband superiority. In contrast, there is a strong bias in favour of the educational equality of spouses in Confucian societies in South East Asia. Christian societies fall between these two extremes (Smits, Ultee, and Lammers 1998: 280). Moslem men dislike women who 'argue back', whereas Confucian cultures expect marriage to be a dialogue.[9]

Although there is an extensive literature on marital homogamy, only a small part of it is concerned specifically with educational homogamy, more particularly with long-term trends in educational homogamy and the impact of the equalization of educational attainment on marriage patterns (Berent 1954; Michielutte 1972; Rockwell 1976; Sixma and Ultee 1984; DiMaggio and Mohr 1985; Shoen and Wooldredge 1989; Ultee and Luijkx 1990; Kalmijn 1991, 1994; Mare 1981, 1991; Shoen and Weinick 1993; Blossfeld, Timm, and Dasko 1996; Uunk 1996; Smits, Ultee, and Lammers 1998). The educational (in)equality of spouses, and its social and psychological impact within the family, has attracted little attention among sociologists because theory directed their attention instead to social stratification and social mobility as the main issues for research. This body of research considered whether spouses were more similar in social class of origin or education, in ascribed or

[9] Further evidence comes from a cross-national comparative study of fertility based on the World Fertility Survey datasets. Cain (1993) used the median age gap between spouses as an indicator of patriarchal regimes in less-developed countries, and found it to be strongly associated with a preference for sons and with fertility levels, with a few exceptions. The median age gap between spouses did not vary between socio-economic groups within countries, and did not vary with the wife's education, the husband's occupation, or urban/rural residence. Moslem societies were the most patriarchal, with the largest age gaps between spouses, and strong preferences for sons. The Buddhist and Confucian societies of South-East Asia were the least patriarchal. Christian societies fell between these two groups. This conclusion parallels that of Smits, Ultee, and Lammers (1998: 280) based on the incidence of relative educational homogamy in these three cultural groups.

achieved status, as a measure of the 'openness' of society (for example, Kalmijn 1991; Smits, Ultee, and Lammers 1998). Other studies considered whether people chose spouses with high earnings potential or with high education, whether economic or cultural capital are more important (Kalmijn 1994). Some studies looked at women's upward social mobility through the labour market, or through the marriage market, by comparing the social class of a woman's father with her own occupational class or that of her husband (for example, Erikson and Goldthorpe 1993: 231–77). Her own occupation prior to marriage and her own education were treated as irrelevant. More recently, there has been some interest in the educational and occupational (in)equality of spouses and its effects (for example, Benham 1974, 1985; Richardson 1979; Hout 1982; McRae 1986; Arber and Ginn 1995; Bernasco, De Graaf, and Ultee 1998; Robert and Bukodi 1998), with growing recognition that many outcomes are the result of selection effects as well as interactions between husband and wife, because like marries like. For example Benham (1974, 1985) shows that an educated wife helps her husband to achieve higher earnings.

Because we are interested in long-term trends at the societal level, the absolute, national rates of educational homogamy are most relevant.[10] They are also easy to compare across countries, as shown in Tables 7.1 to 7.7. We would expect to see women's rising level of education reflected in a long-term trend towards educational homogamy. Some social scientists also report the 'expected' proportion of homogamous marriages under a model of chance mating; in analyses of trends over time this reflects the impact of changing educational distributions for men and women in the absence of any preference for homogamy.

Contrary to expectation, educational homogamy *declined* steadily in the first half of the 20th century in the USA. In the post-war decades there was a gradual increase, but the level remains well below rates at the start of the century. In the cohort married before 1910 and still alive at the 1970 Census, 71% of marriages were educationally homogamous, compared to just half (46%) in the 1966–1970 marriage cohort (Table 7.1). A study of newlyweds found that half (53%) of marriages in the USA were homogamous by 1985–87 (Mare 1991: 20), leaving the overall trend one of a decline in educational homogamy.

This decline is balanced by a steady rise in marriages where the husband was better educated than the wife. In the cohort marrying before 1910, only

[10] Absolute measures of homogamy report the percentage of all marriages—or the proportion of married women and men taken separately—where spouses have the same level of education, with educational qualifications grouped into 4, 5 or 6 levels. Rockwell (1976) used 6 levels in his analysis for the USA in Table 7.1, thus obtaining slightly lower absolute levels of homogamy than if 4 or 5 levels were used. Blossfeld, Timm, and Dasko (1996) used only 4 levels of education, thus slightly inflating the level of educational homogamy in Germany in Table 7.5, as compared with the USA analysis.

TABLE 7.1. *Long-term trends in educationally homogamous marriages and in women marrying up in the USA*, 1890–1970*

Marriage cohort	Homogamous marriages			Women marrying up		
	Actual %	Expected %	Ratio Act/Exp	Actual %	Maximum %	Ratio Act/Max
1966–1970	46	26	1.8	33	61	0.55
1961–1965	45	26	1.7	35	60	0.59
1956–1960	43	26	1.7	35	60	0.58
1951–1955	43	24	1.7	33	61	0.54
1946–1950	43	24	1.8	29	61	0.48
1941–1945	42	23	1.8	29	63	0.46
1936–1940	45	24	1.9	26	67	0.38
1931–1935	48	26	1.9	23	58	0.40
1926–1930	50	30	1.7	21	49	0.44
1921–1925	56	37	1.5	19	40	0.47
1916–1920	62	43	1.4	18	36	0.50
1911–1915	68	50	1.4	16	30	0.52
up to 1910	71	58	1.2	13	23	0.58
All cohorts	46	23	2.0	30	65	0.46

Note: * White-white marriages, both married once only, and still alive at the 1970 Census. Marriage cohort is the year of first marriage. All percentages have been rounded here. Educational qualifications are grouped into six levels.

Source: Extracted from Table 4, reporting an analysis of 1970 Census 5% Public Use Sample data, in R. C. Rockwell, 'Historical trends and variations in educational homogamy', *Journal of Marriage and the Family*, 1976, 38: 83–95.

13% of wives married 'up', to someone better educated than themselves; in the 1966–1970 marriage cohort this had risen to one-third of all marriages. These unexpected results reveal that, in the USA, where there was a tradition of equal education for sons and daughters, rising educational heterogeneity was the dominant trend. At the start of the century few people were educated beyond primary school level, and most marriages were homogamous. By the end of the century, there was far greater differentiation in educational qualifications, so for a woman at any level of education there were an increasing number of possibilities to marry a man at an even higher level. The changing patterns of marriage were dominated by the increasing heterogeneity of educational attainments, among men and women. The ratio of actual to 'expected' marriage rates in Table 7.1 shows that the bias in favour of homogamous marriage over other types increased over the century, whereas the increase in women marrying up was due largely to changes in the educational

TABLE 7.2. *Educational homogamy by highest qualification, Britain, 1949*

Highest qualification obtained	Husband's education is:			Base	
	Higher	Equal	Lower	N=100%	%
All wives aged 18 and over	18	72	10	5533	100
University degree and equivalent professional qualifications	0	42	58	84	2
Other higher education	6	44	50	808	15
Secondary education	39	29	32	344	6
Primary education	19	81	0	4297	78
	Wife's education is:				
	Higher	Equal	Lower		
All husbands aged 18 and over	10	72	18	5533	100
University degree and equivalent professional qualifications	0	20	80	171	3
Other higher education	2	32	66	1118	20
Secondary education	26	32	42	310	6
Primary education	12	88	0	3934	71

Source: Calculated from Table 6, p. 331, in J. Berent, 'Social mobility and marriage: a study of trends in England and Wales', pp. 321–38 in D. V. Glass (ed) *Social Mobility in Britain*, London: Routledge, 1954, which reports analyses of a 1949 national survey of 10,000 adults aged 18+ living in Great Britain.

distribution (Rockwell 1976: 89). A subsequent study found that cultural homogamy remained the dominant feature of new marriages in the 1970s, accounting for half of all marriages, but still only half (Kalmijn 1994). Another study confirmed that there was a small but statistically significant increase in the bias towards educational homogamy in the post-war decades, after taking account of changes in educational attainment (Kalmijn 1991: 516).

Due to sharply increasing educational heterogeneity of the population, the small convergence of men and women's educational attainments coexisted with an increasing proportion of wives marrying someone higher on the educational ladder, and hence, almost certainly, marrying a man with higher occupational status and earnings as well. By the end of the century, about half of marriages in the USA were educationally homogamous, and at least one-third included an educationally, and no doubt occupationally, superior husband.

Information on trends in Britain comes from three national surveys, carried out in 1949, 1992, and 1996 (Tables 7.2 to 7.4). Here too, there is a

TABLE 7.3. *Educational homogamy in three age cohorts, Britain, 1992*

	Husband's education is:			Base N=100%
	Higher	Equal	Lower	
All wives aged 20–65 years	37	42	21	4669
aged 20–35	35	41	24	1537
aged 36–50	40	38	22	1874
aged 51–65	35	49	16	1258

Source: Calculated from special analyses of 1992 General Household Survey data for married and cohabiting women aged 20–65 years, supplied by Colin Mills, LSE, London.

steady *decline* in educational homogamy across the 20th century. An early analysis by Berent (1954: 330–8) showed homogamy to be the dominant pattern before World War I: three-quarters of all couples had a similar level of education (Table 7.2). However he found a decline in educational homogamy over the first half of the century, even before the dramatic expansion of educational opportunities in the post-war decades. Within the cohort married before 1915, 84% of couples were educationally homogamous; the level fell to 73% among the cohort that married in 1915–1939, and to 62% in the cohort married in the decade 1940–1949. As in the USA, there was a counter-balancing rise in women marrying up (Berent 1954).

By the 1990s, less than half of all married and cohabiting couples had equal levels of education: 42% of wives in 1992 and 1996 (Tables 7.3 and 7.4). The proportion of women marrying up had risen to more than double the level before 1950 (38% compared with 18%) and was beginning to equal the share of homogamous marriages. This was assisted by the fact that the convergence of men's and women's qualifications was never as complete as it appears in national surveys with samples of less than 5,000 persons. Larger data collections, such as the 1991 Census, reveal that the sex differential in educational qualifications remained within higher education (Hakim 1998a: 33–9; see also Table 5.1). It was reinforced by sex differences also in the quality of the educational institution attended and in the economic value of the degree subject chosen (Dale and Egerton 1997; ONS 1998: 94). The GHS also reveals that the qualifications gap stopped shrinking by 1991 and remained stable in the 1990s (ONS 1998: 89, 92). Roughly equal proportions of men and women have tertiary level qualifications, but within this group there are substantial differences, in cultural and economic capital, between the qualifications of a nurse, primary school teacher, surgeon, university professor, and company manager with an MBA. Analyses which group all tertiary level qualifications together will

TABLE 7.4. *Educational homogamy by highest qualification, Britain, 1996*

Highest qualification obtained	Husband's education is:			Base	
	Higher	Equal	Lower	N=100%	%
All wives aged 25–69 years	38	42	20	3715	100
University degree and equivalent	0	58	42	318	9
Other higher education	29	21	50	397	11
GCE A-levels*	35	23	43	317	8
Basic secondary education	42	37	21	1349	36
None+	45	55	0	1334	36
	Wife's education is:				
	Higher	Equal	Lower		
All husbands aged 25–69 years	21	42	37	3835	100
University degree and equivalent	0	35	65	543	14
Other higher education	7	17	76	491	13
GCE A-levels*	18	16	66	488	13
Basic secondary education	22	46	32	1165	30
None+	37	63	0	1148	30

Notes: * equivalent to the *Arbitur* and the *Baccalaureat*.
+ this category includes a tiny number of people with foreign and unclassifiable qualifications.

Source: Calculated from Table 7.5 in *Living in Britain 1996*, reporting General Household Survey, data for married and cohabiting people aged 25–69 not in full-time education in Britain.

identify more homogamy and lower rates of women marrying up, because the nurse who marries the surgeon is classified as having an equal level of education to her husband. In reality, such cases should be classified as wives marrying up. The analyses in Tables 7.2 and 7.4 differentiate between higher education qualifications *below* degree level (for example, nursing, teaching, and certain vocational qualifications), and those at university degree level or above (including equivalent higher vocational qualifications), to show that a substantial amount of marrying up occurs within the tertiary level. They also show that husbands, collectively, are consistently better educated than wives, collectively, both in 1949 and 1996 (Tables 7.2 and 7.4).

The long-term decline in homogamy continued in the second half of the century. By 1992, 49% of the oldest couples were equally educated compared to 41% of the youngest couples (Table 7.3). There is a simultaneous increase in wives marrying up and down, but by 1996 wives marrying up are twice as common as wives marrying down in Britain (Table 7.4). It is worth noting that the cohort of women aged 20–35 years in Table 7.3 had the full benefit of the equal opportunities revolution, the contraceptive revolution, and other features of the new scenario. Yet even in this age cohort, fully one-third of young women used the marriage market for upward social mobility.

The discrepancy between the results for 1949 and for the oldest age cohort in 1992 requires comment. There are several factors that could produce small discrepancies between the two surveys: small differences in the two educational classifications, the social class differential in mortality and the exclusion of widows from all these tables.[11] However the main explanation, in our view, is the dramatic expansion in education that took place after World War II, combined with men's greater propensity to upgrade their qualifications during their working life. Many men whose education was equal to their wives' education at the time of the 1949 survey subsequently upgraded their qualifications by returning to education as mature students, on a full-time or part-time basis. Overall, more adult men than women do this. Thus by the time of the 1992 survey, 35% of the oldest wives had a better educated husband whereas only 18% reported this in the 1949 survey.

A recent study for West Germany (Blossfeld, Timm, and Dasko 1996) shows quite different trends in marriage patterns. As noted earlier, women were on average far less educated than men in Germany, and the qualifications gap was only eliminated towards the end of the 20th century. As a result it was 'traditional' for wives to marry better-educated husbands and to become full-time homemakers (Blossfeld, Timm, and Dasko 1996: 17). In Germany, educational homogamy *increased* substantially over the century, while the custom of women marrying up declined sharply (Table 7.5). In the cohort of people born in 1900–1918 (and still alive in 1984 when the first German SOEP panel study survey was conducted), women were just as likely to marry up as to marry someone of equal education—48% and 50% respectively. In the 1964–1978 birth cohort (that would have reached adulthood around 1984–98), 70% of marriages were homogamous and only 22% involved a bride marrying up. So-called 'expected' marriage rates, based on the assumption of random mating, are close to observed marriage rates, showing that the changing patterns of marriage could be explained by the trend towards educational equality in West Germany.

[11] Men in the lower, manual social classes tend to be less well educated, are more likely to marry homogamously, and are more likely to die early. Their widows would be excluded from the analyses, which are restricted to married and cohabiting couples. This means that educational homogamy would be slightly understated in the oldest age group of women. On the other hand, the 1949, 1992, and 1996 surveys were all carried out by the same government survey organization, so there would be no major methodological differences between them.

TABLE 7.5. *Long-term trends in educationally homogamous marriages and women marrying up in West Germany, 1900–1978*

Birth cohort	Homogamous marriages			Women marrying up		
	Actual %	Expected %	Ratio Act/Exp	Actual %	Expected %	Ratio Act/Exp
WIVES						
1964–1978	70	49	1.42	22	28	0.79
1959–1963	70	58	1.20	22	25	0.88
1954–1958	71	55	1.28	24	27	0.88
1949–1953	69	53	1.31	27	33	0.81
1944–1948	66	53	1.25	27	33	0.80
1939–1943	58	51	1.15	37	40	0.93
1934–1938	56	47	1.19	38	42	0.90
1929–1933	41	38	1.08	54	51	1.06
1924–1928	49	42	1.19	47	50	0.93
1919–1923	44	39	1.13	52	54	0.97
1900–1918	50	40	1.25	48	51	0.96
HUSBANDS						
1964–1978	65	49	1.33	21	28	0.75
1959–1963	72	58	1.22	21	25	0.85
1954–1958	74	55	1.34	23	27	0.83
1949–1953	71	53	1.35	23	33	0.69
1944–1948	67	53	1.27	28	33	0.83
1939–1943	62	51	1.22	33	40	0.84
1934–1938	58	47	1.22	37	42	0.87
1929–1933	46	38	1.21	49	51	0.95
1924–1928	43	42	1.02	53	50	1.06
1919–1923	45	39	1.16	49	54	0.92
1900–1918	52	40	1.29	47	51	0.92

Note: All percentages have been rounded here. Educational qualifications have been grouped into four levels.

Source: Extracted and calculated from Table 1, reporting analyses of German Socio-Economic Panel (SOEP) data from waves 1984–94, in H-P. Blossfeld, A. Timms and F. Dasko, 'The educational system as a marriage market', Working Paper No. 46, University of Bremen Sfb 186, 1996.

In sum, Germany displays the expected large increase in educational homogamy, and a sharp decline in wives marrying up, as a result of the closing of the qualifications gap between men and women. In contrast, the USA and Britain display a *rising* trend in wives marrying up and a decline in homogamy over the century, due to educational heterogeneity.

TABLE 7.6. *Trends in educational homogamy at marriage in Hungary, 1950–1992*

Marriage cohort	Wives marrying up (%)	Homogamous marriages (%)	Wives marrying down (%)
1980–92	32	42	26
1970–79	35	42	23
1960–69	29	52	19
1950–59	25	65	10
All marriages	31	48	21

Note: Educational qualifications are grouped into six levels: less than primary school completed; primary school completed; vocational secondary school education; academic secondary education; college; and university.
Source: Calculated from special analyses of the 1992 Social Mobility and Life History Survey of the Hungarian Central Statistical Office supplied by Peter Robert, TARKI, Hungary.

It is instructive to compare these countries with an egalitarian socialist country, especially as Hungary always had relatively low sex differences in educational attainment (Robert 1991: 221). Here too, educational homogamy *declined* among post-war marriage cohorts, with corresponding increases in wives marrying up and marrying down (Table 7.6). By the end of the 20th century, there was a remarkable similarity between the USA and Hungary in absolute rates of homogamy and heterogamy (Tables 7.1 and 7.6). Both analyses group educational qualifications into six levels; they find one-third of wives marrying up and less than half homogamous. If qualifications are grouped into just four levels, the level of homogamy in Hungary is higher,[12] but it is still on a declining trend, replaced by more women marrying up (Table 7.6). The relative incidence of wives marrying up, or on an equal level, is much the same in Britain, when qualifications are grouped into five levels (Table 7.4). Economic systems and political ideologies seem to have little effect on marriage patterns, which are determined by private preferences and cultural factors. Given that homogamy is *not* increasing in Hungary, it appears that here also rising educational heterogeneity has a greater impact than increasing educational equality between men and women.

[12] Results for Hungary in Table 7.6 are not very different when qualifications are grouped into four levels: among all marriages, 55% were homogamous, 27% had wives marrying up, and 18% had wives marrying down in terms of educational qualifications. For the 1980–92 marriage cohort, these proportions were 46%, 29%, and 25% respectively.

TABLE 7.7. *Trends in educationally homogamous marriages and women marrying up in 23 industrialized nations, 1949–1983*

		Wives marrying up	Homo-gamous marriages	Wives marrying down	Total marriages Base=100%
Australia	1966	18	70	12	2,333,000
	1981	23	56	21	30,276
Austria	1971	12	81	7	1,705,205
	1981	14	75	11	1,729,065
Belgium,	1976	33	48	19	3,984
Flanders	1983	28	53	19	2,432
Canada	1971	19	64	17	4,605,495
	1981	21	64	15	1,122,304
England & Wales	1949	18	72	10	5,533
	1972	26	60	14	8,513
West Germany	1972	47	45	8	126,573
	1982	47	44	9	6,670
Finland	1972	16	67	17	617
	1981	22	55	23	5,522
France	1959	19	69	12	1,646
	1969	19	66	15	7,304
	1981	23	59	18	60,000
Hungary	1960	15	75	10	2,388,007
	1970	19	68	13	2,324,608
	1980	21	64	15	2,686,441
Japan	1955	31	57	12	1,586
	1965	28	58	14	1,704
Norway	1957	17	70	13	1,113
	1972	35	51	14	747
The Netherlands	1959	28	67	5	10,000
	1971	32	56	12	300,000
	1983	39	43	18	2,808
Sweden	1972	26	61	13	735
	1981	24	55	21	4,148
USA	1962	23	51	26	9,763
	1973	24	55	21	19,527
	1983	24	57	19	1,368
Czechoslovakia	1980	32	54	14	30,299
Denmark	1972	22	67	11	733
Irish Republic	1973	11	81	8	1,437
Northern Ireland	1973	12	83	5	1,759
Italy	1979	24	66	10	2,325
New Zealand	1981	25	54	21	643,521
Poland	1982	24	51	25	1,880
Scotland	1973	19	68	13	3,844
Yugoslavia	1971	15	75	10	2,622

Note: Educational qualifications have been grouped into four levels.

Source: Calculated from Table 1 in W. C. Ultee and R. Luijkx, 'Educational heterogamy and father-to-son occupational mobility in 23 industrial nations: general societal openness or compensatory strategies of reproduction?', *European Sociological Review*, 1990, 6: 125–49.

The contrast between trends in the USA and Europe is confirmed by the analysis in Table 7.7. This is based on data from a unique cross-national comparative study of educational heterogamy in the post-war decades by Ultee and Luijkx (1990). Whereas Tables 7.1, 7.3, 7.5, and 7.6 present cohort data, Table 7.7 presents national cross-sectional data for all married couples at two or three points in time around 1970 and 1980 or, for some countries, at a single point in time. This analysis classifies the highest qualification obtained into just four levels: primary education or no more than compulsory schooling; lower-level secondary education; higher-level secondary education; and all types of tertiary education grouped together along with equivalent professional qualifications obtained after higher-level secondary education. This simplified classification inflates the level of educational homogamy observed, and understates the rates for wives marrying up, as noted earlier.

The comparisons in Table 7.7 confirm that the USA is unusual in having a slightly *rising* level of homogamy in the second half of the twentieth century. There appear to be only three other cases: Japan 1955–65, Belgian Flanders 1976–83, and West Germany, as we have already seen, although the rates appear constant for 1972–82 in Table 7.7. In all other modern societies for which we have data at two points in time there is a *decline* in the proportion of marriages where the spouses have equal levels of education. The largest falls are in Australia 1966–81 (70% down to 56%), Finland 1972–81 (67% down to 55%), Hungary 1960–80 (75% down to 64%), Norway 1957–72 (70% down to 51%), and the Netherlands 1959–83 (67% down to 43%). These societies include a wide spectrum of political, economic and social characteristics. The decline in educational homogamy is balanced by increases in the percentage of wives marrying up and, to a lesser extent, in wives marrying down. For example in the Netherlands, the percentage of wives who had married up rose from 28% to 39% by 1983, and this type of marriage appears to be overtaking homogamous marriages as the dominant choice. In contrast, in the USA, there was only a small increase in wives marrying up and a larger increase in homogamous marriages in the post-war decades.

Table 7.7 also shows that there is enormous variation among affluent modern societies in preferences for homogamous marriages or for marriages in which the husband has educational superiority. There is certainly no single convention on this point, and no sign of convergence between modern societies.

West German society stands out in Table 7.7 for its clear preference for less-educated wives over equally-educated wives—the only country of its type. It also has the lowest percentage of marriages where the husband is less educated, 8%–9%, as implied also by Table 7.5. As noted earlier, educational equality was achieved in West Germany, as elsewhere in Europe, in the period covered here, so the high percentage of wives marrying up can be read as a clear social, economic, and cultural preference.

In most other countries, marriages with educational equality greatly outnumber those with less-educated wives: rates vary around 60% and 20% nationally in the 1970s. However the balance is more even, or is becoming more even, in some countries, due to the growth in wives marrying up. By 1983, in the Netherlands, 39% of marriages involved a less-educated wife, with similar percentages in Norway (35% by 1972) and Japan (28% in 1965). If these trends persist, we can expect marriages with less-educated wives to outnumber homogamous marriages by the start of the 21st century in at least some countries. In the most economically developed countries there is a trend towards wives marrying up instead of educational homogamy, both absolutely and after controlling for differences in the educational distributions of husbands and wives; this trend became apparent from the mid-1970s onwards (Ultee and Luijkx 1990; Smits, Ultee, and Lammers 1998).[13]

A further analysis of these data by Uunk (1996) paints a slightly different picture. Uunk breaks down cross-sectional data on the stock of all married couples to present trends across birth cohorts from 1900 onwards. Because of smaller base numbers in this analysis, trends are somewhat erratic. Uunk concludes that, overall, levels of educational homogamy are fairly stable across cohorts, contrary to Ultee and Luijkx's conclusions based on stock data (Uunk 1996: 141). However this oversimplifies the picture. Using absolute measures of homogamy—what Uunk calls single trait measures—only the USA and Hungary were shown to have a stable level of homogamy. In almost all other countries, homogamy declines in the *youngest* cohorts, for example in Austria, Bulgaria, Czechoslovakia, Russia, Finland, Sweden, Norway, Denmark, the Netherlands, and Italy. Only in Japan and Malaysia were there small increases in educational homogamy across birth cohorts (Uunk 1996: 72). Uunk's analysis confirms that the level of educational homogamy varies across countries in the 20th century, as is clear from Table 7.7. The highest levels were in Hungary, Italy, and the USA. the lowest levels were in Russia, Holland, England, and Austria (Uunk 1996: 72). Unfortunately France and Germany were not included in the study.

Uunk makes the mistake of claiming that his cohort data are more 'correct' than cross-sectional data. But stock and flow data are equally valid; they answer different questions. Cohort data are best for identifying trends over time at the micro-level. National data on the stock of marriages gives an overview of the incidence of educational equality and inequality within marriages, complementing national data on the polarization of women's employment, and of wives' earnings, in Chapters 4 and 5.

[13] These two studies employ a simple homogamy/heterogamy dichotomy as an indicator of a closed/open society. In practice most educationally heterogamous marriages consist of wives marrying up, as the authors recognize (Smits, Ultee, and Lammers 1998: 274) and as is evident in Table 7.7.

In sum, the relationship between (trends in) educational heterogeneity, educational equality, and educational homogamy is more complex than was anticipated, and there are substantial differences between countries in marriage patterns. Overall, the evidence reviewed here shows an increase in wives marrying up at the expense of educational homogamy in most modern societies in recent decades—the USA and Japan are the two major exceptions. This would be consistent with the 'traditional' sexual division of labour being maintained in many families, with wives being full-time homemakers or secondary earners earning a substantially lower share of total family income. It appears that the educational equality of men and women achieved in the post-war decades has not eliminated women's preference for marrying 'up' whenever possible, by choosing husbands with greater education and earnings potential than themselves.[14]

Tables 7.2 and 7.4 illustrate the point that a considerable amount of women marrying up the educational ladder persists, or even increases, despite the increasing educational equality of men and women at the macro-level, due to increasing educational heterogeneity. Overall, the less qualified a woman is, the more likely she is to use the marriage market to acquire a husband with better qualifications, higher earning power, and better career prospects. The more educated a woman is, the more likely she is to achieve 'equality' in her marriage by being at least equally educated, or even better educated than her husband.[15] For men, the pattern is the exact opposite. The more qualified a man is, the more likely he is to marry a *less* educated woman. Two-thirds of university graduate men have wives who are significantly less qualified, and are thus likely to take on a supportive homemaker role, full-time or part-time. The differences between women with no more than basic secondary education and women with university degrees, or the equivalent, are so marked that we can talk of two different marriage markets and marriage patterns. It seems likely that the apparent impact of educational qualifications on female workrates is in reality confounded with the impact of the varying incidence of marrying up at each level of the educational ladder. This tentative conclusion remains to be tested in future research.

Additional research would also be helpful to test our thesis that educa-

[14] One hypothesis is that the trend towards serial monogamy in modern societies helps to maintain and even increase the proportion of all marriages that consist of a (young) wife marrying a more educated husband. This hypothesis states that the educational and occupational inequality of spouses is greater, on average, in men's second and third marriages than in men's first marriages. In other words, men do not only prefer younger wives for their second marriages, they also choose less-educated wives, all else equal. This hypothesis remains to be tested.

[15] Another way of interpreting these results is to say that women use the educational system to achieve entry to a better marriage market. Nationally, only 6% of wives married a university graduate man in 1996. The higher a woman's own qualifications, the greater the likelihood of her marrying a graduate man. Attending university herself almost guarantees a graduate husband: in 1996, two-thirds of these women married a man with equal or better qualifications. However the exact opposite is the case for men, suggesting that far fewer of them use the education system as a marriage market.

tional homogamy is more important than occupational or earnings equality in shaping marital relationships, and that educational homogamy produces a more 'egalitarian' climate in marriage than is found in couples where the husband is better educated than the wife. We already know that educational inequality between spouses leads to role segregation in the family.

Role Segregation and Family Relationships

It is notable that studies of married couples focus on spouses' occupations and earnings far more often than on spouses' educational level and its influence on family relationships (Menaghan and Parcel 1990). The available studies show that the degree of conjugal role segregation is strongly linked to the degree of educational equality in marriage: wives who are less educated than their husbands are most likely to be full-time homemakers, most likely to have the main responsibility for domestic and family work, and least likely to share tasks with their husbands. This has been found in a study of British managers (Pahl and Pahl 1971), a study of higher and lower professional men and their wives (Edgell 1980), a study of marriage in France (Singly 1996: 150–3), a study of working class and middle class couples in the Netherlands (Komter 1989), a survey of married couples in Belgium (Jacobs, De Maeyer, and Beck 1999), and a study of second generation immigrant Puerto Rican couples in New York in the 1980s (Rogler and Procidano 1989), for example. The 'hidden power' in marriage turns out to be nothing more exotic than a husband who is superior to his wife in education, occupation, and social status (Komter 1989: 194, 211). This may be the reason why surveys in France show that young women today prefer and hope to marry a man of equal education, whereas young men are often content for their wife to be less educated (Singly 1996: 41–2, 173–5).

Role segregation does not automatically equate with a sense of 'inequality' in the couple. An interesting study of young professional couples in the late 1980s in the USA (Sexton and Perlman 1989) found no evidence that full-time homemakers with 'traditional' sex-role attitudes had less marital power than career-oriented wives who had worked continuously, full-time, since graduating. The two groups of wives were equally likely to perceive themselves as active, assertive people—which the researchers labelled a masculine characteristic. Almost all wives perceived themselves as contributing 'more' to the marriage than their partners did. It may well be that the large degree of educational equality in these marriages eliminated differences observed in the past between single-breadwinner couples and dual-career couples. Virtually all the wives, as well as the husbands, were university graduates, and most of the wives in dual-career couples also had higher degrees. Sexton and Perlman express surprise at their findings, which contradicted all their expectations, but never notice the probable effects of relatively high educational equality in their sample, irrespective of whether the wives were working or not. Similar results are reported by Whyte (1990: 153–4) from a broader study of ever-married women in the Detroit Area Study in the 1980s. He found that 11% of wives earned significantly more than their husbands; 24% earned broadly the same; and 65% earned significantly less. However a wife's relative income, or relative financial dependence, was *not* related to marital power, and was *not* linked to marital success and satisfaction (Whyte 1990: 153–4, 161, 187–8). Similar results are reported for the 1970s from the West German housewife survey, which asked the women for a subjective estimate of the balance of power in their marriage. Wives with some income of their own, whether non-wage income or casual earnings, had more power within the marriage. But a non-working wife with high school education or higher education had an even more powerful position, suggesting that education can be as important as income in establishing bargaining power in marriage (Kuiper and Sap 1995: 91–2).

McRae (1986) carried out a study in England in the 1970s of wives who were teachers and nurses married to blue-collar workers, most of them skilled craftsmen. Here too, the focus was on the occupational status inequalities within these couples, and the social and psychological problems that often followed from this. However, the problems these couples confronted could have been due to their educational inequalities as much as to occupational and class differences. Within the tiny subgroup of couples where the spouses were equally qualified, but the husband had been far less successful in his career, there was a much higher level of amicable and explicit role reversal and less friction than in the marriages with educational inequality, where the majority of wives assumed personal responsibility for domestic chores, despite their main breadwinner role, as an expression of their femininity (McRae 1986: 125). Similar results were obtained from a study in the USA of wives who earned substantially more than their husbands (Atkinson and Boles 1984).

There is more information on the influence of spouses' educational level on their children's attainments in school, because this is treated as a sub-topic within social stratification and social mobility studies rather than as an indicator of the quality of family life and family relationships. All the evidence points to a profound influence of the mother's education, as well as the father's education, on the aspirations and achievements of children in the educational system. For example De Graaf (1986) demonstrated the strong effect of parental cultural capital on children's educational attainment in the Netherlands, and Singly (1996: 55–67) presents similar results for France. Mare (1981) has shown the importance of mother's education in the USA. Dale and Egerton (1997: 47–53) found that the mother's education can be even more influential than the father's education and occupation in shaping parental aspirations for their children's education. Maternal education was also more important for the educational achievements of daughters than was paternal education.

One of the factors with the strongest impact on a child's achievements in the educational system, and hence in the labour market beyond it, is learning to read at home *before* starting school. Being taught to read on a one-to-one basis, gradually, in the far less stressful environment of the home, before entering the more public and competitive social environment of the school, gives a child a permanent confidence in his or her ability to learn, and to master new skills which are socially valued. In Japan, all children learn to read at home, and often to write as well, using the *hiragana* script[16] around the age of 3 or 4, well before starting primary school at age 6, a phenomenon unique in the world, and which contributes significantly to the high school attainments of Japanese children. Taking the time to teach a child to learn to read is far more common in western European societies, especially in working class households, when mothers stay at home while their children are small. This crucial factor is overlooked in many studies of education, where the emphasis is on the contribution the school makes to a child's attainment (Rutter 1979). It helps to explain research results that are otherwise puzzling. For example, Dronkers (1995) found that children's attainment in primary school in the Netherlands was substantially better if the mother was a full-time homemaker than if she had a blue-collar job, after controlling for other relevant characteristics. The impact of the mother's occupation did not change over the 1970s and 1980s. In addition, he found that the educational level of the mother and father were equally important as determinants of the child's attainment (Dronkers 1995: 240–3).

Consistent results emerge from studies in Britain. Young mothers in the NCDS cohort study were less likely to read frequently to small children if they had a full-time job (Ferri and Smith 1996: 38). O'Brien and Jones (1999) found that in poor working class areas, mothers in *part-time* employment had the greatest beneficial impact on teenagers' educational attainment, doubling the likelihood of high grades in school exams when compared with mothers in full-time jobs. A mother's part-time job raised the family's standard of living while still leaving plenty of time for maternal supervision and encouragement of children's activities. The study also found that maternal praise for teenagers' achievements was a powerful determinant of subsequent success in school exams, increasing the odds of

[16] The *hiragana* is a phonetic and cursive alphabet with only 51 signs, which is much easier to learn than the full ideographic script, with a minimum of 3,000 characters regarded as necessary for everyday life. Teaching a child to read is regarded as just one of a mother's educational tasks before a child starts primary school in Japan, and it is one of the arguments offered in favour of women staying at home full-time while children are young.

achieving high grades by a factor of four. However the most important factor was the teenager's own motivation and educational aspirations (O'Brien and Jones 1999: 616).

In conclusion, an equally educated wife remains an intellectual equal even if she does not do paid work and contributes in time and effort, rather than in money, to the family income and well-being (Benham 1974, 1985). In effect, our thesis is that the educational equality of men and women, husbands and wives, is just as important, possibly more important, than the occupational equality or earnings equality on which attention has been focused up to now. This theory would explain why we perceive some fundamental shift towards 'equality' to have happened among younger couples, even when wives continue to be economically dependent on their husbands. In modern society, young wives are no longer psychologically subordinate even if they are financially dependent. And their educational qualifications provide an insurance policy against the need to be self-supporting if the marriage should end in divorce[17] or widowhood. One profound effect of opening up the educational system to women after the equal opportunities revolution was to dramatically increase the possibility of educational equality within marriage, especially when educational institutions function as marriage markets as well as places of learning.[18] In practice, this does not appear to have happened in Europe, except in West Germany. Only in the USA is there a small trend towards homogamous marriages, possibly because educational institutions function more effectively as marriage markets than they do in Europe, where this is a new development.

This theory requires to be further tested and refined. If confirmed, then this might be a sixth factor to be added to the other five causes of the new scenario reviewed in Chapter 3. We might even think of it as the educational revolution for women, alongside the contraceptive revolution and the equal opportunities revolution.

[17] There is a lot of emphasis on rising divorce rates in modern societies. However the fact remains that in most countries the *majority* of marriages do not end in divorce, and divorce is most often instigated by women rather than by men in modern societies. In addition, Jacobs and Furstenberg (1986) show that women who marry a second time achieve the same social status, on average, as in their first marriage. This result was polarized by the presence or absence of children from the first marriage. Women who did not have children from the first marriage achieved a notably *higher* socio-economic status in their second marriage, while divorced mothers had sharply reduced status in any second marriage. In contrast, Whyte (1990: 225) found that most women who remarried achieved higher socio-economic status than they would have had if they remained in their first marriage.

[18] People can meet potential marriage partners in the workplace. But this setting is more likely to produce inegalitarian marriages, of surgeon and nurse, manager and secretary, headmaster and teacher. Research shows that the percentage of homogamous marriages is highest for marriages contracted during, or immediately after full-time education, and for highly qualified women (Mare 1991).

Conclusions

Educational equality has given women and men the option of marrying equally qualified spouses. In practice, an increasing proportion of all marriages involve a wife who has married up, marriages of unequals that will normally give the husband superiority in cultural *and* economic capital. For our purposes, the key dividing line is not between homogamous and heterogamous partnerships, as in social stratification research, but between partnerships where the wife is less educated, and those where her qualifications are equal to or better than her husband's qualifications. In the second case, there is the real possibility of symmetrical family roles being chosen and implemented. In the case of wives marrying up, it is almost guaranteed that the couple will adopt a 'traditional' lifestyle with a clear division of labour, the husband being responsible for income-earning and the wife being primarily a homemaker. These two preferences must have complex causes, given the substantial cross-national variation in homogamy. For example, West Germany has an exceptionally high incidence of wives marrying up, the highest in Europe, whereas neighbouring Austria has the lowest percentage of such marriages in Europe. Despite the egalitarian ideals of socialist and Scandinavian countries, Britain, the Netherlands, Norway, and Czechoslovakia all have one-third of wives marrying up, and Sweden and Poland have one-quarter of wives marrying up by 1980, much the same level as in the USA. Only Hungary and Yugoslavia have low levels of wives marrying up.

We have to ask *why* do women continue to marry up when they now have the option of marrying equally? One answer must be that (partial or complete) role segregation in marriage is attractive to many people, over and above the productivity and efficiency gains set out by Becker (1991). This is usually labelled the 'traditional' family, but the label is arguably incorrect. It is a uniquely modern form of the family. Throughout history, wives, and often children as well, have worked alongside husbands to ensure survival and to rise above poverty. Throughout history, it is the *non-working* wife who has been seen as a sign of affluence and well-being. And large numbers of families with a non-working wife only became possible in the prosperous societies of the modern world. Partnerships with both spouses in employment are more correctly labelled 'traditional' families, and partnerships with role segregation are more correctly labelled 'modern' families.

A second answer is offered by Goldberg's theory of patriarchy in public and private life (Goldberg 1993). Goldberg argues that physiological differences between men and women, in particular the effect of male hormones such as testosterone on physical and emotional development, make men more self-assertive, aggressive, dominant, and competitive, *on average*, than women are. Sex differences that have their root in physiology are then amplified by the socialization process in childhood and adolescence to produce significantly different styles of behaviour in adults. In particular, heterosexual relationships involve an expectation or preference for male dominance in personal or sexual relationships. Over time, rituals and customs evolve which institutionalize male dominance—as illustrated by men paying the bill in restaurants, rather than women, or by men proposing marriage, rather than women. Male dominance in private, sexual relationships is readily achieved when the man ranks higher than the woman in economic and/or cultural capital from the start. In consequence, most women prefer to marry up if the opportunity arises. As educational heterogeneity increases, so do opportunities for marrying a man at least one level up in the educational and occupational hierarchy. Hence, in most modern societies, the rise in women marrying up is a close parallel to the increase in educational heterogeneity.

Whichever explanation is preferred, and the evidence is consistent with both, the fact remains that women today continue to prefer marriage to men who have money, status, and power, even when they themselves have achieved high earnings, whereas men continue to prefer young and attractive women, other things being equal. This long established exchange of complementary status and assets has been weakened by the educational equality of women and men, but it has not disappeared completely. If we use current patterns in educational inequality in marriage as a rough indicator, the feminist thesis, that women seek equality in private relationships, gets twice as much support as the evolutionist or Darwinian thesis that women seek wealthy or powerful men to be good providers while women focus on childrearing, because at present only one-third of women marry up. This is a minority, but a substantial one.

This chapter points attention to topics that have so far received far less research attention than the relative occupational status and incomes of spouses. Arguably, the relative educational status of partners is even more important, so the lack of interest in this topic is puzzling, especially as relevant data are readily available in household surveys and censuses. New research in this field is likely to be fruitful; it could shed light on the pay gap and the 'family gap' as well as on women's employment decisions—reflected in Table 4.4, for example—and work-lifestyle preferences.

8

Policy Applications

Social policies work best if they go 'with the grain of the wood' rather than against the grain. The presence of three separate preference groups among women complicates the policy process. Chapter 6 explored the *conflicting* interests of home-centred, adaptive, and work-centred women. This chapter extends the analysis by showing how policies have varying relevance to, and impact on the three groups. We cannot attempt a comprehensive review of *all* fiscal, social, family and welfare policies and their impact on women, but we discuss examples of each of them, to show their differential impact on the three groups of women. We focus on national government policies, because these affect everyone. Pronatalist policies are discussed first, because these affect all women, whereas labour market policy usually affects working women only. Employer policies are then examined more briefly, mainly to discuss how *differentiated* policies might operate, or do so already under other labels. Trade union policies are also considered, to underline the point that the difficulties of fair and even-handed support for all three groups of women are not restricted to employers and national governments.

In Europe, especially, governments have swung dramatically from a bias in favour of full-time homemaker mothers who almost never did paid work after marriage, to a bias in favour of women adopting the male work history of full-time, permanent, life-long employment with only the briefest of interruptions for childbirth and/or the care of elderly parents. Preference theory suggests that both strategies are equally partial, and fail to address the needs of all women.

The Rhetoric and Reality of Pronatalist Policies

Countries that have long relied on immigration as the principal source of additional labour and population growth, such as the USA, Canada, Australia, and New Zealand, have rarely felt the need to develop pronatalist policies. There is a similar situation in countries like Britain, where immigration—

mainly from Commonwealth countries, in particular the Indian subcontinent and the Caribbean—has been an important source of population increase, never fully compensating for the even larger volume of emigration from Britain to Canada, Australia, New Zealand, and the USA throughout the twentieth century. In contrast, countries such as France and Germany have been reluctant to offer permanent residence and citizenship rights to the large inflow of guestworkers, legal, and illegal immigrants from North Africa and Turkey, and they have been far more inclined to develop overtly pronatalist policies or the weak alternative of policies that support full-time homemakers and non-working wives. The degree of government support for the procreative activities of couples, or mothers, is often labelled as 'egalitarian' or 'family-friendly' rather than pronatalist. But support for native procreation in preference to immigration as a source of population increase can also be regarded as an indicator of ethnocentrism and xenophobia.[1] In some commentaries, the two alternatives are openly contrasted within such a perspective (Chesnais 1995). It could be argued that countries such as Sweden adopted an energetic 'sex equality' rhetoric for pronatalist policies in part to avoid this alternative presentation of the issues,[2] whereas a multicultural, multi-ethnic society like Singapore is frank and explicit about the rationales for successive antinatalist and pronatalist family policies (Hill and Fee 1995: 145–58).

The second important point is that countries without any explicit pronatalist policy objectives may still produce *de facto* pronatalist policies: policies that were originally developed for some other purpose but in practice produce pronatalist outcomes as a side-effect. Britain and the USA are again examples. Policies whose origin and rationale lie in the alleviation of poverty usually become pronatalist in their outcomes and effects. A frequent weakness of policy analysis is the failure to acknowledge both the *direct* and *indirect* impacts of policies. Too often, policies are assessed exclusively in terms of their aims and supporting rhetoric, and not in terms of usage rates and the full range of actual consequences. Also, there is a tendency for policy researchers to assume that policies are effective and produce their intended results. In reality, most social policies, including pronatalist policies, have

[1] The ISSP has shown that, across Europe, people with high levels of national pride tend also to have negative attitudes towards 'outsiders', particularly immigrants and other 'outgroups' (Jowell *et al.* 1998: xii). Definitions of 'outsiders' vary enormously. For example, Swedes point out that their population already includes a relatively high proportion (15%) of ethnic minorities, half of whom are Finns.

[2] However Haas (1992: 26) and Gustafsson (1994) claim that Swedes were always explicit and frank about their preference for employing native wives and mothers rather than immigrant males, in times of labour shortage, in contrast with the policy in Germany. The objections to immigrant males were that they arrived with their families, and created linguistic and cultural problems. Gustafsson also says that, from the 1930s onwards, there were political reasons for conflating pronatalist and social welfare policies in Sweden. McIntosh (1983: 163) is also clear that Sweden promotes pronatalist policies under the 'sex equality' label.

small effects, because there is often insufficient political support and/or insufficient economic resources for strong and effective measures (Demeny 1987; Gauthier 1996a, 1996b). And unintended consequences are commonplace.

In the 1990s, there was a lively debate in the USA over a new policy, the *family cap*, which attempted to overcome the pronatalist side-effects of welfare policies aimed at alleviating poverty (Donovan 1995). Because of the federal system, some states had already introduced the family cap, and had started assessing its impact, when the idea was discussed as a policy modification at federal level. The family cap is the rule that denies higher cash payments, such as Aid to Families with Dependent Children benefits, to a woman who conceives and bears a child while she is financially dependent on public welfare. Without the family cap, a mother's welfare income rose after each birth, in recognition of the family's expanding needs. The policy had an intuitive appeal, arguing that it was wrong for benefit dependents to be rewarded for having more children at public expense, and that they should be using effective contraception. The debate on the ethical and political issues was supplemented by a second debate, on whether the policy had any real impact on birthrates among solo mothers receiving welfare payments, and on whether a precise measure of the impact of such policies was in reality technically feasible (Donovan 1995).

Similar debates arise in other countries that provide destitute citizens, and sometimes foreigners—in the case of Britain—with means-tested welfare payments. In Britain, policy in the 1990s was directed at eliminating two other side-effects of anti-poverty policies, which might also be regarded as other examples of the free-rider problem in public goods. First, there were measures to prevent 'benefit tourism': non-resident visiting non-citizens who declared themselves destitute and thus eligible for all the welfare payments and social support available to resident citizens. Second, there were measures to force absent fathers to pay income maintenance to divorced and separated mothers who had become welfare dependents. Finally, there was debate over the need for new policies to prevent women without partners choosing to get pregnant and have a baby on their own, in the secure knowledge that after the child was born their earnings would be replaced by state welfare payments and housing support.

Public sector subsidized housing, or a cash housing subsidy, is as important as cash benefits in British anti-poverty policies, and there is evidence that public sector housing can have equally important pronatalist side-effects. In East Germany prior to reunification, housing policy was an essential element of pronatalist policies. In the context of housing shortages, women married and had at least one child in order to be eligible for separate accommodation (Duggan 1992; Einhorn 1993: 58). The poor results of Russian pronatalist policies seem to be due in large part to the government's failure to provide adequate housing for families: one-room flats in particular discouraged couples from having more than one child in urban areas (Lapidus 1988). Small homes also discouraged women from wanting to be full-time homemakers and fuelled a preference for going out to work.

A 1993 Eurobarometer survey on *Europeans and the Family* also pointed to the primary importance of housing and the economic situation, across the EU, in decisions about how many children to have, a result consistent with a 1989 Eurobarometer survey (European Commission 1993: 109, 115). Asked to choose the top three priorities for government action to help families, housing and the economic situation came top of the list, chosen by 49% and 43% of adults respectively. There was substantially lower support for reducing the cost of children's education (34%), flexible working hours (33%), improving childcare services (31%), offering tax allowances for dependent children (25%), improving family allowances (23%), and extending parental leave (22%), in contrast with the Commission's focus on childcare and parental leave as the main policy issues (European Commission 1993: 109–122).

'Egalitarian' policies for women often have pronatalist effects, just like poverty-alleviation and housing policies. This explains why birthrates in Britain are as high as in France, despite the lack of explicit pronatalist policies and other supports for (working) mothers which are offered in France (Hantrais 1992; see also Hantrais 1990, 1993, 1994, 1997), because financial support for the poor—or people suffering from social exclusion, in current terminology—is better in Britain than in France. The relatively high fertility rates of Sweden and other Nordic countries are also due to the pronatalist substance of 'egalitarian' policies that were initiated in the 1930s to reverse the population decline (McIntosh 1983, 1987; Gustafsson 1994; Gustafsson and Stafford 1994).

Preference theory clarifies why certain policies will always have side-effects that may be impossible to eliminate. Given a substantial group of home-centred women in the population, there will always be a minority of women who take up the opportunities for motherhood and homemaking as a full-time career that can be found within liberal policies to support the poor. It may not be a comfortable living, and many will dislike state dependence, but it does at least offer the benefit of doing what these women enjoy most, and probably do best. Preference theory also clarifies why certain policies are likely to fail. Work-centred women are unlikely to respond to pronatalist incentives, adaptive women will respond more readily, and home-centred women will be most enthusiastic in their response. Unfortunately, governments usually want to promote fertility rates among the most highly educated groups, following a eugenic logic (Lapidus 1988: 100–3; Hill and Fee 1995: 152).

Policies for Home-centred Women

Fiscal policy is one of the most effective tools of social engineering. It is often overlooked by sociologists because it poses greater technical difficulties for research than, say, attitudes to childcare, and because some fiscal systems are so complex that their underlying policy aims become unclear (Parker 1995; O'Donoghue and Sutherland 1999: 592). One weakness of welfare state research and typologies such as Esping-Anderson's classification, is that taxation is ignored, even though it makes a major contribution to income redistribution (Mitchell 1991: 193–4). Fiscal policy works through the tax and benefit systems. Cross-national comparisons of tax systems are a lot easier than comparisons of benefit systems. The tax system is universal and affects everyone, throughout the lifecycle, with regular annual accounts. In contrast, benefits are often payable only to particular groups of people or types of family, for limited periods or at particular stages of family life; some are lump-sum payments, others are paid in instalments; they may be paid in cash or in kind. Benefits are sometimes means-tested, usage rates are often well below 100%, and they vary hugely between countries. Benefits can be important in raising the income of poorer families. But it is difficult to discuss the effects of all benefits at the aggregate, national level; even more difficult to produce empirical measures of their impact; and extremely difficult to make cross-national comparisons. Gauthier (1996a) was forced to deal separately with child benefits, maternity leave benefits, childcare leave schemes, and public childcare services in order to draw comparisons across OECD countries, and most of the studies she reviews measure the impact—usually very small—of particular cash benefits on fertility, family structure, and women's workrates. As Gauthier (1996a: 326–7) points out, we really want to know the collective impact of all family benefits on household strategies, but studies and datasets have so far been too fragmented and partial to address this question.[3]

In 1985, the European Parliament recommended that the tax system should be neutral as between the married couple with one partner in employment and the married couple with both partners in employment (O'Donoghue and Sutherland 1999: 568). Many countries achieve this objective. Others actively reject this neutrality. When Sweden decided that all non-disabled adults should work throughout life, with individualized welfare benefits, fiscal policy provided the main policy tool. The tax and benefit systems were changed, so that husbands could no longer claim allowances for dependent wives, and women's maternity leave allowance was paid at 90% of their last earnings. From 1986, women remained eligible for paid leave at the

[3] A major study by Mitchell (1991) analysed 1980 data from the Luxembourg Income Study for ten OECD countries to show the aggregate impact of taxes and benefits on income distribution in each country. But she did not address the impact of fiscal policy on families with children.

90% level for 30 months after their first birth, thus encouraging women to plan two births in quick succession, a policy that had marked effects on child-bearing patterns in Sweden. As a result, female workrates are among the highest in Europe, most women are in full-time employment prior to childbirth, and most women return to paid work when they have exhausted their maternity leave entitlement, leaving their children in public daycare centres. The obligation to work is defined primarily through fiscal policy, and applies to everyone, people with dependent children as well as people without children. Gustafsson estimates that Swedish women's workrates would fall from 80% to 60% if they were confronted with West German tax rates. Subsidized child-care services support the policy for those with young children. Only one-third of Swedish children under 6 years old are cared for at home by a mother without a paid job, compared to about half of children under six in the USA, and three-quarters of children under six in the Netherlands. The individualization of work obligations and welfare benefits has a defamilializing impact, and divorce rates are high in Sweden (Gustafsson 1994: 350, 1995: 48, 112; Gustafsson and Stafford 1994; Sainsbury 1996: 86; Blossfeld and Hakim 1997). But despite policies that give no priority to the family and discourage dependent wives, about 10%–15% of all mothers remain continuous full-time homemakers in Sweden, compared to almost half in Britain and West Germany (Wetzels 1999: 50, 116).

In contrast, the German income-splitting tax system supports role-segregated households, where one partner specializes in income-earning while the other partner specializes in family work and homemaking. In the income-splitting system, the earnings of both spouses are aggregated and then split into two to compute the tax rate for each spouse (OECD 1995; O'Donoghue and Sutherland 1999). This tax system reflects the idea that a single bread-winner's earnings belong to both spouses equally, just as the domestic work of the homemaker spouse benefits both partners equally. Whereas Swedish fiscal policy encourages all adults to be economically self-supporting, the income-splitting tax system leaves it to spouses to decide how to divide roles and work within the family. For example couples who decide that both partners will hold part-time jobs and share family work equally are not penalized in comparison with couples who choose complete role segregation. As a result, women's workrates in West Germany are lower than in Sweden, but they are still close to the EU average (see Table 3.3). It is clear that the income-splitting tax system gives couples greater freedom of choice, without depressing female workrates to a low level. It treats married couples as a single unit for tax purposes, unless they choose to be taxed separately, and is thus consistent with most welfare benefit systems which deal with families or households as a unit, rather than with individuals. One side-effect is to reinforce joint decision-making in couples, just as one side-effect of the Swedish system is to make spouses' work decisions independent of each other (Wetzels 1999:

52, 117) and thus to facilitate and encourage separation and divorce, since individuals already function as separate financial units anyway.

The population crisis that Sweden confronted from the 1930s onwards may now be facing Japan, with falling birthrates generating public debate about the family and women's role. Japanese society and culture provide strong ideological support for role-segregation in the family, and women see being a wife and mother as their primary role. Rather than endure the exhausting demands of white-collar jobs in Japan, many highly educated women actively embrace their homemaker role, which is also publicly recognized as a crucial and valued activity. Most government policies assume and support complementary family roles, and jobs are organized almost exclusively for primary earners, who often work long hours of overtime, commit time to work-related socializing, and are always 'on call' for the company. Even part-time jobs can require over 30 hours a week. Japan has the lowest divorce rate of any developed nation: 1.52 per thousand in 1993, but women's employment rates are fairly average at 58% in 1997 compared to 51% in the EU and 67% in the USA (Boling 1998; OECD 1998: 193).

These family values are reflected in, and supported by the fiscal system, and by company pay systems (Shibata 1992). The Japanese tax system requires separate returns from each spouse, but allows husbands to deduct substantial tax allowances for himself, a dependent wife, and other dependents. In addition, wage structures in private companies give their married employees extra payments called spouse benefits, which are usually conditional on the wife having no earnings, or earnings below a level which is the same as the basic tax threshold for spouses—just over 1 million yen in the late 1990s. The larger the company, the larger the value of spouse benefits. The effect is to polarize married women's employment. Most wives take part-time jobs and keep their earnings below the threshold at which the wife must pay taxes and stops being carried on her husband's insurance policy, and her husband loses the tax deduction for a dependent wife as well as any spouse benefits from his employer (Shibata 1992; Boling 1998). About one-third of all female employees earn less than this threshold. At the other extreme, married women in professional and technical jobs with relatively high earnings, such as academics, are not deterred from continuing with their careers, and may themselves benefit from special family allowances paid by employers.

Table 8.1 illustrates how fiscal support for the family varies hugely, even within the small group of OECD economies. Average tax rates are shown for an unmarried single earner without dependents and a one-earner couple with two children aged between 5 years and 12 years. The information is presented for full-time production workers in manufacturing industries because this is the data most readily available, and comparable, for all member countries of the OECD. Manufacturing workers may not be representative of taxpayers

TABLE 8.1. *Average tax rate paid by an adult full-time production worker on average earnings in the manufacturing sector, 1994*

	One-earner couple with two children	Single earner
Countries with strong fiscal support for the family		
Luxembourg	0	13
France	2	9
Austria	2	8
Iceland	3	21
Japan	3	9
Portugal	4	7
Holland	5	8
Spain	6	13
Switzerland	6	11
Germany	8	19
Canada	11	22
USA	11	18
Belgium	12	24
Countries with minimal fiscal support for the family		
Greece	1	2
Italy	13	17
Norway	16	21
Ireland	16	23
Denmark	30	38
Countries with no fiscal support for the family		
Mexico	7	7
Britain	16	18
Australia	21	22
New Zealand	24	24
Turkey	26	26
Finland	29	29
Sweden	29	29

Note: Couples are married, with two children aged between 5 years and 12 years. Single earners are unmarried men and women with no dependent children. The average tax rate reflects a combination of federal, state, and local taxes.

Source: OECD, *The Tax/Benefit Position of Production Workers 1991–1994*, Paris: OECD, 1995.

generally within a country. They generally constitute a minority of employees, ranging from a low of 15% in Canada and 16% in Australia and Norway, to a high of 33% in Switzerland and Luxembourg, and 31% in Germany (OECD 1995: 11).

In countries with strong fiscal support for the family, single earners pay on average twice as much income tax as one-earner couples with children, and sometimes four times more (Table 8.1). At the extreme, Luxembourg levies no tax at all on a family of four compared to a 13% tax rate on a similar single earner's income. At the other extreme, a single earner in the USA pays only 60% more tax than someone with a wife and two children to support. A few countries are classified as offering only minimal fiscal support for families because there is a small difference between the two tax rates. In the third group, tax rates are virtually identical for the two types of earner. It is notable that the Nordic countries vary in financial support for the family: Sweden and Finland offer none at all, while Norway and Denmark offer minimal support. Although Anglo-Saxon countries are often grouped together, they too vary: Australia, New Zealand, and Britain offer no fiscal support for the family while the USA and Canada offer strong support for the working class family. Given the data available, the analysis necessarily offers an imprecise indicator of national differences in fiscal policy, but it does show how financial support for the family varies independently of income tax levels.

Another classification of advanced economies is presented by O'Donoghue and Sutherland (1999: Table 6). They compare the fifteen EU countries on the basis of the main types of income tax applied which should favour families with children. Their study did not look at the *outcomes*, in practice, of each tax system. None the less, their four-fold classification overlaps broadly with that presented in Table 8.1 as regards the EU countries.

There are several mechanisms used to provide financial support for families. Some form of income-splitting is used in Germany, Portugal, Luxembourg, Belgium, and France, with France having the most generous scheme. In the USA, Switzerland and Spain, tax bands are widened for a married couple's joint assessment, if they choose it, so as to produce much the same effect as from income-splitting. In other countries, substantial tax credits, cash transfers, or tax allowances are employed to assist families compared with unmarried single earners (OECD 1995; Gauthier 1996a; O'Donoghue and Sutherland 1999). There are clearly many different fiscal instruments available to support families, both in countries with high and low personal income tax. And there is no sign of convergence in tax regimes, even within western Europe. O'Donoghue and Sutherland (1999) simulated the impact of the French, German, and Spanish versions of income-splitting on family welfare in Britain. They concluded that most of the benefits in lower taxation would go to families with children rather than childless couples. They concluded that the French system was best, in terms of benefits for families with children. In addition, it treats secondary earners and non-working spouses more equitably than in independent taxation.

Social policies can also offer active and direct support for women who wish to concentrate their energies on home and children, for example by paying mothers a homecare allowance. Here, it is important to underline the distinction between benefits for dependent children and a homecare allowance for the mother.[4] *Benefits for dependent children*, or family allowances, are offered to all parents, to help with the extra costs of children's food, clothing, schooling, and so forth. They are normally paid *pro rata* to the number of dependent children, and may also take account of their ages, as teenagers cost more than babies. A *homecare allowance for the mother*, or father, who stays at home full-time to care for children does not need to be tied to the number of children. The money can be regarded as a wage for childcare at home, as a partial replacement for earnings foregone, or it can be used as a subsidy for purchased childcare services which enable the parent to return to work, either on a full-time or part-time basis. Most welfare states offer benefits for dependent children in some form or another (Hantrais and Letablier 1996: 144–6). The weakest form of child benefit consists only of tax deductions for parents in employment, reducing their tax burden somewhat. More positively, tax credits or cash payments can be offered, and cash benefits may be taxable or tax-free. Cash benefits inevitably have a larger effect on low-income families than on high-income families, because the benefits represent a larger proportion of the total household budget. Gauthier (1996a: Table 9.1) shows that the value of child benefits/family allowances varies hugely between countries, and is not necessarily linked to support for the family through the taxation system (see also Kamerman and Kahn, 1978, 1997).

As yet, few welfare states offer a homecare allowance to parents, although the idea is certainly popular. For example, in the late 1980s, Finland introduced a new policy that gave parents the right to choose between publicly provided childcare services and a cash benefit for childcare at home. For two decades previously, Finnish policy had prioritized public daycare services and lengthening maternity leaves with earnings-related benefits which allowed mothers to stay at home during the first year after childbirth, similar to the Swedish model (Ilmakunnas 1997). The new Home Care Allowance (HCA) is paid to all families who do not use the public daycare services, effectively providing a subsidy to fund one parent at home full-time or to help pay for private childcare services.[5]

In addition to a basic benefit for one child, there are 20% supplements for

[4] The fact that child benefit has to be paid to a parent, often the mother, means that these two benefits are often conflated in policy analyses, with child benefits being treated as if they constitute part of the mother's income. Similarly child benefits are often called 'family allowances', leaving it unclear who the intended beneficiary is.

[5] The Finnish HCA is a complex benefit, which is fully described by Ilmakunnas (1997). A simplified picture is presented here.

each additional sibling under school age. Some municipalities, including all the big cities, provide their own homecare allowances, in addition to the statutory, nationwide scheme. The income is taxable. Finnish labour law provides job-protected parental leave until a child is three years old. With closely-spaced children, quite long periods of absence from work are possible. The scheme was introduced when demand for labour was strong; unemployment has risen since then.

Funding is generous. While the exact value of the HCA varies according to family and local circumstances, as noted above, the allowance for one child can amount to the equivalent of some \$700–\$1000 a month, about \$8,000–\$12,000 a year. The maximum HCA for one child amounts to 40% of the average monthly earnings of female employees in Finland.

The scheme is popular and successful. From the start, two-thirds of all mothers with a child under three used the scheme. By the mid-1990s, three-quarters used the scheme in preference to the high quality public daycare services. Mothers with several preschool children were most likely to use the scheme. Usage is twice as high among mothers with low usual earnings as among higher-paid women. Popularity of the scheme was immediately reflected in a fall in workrates among women aged 20–39 (Ilmakunnas 1997). A similar scheme was introduced in mid-1998 in Norway, again offering a homecare allowance to mothers, or fathers, who did not use public daycare nurseries. The allowance is not taxable, is worth about £300–£400 a month, and at present is payable for children up to the age of two. Again, the logic of the scheme is that it expands choice, and offers an equivalent cash subsidy to those parents who choose not to use public nurseries. One expected consequence is that mothers' employment patterns will become more polarized.[6]

A similarly generous French scheme, introduced in 1986 and expanded in 1994, has also proven popular with mothers. The *Allocation Parentale d'Education* (APE) was initially a pronatalist measure, offered only to parents with three children, as an inducement to have a third child. When introduced in 1986, the APE was a flat-rate benefit of about £300 a month, not means-tested and not taxable, which was paid for three years, until the youngest child's third birthday. It was paid only if the mother had worked at least two years in the previous decade and she stopped working completely. The scope of the scheme was widened in 1994, and the APE is now paid from the birth of a second child. The value remained at around £300 a month in the 1990s (OECD 1995: 139).

By 1997, usage of the APE surpassed all other childcare subsidies and services. About one-third of mothers stopped working at the birth of their second child. The scheme contributed to a sharp drop in workrates among

[6] The ethnic minority population has recently been growing in the Nordic countries, and this seems to have prompted a diversification of policies and an expansion of choice, according to some commentators.

mothers of young children, and also helped to keep down unemployment rates. The popularity of the APE scheme, and of two other schemes—known by the acronyms AGED and AFEAMA—that provide subsidies for individualized childcare in the child's own home or in a childminder's home, can be seen in part as a criticism of public daycare services in France, which are not flexible enough to meet the needs of working parents. A 1987 national survey found that, given a choice, 80% of French adults preferred a policy of financial incentives for mothers to leave the workforce temporarily to care for their children over an improvement in childcare services and facilities for mothers of young children who continue working (Hantrais 1993: 135). It is clear that public policy can sometimes be wildly out of sympathy with the preferences of parents and citizens. The APE and similar schemes for individualized home-based childcare are successful because they fit the preferences of adaptive women as well as home-centred women, rather than being targeted on a single group.

An extension of the idea of a homecare allowance for active parenting is the idea of pension credits also being awarded for this period, so that the carer retains entitlement to an old-age pension. In the Netherlands, they go further still: women who have been full-time homemakers for most of their life are still entitled to a full pension in their own right, rather than on the basis of their husband's employment record and contributions. Similarly, in Japan, full-time homemakers receive a pension without having to contribute to the national pension scheme, an arrangement which many working women resent.

The two pioneering homecare allowance schemes in Finland and France[7] confirm that most mothers prefer to care for their young children themselves, and that financial considerations, rather than a strong personal commitment to paid work, are often the prime motivation for mothers' return to employment soon after childbirth, as noted in Chapter 4. Another factor is mothers' fear of losing their place on the jobs ladder. Some commentators also argue that personalized homecare serves children's interests better than collective daycare. It is notable that even in Sweden, only half of children under 6 attend subsidized daycare centres, and this figure includes babies under one cared for at home by a parent on parental leave (Gustafsson 1994: 51). There is also some evidence that the homecare allowance can be cheaper, overall, than public daycare nurseries.[8] Childcare subsidies paid for out of general

[7] Gauthier (1996a: Table 9.3) identifies seven western European countries, including Finland and France, with job-protected childcare leave schemes of 12 to 36 months duration which are at least partially paid, and nine western European countries with job-protected childcare leave schemes that are unpaid. Some of these schemes have eligibility conditions, and payments are sometimes restricted to people on low incomes. The schemes in Finland and France are distinctive in being long and covered by universal and generous payments to the stay-at-home parent.

[8] Einhorn (1993) reports that in the former East Germany and other socialist countries, children had higher sickness rates due to contagion in state nurseries, and in consequence mothers had to

taxation force women who want to look after their own children to pay for those who do not. The homecare allowance scheme redresses this imbalance.

The 1980s and 1990s saw a new stream of writing that explores what is lost in a society where parents are typically out at work most of the day, where parenting is a part-time or weekend activity at best, and where many children grow up with only one parent, usually in mother-alone families. These essays and studies usually conclude that social policy needs to re-evaluate the contributions of full-time mothers, and fathers, to society and communities in the aggregate as well as to the social and psychological development of children. This literature concludes that active parenting has become devalued (O'Donnell 1985; Umansky 1996; Benn 1998); that for most women motherhood remains central to their identity and is a positive experience (Ruddick 1989; McMahon 1995; Benn 1998); and that communities as well as individual families lose something from the trend towards dual-earner households that leaves residential neighbourhoods empty by day (Etzioni 1993a, 1993b). The new stream of writing on motherhood as a positive experience for women, and caring work as an important social contribution, represents a significant change of perspective from an earlier, feminist literature which presented motherhood and the family as noxious, imprisoning women in roles they did not choose or want (O'Donnell 1985; Umansky 1996). It is notable that many of these authors admit that their own perspective on motherhood changed radically after they had children themselves, and discovered that the feminist thesis was simply not borne out by reality. Several studies point out that working class women's expectations of motherhood are close to reality, while the expectations of women with higher education and professional experience are divorced from reality, so that motherhood becomes a more pivotal experience for them, altering priorities and life goals (O'Donnell 1985: 4–5, 57–9; McMahon 1995: 71–2, 99, 162, 267). This probably explains why even modest homecare payments to mothers attract an immediate, positive response. Such payments provide public recognition for the parenting role, and renew its legitimacy and social value by providing the mother with a minimum 'salary' for this work. Also, for mothers on low earnings, the allowance represents an adequate replacement income.

It is notable that pronatalist policies separate child-bearing and motherhood, and support the first but not the second. In Sweden, for example, reproduction is valued, but motherhood is probably just as devalued as in other western countries, in sharp contrast with Japan.

While there is general agreement that motherhood has become devalued

take a lot of time off work to care for them at home. It was calculated that in Hungary, mothers with young children spent up to 50% of their annual worktime at home on maternity or (child) sick leave, or 30%–40% on child sick leave alone. One Hungarian study found that the cost of homecare allowances for mothers was one-third the cost of providing public childcare facilities (Einhorn 1993: 34–5, 47).

in public opinion in modern society, there seems to be even less appreciation of the important contribution of fathers to their families and to wider communities (Blankenhorn 1995; Etzioni 1993a, 1993b; Dennis 1997). Families need fathers just as much as they need mothers. The father's role seems to be especially important during adolescence, particularly for boys. Girls can do well in school, for example, without a father's support, but they get a big boost if they have it, as noted in Chapter 6. For boys, the impact of a man taking an interest in their activities and achievements is much bigger. This suggests that it might be more fruitful to offer men paid parental leave when their children are teenagers rather than when they are small babies. In any event, usage rates for paternal leave in the early years of a child's life are very low, even in Nordic countries, as noted in the next section.

Policies for Adaptive Women

Adaptive women are characterized by divided loyalties, so they are responsive to all and any policies and schemes which tip the balance towards paid jobs or towards homemaking. This group benefits from all the schemes that recognize and reward individualized child-rearing in the home described in the previous section, *and* from all the equal opportunities policies that are so important to work-centred women. Adaptive women benefit just as much as home-centred women from the fiscal policies described above that leave couples free to decide for themselves how to divide family work and paid work. Income-splitting, for example, offers a degree of flexibility that is helpful to women who move in and out of the workforce, and who move between full-time and part-time work. Subsidized collective childcare services are of particular interest to adaptive women. Indeed, it appears that virtually all the pressure for public childcare services comes from this group. Part-time jobs, and long career breaks of 5–10 years are especially attractive to adaptive women, but these are employer schemes, and are discussed in a later section. As regards public policy, many small things can make a big difference to the co-ordination of family life and jobs, including school timetables. It is puzzling that there has been more public debate about the need for employers to develop family-friendly policies than about the need for governments to insist that the public institutions under their control must offer family-friendly services and timetables.

The most obvious example is the failure of schools to offer family-friendly timetables and services. In most countries schools do not take charge of children for the whole day, including providing lunch at midday, throughout the week, throughout the school term, and throughout the year. School timetables often assume the presence of a parent at home, on a daily or periodic basis, even during school terms: for example to provide lunch at home every day in the Netherlands, to provide lunch at home and homework supervision every afternoon in West Germany, to provide home supervision for Wednesday school closures in France, and to provide parental supervision for one-week holidays in the middle of every school term in Britain. The long school holiday in the summer was originally designed to meet the needs of agricultural communities where children helped with harvests. It is not suited to urban lifestyles and to dual-earner families, and it appears also to be educationally dysfunctional. It is surprising that public policy puts pressure on employers to be family-friendly, while failing to achieve school timetables and services that are better co-ordinated with the needs of working parents. Similarly, in some countries public policy has accepted rigid shop hours that are ill-suited to the needs of working parents. We might conclude that debate about employers' policies has become a smoke-screen that conceals the absence of family-friendly services and timetables in the public sector, which is often due to trade union resistance as well as to lack of imagination at management level.

Adaptive women are likely to be heavy users of public adult education courses offering technical updating or more substantial additional qualifications. Work-centred women, like men, are more likely to attend their employer's updating courses, on-the-job, or to invest their own money in extra qualifications, such as an MBA. Because their commitment to work is limited, most adaptive women will not be prepared to invest their own money, or to take out loans for education; instead they will expect courses to be free or heavily subsidized, as well as being family-friendly in timetables and other arrangements such as on-site crèches.

It is often argued that the Nordic model offers the best collection of social policies for adaptive women, who want to combine employment with family activities, policies that give women equal access to jobs in the labour market, financial independence, and high-quality subsidized childcare services that mean women do not have to choose between a job and having children. This perspective is promoted by Nordic social scientists, who have devised several classifications of welfare states that always place the modern Nordic welfare-state at the apex of typologies, as the best-practice model, or even the 'model country' which other countries should emulate (Esping-Andersen 1990; Julkunen 1992; Melkas and Anker 1997: 343, 1998: 8). This idea is also promoted by some social scientists outside the Nordic countries (such as Sainsbury 1996) and it has achieved an informal orthodoxy in certain circles. Some politicians go further still. In a 1996 interview, Allan Larsson, Director General of DGV in the European Commission complained that women's workrates in the EU were still much lower than men's employment rates; he insisted that the days of the male breadwinner taking responsibility for household financial well-being throughout working life, while women assume the bulk of domestic responsibility, had effectively gone; and he dismissed the 'old social contract' with a division of responsibilities between spouses, as 'no longer valid' (European Commission 1997d: 4). Larsson effectively stated that Commission policy was to outlaw the so-called 'traditional' —in fact modern—sexual division of labour in the family, and insist that the Scandinavian model must be extended to all EU citizens, irrespective of preferences. It is thus worth looking at the outcomes of Nordic policies fairly carefully. Sweden is usually taken as the best, or most extreme, illustration of Nordic policies. As noted earlier, there are in fact substantive policy differences between Iceland, Norway, Sweden, Finland, and Denmark, as illustrated by variations in fiscal policy and the homecare allowance. But most typologies insist on their policy similarities, over and above the cultural similarities, and that Sweden is the best exemplar of the type.

For most social scientists, linguistic barriers have impeded a close examination of policy outcomes in any of the Nordic countries. This may explain the heavy reliance on female workrates as the main, or even the sole social indicator in cross-national comparisons. As shown in Table 3.3, Denmark and Sweden have the highest female employment rates in the EU; together with Finland, they have the highest FTE employment rates at 56%–60% of all women of working age.[9] These high workrates have been interpreted as reflecting women's preference for paid work over family work, and for financial independence over dependence on a spouse. Recently, however, there has been greater recognition that high workrates are also forced on Nordic women, by fiscal systems that undermine men's ability to be the sole economic supporter of their household, and that oblige all adults to be gainfully employed, thus reducing the need for immigrant labour (Melkas and Anker 1997: 344, 1998: 9). Dual-earner families have been made a structural necessity, not a choice among several options. However these policies are generally described and evaluated as 'gender equality' policies (Sainsbury 1996; Melkas and Anker 1998). On this criterion, they can be judged of dubious value, at best, and as failures, at worst. As studies in the 1990s finally recognized, the Nordic countries have achieved less than other western European countries, less than North American countries, and less even than Asian countries, in their aim of integrating women into the workforce as equals with men (Wright, Baxter, and Birkelund 1995; Anker 1998; Melkas and Anker 1997, 1998). Parental leave schemes, and other policies designed to promote greater sharing of child-rearing and family work between spouses are also a failure (Moen 1989; Haas 1992; Hoem 1995). The huge and instant-

[9] Table 3.3 presents employment rates. These are slightly lower than labour force participation rates, which include the unemployed. For the age group 15–64 years, and for the period 1991–93, Melkas and Anker report labour force participation rates of 70% in Finland, 77% in Sweden, 78% in Denmark, and 80% in Norway and Iceland. Melkas and Anker (1998: 8–28) provide a statistical summary of the labour market position of women in the five Nordic countries and how it compares with other OECD countries.

aneous success of homecare allowance schemes, noted above, testifies to the failure to inculcate egalitarian sex-roles, despite decades of public education, advocacy research, public rhetoric, and advertising.

The most comprehensive cross-national comparative study of the sex segregation of occupations was completed by the ILO in 1998 (Anker 1997, 1998; Melkas and Anker 1997, 1998). The study used data on the occupational structure of 41 countries for the two decades 1970–1990 from population censuses or labour force surveys. Unlike most previous comparative studies, that used aggregated classifications with only 9–20 occupation groups (Hakim 1992: 132), this study employed detailed occupational data, using classifications with 187–461 separate occupational groups. Several measures of occupational segregation were employed, and the study explored vertical segregation as well as horizontal segregation.[10]

The results showed that, after excluding agricultural occupations,[11] the level of occupational segregation in Nordic countries was substantially higher than in other OECD countries, and substantially higher than in Asian countries such as China, Hong Kong, Malaysia, and India. Only the predominantly Islamic Middle East and North Africa, and certain developing countries, had similar or higher levels of occupational segregation (Anker 1998: Table 9.1). These unexpected results led the ILO to carry out fuller analyses of the data for Sweden, Norway, and Finland, which were presented within the context of Nordic gender equality policies (Melkas and Anker 1997, 1998). These reports highlighted some meagre achievements and, by restricting comparisons to the OECD countries, avoided the embarrassing conclusion that in particular respects sex equality in the Nordic labour markets was on a level with some poor developing countries. It might be argued that the level of occupational segregation is not the only measure, or the best indicator, of women's position in society. However the ILO's presentation of their research results insisted that occupational segregation is an important measure of gender equality in the workforce; that it produces serious inefficiencies in the economy; and that policy should aim to repudiate, if not eradicate it in all civilized societies (Anker 1998: 5–9).

What this means in practice is that about half of Nordic women are in female-dominated occupations compared to about one-quarter of women workers in other industrialized countries. In this study, female-dominated occupations are those with 80%+ female workers. They generally constitute lower-status, less qualified, and lower-paid jobs in any industry—even in the Nordic countries. Women are nurses while men are doctors; women are primary school teachers while men are university lecturers; women are secre-

[10] See note 3 in Chapter 1 for definitions of these terms.

[11] Including agricultural occupations usually reduces the level of occupational segregation in a country, given that women and men both do agricultural work, and agricultural occupations are never finely differentiated in occupational classifications.

taries while most managers are men, and these patterns are much stronger in the Nordic countries than in other OECD countries.[12] In sum, both the horizontal and vertical sex segregation of occupations are higher in the Nordic countries, despite welfare state policies that promote sex equality and allow women to combine paid work with family work.

To counterbalance these results, the authors emphasized that the pay gap is smaller in Nordic countries than in other European countries (Anker 1998: 34; Melkas and Anker 1998: 19). However this is largely due to the fact that earnings differentials generally are smaller in Nordic countries than in the USA and most European countries (Blau and Kahn 1994). It is also due to the ILO report presenting earnings data only for manual workers in manufacturing industries, where few women work. Manufacturing industries account for about one-fifth of all employees in the five Nordic countries (OECD 1995: 11), so they are not representative of the whole workforce anyway. When earnings data for *all* workers are obtained from household survey microdata, the pay gap in Sweden and Norway is shown to be very close to that found in Italy, Austria, West Germany, and Australia in the 1980s.[13] Recent research shows no change by the 1990s. Petersen *et al.* (1997) report a pay gap of 21% in 1990 in Norway, which was due mainly to the high level of occupational segregation. They point out that the pay gap in Norway thus differs little from that in the USA, despite institutional and ideological differences. An analysis of aggregate hourly pay statistics for full-time employees in the early 1990s found pay gaps of about 20% in Norway, Britain, France, and Australia, about 25% in the USA and Canada, and about 30% in West Germany (Grimshaw and Rubery 1997: Table 7). It appears that the pay gap in Nordic countries is no different from that in other advanced economies. One study identified a pay threshold in the Nordic countries below which are eight out of ten women, and above which are eight out of ten men (Anttalainen 1986, quoted in Melkas and Anker 1998: 19). In sum, Nordic women have not achieved any significant degree of equality with men in market work, in terms of access to the top jobs, occupations with authority, or higher pay.

In consequence, Nordic couples differ little from couples in other advanced economies as regards wives' financial dependence on the husband.

[12] A comparative study of Britain and Sweden concluded that they had similar levels of horizontal occupational segregation by the late 1990s (Meadows 2000). It appears that occupational segregation fell sharply in Sweden in the 1990s, after it joined the EU, and after a deep recession in the early 1990s. However levels of vertical occupational segregation remain unchanged, and are still much higher in Sweden than in other modern societies. For example less than 3% of working women hold management and senior government jobs in Sweden compared to 11% of working women in Britain (Meadows 2000).

[13] Blau and Kahn present earnings data for the mid-1980s for all workers, adjusted only for hours worked. They show average female earnings as a percentage of male earnings to be 82% in Italy, 77% in Sweden, 74% in Austria, 73% in Australia, 71% in Norway and West Germany, 67% in the USA, 65% in Switzerland and Hungary, and 61% in Britain (Blau and Kahn 1994: 109). The ratio for Britain is reduced by the inclusion of a large part-time workforce; the ratio was 74% in the mid-1980s when analysis is restricted to adult full-time employees (Hakim 1996a: 175).

As shown in Table 4.7, husbands contribute about 62% of total earnings in Nordic countries compared to 67% in North America, and about three-quarters in other European countries. A fuller analysis by Hobson (1990), using data for the mid-1980s, shows that the Nordic countries differ in having much lower proportions of wives with no earnings at all who are totally dependent on their husband: 11% in Sweden and 25% in Norway, compared to 68% in Holland, 53% in Switzerland, 49% in West Germany, 40% in Australia, 36% in Canada, and about 30% in the USA and UK. However the Nordic countries have not produced substantial proportions of couples where spouses have roughly equal earnings: 12% in Sweden and 8% in Norway, compared to 10% in the USA, 8% in Canada and Australia, 6% in Germany and the UK, and 3% in Switzerland and The Netherlands (Hobson 1990: Table 1; see also Sorensen 1994: Table 5). Wives' economic dependency is reduced, but certainly not eliminated in the Nordic countries. Nordic wives are typically secondary earners, just as they are in other advanced economies.

Contrary to expectation, the ILO found that the USA and Canada had the lowest levels of occupational segregation within the OECD. These are liberal and *laissez-faire* economies with few welfare state and family-friendly policies, but with a fierce commitment to the sex and race equality that is the hallmark of meritocracies. The ILO concluded that the sex segregation of occupations is not related to socio-economic development, and that social, cultural, and historical factors are the main determinants of the sexual division of labour (Anker 1998: 409). Another interpretation of their results is that the pronatalist element in Nordic policies negates and outweighs the impact of the equal opportunities element, or that policies that push all women into employment, irrespective of preferences, are incompatible with sex equality in the workforce. A study of nine western European nations[14] by Charles (1998) led her to conclude that gender-equality norms facilitate the integration of women into professional and managerial occupations, but high levels of female employment are associated with greater segregation of women into female-dominated service sector occupations, which are generally low status. The Nordic countries' failure to achieve sex equality in the workforce, despite high female workrates, is duplicated in the socialist USSR (Lapidus 1988) and egalitarian Israeli *kibbutzim* (Agassi 1989), but not in socialist China, which has the lowest level of occupational segregation in the world, even after excluding agricultural occupations (Anker 1998: Table 9.1). The USSR and Israeli *kibbutzim* combined pronatalist policies with a requirement that all women do 'social work'. In contrast, overpopulation and periodic famines meant China did not need pronatalist policies. On the contrary, antinatalist policies allowing only one child per woman were implemented in the 1980s

[14] Charles (1998) analysed data for Sweden (1990), Britain (1991), Belgium (1991), France (1990), Luxembourg (1991), Germany (1993), Switzerland (1990), Italy (1991), and Portugal (1991).

and 1990s, to reduce the population to a manageable size. It appears that egalitarian or socialist policies can achieve sex equality in the workforce, if used in isolation, as illustrated by China. However if pronatalist and family-friendly policies are implemented at the same time, they negate and outweigh the impact of gender-equality policies, as illustrated by the Nordic countries, Israeli *kibbutzim*, Russia and the socialist countries of Eastern Europe prior to 1989.

Sex equality within the family appears to be no more of a success in the Nordic countries. As Haas (1992) points out, Sweden provides a strategic test of the impact of parental leave policies, as Sweden has the most generous schemes of all, with 80%–100% replacement of earnings for the first 12 months after a birth (since extended to 18 months), reduced pay for another 3 months, and entitlement to a further 18 months of job-protected unpaid leave (Gustafsson and Stafford 1994: 344; Meadows 2000). Despite this, half of all fathers took no parental leave at all, so that the mother alone cared for the new baby. Among couples who shared the leave, fathers took about 15% of the total. Nationally, fathers take only 5%–8% of all parental leave days taken in Sweden. Haas concludes that the scheme has been a failure, and that the egalitarian polemics used to promote it failed to persuade men to become involved in the care of small babies (Haas 1992: 61, 224). The Swedish experience is typical of other Nordic countries. Men's usage rates for parental leave are just as low elsewhere: 1% in Norway, 2% in Denmark, 3% in Iceland, with a maximum of 13% in Finland (Haas 1992: 61–3). Surveys of new parents showed that most Swedish mothers preferred *not* to share care of a newborn with the father, and that men with high work commitment and those in professional and managerial occupations were least interested in using parental leave. Although they routinely endorsed egalitarian values, most Swedes still held conventional ideas about roles within the family: 77% of fathers and 57% of mothers thought the father should be the primary income-earner; 66% of fathers and 54% of mothers thought success in the job ought to be a man's main goal in life. Many of the women, including professionals, gave priority to motherhood over market work (Haas 1992: 76, 80, 88, 177–9). Moreover, three-quarters of mothers and fathers were against any compulsion for men to take parental leave (Haas 1992: 75).

Despite this, the scheme was altered in the 1990s to introduce a compulsory period of 30 days' parental leave for fathers. If the father does not use his one-month minimum share of parental leave, it cannot be transferred to the mother, and is thus lost. The new rule had only a tiny impact. By the late 1990s, fathers were taking only 11% of all parental leave days, and half still took none at all; most of the fathers taking any leave were in the public sector and had wives in higher status jobs (Meadows 2000). Despite the 'egalitarian' rhetoric, the private sector—where most men work—is hostile, in practice, to one-month absences from work for workers who have scarce expertise or hold key posts, just as in the USA (Fried 1998).

It is clear that Swedish policy-makers adopt policies that work 'against the grain' and are using social engineering to attempt to redesign family roles and sex-roles. It also appears that these efforts are not really successful, unless an element of compulsion is introduced that literally forces choices and behaviour, and not even then.

Some scholars are now concluding that Nordic egalitarian policies have failed, that the aim of complete gender symmetry is probably unattainable, and that policies acknowledging women's greater involvement in child-rearing would be preferable (Hoem 1995: 295). Family-friendly policies certainly help adaptive women to combine employment with family work. But it appears that they cannot, as some have hoped, also produce complete equality of men and women in the labour market, and apparently not even in the family either. This second objective is feasible, but only for work-centred women, an entirely different group. In sum, the policy failed to distinguish between adaptive and work-centred women. The achievements of the two groups differ because adaptive women have divided loyalties that cannot be resolved by time flexibility alone.

National policies that offer mothers substantial periods of paid and unpaid maternity leave, the right to work shorter hours, and other benefits to help reconcile work with family life do have unintended side-effects. One effect is that employers in Sweden, for example, have come to regard women of child-bearing age as unattractive employees (Haas 1992: 174). Similarly, prior to reunification in 1989, East German employers regarded women as 'unreliable' workers, because of their entitlement to frequent absences to care for sick children and for other family obligations. This meant that women were far less likely to be promoted to management positions (Einhorn 1993, 1997: 69). It is no accident that in Sweden the majority of women work in public sector jobs, while most private sector jobs are held by men. Chapter 9 considers wider responses among men to women's newly-gained special advantages in the workforce.

Policies for Work-centred Women

No special social or family policies are required for work-centred women. Apart from entitlement to basic job-protected maternity leave, their needs and interests are much the same as for men. However, active policies to prohibit and prevent discrimination on grounds of sex, race, and marital status are crucially important for this group, especially in relation to the secretive, private processes of promotion systems within organizations and occupational careers. Even in the 1990s, women continued to be 'frozen out' of management jobs by the sex-role stereotyping that continues to profile managers and senior posts in masculine terms (Hakim 1996a: 184). In a sense, work-centred women have moved beyond sex and gender. Their problem is that they continue to be labelled as women, stereotyped as having the divided loyalties of adaptive women or the marriage career ambitions of home-centred women. The problem for work-centred women is statistical discrimination (Phelps 1972). The difficulty of avoiding this discrimination is reinforced by the fact that there are no agreed conventions for identifying and distinguishing the three preference groups, to enable employers to devise differentiated policies for them, where appropriate. On the contrary, it has now become conventional for all women to protest their complete commitment to their jobs and careers, and to deny that they feel any competing loyalties to their families. In some cases, organizational procedures and the law force this position on women. As noted in Chapter 4, virtually all women who are eligible for job-protected maternity leave in Britain tell their employer that they want to return to their job after childbirth, but only about half do so in practice. Even today, the successful outcome of a pregnancy cannot be guaranteed, so it is rational for all women to promise to return to their jobs, just in case. At the same time, employers are left with the difficulty of trying to predict *which*, if any, of their employees will in fact return to their jobs. And only a minority of mothers of small children return to full-time work (see Table 4.8). Policies which permit, or endorse, women's self-identification as work-centred and career-committed, as the basis for mutually-enforceable contracts, might be helpful, but they are likely to be seen as controversial. Such policies have already been introduced in large companies in Japan. About half of the young women selected for entry to the 'male' career tracks—which generally involve geographical mobility as well as long hours of work—drop out within a couple of years, complaining of exhaustion and/or sex discrimination. It is too early to see the long-term effects. However the situation in Japan may not have close parallels in Europe.

In Europe, it is already evident that up to half of women who achieve the highest grade professional and managerial jobs remain childless, thus avoiding all the work–family conflicts that men deal with by having homemaker wives who take the main responsibility for domestic and family work, or else by remaining single. For example a study of women in the top jobs of the British National Health Service found that half were childless, although the majority had married at some point (Wyatt and Langridge 1996). Similarly, Coatham and Hale (1994) found that the majority of women in top management jobs in housing were childless. In both cases, the women reported that their jobs and careers necessarily involved long hours of work and substantial geographical mobility, which men accept but are incompatible with the more 'balanced' combination of employment and family work that adaptive women prefer. For those work-centred women who do have children, childcare is simply not an issue, as they do not hesitate to pay for substitute childcare so that they can continue doing their own job, at whatever level of pay. A recent cross-national comparative analysis of EU and OECD countries by Dex and Sewell (1995) concluded that the provision of childcare for preschool children had no effect at all on women's chances of reaching the top professional and managerial occupations. On the contrary, childcare provision was positively related to women's concentration in low-paid jobs (Dex and Sewell 1995: 386–8), a finding consistent with the ILO study's results described earlier.

The policies needed by work-centred women are already in place in most advanced economies: the argument against sex and race discrimination has already been won in principle, even if it takes some time for attitudes and practices to fully adapt, among trade unions as well as employers, as we see in the next section.

Employer and Trade Union Policies

Employers, in consultation with trade unions, generally offer their workers a range of benefits in addition to basic pay, such as paid holidays or paid sick leave, at the minimum, extending to a variety of other benefits, such as low-interest loans or private health insurance. As a result of increasing numbers of women in the workforce, attention has started to focus on employers' family-friendly policies and benefits. These can be grouped into four broad categories:[15] flexible working hours, time off work and holidays, dependent care and related services, and other benefits.

Flexible working hours and alternative work schedules constitute the largest and most diverse group, offering benefits to all workers, potentially, as well as to those with young children. This category includes temporarily reduced working hours, permanent part-time hours, job-sharing, flexitime arrangements, school term-time working, annual hours arrangements, the option of working at home on a regular or occasional basis, and any other modification of the standard full-time year-round working week with fixed daily work hours. Shiftwork in all its many forms is usually excluded, because it is dictated primarily by the needs of the employer's business rather than the worker's needs. For example rotating eight-hour shifts have always been a necessity in police work and in hospital nursing, and were later introduced into factories operating continuous processing. Shiftwork is usually unpopular with workers. However shiftwork can sometimes be attractive to workers as well, if they are able to work one particular shift on a regular basis which fits in with family work. For example some nurses prefer to work regular night

[15] This classification is a modified version of the classification presented by Guerin *et al.* (1997).

shifts while their children are young. If a substantial premium is paid for shifts at unsocial hours, men can also find them attractive when they have a family to support. Shiftwork and overtime are the oldest forms of flexible working hours. The newer forms, listed above, have generally been developed to suit the needs and preferences of *both* worker and employer, producing mutually advantageous arrangements in most cases (Bosch, Dawkins, and Michon 1994: 27).

Time off work (paid and unpaid) normally constitutes an addition to annual paid holiday allowances, which vary between countries from the two-week norm in the USA and Japan to the 5–6 week norm in some European countries. This category includes paid and unpaid maternity leave around the time of a birth or adoption (which can vary from 1–12 months); paid or unpaid paternity leave (which can vary from 1 day to 4 weeks); parental leave (longer periods of up to three years' absence from work which may be reimbursed by state benefits); career breaks (unpaid leave of up to five years); and special leave for family needs and emergencies. This last is the most variable category, ranging from being allowed the occasional day off work to attend a funeral, for example, to a fixed allowance of 5 paid days a year for family needs (such as sick children or childcare arrangements breaking down), to up to 10 unpaid days' absence a year to deal with family needs. In Sweden, parents are entitled to 120 days' paid leave per child per year to look after sick children, as well as the right to work part-time (Gauthier 1996a: 310; Meadows 2000), rights that are used almost exclusively by mothers. In the former USSR and Eastern European countries, mothers were often allowed an unlimited number of paid days special leave to care for sick children, a practice that led to women being regarded as unreliable workers and unsuitable for promotion to management grades.[16] Inevitably, if family-friendly benefits are used very extensively, workers risk being informally devalued by employers and colleagues, just like a worker who is perennially absent on sick leave. In Japan, fear of informal hostility from their colleagues and superiors leads many women not to use maternity leave and other rights and benefits that are formally available to them. In Sweden, men rarely use paternal leave, as noted earlier. In the USA, in many corporations, parental leave is rarely used by men and women in senior management (Fried 1998).

Dependent care and related services provide assistance, in cash benefits, free or subsidized services, for childcare and the care of elderly dependents. This category includes crèches and childcare services provided on-site at the workplace, sometimes free of charge or at subsidized low charges; cash benefits to assist with childcare services chosen by the worker; information and referral services concerning care for children and/or elderly dependents; and help in

[16] Children in day-care nurseries had high sickness rates due to higher rates of contagious illnesses, so that mothers did, in practice, need to take large amounts of leave to care for sick children (Einhorn 1993).

dealing with domestic emergencies. Until recently, the emphasis has been on childcare services and benefits, but the equivalent pressures on older workers with elderly dependents are now being recognized by employers.

The fourth category consists of a miscellaneous range of *other benefits*. In countries where health services are not provided free by the state, such as the USA, medical insurance that covers all members of a worker's family can be a crucially important employer benefit. Among employers who periodically relocate workers to another city or to another country, various family benefits may be supplied in addition to refunding the essential costs of a transfer—such as providing information and advice on schools and on job opportunities for trailing spouses in the new location; free trips to visit the new location; assistance with the costs of house purchase, and so forth. Employers sometimes provide benefits specific to their business or industry. For example, employers in the financial services industry often provide cheap loans to assist with house purchase. Educational institutions sometimes provide free or subsidized educational courses for staff or their children. Manufacturers may offer their products to employees at discounted prices.

It should be clear that family-friendly policies shade into the many other benefits and options that employers provide (Cobble 1993). They are not a distinct group, if only because male employees have always had families to support. Furthermore, many of the options and benefits now labelled as family-friendly were previously introduced for other reasons, and they can be just as advantageous to employees without young children as to those with responsibility for children. The impetus for change may initially be the problems of mothers. But new schemes can be designed to apply to all workers rather than being exclusive to one subgroup of employees.

One example is the career break: unpaid leave for a period up to five years. The idea of the career break first arose in relation to mothers who prefer to stay at home to care for a pre-school child, returning to paid work after the child starts school. Once the option was formalized, it proved attractive to other workers as well, for different reasons. For example, it allows employees to take unpaid leave to return to full-time education and gain extra qualifications. In Britain, the career break proved attractive to the children of immigrant families, who wanted the opportunity of extended visits to their parents' country of origin, to visit relatives and explore their cultural roots. Career breaks are also used for a variety of personal initiatives, where people want the security of being able to return to their previous job if the new venture is unsuccessful.

An older example is part-time jobs. In some countries, such as Italy and Greece, male-dominated trade unions prevented the introduction of part-time jobs on the grounds that male workers had no interest in them (Bosch, Dawkins, and Michon 1994; Blanpain and Rojot 1997; Blossfeld and Hakim 1997). Indeed, part-time jobs, flexible working hours and novel working arrangements generally were decried by trade unions as exploitative and unfair. In many European countries, trade union resistance persists to this day (Hakim 1997: 47–52). After trade unions began to recognize women's interests, part-time work and other forms of flexible working began to be not merely accepted, but even welcomed under the new label of family-friendly working practices. Part-time jobs are especially attractive to adaptive women, who seek a balance between employment and family life, but they are also attractive to home-centred women who may find it necessary to do paid work at particular times of the family lifecycle. Similarly annual hours contracts allow adaptive women to concentrate their working time during term-time, when children are at school, leaving them free to stay at home during the school holidays. These arrangements can also be attractive to other people for quite different reasons.

In general, family-friendly benefits are most likely to be welcomed when they are formulated in sufficiently general terms as to make them accessible and attractive to *all* workers in an enterprise, rather than to workers with young children only. This can be done with virtually all benefits except maternity and paternity leave, the only benefits that are tied specifically to childbirth or, more recently, adoption. There is evidence that benefits that are strongly targeted on families with young children can cause resentment and dissatisfaction among other workers in an enterprise. Older workers whose children have grown up can feel resentful that they were obliged to manage without the benefits, so younger families should do so also. Workers without any children are often ambivalent about targeted benefits.

There is now a growing research literature on the advantages and disadvantages of family-friendly benefits, the relative incidence of the four types of benefit, the causes of their introduction, usage rates, and the consequences for the employer, such as the impact on recruitment, absenteeism, turnover, and productivity (for example Auerbach 1988; Fernandez 1990; Wolcott and Glezer 1995: 156–69; Blau and Ehrenberg 1997; Callender *et al.* 1997; Forth *et al.* 1997; Guerin *et al.* 1997; Parasuraman and Greenhaus 1997; Cully *et al.* 1998, 1999; Guthrie and Roth 1999). In most countries, the provision of family-friendly benefits remains at a level low enough to be invisible in national statistics unless one or more of the following conditions are met:

(1) there is a statutory obligation on employers to provide a particular benefit, such as job-protected maternity leave;
(2) the scheme is mutually beneficial to employer and worker, such as part-time work; and
(3) the benefit is defined broadly enough to apply to all workers, men as well as women, younger and older workers, so that employee representatives will campaign for the benefit through collective bargaining. Trade unions have generally focused their efforts on bargaining for better pay because this benefits everyone, rather than for benefits applicable only to particular groups.

At enterprise level, the circumstances of individual organizations can determine the benefits offered, or not. Firms with a high proportion of female employees can find it advantageous to offer a range of family-friendly benefits. Firms operating in a rapidly-changing business environment usually rule out extended parental leave. Working at home is generally not an option in retail companies. The long-hours culture may be consciously rejected in enterprises that aim to employ creative people, on the grounds that people with no interests outside their work are less useful, socially knowledgeable, and creative. In certain circumstances, firms can obtain substantial public relations benefits from family-friendly policies.

It is probably fair to say that the majority of family-friendly benefits are designed for adaptive women, who want to combine employment with a major role in the family, and thus have 'the best of both worlds'. However if such benefits are drawn broadly enough, they can be attractive to work-centred women as well, and hence to men as well as women.[17] This approach avoids the problem of an apparent bias in favour of mothers, or parents, which can appear to be divisive or unfair to other groups of workers. In smaller organizations with a relatively homogeneous and mainly female workforce it may be feasible to have benefits that are targeted on particular types of workers, or particular needs, such as childcare. But family-friendly policies are more common in larger employing organizations, especially in the public sector, with large and heterogeneous workforces, where targeted benefits can cause resentment among those employees who are excluded from them. Putting it another way, benefits should be designed to be attractive to work-centred women (and men) as well as to adaptive women (and men) if the schemes are to work successfully.

To take the example of the option of reduced hours of work, with a corresponding reduction in pay, for mothers of young children. Framed in this way, the scheme offers more options to mothers than to other workers and risks being regarded as unfair. This may be expressed as resentment against the mothers who use the scheme, resentment that may take hidden and even unconscious forms in day to day working life, from other women as well as from men. The scheme can be redesigned to offer the option of a temporary reduction in working hours and pay to all workers for a limited period of time, such as six years. The scheme could potentially be used by career-centred employees, for example to take part-time courses to gain extra qualifications. In practice, very few work-centred women and men are likely to use such a scheme, but the problem of overt bias is overcome.

[17] There is some debate about whether trade unions remain male institutions serving male interests, or whether they now serve women's interests as well—a debate that is often illustrated by trade union response to the special needs of mothers (Cobble 1993; Cunnison and Stageman 1993). The preference theory perspective suggests that the issue is rather trade unions' ability to represent the interests of secondary earners as well as primary earners, of adaptive women and men as well as work-centred women and men.

This approach, of designing all employee benefits so as to be open to all workers within each occupational grade in an organization is consonant with, but different from, the idea of 'cafeteria benefits', also called 'flexible benefits'. The essential idea of cafeteria benefits is that workers are given a fixed benefit allowance, which may vary by grade, which they can 'spend' each year by selecting from a list of priced benefits offered by the employer (Merrick 1994). Both schemes recognize that the increasing social and cultural diversity of the workforce entails very different interests and values among workers. But cafeteria benefits are probably less flexible than our approach, which includes schemes and choices with no visible price attached, such as career breaks.

In some cases, employers may wish to offer targeted benefits to attract and retain particular types of worker. Preference theory offers a framework for designing targeted benefits that should achieve high usage rates. Any scheme that is little used is probably misdirected in some way, designed for a type of woman who does not exist. For example, many organizations design career break schemes that are offered only to 'high flyers' who have already achieved a relatively high grade in the organization and who are predicted to rise rapidly in future years. Understandably, such schemes have almost no users. Work-centred women rarely take career breaks, and certainly not at a crucial stage in their career development. Career breaks are most attractive to adaptive women, who are unlikely to be identified as 'high fliers' during the child-bearing phase of their life, though this can sometimes happen at a later stage in life when their children have grown up and adaptive women devote more energy and effort to their worklife. Benefits and schemes targeted at adaptive women should be designed for the 'loyal employee' who will stay with the company for many years and acquire firm-specific expertise and loyalty. Benefits and schemes targeted at careerist women probably do not need to differ at all from those that would be attractive to men.

In sum, it is a mistake to assume, as many trade unions have done so far, that women and men have conflicting interests. The more important divide is between adaptive women and careerist women, as the interests of careerist women coincide very largely with those of men. The one major exception to this rule is the sexual harassment of female workers by male managers and colleagues. When both parties belong to the same trade union, this poses major problems of divided loyalties for trade unions (Lawrence 1994).

Finally it may make sense for some employers to develop separate career tracks for adaptive women and careerist women, if they have large workforces and substantial numbers of women. Public sector health and education services would be an obvious example. Careerist women, like most men, will welcome fast-track career development throughout their working life but particularly in the early years. In contrast, adaptive women often prefer to have a long plateau phase during the child-bearing years, if they work at all in this period, with the option of returning to active career development later on, when their family role is less demanding. Differentiated career tracks could prove very acceptable, so long as there are opportunities to switch from one career track to the other, for those women who make the wrong choice or whose circumstances change fundamentally, for example, if a husband dies. To some extent, the two career tracks already exist, informally, with some women switching permanently to part-time work after they have children, while other women work full-time continuously and may not have children at all. Adopting formal policies for separate career tracks would acknowledge the existing polarization of women's employment shown in Chapters 4 and 5. This could also improve working conditions and career prospects for adaptive women, who are sometimes treated as second class workers purely because they do not behave like careerist primary earners. Offering a separate 'loyal employee' career track to people who prefer a balanced life should legitimize and validate this alternative work-lifestyle instead of implicitly treating such workers as failed or inadequate careerists.

Conclusions

One current trend in social policy research is to classify welfare states according to their policy bias in favour of the male breadwinner family with complete role segregation or in favour of the dual-career family with shared family work (for example Lewis 1992; Sainsbury 1996). Countries with multiple biases, such as France, can be difficult to classify meaningfully in these schemes. As a result of alternating governments, French policy supports the non-employed mother with two or more children through fiscal policy, and it *also* supports the mother in full-time employment by providing high quality childcare services for very young children. The new perspective offered by preference theory suggests that countries that are difficult to classify may be supporting several different work-lifestyles at the same time, through different policy tools, thus giving citizens greater freedom to pursue the work-lifestyle of their choice.

Most governments are biased towards social uniformity rather than diversity, towards a single model of the family and sex-roles rather than a plurality of models. Uniformity greatly simplifies the politicians' and policy-makers' task; diversity hugely increases their workload. Preference theory is problematic because it argues that policies should be devised to support three major contrasting work-lifestyles. The assumption (usually implicit) of a homogeneous group of women with common interests is overturned by the solid body of evidence showing the polarization of women's work orientations and employment patterns in all affluent modern societies.

Governments, like other organizations, have vested interests. The idea of homogeneous female interests seems to be readily accepted because it helps to simplify politicians' difficult task. The preference theory perspective complicates things. Small states with ethnically and culturally homogeneous populations may be able to successfully implement policies based on a single model of the family and sex-roles. Such an approach is less likely to be acceptable or practical in nation-states with large populations, which will almost inevitably be socially, culturally, and ethnically heterogeneous. In this context, the preference theory perspective could prove a more acceptable basis for policy development, because it recognizes the inevitable heterogeneity of work-lifestyle preferences, and is not associated with the perspective of any particular subgroup in the population.

Our analysis has shown that it is possible to design new policies, or to modify existing policies, to offer advantages to women and men generally, rather than to narrowly-defined subgroups. Targeted policies can often be drawn more widely so as to offer benefits to more than one group. One example of a broader policy is taxation based on income-splitting, which offers benefits to adaptive women as well as home-centred women. The only group to benefit from the enforced separate taxation of spouses and individualized welfare benefits seems to be work-centred women, a minority group in any society. The apparent popularity of the idea of individualized welfare benefits derives from a widespread misunderstanding of the proposal: many women believe that individualized benefits are obtained as a citizenship right, irrespective of work history and contributions record. They do not realize that the price they have to pay for such benefits is full-time lifelong employment. Once this is made clear, many women are happy to return to benefits earned by their spouse's full-time lifelong employment.

Another example of open-ended instead of targeted benefits would be an allowance paid to *all* mothers, irrespective of their employment record, for three or more years after each birth. Such an open-ended scheme would leave mothers free to decide whether to use the money as a replacement for lost earnings while they stay at home to raise their child, as a salary for this alternative occupation, or as a subsidy for any childcare services that they use to enable them to return to part-time or full-time employment. The new home-care allowances introduced in Finland and France begin to offer this kind of neutral, open-ended benefit instead of the benefits with social engineering aims that promote particular choices and behaviours. Flexible, open-ended policies and benefits can be designed if policy-makers decide to move in that direction. The challenge for politicians and policy-makers in the 21st century is to design policies that are neutral between the three preference groups. The challenge for policy researchers is to design research projects that assist and inform this process.

If we accept that women are heterogeneous in their preferences, producing a polarization of work-lifestyles and family models, then we must also accept the polarization of household incomes and lifestyles that follows from this. Policies that privilege the two-earner family will exacerbate this polarization of household incomes. Policies that are neutral between the three preference groups and family models may do little to reduce the polarization of household incomes, but are unlikely to increase it. Other policies, that are not manifestly concerned with women's employment or fertility, may also interact with the polarizing trend, strengthening or weakening it.

9

Preferences among Men

Preference theory was developed first and foremost with reference to women, unlike other sociological and economic theories of labour market participation. This chapter presents a preliminary outline of how the theory applies to men. It is necessarily tentative and exploratory. As in other chapters, the focus is on the attitudes and behaviour of men in rich modern societies *after* the new scenario has given women genuine choices between a life centred on employment and a life centred on family work. Again, the USA and Britain provide our main examples. Will men's work-lifestyle preferences converge with those of women? This seems unlikely in the short term.

The Work-Lifestyle Preferences of Men

Table 9.1 gives estimates of the distribution of work-lifestyle preferences among men, based on recent research evidence. There are two main differences from the distribution of preferences among women, which approximates to a 'normal' distribution, as noted in Chapter 6. First, the majority of men are work-centred, and the family-centred group is tiny.[1] The most 'egalitarian' or 'modern' men are in fact adaptive men, who would like to combine family work with employment. Second, men collectively are a more homogeneous group, with a clear bias towards competitive activities in the public arena rather than non-competitive activities within family life.[2] In consequence, men do

[1] The Australian Family Formation Surveys in 1981 and 1991 are among the few surveys to ask men directly about their employment preferences, if they had a real choice. In 1991, 80% of married and cohabiting men aged 27–43 years preferred full-time work, 16% preferred part-time work, and only 4% preferred no paid work at all. Men's work preferences were not influenced by their occupational status, age, presence of children in the home, age of youngest child, wife's employment situation, the couple's financial situation, or the men's attitudes towards the breadwinner role (Wolcott and Glezer 1995: 81). They seem to be genuinely personal preferences, disconnected from their actual social situation.

[2] Craib (1987) points out that gender identity is central to a person's sense of self, but that gender identity alone does not determine the social roles people prefer or take up. Masculine men can work in 'feminine' organizations and settings, just as feminine women can work in 'masculine' organizations and settings.

TABLE 9.1. *A classification of men's work-lifestyle preferences in the 21st century*

Family-centred	Adaptive	Work-centred
10% of men varies 5%–15%	30% of men varies 20%–40%	60% of men varies 45%–75%
Children and family remain the main priorities throughout life	A diverse group, including men who want to combine work and family, plus unconventional careers, drifters, and innovators	This group is most diverse Main priority in life is employment or equivalent activities such as politics, sport, art, etc.
Prefer *not* to engage in competitive activities in public domain	Want to work, but *not* totally committed to work career	Committed to work or equivalent activities in public domain
Qualifications obtained for intellectual value, cultural capital, or as insurance policy	Qualifications obtained with the intention of working	Large investment in qualifications for employment or other activities, including extra education during adult life

not suffer from the problem of conflicting interest groups to the same extent as do women, and men organize collectively to defend and promote their interests far more effectively than women. The relative uniformity of male preferences, behaviour, and interests contributes to the continuing disproportionate success of patriarchy, even in modern societies.

Men are relatively homogeneous in work-lifestyle preferences and interests, but they also exhibit substantial diversity in the nature of their activities. Work-centred people are focused on competitive achievement in the public domain, in activities exposed to the public gaze, where success is measured by public approval, social status, wealth, power, or fame. At present in market economies, economic activity is the principal route for self-actualization, so market work—that is, work for pay or profit—is by far the most common type of central life activity. But there are many other areas of activity in which men seek competitive achievement and self-expression: politics at the national or community level, amateur or professional sports, artistic activities, religion, or intellectual-cultural activities. The work-centred career and work history does not necessarily involve employment in the conventional sense. Picasso was a work-centred person *par excellence*, but he never held an ordinary job. Other artists may hold ordinary 'day jobs' as teachers, librarians, or government administrators, in order to subsidize their 'real' artistic careers as poets, writers, or painters. High levels of achievement can take many different forms, and work-centred men can have very diverse lifestyles. But when men discuss the choice of life values and priorities for how they want to live, they discuss the pursuit of wealth versus knowledge, politics versus religion, civic virtue versus the arts, as reflected in the choice of their main occupation (Levinson 1978; Mouzelis 1995: 164–8; Zetterberg 1997: 199). They do *not* discuss a career in public life versus full-time family work.

Work-centred people are defined by their aspirations and motivations, not by high ability and success. The unknown artists whose works do not sell—such as Van Gogh, in his lifetime—the politicians who lose elections, the ambitious failures in the corporate jungle; these are all work-centred people just as much as Picasso, Hitler, and Bill Gates. By the age of 50, careers often reach a plateau and work commitment declines sharply (Warr 1982; Hakim 1996a: Table 4.8). The fact that people adjust their aspirations to accommodate reality, work less overtime, or spend more time with their families from their 50s onwards does not deny that a work-centred orientation has been the central driving force of their life. Similarly, working class men are just as likely to be work-centred as men in professional and managerial careers, despite the fact that the rewards and benefits of their jobs are lower and more uncertain. It is precisely because jobs, and the associated earnings and male collegiality, are so central to men's personal identity that unemployment causes psychological and family problems, over and above the financial problems, even if the job lost was boring and low paid (Hakim 1982), as is evident in the NCDS results in Chapter 5.

Table 9.1 does not present speculations about the policy-responsiveness of the three male preference groups because there is as yet insufficient research evidence on this within the context of the new scenario. Just one example will suffice. We have little information on men's preferences for having children or remaining childless, for having large or small families, after the contraceptive revolution introduced real choice in these matters. Virtually all studies of fertility and family planning focus on women. When surveys ask about men's views as well as women's, they show that European women always want more children than men do, no matter how many children they already have (Siegers, de Jong-Gierveld, and van Imhoff 1991: 77). Reproduction is, in a real sense, women's project more often than the joint project of couples.[3] We know that childlessness is equally acceptable to younger men and women (see Table 3.2), but virtually all studies of childless couples focus on women, as noted in Chapter 3. There is some evidence that childlessness is a lifestyle preference for some men as well as women. The men most likely

[3] This is one reason why many men regard it as legitimate to leave the main burden of childcare to women.

to remain childless are the most ambitious, highly educated professional men who do not remain in stable marriages (Kiernan 1989). However we still know very little about the relative importance of children and family life versus career for men, let alone how these preferences might be affected by public policy. Our tentative conclusion is that the responsiveness of men to social and family policies is very low indeed, because the majority of men are work-centred; in contrast, women are extremely responsive to all policies, because the majority of women are adaptive.

There is an overlap between men's and women's work-lifestyle preferences in Tables 1.1 and 9.1, but it is small, even at the macro-level. The two sets of preferences suggest ample room for disagreement and conflict between men and women, especially when social roles are chosen rather than ascribed at birth. The two sets of preferences are broadly consistent with the family role preferences shown in Tables 4.1 and 4.2: male partners are always expected to work and almost invariably want a role in the public sphere, whereas women are split between two possible roles.

In sum, the majority of men are work-centred while the majority of women are adaptive, seeking to combine family work and employment. There are two reasons for the substantial difference between the distribution of preferences among men and among women. First, there are small, but substantively important enduring differences between men and women, in attitudes and behaviour. Second, the globalization of marriage markets allows work-centred men to retain their preference for role-segregated marriage, and to avoid any social pressure to move towards the 'egalitarian' symmetrical roles family model which requires them to do a greater share of family work. As noted in Chapter 7, national marriage markets are still adjusting to the new scenario. By using international marriage markets, men can avoid the need to modify their preferences or behaviour. The evidence on enduring sex differences and on global marriage markets is reviewed below.

Following the two revolutions, women's preferences are potentially realizable, and one can envisage a situation where all women implement their preferred work-lifestyle, working full-time, part-time or not at all. In contrast, men's preferences are *not* easily realizable, even in prosperous modern societies. In this sense, men do not have as many options and choices as do women. For example there are no social conventions that support a family-centred man who does not do paid work (Baker and Bakker 1987: 334, 339). The evidence reviewed in Chapters 5, 6, and 7 suggests that, as yet, very few women are attracted to, or accept, complete role reversal in the family. So family-centred men are unlikely to do well in the marriage market, if they make their preferences clear. It seems likely that most of them simply conform, however unwillingly, to the convention of the breadwinner male.

Adaptive men may have more success in implementing their preference, but again it is likely that many simply conform to the role of primary earner in any marriage, without great enthusiasm for this role, and without any other burning interest outside the home. Voluntary part-time employment remains almost unheard-of among prime-age men. Full implementation of this preference would depend heavily on a partnership of equals with a similar outlook. If we use earnings equality within marriage as an indicator of such an arrangement—admittedly a superficial indicator—the evidence reviewed in Chapter 4 suggests that between 10% and 20% of couples in North America and western Europe have so far adopted this work-lifestyle, at least temporarily. The proportion seems to be no higher than about 20% even in the younger generations described in Chapter 5. We assume that couples with earnings equality are most likely to share domestic work and family work. So up to one-fifth of men may already have achieved the adaptive work-lifestyle.

Work-centred men should have the greatest facility for putting their preferences into practice. Their main problem is finding an appropriate partner, one who takes on all the family work, leaving husbands free to pursue their interests outside the home. Given the shrinking popularity of complete role-segregation in western Europe, some men turn to the international marriage market to achieve their preferred work-lifestyle.

What factors might help to change the pattern of male behaviour in the future, to match the pattern among women more closely? Paradoxically, the stimulus could be jealousy and resentment of women's wider options, leading to male demands for equality with women. Another stimulus could be increasing awareness of the *rising* sex difference in average life expectancy. Men are becoming aware that the pensions they spend a lifetime working for will most likely be enjoyed longest by their widows and not themselves. For the truly determined work-centred person, these facts will make no difference. Others may reassess the current sexual division of labour and begin to demand equal opportunities for men. We turn to this theme in the penultimate section of this chapter.

Enduring Sex Differences

Few social scientists today accept the 'essentialist' thesis that there are fundamental, large, and important differences between men and women that are biological in origin, immutable and universal, such that all men differ from all women. Even evolutionists today accept that sex differences are not absolute but a matter of degree (Browne 1998). However, the small but enduring differences between men and women are important, even though sex differentials in abilities, attitudes, and behaviour generally shrink to a low level in the new scenario.

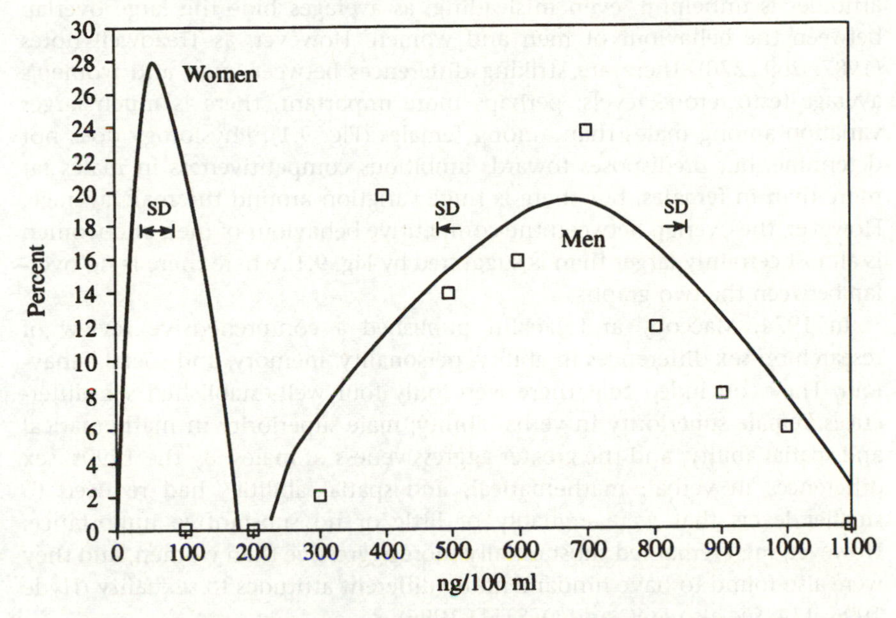

FIG. 9.1. Testosterone levels among men and women

Notes: This figure reports nanograms/100 millilitres of blood plasma. Markings on the figure refer to Standard Deviations, shown as +1 SD and −1 SD separately for women and men.

Source: Figure 1 in P. Treadwell 'Biologic influences on masculinity', in Harry Brod, *The Making of Masculinities*, Boston, MA: Allen & Unwin, 1987, p. 269.

One indisputable difference is the sex differential in aggression, which is sometimes expressed as violence, but more often takes the form of persistence, ruthlessness, energetic activity, drive, and determination. Women are perfectly capable of violence, and sometimes kill their own children. But women use violence far less often than men. Men commit over 80% of all homicides in all societies and all cultures. This does not mean that all men are violent, as some feminists claim. But it does indicate that, at the broadest level, men's capacity for aggression, in all its forms, outweighs women's capacity for aggression by a factor of four to one. Sex differences in aggression, like others, are probabilistic and statistical, but they are substantively larger than in most other domains, and they seem to be permanent, unlike others.

It seems likely that physiological factors contribute to enduring sex differences in aggression, drive and determination. The widespread use of statistical averages to describe and differentiate male and female behaviour and attitudes is unhelpful, even misleading, as averages hide the large overlap between the behaviour of men and women. However, as Treadwell notes (1987: 269, 278), there are striking differences between men and women's average testosterone levels; perhaps more important, there is much larger variation among males than among females (Fig. 9.1). Physiology does not determine, but predisposes towards ambitious competitiveness in males far more than in females, but there is huge variation around the male average. However, the overlap between the competitive behaviour of men and women is almost certainly larger than is suggested by Fig. 9.1, where there is no overlap between the two graphs.

In 1974, Maccoby and Jacklin published a comprehensive review of research on sex differences in ability, personality, memory, and social behaviour. They concluded that there were only four well-established sex differences: female superiority in verbal ability; male superiority in mathematical and spatial ability; and the greater aggressiveness of males. By the 1990s, sex differences in verbal, mathematical, and spatial abilities had reduced to smaller levels that were arguably of little or no substantive importance. However, men remained substantially more aggressive than women, and they were also found to have fundamentally different attitudes to sexuality (Hyde 1996: 114; see also EOC and OFSTED 1996).

Other sex differences are small, but stable and substantively important, for example in explaining the small and stable 20% pay gap in western Europe and North America at the end of the 20th century. Beutel and Marini (1995) monitored trends in the values of young people in the USA from 1977 to 1991. They found persistent sex differences in fundamental values. Men were more competitive and materialistic. Women were more caring and compassionate. These sex differences remained stable across the two decades despite substantial change in other attitudes, at a time when the new scenario was becoming established in the USA.

Similarly, as noted in Chapter 5 (see Table 5.4), the majority of men regard high pay and good career prospects as the two most important criteria in choosing a job, whereas a minority of women emphasize these criteria. Women are more likely to focus on convenience factors, such as an easy journey to work, flexible or part-time hours. These differences emerge early, at the start of careers, and will clearly structure subsequent work histories.

As some men admit, men's lives are all about rivalry, competition, and preferment. Unlike most women, and irrespective of their natural talents, men spend significant amounts of time thinking about how to get ahead, or beat the system. It is a myth that women have superior social skills. Men also have social skills, but use them differently. Men are more adept at interpersonal politics, status games, and diplomacy within organizations. This is sometimes labelled as 'teamwork', rather than a pragmatic attitude to ensuring, first, that the team or game continues in existence so that, second, they can achieve success within it. Like women, men like to be admired, if possible. But if admiration is not attainable, they will make do with the visible signs of success: money, rank, status, power, position, and deferential subordinates. Either way, men seek status among other men, in the public arena, as reflected in material and other rewards (Giddens 1992: 60). This orientation is inconsistent with a primary focus on the private world of the family, and is found among only a minority of women.

Feminists have underestimated the importance of what Goldberg (1993) refers to as psycho-physiological sex differences, and they have overestimated the importance of social and cultural factors. One illustration is the remarkable failure of Swedish policy on paternity leave, which is barely admitted in texts that expound the virtues and value of such schemes (Moen 1989; Haas 1992; see also Hoem 1995). The original idea was that offering maternity leave only to mothers was discriminatory and maintained role segregation in the family. A short paternity leave was introduced for men, to enable and encourage them to get involved in the care and development of their young children. As noted in Chapter 8, hardly any men ever used it. Despite the strongly egalitarian Scandinavian culture, male take-up rates remained under 5% compared to women's 100% take-up of maternity leave. One month's paternity leave was then made almost obligatory, to *force* fathers to get involved in childcare. In practice, men often used it for personal and leisure activities, to go fishing or take training courses, if they used it all. The potential for developing men's interest in very small babies seems limited. The scope for expanding their parenting role with older children, especially teenagers, has so far been overlooked by policy-makers.

It is sometimes argued that men are changing, are more involved with their families than in the past, do more housework, and generally accept less role segregation in the family. There is some evidence of this. However it does not necessarily follow that men become less ambitious and less competitive in the workplace, or other public sphere, as a result of changes in family relationships. Women claim that they do not become inferior mothers as a result of taking paid jobs. Similarly, men do not automatically become less ambitious in the workplace because they cook a meal more often and do the laundry occasionally. As regards parenting, the evidence from longitudinal studies suggests that men in the 1990s are *less* involved with their children than men were in the 1960s, as noted in Chapter 5. The NCDS suggests that young fathers' happiness owes little or nothing to a close involvement with their children. Jobs and activities outside the home seem to be more important, as noted in Chapter 5.

One particular indicator of New Man does not stand up to close scrutiny. The rise in part-time work among men (see Table 3.3) is often interpreted as an indicator of changing work orientations among men. In reality, the rise is due primarily to rapid growth in the number of student jobs throughout

Europe and, secondarily, to part-time work among older men who have taken early retirement and are supplementing an employer's pension (Hakim 1997: 60–1, 1998a: 110–11; Gregg and Machin 1999: Table 6.1).[4] In addition, some countries, notably the Netherlands, have forced young people entering the labour market to take part-time jobs rather than remain in full-time unemployment. Unlike women, the majority of men working part-time hours are doing so involuntarily (OECD 1999: Table 1.13). There is no increase in voluntary part-time work among prime-age men, in any prosperous modern society (Hakim 1997: 60–1, 1998a: 110–11). Such a development would indeed constitute a notable new trend.

Finally, we should recognize that the role of dominant male and sole breadwinner can be imposed on men by women, sometimes to an oppressive degree. Marriages that experience male unemployment are far more likely to break up than marriages where the husband is in continuous employment (Hakim 1982: 454–5). A man's failure to be the major earner, or sole earner, can prove unacceptable to some wives, especially if they have the alternative option of dependence on state benefits. As noted in Chapter 5, among young couples in the 1990s, the highest levels of life satisfaction are reported by couples with a breadwinner husband and a wife at home full-time; the lowest levels of satisfaction are reported by couples where the husband is unemployed, and by role reversal couples with the wife only in employment (Ferri and Smith 1996: 40–7). When a husband is continuously employed, some wives are unable to accept a man's failure to achieve major success and material rewards, even if he offers compensating benefits through his involvement in family life. Even today, some women reject egalitarian marriages and insist on a dominant and successful husband (Pyke 1996: 542–4; see also Giddens 1992). The most recent evidence, shown in Table 4.2, suggests that wives reject fully symmetrical family roles more quickly than men, after a brief honeymoon period of youthful, idealistic support for the 'egalitarian' model of the family.

The Globalization of Marriage Markets

The globalization of labour markets is a well-established trend, which is speeded up by improvements in international travel and communications, by new developments in information technology which allow white-collar work

[4] The number of men with early retirement pensions increased in the 1980s and 1990s, so that almost 30% of British men aged 50–64 years were economically inactive by 1998 (ONS 1999). But the practice has a long history in certain occupations. For example, people working in the British police force usually retire in their 50s, after 30 years' service, and there is a long tradition of retired police officers finding other work, sometimes part-time and sometimes on a self-employed basis, to supplement their police pension after the age of 50.

to be carried out in locations far distant from the employer, and by regional political alliances. What is less well-recognized is that these developments are also producing a globalization of marriage markets.

Elite marriage markets have often been international. Emperors and kings frequently look for spouses within the royal families of other nations. What is new is that ordinary people in prosperous modern societies, including the less affluent, are now seeking spouses outside their own society and culture. As noted in Chapter 7, wealth has always made men attractive marriage partners in women's eyes. Differences in average household income, or annual earnings, between advanced economies and late developing societies are so large that even people with below average incomes in a rich society are fabulously wealthy by comparison with the vast majority of people in less-developed societies. They can afford to pay the extra costs of accessing the global marriage market, where they have the advantage of hugely inflated *relative* value in mating transactions, just as tourists travelling in poorer countries benefit from the inflated value of their holiday funds. The globalization of the higher education market, the holiday industry, business and trade, all contribute to the process by lowering the cultural, linguistic, and information barriers to the globalization of marriage markets. For most of the 20th century, it was men who had travelled abroad to attend university, or on business, who married women from other societies and cultures. By the end of the century, specialist international marriage bureaux had been created, operating along similar lines to national marriage agencies, both of them offering the modern equivalent of the matchmaker role in earlier times (Mullan 1984).

The significance of the globalization of marriage markets is that it counterbalances the apparent small trend towards the 'egalitarian' family model in Table 4.1—though not in Table 4.2. Women living in western European countries are slightly ahead of men in preferring symmetrical roles rather than role segregation in the family. For example, one-third of all men in the EU aged 40–54 years preferred complete role segregation, compared to one-quarter of women aged 40–54, and only one-fifth of women aged 25–39. Marriage to a young woman from a less-developed country allows men, especially older men, to achieve their preference for role segregation in the family without foregoing their preference also for a young and attractive wife. The globalization of marriage markets also allows older women to marry young and attractive men from less-developed societies, as her greater affluence compensates for his lack of resources. In both cases, the wider market gives older people greater choice than they would have within their own society. In addition, awareness of the global marriage market may affect attitudes and expectations in prosperous modern societies to some small extent, although it is virtually impossible to demonstrate the impact of stories in the media.

The almost universal feature of the international marriage market is that it allows people in poorer or late developing societies to achieve upward social mobility and a far higher standard of living than they could normally expect within their own country. This usually means that marriages are based more on compensating differences than on matching similarities, as is the norm in most national marriage agencies in the western world.[5] Apart from this, the international marriage market is varied, as a few examples will demonstrate.

The collapse of the Russian economy produced a sharp increase in the number of women working as prostitutes inside and outside Russia, and led to large numbers of young women applicants to international marriage bureaux. Although many of these women are divorced and already have a child, they offer attractive partners to older North American men, many of them also divorced, who may lack social skills and physical attractiveness but do have secure incomes and homes. Similarly, young single and divorced women from eastern European countries are increasingly interested in marriage to men in western European countries. In all these cases, the women are typically well-educated and have a profession. A teacher of English would be a typical example. Husbands in western countries invariably offer greater economic resources, and a degree of economic stability often lacking in transition economies. Even without the special situation of the collapse of the command economies, there are dating agencies and marriage bureaux in Europe that specialize in particular combinations, such as men in the USA who want to marry 'an English rose', or German men who want to marry a Brazilian woman.

A somewhat different category consists of men in western Europe and North America who wish to marry a Thai woman, a Japanese woman, or a woman from any society where total role segregation in the family is still regarded as the ideal to aim for, and a sign of affluence. Some men mistakenly believe that this is invariably accompanied by female deference towards the male breadwinner, as distinct from mutual respect based on the mutual dependence of spouses. In these cases, the women are typically young, physically attractive, and not necessarily well-educated. Again, the husbands are older men, but offer a life of comparative luxury for a wife who would otherwise face a lifetime of hard work in the market economy in her own country. In some cases the wife may also send money back to her family, on a regular or occasional basis.

The third example consists of the growing demand for Filipina and Chinese wives among Japanese men, especially among farmers who have difficulty attracting wives who are prepared to live in rural areas, where it is still customary for parents to live in the same home with the couple, so that the wife is expected to care for the husband's parents as well as her own

[5] The classic example is the Dateline company's computer processing of application forms. These are first matched on essential characteristics, such as class—as indicated by own occupation or education—age, height, and area of residence, with a second process of matching on leisure interests, lifestyle indicators, and other preferences (Mullan 1984: 83–4).

family. These women are generally well-educated, but come from families that are significantly less affluent that the Japanese families they marry into. Some do agricultural work on the family farm; some take other paid jobs. Many send money home to their family in the Philippines, on a regular or occasional basis (Jolivet 1997: 147–61). These marriages are generally arranged through marriage bureaux. In addition, from the 1980s onwards, large numbers of Filipina and other women were allowed to travel to Japan to work in the large and lucrative hospitality and entertainment industry. Many of these women also married Japanese men, in this case living in urban areas. Although they can only enter Japan on the six-month 'entertainer' visa, these women are also well-educated; they often continue working after marriage, and often send money home to their family of origin (Piper 1997). They are attracted by the much higher wages available in Japan, even for less skilled work, and by the generally higher standard of living.

In all these cases, language differences do not pose an insuperable problem. Women who are motivated can learn another language. The spread of English as an international language also helps. Even if it is not their first language, many people have English as their second or third language.

The international marriage market does not necessarily recruit uneducated, gullible, and desperately poor women, as some people assume. However such marriages normally involve men who are relatively prosperous and live in countries with a much higher standard of living, so that their wives are usually achieving very substantial upward social and economic mobility. This is usually associated with a marriage based on a complete sexual division of labour, with the wife devoting herself full-time to homemaking activities. The international marriage market, by itself, will ensure the survival of what is often called the 'traditional' marriage but is in fact a modern development, characteristic of affluent modern societies, and especially of higher-class husbands in demanding professional and managerial occupations (Pyke 1996: 541), who benefit from the support services of a full-time homemaker.

Male Responses to the New Scenario

Male responses to the new scenario, in particular to the two revolutions, are decidedly ambivalent and mixed. Some eagerly welcome the prospect of wives sharing responsibility for income-earning. Others resent feminist attacks on the role-segregated family, and respond by extolling its virtues. Two other themes in the debate are the new sex differential in life expectancy and the issue of positive discrimination in favour of women in the labour market.

In the 20th century, women started to live longer than men. The sex difference in average life expectancy only emerged recently, and is increasing over time. For example, in Britain, life expectancy almost doubled over the last 150 years, from 40 years for men and 42 years for women in 1838–54 to 74 and 79 years respectively in 1990–95. The sex difference in average life expectancy has more than doubled in this period, from just under 2 years to 5.4 years in favour of women in Britain. In many countries, the sex difference is even larger. On average, women now live 8 years longer than men in France, 7 years in the USA, 6 years in Germany, Sweden, and Japan, and 5 years in Denmark. Across the EU, the average is 7 years and the sex difference shows no sign of falling in the post-war decades (European Commission 1995: 36). In Eastern Europe, life expectancy was generally about 5 years lower for everyone up to 1990, but the sex differential was just as big as in western Europe: 7 years in East Germany, 7.5 years in Czechoslovakia and Hungary, 8 years in Poland, and 9 years in the USSR (Einhorn 1993: 265). The sex differential is now as large as, or larger than the social class differential in life expectancy—6 years versus 5 years in 1987–91 in Britain—yet only the latter is treated as inegalitarian and a social problem (Drever and Whitehead 1997).

Women only started to live longer than men in affluent societies where the single breadwinner family became the norm. In less-developed countries, sex differentials in life expectancy at age 10 are still zero or very small, and may be in favour of women or men (Federici, Mason, and Sogner 1993: 142–3). This is probably due to women's greater involvement in productive work, as well as the higher risks of childbirth. It is notable that in the 'hoe cultures' of Africa south of the Sahara and certain South East Asian and Latin American countries, it is women who traditionally supply the bulk of agricultural labour; women still bear the largest part of the work burden in more egalitarian communities (Boserup 1970: 15–31). Wives take it for granted that they will support themselves and their children and also cook for the husband (Boserup 1970: 41–50), as do many women of Afro-Caribbean descent today in the USA and Britain (Boserup 1970: 50; Siltanen 1994: 85–7; Dench 1996: 33–8, 45–51). In Europe also, wives traditionally worked just as hard as men in the family business, in agriculture, or trade (Pfau-Effinger 1998: 180). The non-working wife has always been an indicator of relative prosperity and is a recent phenomenon.

Demographers and medical statisticians became aware of the sex differential in life expectancies in the 1950s, and they started to look for explanations in the characteristics of typically-male and typically-female occupations, in the higher stress of market work as compared with the full-time homemaker role, and in lifestyle factors such as diet and smoking patterns (Ehrenreich 1983: 68–87). By the 1990s, it became clear that in modern societies women's health benefits from three advantages over men (Egidi and Verdecchia 1993).

First, women are more concerned with their health and their bodies, make greater use of all health services, and take greater care of themselves than do men. The onset of monthly menstruation, the anticipation and experience of childbirth, and women's concern with their physical attractiveness, all encourage women to take greater care of their bodies and their health. In contrast, most societies and cultures encourage men to disregard their bodies and physical discomfort, to look outward to society, to be active and physically brave, to show endurance and strength. Men are generally less likely to report any health problems, especially chronic problems, and they make less use of health services in modern societies.

Second, women have higher survival rates from disease. This is illustrated by sex differences in survival rates from cancers. At young ages, men have lower incidence rates and lower mortality rates from cancer than do women. From the age of about 40 years onwards, men have higher incidence rates and *much* higher mortality rates from cancer than do women. Overall, male mortality rates from cancer are double the rates among women, and women generally have higher survival rates from disease, possibly helped by their taking greater care of themselves, as noted above.

Third, women's lives in advanced economies expose them to fewer dangerous or stressful occupations and activities as compared with men. This is clearly linked to the fact that for most of the 20th century women benefited from the modern model of marriage that has most wives working at home as full-time homemakers while husbands work full-time, life-long in the market economy. There is evidence that when women adopt the male lifestyle of continuous employment, their mortality rates approximate more closely to those of men than to those of women (Harrop and Joshi 1994).

These three factors cut across social class groups. Some demographers are now concluding that women have a biological or genetic advantage over men that produces greater female longevity, and this is then enhanced by the recent invention of the role-segregated family, which exempted women from market work, and by universal health care, which women exploit fully (Egidi and Verdecchia 1993: 224).[6]

From 1950 onwards, female longevity was sufficiently large for men to notice, and resent, the fact that the modern, role-segregated model of marriage was in many respects advantageous to women and not, as women claimed, beneficial to men only. As a prosperous young man in the USA argued in the 1970s:

> It is high time for women to stop being parasites, and to work until the day they drop dead or retire, as men do, and not expect a man to support them. (Ehrenreich 1983: 159)

[6] In this context, it is puzzling that the European Commission displays more concern with women's health than with men's health (European Commission 1997b).

Similarly, social scientists pointed out that the pensions that men spend a lifetime saving for are more likely to be enjoyed by their wives than by themselves. Davis (1984) noted that in 1900 the sex difference in life expectancy at age 20 was only 1.6 years in the USA; by 1981 it was 7 years. Given that women generally marry men who are three years older (see Chapter 7), wives could expect to outlive their husbands by 5 years in 1900, and by 10 years in 1981, which represented almost one-fifth of their adult, or married, lives (Davis 1984: 409–10).

As Ehrenreich (1983) demonstrates, many men noticed that modern marriage benefited women more than men, and they welcomed the equal opportunities revolution because it re-established a fair distribution of labour between men and women. What has sometimes been described as a 'flight from commitment' among men can also be seen as rejection of a modern sexual contract that is heavily weighted against men's interests (Ehrenreich 1983; Dench 1996; see also Dench 1999). Bernard (1981) was probably the first to point out that the 'good provider' role was not always enjoyed by men. Many men felt it to be an onerous duty, which they resented, even if it also offered rewards. Men who resented their family's economic dependence sometimes deserted their family, or responded with violence. Bernard pointed out that the proportion of working men with a positive attitude toward marriage halved in the USA between 1957 and 1976, from 68% to 39%, while the proportion regarding marriage and children as burdensome and restrictive doubled, from 25% to 58%. It seems likely that changes in women's aspirations contributed to decreasing satisfaction with the institution of marriage among men as well as among women (Bernard 1981: 8). Ehrenreich (1983: 12) argues that the collapse of the breadwinner ethic among white men began well before the second wave of feminism and stemmed from dissatisfactions just as deep, if not as idealistically expressed, as women's discontents. Married people often feel 'trapped', but this feeling was in fact more common among men than among women by the 1970s (Davis, Bernstam, and Ricardo-Campbell 1987: 184–5). Many men welcome the equal opportunities revolution not because it eliminates a serious injustice against women, but because it eliminates a serious injustice against men. It is notable that men are no more likely than women to believe that men *should be* the main income-earner while women do the housework; indeed on some questions women are slightly more in favour of role segregation than are men (see Table 4.3). Men can feel just as oppressed by sex-role stereotypes as women (Lawrence 1994: Table 6.3; Bourdieu 1998: 129–34).

Feminists have championed symmetrical family roles as the ideal which everyone should aim for. In the process, some have denigrated the modern role-segregated family, as illustrated by polemics against women's economic dependency in marriage (Hobson 1990; Lister 1992, 1999). In response, some men mounted a defense of the modern sexual division of labour, pointing out the mutual benefits to wife and husband. For example Dench (1996), a sociologist, argued that role segregation in the family had tremendous advantages for women, especially mothers and their children, as well as for men. He even claimed that patriarchy was created by women to serve their own interests. Like Giddens (1992: 195), he argued that the role-segregated family is one perfectly adequate model among several available, and should not be rejected unthinkingly. Keyfitz (1987), a demographer, argued that male dominance and patriarchy were necessary in the past to ensure high fertility rates and hence societal survival. He accepted that women did not want the large numbers of children they used to bear in the past, and did so because male dominance forced this role on them. Rich societies give people real choices, between working and not working, between childlessness and raising children. The decline of male dominance was a key cause of declining fertility rates, he concluded (Keyfitz 1987: 144, 151). Chesnais (1995) argued that Europe is imploding as a result of women's preference for market work over child-rearing in the new scenario. He argued that more effective pronatalist policies were essential in France, and in Europe generally, to prevent immigration replacing native reproduction of the population. It appears that concern about population decline is often the catalyst for concern about the demise of the role-segregated family.

Other responses to the equal opportunities revolution focus on recent developments in labour policy, with the suspicion of a new bias in favour of women. One continuing problem is the conflation in popular understanding of affirmative action, which is lawful, with positive discrimination, which is generally unlawful. Positive discrimination, or reverse discrimination, consists of active discrimination in favour of a woman in preference to a man, for example in selection for or promotion to a job. Affirmative action, or positive action, consists of activities that generally help women to compete more easily and more successfully with men at some future time, such as education and training designed to remedy women's weaknesses, or to fill gaps in their qualifications and experience. Assertiveness training, mentoring, and mock job interviews would be examples of affirmative action schemes. The dividing line between affirmative action and positive discrimination can become blurred in everyday discussions, and unfortunately some commentators have contributed to this confusion by conflating the two (for example Richards 1994: 32, 36, 132–60). Positive discrimination has always been unlawful in British law, has so far been classified as unlawful in EU law, and prompted a serious 'backlash' when adopted by certain states in the USA. It arouses strong opposition as a matter of principle (Quest 1992: 53–8, 101–14) and is often counterproductive in practice (Hepple and Szyszczak 1992). Suspicions of positive discrimination in favour of women in German länder prompted men to bring a series of legal cases that went to the European Court of Justice (ECJ) in the 1990s. These led, on the one hand, to the affirmation that positive discrimination is contrary to EU law—in the *Kalanke* case—and on the other hand to the affirmation that positive action is lawful—in the *Marschall* case—with the distinction resting on the fine details of a particular employer's personnel policies and selection procedures.[7] Unfortunately the adversarial character of legal cases such as these rarely provides a constructive basis for developing general statements about the personnel policies that are unacceptable, and those that are fair and offer models of best practice. In practice, it is left to employers to invent new rules, guidelines, and procedures which overcome previous biases and are acceptable to all parties. Just one example of creative thinking is the rule of always having at least one woman on all selection and promotion panels in large organizations (Hakim 1996a: 184), a rule that does not prompt the same objections as a quota system in selection processes, but usually has a significant impact on outcomes.

Many men believe that women have, in practice, acquired more employment rights than men in the new scenario, by virtue of demanding that all employment practices be modified to accommodate the special needs of women. Sometimes these special needs are those of mothers with childcare responsibilities or, more recently, women with responsibility for the care of elderly relatives. Sometimes women demand, and get, exemptions from the obligations and constraints of an ordinary job on the grounds that they are secondary earners (Hakim 1996a: 197–8). As noted in Chapters 4 and 5, the great majority of wives continue to be secondary earners throughout adult life (see Tables 4.7 and 5.6). Whether arguing their case as mothers, carers or secondary earners, women are now forcing employers to give them additional rights and freedoms that male workers have never had, such as the right to work reduced hours or half-time hours, the right to job-share with another person even when the employer objects, and the right not to be geographically mobile in management job grades that have always required this. Employers who are fearful of the costs, in time as well as money, of drawn-out court cases sometimes think it is easier to accede to individual requests rather than to challenge them in the labour courts. This may be rational, given the unpredictable and sometimes perverse outcomes of industrial tribunal cases, such as the Edwards case described in Chapter 3 (see page 61) where a single female objection to a new shiftwork system was accepted as proof of sex discrimination by the employer. None the less, from the perspective of male employees, who have not always liked the rules and rigours that the workplace and jobs impose on them, it can appear that women are acquiring additional rights that leave men, collectively, worse off and hence discriminated against. As noted in Chapter 8, it is rare for state policies to be

[7] One indicator of positive discrimination is the creation of quotas for women, for example, in an occupation, or occupational grade, so that the choice of a man or a woman at the next job opening becomes entirely predictable, irrespective of the merits of the candidates who compete for the vacancy.

completely neutral; most policies favour one or another model of the family and associated sex-roles. Similarly, many employer policies are not completely neutral and favour one group or another. Some men now feel that the pendulum has swung too far in favour of women—in practice, this means adaptive women, who are far more numerous than career-oriented women—to the point that men are being discriminated against, overtly or indirectly. For example, by the late 1990s one-quarter of all complaints to the British EOC came from men (EOC 1997).

The final stage of the equal opportunities revolution may thus consist of men demanding access to the special new employment flexibility rights that women are now claiming and winning. The result is likely to be a wider range of worker-friendly flexible work arrangements for men as well as women, which are obtained through individual complaints and demands *via* the adversarial process of labour courts—industrial tribunals in Britain—as well as through the traditional process of collective bargaining between trade unions and employers, which has so far failed to address the interests of female workers (Hakim 1997). As noted in Chapter 8, it is usually feasible to redraw family-friendly policies designed for mothers so as to make them accessible to other employees as well.

Conclusions

Table 9.1 presents our initial estimate of the work-lifestyle preferences of men. It is based on more limited research evidence than the equivalent Table 1.1 for women. It remains to be refined and developed further as new research evidence becomes available. The most relevant new evidence would be nationally representative data on the relative importance of family and career, the importance of competitive achievement, and the working hours and employment arrangements men would choose in an ideal world. In the 1990s, the indications are that the majority of men in advanced economies remain work-centred, so that work-centred men easily outnumber work-centred women in each age group, in the workforce, and in the population as a whole. At present, there is a substantial gap between the work-lifestyle preferences of men and women in the new scenario.

Will the preferences of men and women converge in the future? Probably not, at least in the short to medium term. Few men become seriously interested in babies and very small children, to the point where they are prepared to centre their lives on child-rearing and family work rather than paid work. The evidence from Scandinavian schemes of paternal leave suggests that very few men are prepared to take even a short break from work to spend time with a baby, unless forced to do so by government policy. This still leaves open the possibility that most men may be far more interested in, and successful at parental involvement with teenage children, an option that has not yet been addressed by policy-makers.

Although there are continuing differences between men and women in life-goals and priorities, it appears that the main dividing lines are no longer between men collectively and women collectively, but between the three work-lifestyle groups. Sex and gender may not, in practice, constitute fundamental dividing lines between roles in the future, as they have in the past. Just as our analysis in Chapter 6 revealed important conflicting interests between the three groups of women, it is likely that conflicting perspectives, and interests, will appear between men, especially between work-centred and adaptive men. Developments in the next few decades are likely to be lively and interesting.

10

Conclusions

There has been a flood of new research on women's employment and position in society since the 1960s. Within this rich harvest of new information and ideas, it can be difficult to discern any broad pattern or common conclusions. Preference theory is one attempt to structure the evidence into a coherent perspective that makes sense of the diversity of research findings as well as the common themes. The theory is concerned primarily with the conditions of life for women, and the social changes that are creating a new scenario for women in the 21st century. The underlying theme of theories of social change has so far been 'progress', but the underlying theme of preference theory is 'diversity and choice'.

Preference theory also helps us to resolve several theoretical puzzles, sheds new light on current trends, and identifies methodological problems that must be avoided in future research. For example it provides a new explanation for the disproportionate success of patriarchy and male dominance. It informs cross-national comparisons. The theory also reveals a new form of ecological fallacy in contemporary analyses and points to the increasing importance of selection effects in future research on women.

Work-lifestyle Preferences in the 21st Century

Even Marx accepted that individuals make their own history, although they make it under circumstances that are given, not chosen (Marx 1977: 300, quoted in Lawson 1997: xiv). Our thesis is that the circumstances that women face after the two revolutions, in the new scenario, are fundamentally different from what went before, and permit a real choice of personal histories. The argument of this book has been that, in modern society, work-lifestyle preferences and the roles played by women and men are not only the product of contextual influences, but also the expression of chosen gendered identities. Women today are divided in their work-lifestyle preferences, and possibly always have been. Affluent and liberal modern societies provide opportunities for diverse lifestyle preferences to be fully realized. The results are displayed in women's varied employment profiles. In addition to the single women who have always worked continuously to support themselves, there is now a minority of wives who also behave like primary earners and are financially independent, continuing their careers irrespective of their husband's career.[1] However the majority of women seek a more equal balance between family work and market work. They tend to regard their work as a job rather than a career, especially after marriage and motherhood. Many work intermittently and/or part-time if such jobs are available; others work full-time in a job that offers other convenience factors, such as relatively low and fixed hours, a location close to home or with a convenient journey to work. They readily reject promotion if it imposes burdensome additional responsibilities, requires substantial travel, or relocation to another area. Most regard themselves as secondary earners, and become financially dependent on their partner to some degree. The minority of women who choose the marriage career usually become fully financially dependent on their partner, as they rarely work after marriage except in emergencies. Their lives are centred on child-bearing, childcare, and family work, and they often have many more children than the other two groups. Since these family models are chosen voluntarily by couples, there is no reason for third parties to deplore wives' financial dependency, as some social scientists have done (Hobson 1990; Lister 1992, 1999; Orloff 1993), and insist that all women *must* be self-supporting, as the European Commission has done.

The three groups of women, work-centred, adaptive, and home-centred, only become clearly visible after the equal opportunities revolution and the contraceptive revolution give women genuine choices as to what to do with their lives, in the new scenario. Before that, pregnancy was an uncontrollable hazard of women's lives, and child-bearing was the almost inevitable consequence of marriage. Women's fertility made it more difficult for them to pursue careers outside the farm or family business, except in prosperous families where childcare could be delegated to others. The contraceptive revolution allows child-bearing to be disconnected from sexual activity and marriage; gives women independent and reliable control over their fertility; and allows women to control the timing of child-bearing so as to fit in with other activities and priorities. The equal opportunities revolution means that the full range of occupations and activities become accessible to *all* women, if they wish to get involved in market work and other activities in the competitive public domain. In addition, a series of changes in the labour market are producing a more attractive range of jobs for women, and prosperity increases lifestyle choices. In the context of this new scenario, which was achieved early in the USA and Britain, women's (and men's) work-lifestyle

[1] Just one example is Cheri Booth, who continued her career as a lawyer after marriage, even after her husband Tony Blair became British Prime Minister, and who always earned substantially more than her husband.

preferences become an important determinant of behaviour, certainly more important than in the past. Indeed there is evidence that attitudes are becoming increasingly important over time, producing the gradual polarization of women's employment patterns now observed in the USA, Britain, and many other industrial societies.

Contextual influences and institutional constraints remain, but they are becoming less important.[2] Accidents of time and place shape options and opportunities for everyone, men and women, young and old. However for those with the necessary talents, it is more and more the case that the key factors are attitudinal: work-lifestyle preferences, motivation, aspirations, and determination to achieve goals within the highly competitive public sphere of the marketplace, politics, and other arenas.

Several arguments are raised against this conclusion. Some feminists argue that women regard themselves as secondary earners only because they cannot get the well-paid jobs that are offered to men. They claim that women's attitudes are a consequence of sex discrimination and women's weak position in the labour market. The evidence contradicts this argument. Women who aim for qualifications and good jobs have been able to achieve them in the new scenario. Women's concentration in lower-paid and part-time jobs is the consequence, not the cause, of most women's expectation of marriage and financial dependence on a man. Longitudinal studies show this clearly. Even graduate wives who have well-paid professional jobs still regard themselves as secondary earners who are dependent on a man, whereas a man in the same occupation regards himself as the main breadwinner for his family. In the new scenario, self-classification as a primary earner or as a secondary earner is determined by chosen identities rather than imposed by external circumstance or particular jobs.

Another argument is that women do not have fixed preferences, that they change their priorities repeatedly over the lifecycle. Life history research shows this to be true, but only for adaptive women, who are torn between the competing attractions of family life and market work. In contrast, home-centred women and work-centred women maintain a consistent commitment to their chosen life-goals which, in the new scenario, can generally be achieved.

Preference theory also challenges the argument that male-dominated trade unions and employers are mainly responsible for continuing sex differences in labour market outcomes and for women's lower pay and lesser employment benefits at the aggregate level. The poor compatibility of work and

[2] This is illustrated by the contrasting opportunities facing the wives of politicians, traditionally an occupation that permitted full-time homemaking as the only activity. In Britain, Cheri Booth was able to continue her own career as a lawyer after her husband became Prime Minister in 1997. In the USA, Hilary Rodham Clinton, also a lawyer, found it impossible to do the same after her husband, Bill Clinton, was elected President, and she had to channel her talents and energies into other activities during his Presidency.

family for women is not exclusively a matter of excessively long hours, sex discrimination, and the absence of family-friendly employer policies, but of who deals with family crises and deadlines, and who deals with crises and deadlines at the workplace. Professionals and managers are expected to be committed to their work, and blue-collar jobs are physically demanding. Adaptive mothers still choose to give equal or greater priority to their children and families, so the normative expectations of the workplace and the family necessarily come into conflict at times. The conflict is one of allegiance, personal identity, and normative priorities, not simply a practical problem of daily time management. Employer policies can certainly help, by offering flexible hours, reduced working hours while children are small, part-time jobs, and time off for domestic crises. But the wider problem is ultimately not one that employers create or can solve. Open recognition of the diversity of women's work-lifestyle preferences could provide the foundation for employers developing policies selectively adapted to one or more of the three groups, or for designing policies that are general enough to offer benefits to all three groups rather than being unintentionally biased towards one group only. The relative failure of gender-equality policies in the Nordic countries, discussed in Chapter 8, suggests that it is not simply a matter of producing the right policies and the political will to overturn patriarchy. In the new scenario, work-centred women are able to compete with men as equals. But adaptive women are less likely to achieve significant success in the labour market simply because they do not aim for it, consistently, as they prefer a balanced life instead. And it is adaptive women, rather than work-centred women, who constitute the majority of the female workforce in most countries.

In sum, the combination of two revolutions and other major changes will give all women in affluent modern societies opportunities and choices they did not have in the past. In the new scenario, work-lifestyle preferences become the main determinant of women's choices between family work and market work, and the principal determinant of employment patterns. Women's success in the labour market, as indicated by occupational grade, earnings and status, will be determined by the same factors that shape men's achievements: talent and ability, qualifications, hard work, the particular industry and career path chosen, an element of luck. Sex discrimination does not disappear overnight, but will eventually cease to be a major factor at the national level, even if it can have serious consequences for the particular individuals who occasionally experience it. Work-lifestyle preferences, and related investments, become more important, overall, than sex discrimination as a determinant of success in market work and, eventually, other domains as well.[3] This means that it will no longer be possible to automatically interpret data on differential outcomes in the labour

[3] Politics seems to be the public domain where discrimination is likely to persist the longest, due to the stereotyping of authority as masculine in patriarchal cultures, and because the application of equal opportunities laws is more uncertain in this field.

market, such as the pay gap, as evidence of hidden and indirect sex discrimination, unless controls have been added for work-lifestyle preferences and related investments. The USA and Britain have already reached this stage, and so will many other modern societies in the near future.

Preference theory predicts that women will remain a minority within the very top echelons of any society because only a minority of women are work-centred in the way that most men are, and because competitiveness increases as one moves up the occupational ladder. Some proportion of adaptive women will also reach the top jobs, if only because so many of them are concentrated in public sector industries and occupations where women predominate. Research to date suggests that work-lifestyle preferences are only weakly associated with ability and with qualifications obtained. So we can expect to find some combination of both work-centred and adaptive women achieving the highest positions in their chosen sphere of activity—be it market work, politics, religion, the arts, or sports.

Preference theory predicts that the polarization of women's employment patterns, earnings and status attainment in the labour market will intensify in future decades. The new trend is already found, to varying degrees, in many advanced economies, usually associated with increasing inequalities of household income. This means that the marriage premium for men (Daniel 1995) will remain, although it may decline in future decades. However the 'family gap' for women (Waldfogel 1998) will increase gradually, with the polarization of work-lifestyles between childless career women and adaptive mothers with jobs. It also means that there will be no convergence on the 'egalitarian' model of symmetrical conjugal roles, as some social scientists expected. Policy-making becomes more complex as a result, as policy-makers need to make allowance for at least three distinct household work strategies. This is certainly feasible, although it does require a change of strategy, and a lot more imagination. For historical reasons, France has achieved an approach of this kind, with a combination of fiscal policies that support the single breadwinner household and social policies that provide childcare services and other benefits for mothers in continuous full-time employment. In the French case, this balanced spectrum of policies seems to be the result of alternating governments, each with a very different policy bias. Balanced policies that are fair to all groups can also be designed intentionally.

We have yet to discover all the social consequences of the polarization of women's preferences and employment patterns. Just one example is the polarization of childcare patterns between do-it-yourself mothers, and fathers, and parents who delegate childcare to paid professionals, or amateurs, while continuing with their own careers.[4] Etzioni raises this issue in *The*

[4] The risks of employing others, whether professionals or amateurs, were highlighted in the 1990s by several well-publicized cases of small children who died while in the care of their child-minder, both in the USA and in Britain.

Parenting Deficit, where he discusses the wider implications of the rise of dual-career families for the quality of community life as well as for children's social development (Etzioni 1993a, 1993b). He argues that children become devalued in consumerist and individualistic societies, and that new policies are needed to support the family. Similar arguments are offered by Wilkinson and Briscoe (1996) when making a case for state-funded parental leave. They point to research showing that young children need close and secure relationships in their first one to three years of life to achieve good cognitive and social development, which in the long run can help to avoid problems in school, low educational attainment, deviancy and crime. At present, the policy emphasis is almost exclusively on women's right to work, with little regard paid to the potentially conflicting needs of young children for good quality parenting.

After the two revolutions, women are at the forefront of changing gender roles. They can adopt a male work-centred lifestyle if they wish, and socially their gender becomes male rather than female. They can also choose to remain dependent, in whole or in part, on a male breadwinner. There is also nothing to stop them switching between these options over the lifecourse, in response to exceptional opportunities in either direction. As yet, men do not have the same options, but they are likely to demand them eventually. It may seem paradoxical for men to demand 'equality with women', but in practice this will be one result of the equal opportunities revolution. It is notable that in Britain, for example, a large proportion of complaints to the EOC now come from men, indicating that men are already beginning to feel disadvantaged compared with women.

Preference theory was developed explicitly to explain women's employment choices today and tomorrow. It constitutes a break from past theories because it insists that women are not a homogeneous group but heterogeneous in tastes and preferences as between market work and home activities. It argues the need for a diversified theory instead of hoping that one theory will fit everyone. Preference theory can explain important exceptions to the rule as well as the central tendency. It identifies one group that is highly responsive to social structural constraints, social pressures, social conventions and social rules, and two groups that are relatively unresponsive. It identifies the limits to economic theory by identifying two groups in which choices disregard purely financial cost-benefit analysis. It goes beyond economics by identifying the nature of differing tastes and preferences among women, and the degree to which these preferences can be moulded by socialization processes or shaped by social structural factors. Preference theory suggests that a change of emphasis is needed in sociological research, away from the structural factors that have been its focus in the 20th century, towards the values and preferences that will shape behaviour in the new scenario in modern society in the 21st century. Values and preferences are becoming increasingly important determinants of lifestyle choices and behaviour in prosperous modern societies. Sociologists are better placed than social psychologists and economists to study lifestyle preferences. Sociological theory needs to be reoriented and updated in order to remain relevant to the modern world and to changing social conditions.

The domestication of women was a social experiment that lasted little more than a century in western Europe and North America (Bernard 1981; Rogers 1981; Hakim 1996a: 79–82). With it went an ideology that valued a wife's domestic contribution and a greatly extended mothering role. A wife's job was different, but it was none the less valuable and gave her 'equality' alongside her husband. This ideology is now being cast aside in favour of the argument that 'equality' requires an independent source of income and hence a job. But education is another source of 'equality' and its importance seems to have been overlooked in the current emphasis on women's increasing participation in the labour market. Our review suggests that social scientists must in future consider a wider range of sources of equality in interpersonal relationships and in marriage. Economic theory, with its emphasis on monetary rewards and financial status has perhaps blinded us to equally important changes that are taking place in other aspects of women's position in the family and in society.

Preference theory is a universalistic theory of the social development of gender roles. It predicts that, in any culture where the two revolutions and labour market changes create a new scenario, the full heterogeneity of women's work-lifestyle preferences will emerge, and women's employment patterns will polarize in consequence. However it is a time-specific theory, which is unlikely to remain useful for much longer than about fifty years after the new scenario is achieved, given the pace of change in all the sciences and the way this will alter the basic conditions of life in the 21st century.

The theory is thus historically situated and adopts a holistic perspective, as advocated by Ragin (1987). The theory is also consonant with complexity theory, allocating a specific role to agency which determines which of several options women and men will favour. The identification of three preference groups is consonant with complexity theory's identification of 'strange attractors' and the emergent properties of systems (Byrne 1999; see also Ormerod 1998). Complex causal processes do not have singular outcomes, but multiple outcomes. Complexity theory does not predict convergence, nor does preference theory.

Beyond Sex and Gender

The distinction between sex and gender, and their exact relationship, were the subject of protracted debate in sociology from 1972 onwards (Hood-

Williams 1996; Willmott 1996). Preference theory suggests we can now move beyond sex and gender, to look instead at the social roles that women and men prefer and adopt for their own lives. In this sense, preference theory is a 'unisex' theory. For example the contraceptive revolution means we can no longer take it for granted that all women will become mothers and spend an important part of their adult life in child-rearing activities. The equal opportunities revolution means that work-centred childless women can have lives that are indistinguishable from those of work-centred men, who do not *all* achieve highly-paid top jobs. Employment and other roles in the public sphere can now be chosen by women as well as men. If men are successful in gaining equal rights with women, they too may be able to freely choose to lead home-centred lives, or adaptive lives in the future.

The three preference groups cut across sex and gender, making these concepts redundant. They define 'unisex' work-lifestyle goals and priorities. Home-centred women are happy to choose a life centred on marriage, children, and family work. If they work at all after marriage, it will usually be prompted by desperate economic necessity or by some crucial family goal. Employment is an extension of their family role rather than an alternative to it. Work-centred women are happy to choose the public arena as the focus of their energies, through careers in market work, politics, sports, or the arts. If they have children, it will be in the same way as among men, as an expression of normality and a weekend hobby. Adaptive women are the only group who do *not* want to have to choose between family and employment, who insist on wanting *both*, albeit with different emphases at different points in their life. Adaptive women are distinctive in being unwilling to choose a single life focus. If they give priority to family or to paid work, it is a temporary emphasis rather than a lifetime commitment.

These conflicting values and contrasting work-lifestyle preferences may not always be visible,[5] but they are real in their consequences, and they will become increasingly important in the 21st century. This means there will be no convergence in values and work-lifestyle choices in rich modern societies, except for the agreement to differ. The polarization of family models leads to widening disparities in family incomes; even in prosperous societies, there will be greater inequality of household incomes. The challenge for policy-makers is to design diversified and neutral policies that support all three preference groups and all three family models—a task that requires greater imagination and skill than producing policies that prioritize one single model of the good life.

[5] They are often readily declared. Many working women find it necessary to declare themselves to be mothers immediately on first acquaintance, indicating that this constitutes their primary self-identity. Conversely, other working women (and many men) fail to give any indication of their marital and parental status, even after many years of acquaintance, because these are not central to their self-identity.

Explanations for Patriarchy and its Success

The major theoretical contribution of feminism has been to elaborate the concept of patriarchy and to develop explanations for the universal subordination of women. As Lerner (1986: 239) points out, the feminist concept is wider than the narrow, traditional meaning of patriarchy, which refers to a male head of household's absolute legal and economic power over his dependent female and male family members. The feminist concept of patriarchy refers to the institutionalization of male dominance over women in society in general as well as in the family. It directs our attention to the unequal power relations between men as a group and women as a group and therefore, very often, between individual men and women, and to the social institutions that maintain the subordination of women.

Lerner (1986) reviews a succession of theories offered from Engels onwards to explain the creation of patriarchy during the transition from hunter-gatherer societies to the creation of kingships and archaic states, and finds all of them either theoretically unsatisfactory or else unsupported by the evidence. Her own explanation of the historical origins of patriarchy rests on the idea that men's control of women's sexuality and reproductive capacity was crucial to the foundation of private property and inheritance. This entailed the artificial division of women into 'respectable'—that is, attached to one man—and 'not respectable'. Sexual subordination and control were eventually extended into economic subordination and control. This thesis states that men have been concerned primarily with controlling women's sexuality and reproductive work rather than their productive work.

Other social scientists seek to explain why patriarchy has persisted in the very different social and economic conditions of modern industrial society. They focus on how patriarchy functions in the modern world, in particular how it constrains and controls women's participation in the labour market. Hartmann (1976) defined patriarchy as men's domination of women, more specifically men's control over women's labour, as illustrated by developments in trade union policies in Britain and the USA in the 19th and 20th centuries. Her analysis emphasized occupational segregation as the principal mechanism used by men to restrict and constrain women's access to earnings and financial independence. Walby (1990) attempted to develop Hartmann's thesis into a more extensive and complex theory of patriarchy, but again occupational segregation was a crucial mechanism for ensuring women's subordination. Walby claimed that the exclusion strategy was dominant in 19th century Britain and elsewhere, while the segregation strategy was most influential in twentieth century Britain (and elsewhere). This was the basis of her thesis that patriarchy had changed and developed over time, from the private patriarchy of the 19th century, when women were excluded from paid work and restricted to the domestic sphere, to the public patriarchy of the

20th century, in which women are collectively exploited by employers who restrict them to low grade and low paid work, often in part-time jobs, which ensures they cannot be financially independent.

Unfortunately, the empirical research evidence for the USA and Britain does not support either Hartmann's or Walby's theses on the social mechanisms used by men to control women's labour. There are now many new studies on long-term trends in female workrates, the pattern of occupational segregation and its relationship to unequal pay for women workers, long-term trends in occupational segregation, cross-national comparisons of occupational segregation, sex differentials in work orientations and behaviour, and reasons for the expansion of part-time jobs in all rich modern societies (Milkman 1987; Grint 1988; Hakim 1991, 1993a, 1993b, 1994, 1996a: 9–13, 79–82, 186, 1996b, 1998a; Rubery and Fagan 1993; Blossfeld and Hakim 1997; Tam M. 1997; Anker 1998; Melkas and Anker 1998). These show that occupational segregation did not play the role hypothesized; that large sex differentials in pay for the same job were created directly and maintained consciously by male trade unionists and employers, right up to the imposition of legislation outlawing sex discrimination and promoting equal opportunities in the labour market from the 1960s onwards; and that occupational segregation is actually higher in Nordic countries pursuing gender equality policies than in competitive and relatively unregulated liberal economies. These two theories of patriarchy have so far failed on the evidence. However they both point our attention to the way men organize collectively to further their interests against the interests of women—trade unions being just one of many male organizations developed to serve male interests.

As several theorists have pointed out (Fine 1992: 42; Goldberg 1993: 148; Hakim 1996a: 210) feminist patriarchy theory has so far failed to identify a *cause* for patriarchy, male dominance and male solidarity, as distinct from a description of the *mechanisms* used to dominate women. Goldberg's explanation, which cannot be refuted on the evidence, focuses on the impact of psycho-physiological factors on social attitudes and behaviour, in particular the effect of male hormones such as testosterone as a source of sex differences in motivation, ambition, and competitiveness. He argues that men as a group are on average more self-assertive, aggressive, dominant, and competitive than women as a group. This means that men collectively work harder than women collectively to achieve the top positions in any hierarchy, including the highest status and highest paid jobs or roles in the workforce. As a result, patriarchy is universal in that authority and leadership are, and always have been, associated with the male in every society, and the majority of higher positions in hierarchies are occupied by males (Goldberg 1993), a conclusion drawn also by Lerner (1986: 30–1) and, with small qualifications, by Whyte (1978). Goldberg points out that differences between men and women are statistical and probabilistic, rather than absolute, with substantial variation around the male average and the female average on any characteristic, and substantial overlap between the two distributions. Socialization processes in the family, school, and community can either promote or reduce, encourage or ignore sex differences that emerge during childhood, and they may assign greater weight to masculine or feminine values. From his study of 53 countries across all continents, Hofstede (1980, 1991) showed that societies differ in promoting masculine values (with an emphasis on dominance, challenge, and material success) or feminine values (concerned with the quality of life, good social relations, modesty, and tenderness). Societies such as Japan, Austria, Germany, Britain, Italy, and Mexico have masculine work cultures, whereas the Scandinavian societies, the Netherlands, and Costa Rica have feminine work cultures. Interestingly, many countries of South East Asia have scores almost exactly in the middle of the masculinity-femininity scale: notably Malaysia, Singapore, and Indonesia (Hofstede 1980: 279–85, 1991: 81–6).

Preference theory provides an explanation for the remarkable success and effectiveness of male solidarity and male organization in *all* modern societies, whether they have masculine or feminine cultures. Women are fundamentally divided in their preferences and interests. Conflicting interests make it difficult for women to organize around any single set of common aims, and women often find themselves in fundamental conflict over *which* policies genuinely benefit women. Men collectively gain a huge tactical advantage from women's diversity, an advantage that they need do nothing to create, but can simply exploit to further their own *relatively homogenous* interests. The heterogeneity of women's preferences, for a lifestyle centred on the home, or on public life, with or without role segregation, opens up a fatal weakness in women's representation of their interests. Women's *conflicting interests* are most clearly exposed in the USA, where there are two women's movements in conflict with each other, the maternalist movement and the women's liberation movement, effectively cancelling out the potential power of the female vote on matters of concern to women. But in other countries also, the same divisions and conflicts weaken women's public voice, even if the process is more chaotic and less visible. Preference theory explains why small and variable statistical sex differentials in motivation, aggression, competitiveness, and determination to succeed can produce disproportionately large differences in outcomes in the long term. Patriarchy is disproportionately successful because women are sharply divided in their preferences and goals. These conflicting preferences are now emerging clearly in affluent modern societies. The polarization of women's central life interests and activities suggests that male dominance will continue to be a feature of modern societies, long after the equal opportunities revolution.

Methodological Implications

In virtually all advanced societies, women are becoming better educated, female workrates are rising and the pay gap between men and women in employment is declining slowly. These trends produced an expectation of increasing equality within marriage and among cohabiting couples: educational equality, equality in the extent of spouses' employment, and financial equality. The very small reductions in wives' economic dependence on their husbands shown in Chapters 4 and 5 came as a surprise to many scholars. The problem is of course that they made incorrect deductions about the behaviour of individuals from trends in national statistics. In reality, educational homogamy has been declining, rather than rising, in many countries. More important, women continue to prefer to marry men who are at least a little taller and a little older than themselves, and many marry men who are better educated as well. The small advantage of three years' extra work experience can translate into an important *relative* advantage for husbands, given that most couples marry and start child-bearing when they are young, when they have both accumulated relatively little work experience. The apparently innocuous and universal preference for a husband who is about three years older, on average, quickly translates into the rational decision to give his career priority as soon as the first child is born. A small initial difference grows quickly over the years into substantial financial inequality. At the extreme, the wife stops work permanently.

Marriage patterns seem to have changed little, if at all, after the two revolutions. Possibly, they may change in the future, although there are currently few signs of change. Further research would be helpful here. Unless and until women find dependent househusbands or complete equality with men just as attractive as marriage to successful, rich, and powerful men, we can expect financial inequality to remain the norm in most marriages in most countries. Over the lifecycle the degree of inequality will tend to grow. It appears that labour market trends at the national level can develop quite independently of trends in marital selection at the micro-level. The often implicit assumption that the trend towards the equality of men and women observed in national statistics, entails a similar trend towards the equality of spouses at the micro-level, is a new example of the ecological fallacy.

The classic exposition of the ecological fallacy given by Robinson (1950) has led to us seeing it primarily as a problem in social geography. She pointed out that aggregate units, such as regions or cities, can display correlations between social indicators, such as unemployment rates and crime rates, without there necessarily being any causal link between these factors at the individual level. If one is really interested in establishing causal processes at the micro-level, then studies of individuals are required; macro-level analyses based on national statistics are inadequate. The ecological fallacy is now recognized as a potential hazard in social geography research. But it emerges also in research on women, in the contradictions between trends at the national level and trends at the micro-level.

Preference theory also points up three other methodological points. First, we need to be sensitive to research dates, to whether research evidence for any country was collected *before* or *after* the two revolutions were fully implemented, *before* or *after* the new scenario was achieved. Research results for earlier periods may not necessarily apply at all, or in the same way, in the new scenario. Some research data for the USA and Britain are now very dated, effectively historical, as the new scenario was achieved very early in these two countries.

Second, preference theory suggests that sample selection bias will always arise unless the entire female adult population is covered by a study, including women who have been out of employment for many years. This theoretical argument is consistent with the technical arguments offered by Stolzenberg and Relles (1997), that while tools exist to help in the identification of sample selection bias, no techniques currently exist to eliminate or overcome the problem. They argue further that the popular two-step estimator of Heckman (1976, 1979a) can sometimes further reduce the accuracy of regression estimates instead of improving matters. In addition, we might expect selection effects to become more important, even dominant, in the social processes of a meritocratic society. If men and women are selected for top jobs on the basis of talents, ability, motivation, and hard work more than on the basis of social origins and social capital, we can expect increasing polarization within the whole workforce, in addition to the previously noted polarization of female employment. Given that selection effects are a substantive issue and cannot, ultimately, be controlled for or eliminated, multivariate analysis becomes even less attractive as an analysis tool, because a fundamental underlying assumption is breached. The general point has already been made with some force by Lieberson (1985: 14–43, 200–17), but the increasing polarization of women's employment gives it additional force today.

Third, preference theory warns us against studies that seek to identify the average or representative woman, or that use measures of central tendency—such as averages—to describe 'typical' patterns of behaviour. Such studies inevitably focus on adaptive women, and fail to notice or report results for home-centred and work-centred women, who remain minorities everywhere. This problem arises with case studies and qualitative research just as often as with quantitative studies based on national datasets. Studies tend to focus on the working mother with one or two children, for example, overlooking childless career women and non-working mothers of large families. These two groups may be much smaller, but they are nevertheless important and should be identified in studies.

Finally, the most important lesson of preference theory for research methodology is that the 'silent movie' era of social science must finally come to an end. It is no longer acceptable for research surveys and statistical surveys to collect extensive data on behaviour without also collecting adequate data on motivations, values, preferences, and life goals. It is no longer acceptable for scholars to impute motives and reasons for the choices and decisions reflected in the results of a multivariate analysis. Social science research must finally start asking people directly about the values and preferences that inform behaviour, and that cannot reliably be deduced from behaviour.

Cross-national Comparisons

Cross-national comparisons of work-lifestyle preferences display clearly the impact of social and cultural contexts on ideal models of the family and gender roles, and show also that all three preference groups exist in all countries. This means that home-centred women in the USA may have more in common with home-centred women in Japan, Singapore, and France than with work-centred women in the USA. The three preference groups cut across national boundaries as well as across class and ethnic groups, in the same way that social and political movements are becoming globalized (Albrow 1996: 140–1, 152–3).

Cross-national comparisons also display the limitations of social and institutional constraints. In the former USSR, eastern Europe and the Nordic countries, public policy forced women into the labour market and into financial independence, but this did not produce the expected equalization of male and female employment patterns, because it did not change underlying work-lifestyle preferences, which favoured the full-time homemaker role almost as often as in many western European countries. The diversity of work-lifestyle preferences *within* as well as across European societies suggests that it is not very fruitful to seek to identify the ideal welfare state for women—a goal that is implicit in most of the social policy and gender classifications currently on offer (such as Esping-Andersen 1990; Lewis 1992; Mósesdóttir 1995; Sainsbury 1996) and in the convergence thesis of the European Commission (Hakim 1999). It is more meaningful, and constructive, to seek to identify those policies that are framed broadly enough to offer benefits to all three groups of women, and that do not actively discriminate against any of them.

From the perspective of preference theory, societies could be classified into a simple dichotomy, or on a continuum. At one extreme are societies that are ideologically hegemonic, where one set of ideas, norms, and rules dominate public and private life. Although these societies vary a lot in *which* particular ideology is dominant—socialism or capitalism, one religion or another—they all offer women (and men) only *one* model of the family and of women's role in society. In that sense they are all equally oppressive, in eliminating choice. At the other extreme are societies that are pluralist in ideology, where no single set of ideas and values is hegemonic, where a variety of ideologies are permanently in competition with each other. These societies allow a diversity of family models and of women's roles to flourish, thus offering women more open choices between alternative role prescriptions. These societies often look 'chaotic' or conflict-ridden in comparison with the hegemonic societies.

On this analysis, there is little difference between the patriarchy of Japan and the egalitarianism of Sweden: both offer women only one model of women's role that is publicly admired, supported and valued, so that all women are pushed into a single lifestyle. Britain and the USA are examples of the 'chaotic' pluralist societies. Sweden and Japan are examples of hegemonic societies. Some societies fall half-way between the two extremes. For example, the Netherlands in the 'pillarization' era prior to the 1990s was *both* hegemonic, within each religious community, and pluralistic, taking Dutch society as a whole. At present, pluralist liberal societies are most likely to offer women choices between alternative gender roles and work-lifestyles. So it is in these societies that we can expect the fastest and fullest emergence of the three preference groups, with ensuing policy implications. Our review of recent developments in the USA and Britain suggests that they will continue to be in the vanguard of future developments, and will repay close study.

Theorizing Social Change

Although we live in a century of constant and accelerating change, the social sciences have not been very successful at theorizing social change. The broadest sociological theories interpret social change within an evolutionary perspective, which presents contemporary industrial society as the highest or most complex stage of human social development. Even historical materialism can be seen in this light, with socialist society presented as the culmination of social and economic development. By adopting Mouzelis' conceptual framework of the modern society, we have sought to avoid a theoretical tradition that has generally equated modernization with westernization. Similarly, we have sought to avoid an evolutionist perspective within feminist research that tends to classify the Nordic countries as the 'model' societies that all other countries should seek to emulate.

Within the context of prosperous modern societies, preference theory identifies five changes that collectively create a new scenario for women, and hence, consequentially, for men also. The theory is centred first and foremost on the conditions of life for *women*, even though it can potentially be extended to cover men as well. In this respect, it differs from most social science theorizing to date which has more or less explicitly focused on men and their activities, with reproduction taken for granted as unproblematic. Preference theory is an empirically-based, multidisciplinary theory for explaining and predicting current and future patterns of women's choices between family work and market work, or equivalent activities in the public sphere. Ultimately, it provides a theory of changing gender relations. It does not carry any value judgements, overt or hidden, about which choices and which work-lifestyles are 'better' or 'worse'. It treats all three lifestyle choices as valid and beneficial, in different ways, for those who freely adopt them. Our aim is a genuinely social scientific theory, rather than political advocacy masquerading as social science. Preference theory also contradicts convergence theories of women's position in society. These have usually relied heavily on comparisons of economic activity rates to conclude that European societies, or modern economies more generally, are converging on a single, 'egalitarian' model of the family with symmetrical sex-roles. As we have shown, the empirical evidence reveals more complex, polarizing trends.

Modern societies do not automatically make the transition to the new scenario. The two revolutions and the three other changes required do not necessarily occur together, and may even be intentionally delayed or prevented by governments. One example is the contraceptive revolution which is, for women, probably more important than any other single technological or social change. The contraceptive revolution has been delayed in some countries, such as patriarchal Japan and several Catholic countries, so that women still do not have reliable personal control over their fertility in these countries. In this sense, the contraceptive revolution and the equal opportunities revolution are both *social* revolutions, reflecting a new consensus that women can and should determine their own lifestyles, with one revolution removing barriers and the other revolution creating new opportunities.

Preference theory also differs from many theories of social change in its greater emphasis on personal attitudes, values, and preferences as driving forces in their own right. Until now, attitudes and preferences were treated as the separate domain of social psychologists, while sociologists and economists focused on social structural, political, and economic factors. A multidisciplinary approach demands that all these threads are brought together, to produce a holistic, rather than fragmented theory of social change.

Most theories of social change, and social science theory more generally, have focused on the technology and social relations of productive work, with reproduction taken for granted and ignored. We argue that the technology and social relations of reproduction are equally important. For women, they are arguably more important, given that women's lives have so far almost invariably included reproductive as well as productive work. As noted above, it seems likely that the original cause of patriarchy was men's need to control women's reproductive activities, not their productive activities *per se*. The contraceptive revolution is just the first of a series of technological changes to human reproduction which will necessarily entail major changes in the social relations of reproduction and, potentially, in the social relations of production. For example, DNA testing now allows the paternity of a child to be reliably identified even in the context of sexual promiscuity, so there is no longer any need for men to control women's sexuality. Within the next 50 years, it will become feasible for women to produce babies even after the menopause, for sexual activity and reproduction to become completely separated, and for most babies to be born *in vitro*, with their characteristics 'designed' rather than unpredictable. If there are further declines in fertility, women's reproductive work could at last come to be valued as highly as many occupations in the market economy, and may even enter the market economy—as illustrated by women who become surrogate mothers for a fee. The impact of these technological changes in reproduction on the social and economic relations of reproduction cannot be predicted: much depends on how men and women organize to use and regulate these developments. Women's fragmentation into three groups could weaken their ability to present a united front, as illustrated already by the abortion debate in the USA. Within the social sciences, the important job now is to develop theories of social change that address the social relations of reproduction as well as the social relations of productive work. Preference theory provides the first element of such a theory, as it addresses the social changes consequent on the contraceptive and equal opportunities revolutions. But further changes in the next 50 years will require the rapid development of new social science theories of change.

REFERENCES

Abramson, P. R. and Inglehart, R. (1995) *Value Change in Global Perspective*, Ann Arbor: University of Michigan Press.

Adler, L. L. (ed) (1993) *International Handbook on Gender Roles*, Westport CN: Greenwood Press.

Adnett, N. (1996) *European Labour Markets: Analysis and Policy*, London and New York, NY: Longman.

Agassi, J. B. (1979) *Women on the Job: The Attitudes of Women to Their Work*, Lexington MA: Lexington Books.

—— (1982) *Comparing the Work Attitudes of Women and Men*, Lexington MA: Lexington Books.

—— (1989) 'Theories of gender equality: lessons from the kibbutz', *Gender and Society*, 3: 160–86.

Ajzen, I. and Fishbein, M. (1977) 'Attitude-behaviour relations: theoretical analysis and review of empirical research', *Psychological Bulletin*, 84: 888–918.

Albrow, M. (1996) *The Global Age: State and Society Beyond Modernity*, Cambridge: Polity Press.

Allen, I. (1994) *Doctors and Their Careers*, London: Policy Studies Institute.

Almquist, E. M., Angrist, S. S., and Mickelson, R. (1980) 'Women's career aspirations and achievements: college and seven years after', *Sociology of Work and Occupations*, 7: 367–84.

Alwin, D. F. (1973) 'Making inferences from attitude-behaviour correlations', *Sociometry*, 36: 139–81.

—— Braun, M., and Scott, J. (1992) 'The separation of work and the family: attitudes towards women's labour-force participation in Germany, Great Britain and the United States', *European Sociological Review*, 8: 13–37.

Anker, R. (1997) 'Theories of occupational segregation by sex: an overview', *International Labour Review*, 136: 315–39.

—— (1998) *Gender and Jobs: Sex Segregation of Occupations in the World*, Geneva: ILO.

Antonides, G. (1991) *Psychology in Economics and Business*, Dordrecht and London: Kluwer Academic.

Anttalainen, M-L. (1986) *Sukupuolen Mukaan Kahtiajakautuneet Työmarkkinat Pohjois-Maissa* (Gender-based labour market segmentation in the Nordic countries), Working Paper Naistutkimusmonisteita 1: 1986. Helsinki: Tasa-arvoasiain Neuvottlukunta (Council for Equality between Men and Women).

Arber, S. and Ginn, J. (1995) 'The mirage of gender equality: occupational success in the labour market and within marriage', *British Journal of Sociology*, 46: 21–43.

Archer, J. and Lloyd, B. (1982) *Sex and Gender*, Harmondsworth: Penguin.

Ashenfelter, O. and Layard, R. (eds) (1986) *Handbook of Labor Economics*, Amsterdam: North Holland.

Atkinson, D., Dallin, A., and Lapidus, G.W. (1978) *Women in Russia*, Hassocks: Harvester Press.

Atkinson, M. and Boles, J. (1984) 'Wives as senior partners', *Journal of Marriage and the Family*, 46: 861–70.

Auerbach, J. D. (1988) *In the Business of Child Care: Employer Initiatives and Working Women*, London: Praeger.

Axelrod, R. (1984) *The Evolution of Cooperation*, New York, NY: Basic Books.

Badcock, C. (2000) *An Introduction to Evolutionary Psychology*, Cambridge: Polity Press.

Badinter, E. (1981) *The Myth of Motherhood: An Historical View of the Maternal Instinct*, translated by R. DeGaris, London: Souvenir Press.

Baker, M. and Bakker, J. I. H. (1987) 'The double-bind of the middle class male: men's liberation and the male sex-role', pp 331–46 in E. D. Salamon and B. W. Robinson (eds) *Gender Roles: Doing What Comes Naturally?*, Toronto and London: Methuen.

Baker, P. and Eversley, J. (eds) (2000) *Multilingual Capital*, London: University of Westminster Press.

Baker, R. (1999) *Sex in the Future: Ancient Urges Meet Future Technology*, London: Macmillan.

Barnard, C. and Hepple, B. (1999) 'Indirect discrimination: interpreting Seymour-Smith', *Cambridge Law Journal*, 58: 399–412.

Bartlett, J. (1994) *Will You Be Mother? Women Who Choose To Say No*, London: Virago.

Baum, F. (1982) 'Voluntary childless marriages', *International Journal of Sociology and Social Policy*, 2: 40–54.

—— (1983) 'Orientations towards voluntary childlessness', *Journal of Biosocial Science*, 15: 153–64.

—— and Cope, D. (1980) 'Some characteristics of intentionally childless wives in Britain', *Journal of Biosocial Science*, 12: 287–99.

Baxter, J. and Kane, E. W. (1995) 'Dependence and independence: A cross-national analysis of gender inequality and gender attitudes', *Gender and Society*, 9: 193–215.

Beck, U. (1986/1992) *Risk Society: Towards a New Modernity*, London: Sage.

—— and Beck-Gernsheim, E. (1995) *The Normal Chaos of Love*, translated by M. Ritter and J. Wiebel, Cambridge: Polity Press.

—— Giddens, A., and Lash, S. (1994) *Reflexive Modernization*, Cambridge: Polity Press.

Becker, G. S. (1965) 'A theory of the allocation of time', *Economic Journal*, No. 299, 75: 493–517.

—— (1981, 1991) *A Treatise on the Family*, Cambridge MA: Harvard University Press.

Beckmann, P. (1998) *Working Hours and Wishes Concerning Working Hours among Women in Western and Eastern Germany*, Labour Market Research Topics No. 27, Nuremberg: IAB

Beere, C. A. (1979) *Women and Women's Issues: A Handbook of Tests and Measures*, San Francisco, CA: Jossey Bass.

Benham, L. (1974) 'Benefits of women's education within marriage', *Journal of Political Economy*, 82: S57–S71.

—— 1985) 'Non-market returns to women's investment in education', pp 293–309 in C. B. Lloyd (ed) *Sex Discrimination and the Division of Labour*, New York, NY: Columbia University Press.

Benn, M. (1998) *Madonna and Child: Towards a New Politics of Motherhood*, London: Jonathan Cape.

Berent, J. (1954) 'Social mobility and marriage: a study of trends in England and Wales', pp 321–38 in D. V. Glass (ed) *Social Mobility in Britain*, London: Routledge.

Berger, P. A., Steinmüller, P., and Sopp, P. (1993) 'Differentiation of life-courses: changing patterns of labour-market sequences in West Germany', *European Sociological Review*, 9: 43–65.

Bernard, J. (1981) 'The good-provider role: its rise and fall', *American Psychologist*, 36: 1–12. Reprinted in E. D. Salamon and B. W. Robinson (eds) *Gender Roles*, New York, NY: Methuen, 1987, pp 177–92.

Bernasco, W., De Graaf, P. M., and Ultee, W. (1998) 'Coupled careers: effects of spouse's resources on occupational attainment in the Netherlands', *European Sociological Review*, 14: 15–31.

Bernhardt, E. M. (1993) 'Fertility and employment', *European Sociological Review*, 9: 25–42.

Betz, N. E. and Fitzgerald, L. F. (1987) *The Career Psychology of Women*, Orlando, FL: Academic Press.

Beutel, A. M. and Marini, M. M. (1995) 'Gender and values', *American Sociological Review*, 60: 436–48.

Bielby, D. D. and Bielby, W. T. (1984) 'Work commitment, sex-role attitudes and women's employment', *American Sociological Review*, 49: 234–47.

Blackburn, M. L. and Bloom, D. E. (1994) *Changes in the Structure of Family Income Inequality in the United States and Other Industrial Nations During the 1980s*, Working Paper No. 4754, Cambridge MA: National Bureau of Economic Research.

Blake, J. (1979) 'Is zero preferred? American attitudes toward childlessness in the 1970s', *Journal of Marriage and the Family*, 41: 245–57.

Blank, R. M. (1998) 'Labour market dynamics and part-time work', pp 57–93 in S. W. Polacheck (ed) *Research in Labor Economics*, vol 17, Greenwich CN: JAI Press.

—— (1999) 'Labour market dynamics and women's part-time work in the United States', *Focus*, 20: 37–40.

Blankenhorn, D. (1995) *Fatherless America*, New York, NY: Basic books.

Blanpain, R. and Rojot, J. (eds) (1997) *Legal and Contractual Limitations to Working Time in the European Union*, Leuven: Peeters Press.

Blau, F. D. and Ehrenberg, R. G. (eds) (1997) *Gender and Family Issues in the Workplace*, New York, NY: Russell Sage Foundation.

—— and Ferber, M. A. (1992) *The Economics of Women, Men and Work*, Englewood Cliffs, NJ: Prentice-Hall.

—— and Kahn, L. M. (1994) 'The gender earnings gap: some international evidence', pp 105–43 in R. B. Freeman and L. F. Katz (eds) *Differences and Changes in Wage Structures*, Chicago, IL: Chicago University Press.

Blau, P. M. and Duncan, O. D. (1967) *The American Occupational Structure*, New York, NY: Wiley.

Blaug, M. (1980) *The Methodology of Economics: Or How Economists Explain*, Cambridge and New York: Cambridge University Press.

Blitz, R. C. (1974) 'Women in the professions: 1870–1970', *Monthly Labor Review*, 97/5: 34–9.

Bloom, D. and Pebley, A. R. (1982) 'Voluntary childlessness: a review of the evidence and implications', *Population Research and Policy Review*, 1/3: 203–24.

Blossfeld, H-P. (1997) 'Women's part-time employment and the family cycle: a cross-national comparison', pp 315–24 in H-P. Blossfeld and C. Hakim (eds) *Between Equalization and Marginalization: Women Working Part-Time in Europe and the United States of America*, Oxford: Oxford University Press.

—— and Hakim, C. (eds) (1997) *Between Equalization and Marginalization: Women Working Part-Time in Europe and the United States of America*, Oxford: Oxford University Press.

—— Timm, A., and Dasko, F. (1996) 'The educational system as a marriage market: A longitudinal analysis of marriage in the life course', Working Paper No. 46, Bremen University Sfb 186.

Blundell, R., Dearden, L., Goodman, A., and Reed, H. (1997) *Higher Education, Employment and Earnings in Britain*, London: Institute for Fiscal Studies.

Boh, K. *et al.* (eds) (1989) *Changing Patterns of European Family Life: A Comparative Analysis of 14 European Countries*, London: Routledge.

Boling, P. (1998) 'Family policy in Japan', *Journal of Social Policy*, 27: 173–90.

Bonney, N. (1988) 'Dual earning couples: trends of change in Great Britain', *Work, Employment and Society*, 2: 89–102.

Borooah, V. and McKee, P. (1996) 'How much did working wives contribute to changes in income inequality between couples in the UK?', *Fiscal Studies*, 17: 50–78.

Bosch, G., Dawkins, P., and Michon, F. (1994) *Times are Changing: Working Time in 14 Industrialised Countries*, Geneva: International Institute for Labor Studies.

Boserup, E. (1970) *Women's Role in Economic Development*, London: Allen & Unwin.

Bottero, W. (1992) 'The changing face of the professions? Gender and explanations of women's entry into pharmacy', *Work, Employment and Society*, 6: 329–46.

Bouffartigue, P., de Coninck, F., and Pendariès, J-R. (1992) 'Le nouvel âge de l'emploi à temps partiel', *Sociologie du Travail*, 92/4: 403–28.

Boulton, M. G. (1983) *On Being a Mother: A Study of Women with Pre-School Children*, London: Tavistock.

Bourdieu, P. (1972, 1977) *Outline of a Theory of Practice*, translated by R. Nice, Cambridge Studies in Social Anthropology, Cambridge: Cambridge University Press.

—— (1984) *Distinction: A Social Critique of the Judgement of Taste*, translated by R. Nice, London: Routledge.

—— (1989) *La Noblesse d'Etat: Grandes Ecoles et Esprit de Corps*, Paris: Minuit.

—— (1998) *La Domination Masculine*, Paris: Seuil.

—— and Wacquant, L. J. D. (1992) *An Invitation to Reflexive Sociology*, Cambridge: Polity Press.

Bradley, H. (1989) *Men's Work, Women's Work: A Sociological History of the Sexual Division of Labour in Employment*, Cambridge: Polity Press.

Brass, W. (1989) 'Is Britain facing the twilight of parenthood?', pp 12–26 in H. Joshi (ed) *The Changing Population of Britain*, Oxford: Basil Blackwell.

Braun, M., Scott, J., and Alwin, D. F. (1994) 'Economic necessity or self-actualisation? Attitudes toward women's labour force participation in East and West Germany', *European Sociological Review*, 10: 29–47.

Breakwell, G. M. (1986) *Coping With Threatened Identities*, London and New York, NY: Methuen.

—— (ed) (1992) *Social Psychology of Identity and the Self-Concept*, London: Surrey University Press.

Breen, R. and Goldthorpe, J. H. (1999) 'Class inequality and meritocracy: a critique of Saunders and an alternative analysis', *British Journal of Sociology*, 50: 1–27.

Brines, J. (1994) 'Economic dependency, gender and the division of labor at home', *American Journal of Sociology*, 100: 652–88.

Brocas, A-M. (1997) 'Equality of treatment between men and women in social security and in family responsibilities', pp 155–72 in E. Date-Bah (ed) *Promoting Gender Equality at Work*, London: Zed Books.

Brown, G. W. (1993) 'The role of life events in the aetiology of depressive and anxiety disorders', pp 23–50 in S. C. Stanford and P. Salmon (eds) *Stress: From Synapse to Syndrome*, London: Academic Press.

—— and Bifulco, A. (1990) 'Motherhood, employment and the development of depression: A replication of a finding?', *British Journal of Psychiatry*, 156: 169–79.

—— and Harris, T. (1978) *The Social Origins of Depression*, London: Tavistock

—— —— and Hepworth, C. (1995) 'Loss, humiliation and entrapment among women developing depression: a patient and non-patient comparison', *Psychological Medicine*, 25: 7–21.

—— and Moran, P. M. (1997) 'Single mothers, poverty and depression', *Psychological Medicine*, 27: 21–33.

Browne, K. R. (1995) 'Sex and temperament in modern society: a Darwinian view of the glass ceiling and the gender gap', *Arizona Law Review*, 37: 971–1106.

—— (1997) 'An evolutionary perspective on sexual harassment: seeking roots in biology rather than ideology', *Journal of Contemporary Legal Issues*, 8: 5–77.

—— (1998) *Divided Labours: An Evolutionary View of Women at Work*, London: Weidenfeld & Nicolson.

Bruyn-Hundt, M. (1992) 'Economic independence of women in the Netherlands', pp 120–31 in N. Folbre *et al.* (eds) *Women's Work in the World Economy*, London: Macmillan.

Bryson, A., Ford, R., and White, M. (1997) *Making Work Pay: Lone Mothers, Employment and Well-Being*, York: Joseph Rountree Foundation.

—— and McKay, S. (1997) 'What about the workers?', pp 22–48 in R. Jowell *et al.* (eds) *British Social Attitudes—the 14th Report*, Aldershot: Ashgate.

Buckingham, A. (1999) 'Is there an underclass in Britain?', *British Journal of Sociology*, 50: 49–75.

Bundesministerium für Familie, Senioren, Frauen und Jugend (1996) *Gleichberechtigung von Frauen und Männern: Wirklichkeit und Einstellung in der Bevölkerung 1996* (Equal Opportunities for Women and Men: Reality and Attitudes in the Population 1996), Stuttgart: Kohlhammer.

Burchell, B. and Rubery, J. (1994) 'Divided women: labour market segmentation and gender segregation', pp 80–120 in A. M. Scott (ed) *Gender Segregation and Social Change*, Oxford: Oxford University Press.

Burke, R. J. and Weir, T. (1976) 'Some personality differences between members of one-career and two-career families', *Journal of Marriage and the Family*, 38: 453–9.

Burr, W. R. (1970) 'Satisfaction with various aspects of marriage over the life cycle: a random middle class sample', *Journal of Marriage and the Family*, 32: 29–37.

Buss, D. M. (1989) 'Sex differences in human mate preferences: evolutionary hypotheses tested in 37 cultures', *Behavioural and Brain Sciences*, 12: 1–49.

—— (1994) *The Evolution of Desire: Strategies of Human Mating*, New York, NY: Basic Books.

Bynner, J., Ferri, E., and Shepherd, P. (1997) *Twenty-something in the 1990s: Getting On, Getting By, Getting Nowhere*, Aldershot and Brookfield: Ashgate.

—— Morphy, L., and Parsons, S. (1997) 'Women, employment and skills', in H. Metcalf (ed) *Half Our Future*, London: Policy Studies Institute.

Byrne, D. (1999) *Complexity Theory and the Social Sciences*, London: Routledge.

Cain, G. G. (1986) 'The economic analysis of labour market discrimination: a survey', pp 693–785 in O. Ashenfelter and R. Layard (eds) *Handbook of Labor Economics*, Amsterdam: North Holland.

Cain, M. T. (1993) 'Patriarchal structure and demographic change', pp 43–60 in N. Federici, K. O. Mason, and S. Sogner (eds) *Women's Position and Demographic Change*, Oxford: Clarendon Press.

Caldwell, J. C. (1982) *Theory of Fertility Decline*, London: Academic Press.

—— and Caldwell, P. (1997) 'What do we know about fertility transition?', pp 15–25 in G. W. Jones *et al.* (eds) *The Continuing Demographic Transition*, Oxford: Clarendon Press.

Callan, V. J. (1985) *Choices About Children*, Australian Studies Series, Melbourne: Longman Cheshire.

—— (1986) The impact of the first birth: married and single women preferring childlessness, one child or two children', *Journal of Marriage and the Family*, 48: 261–9.

Callender, C., Millward, N., Lissenburgh, S., and Forth, J. (1997) *Maternity Rights and Benefits in Britain*, DSS Research Series No. 67, London: DSS.

Cameron, J. (1990) *Why Have Children? A New Zealand Case-Study*, Christchurch: Canterbury University Press.

—— (1997) *Without Issue: New Zealanders Who Choose Not to Have Children*, Christchurch: Canterbury University Press.

Campbell, E. (1985) *The Childless Marriage: An Exploratory Study of Couples Who Do Not Want Children*, London: Tavistock.

Cargan, L. and Melko, M. (1982) *Singles—Myths and Realities*, Beverly Hills, CA: Sage.

Carrier, S. (1995) 'Family status and career situation for professional women', *Work, Employment and Society*, 9: 343–58.

Cartwright, A. (1976) *How Many Children?*, London: Routledge.

Cassidy, M. L. and Warren, B. O. (1996) 'Family employment status and gender role attitudes: A comparison of women and men college graduates', *Gender and Society*, 10: 312–29.

CELADE and CFSC (1972) *Fertility and Family Planning in Metropolitan Latin America*, Chicago, IL: University of Chicago, Community and Family Study Centre.

Charles, M. (1998) 'Structure, culture, and sex segregation in Europe', *Research in Social Stratification and Mobility*, 16: 89–116.

Chase, I. (1975) 'A comparison of men's and women's intergenerational mobility in the United States', *American Sociological Review*, 40: 483–505.

Chesnais, J-C. (1995) *Le Crépuscule de l'Occident: Dénatalité, Condition des Femmes et Immigration*, Paris: Robert Laffont.

Chisolm, L. and DuBois-Raymond, G. (1989) 'Youth transitions, gender and social change', *Sociology*, 27: 259–79.

Cleland, J. (1985) 'Marital fertility decline in developing countries: theories and the evidence', pp 223–52 in J. Cleland and J. Hobcraft (eds) *Reproductive Change in Developing Countries: Insights from the World Fertility Survey*, Oxford: Oxford University Press.

—— and Hobcraft, J. (eds) (1985) *Reproductive Change in Developing Countries: Insights from the World Fertility Survey*, Oxford: Oxford University Press.

—— and Scott, C. (eds) (1987) *The World Fertility Survey: An Assessment*, Oxford: Oxford University Press.

Coatham, V. and Hale, J. (1994) 'Women achievers in housing: the career paths of women chief housing officers', pp 196–225 in R. Gilroy and R. Woods (eds) *Housing Women*, London: Routledge.

Cobble, D. S. (ed) (1993) *Women and Unions: Forging a Partnership*, Ithaca NY: ILR Press.

Cockburn, C. (1983) *Brothers: Male Dominance and Technological Change*, London: Pluto Press.

—— (1996) *Strategies for Gender Democracy, Social Europe*, Supplement 4/95, Luxembourg: OOPEC.

Cohn, S. (1985) *The Process of Occupational Sex-Typing: The Feminisation of Clerical Work in Great Britain*, Philadelphia: Temple University Press.

Cole, S. and Fiorentine, R. (1991) 'Discrimination against women in science: the confusion of outcome with process' pp 205–26 in H. Zuckerman, J. R. Cole and J. T. Bruer (eds) *The Outer Circle: Women in the Scientific Community*, New York, NY: WW Norton.

Coleman, D. (1996a) 'New patterns and trends in European fertility: international and sub-national comparisons', pp 1–61 in D. Coleman (ed) *Europe's Population in 1990*, Oxford: Oxford University Press.

—— (ed) (1996b) *Europe's Population in 1990*, Oxford: Oxford University Press.

Coleman, J. S. (1961) *The Adolescent Society*, New York, NY: Free Press.

Coleman, M. T. and Pencavel, J. (1993) 'Trends in market work behaviour of women since 1940', *Industrial and Labor Relations Review*, 46: 653–77.

Coleman, S. (1983) *Family Planning in Japanese Society: Traditional Birth Control in a Modern Urban Culture*, Princeton NJ: Princeton University Press.

Collins, P. H. *et al.* (1995) 'Symposium: On West and Fenstermaker's Doing difference', *Gender and Society*, 9: 491–513.

Connell, R. W. (1987) *Gender and Power*, Cambridge: Polity Press.

Cook, A. and Hayashi, H. (1980) *Working Women in Japan: Discrimination, Resistance and Reform*, Cornell International Industrial and Labor Relations Report, New York: Cornell University Press.

Corcoran, M., Duncan, G. J. and Ponza, M. (1984) 'Work experience, job segregation and wages', pp 171–91 in B. F. Reskin (ed) *Sex Segregation in the Workplace: Trends, Explanations, Remedies* , Washington DC: National Academy Press.

Cornwall, A. and Lindisfarne, N. (eds) (1993) *Dislocating Masculinity: Comparative Ethnographies*, London and New York, NY: Routledge.

Corti, L., Laurie, H., and Dex, S. (1995) *Highly Qualified Women*, Research Series No. 50, London: Employment Department.

Cousins, C. (1998) 'Social exclusion in Europe: paradigms of social disadvantage in Germany, Spain, Sweden and the United Kingdom', *Policy and Politics*, 26: 128–46.

Craib, I. (1987) 'Masculinity and male dominance', *Sociological Review*, 35: 721–43.

Cramer, J. C. (1980) 'Fertility and female employment: problems of causal direction', *American Sociological Review* 45: 167–90.

Creighton, C. (1996a) 'The family wage as a class-rational strategy', *Sociological Review*, 44: 204–24.

—— (1996b) 'The rise of the male breadwinner family: a reappraisal', *Comparative Studies in Society and History*, 38: 310–37.

—— (1999) 'The rise and decline of the male breadwinner family in Britain', *Cambridge Journal of Economics*, 23: 519–41.

Crispell, D. (1993) 'Planning no family, now or ever', *American Demographics*, October: 23–4.

Crompton, R. (1997) *Women and Work in Modern Britain*, Oxford: Oxford University Press.

—— and Harris, F. (1998) 'Explaining women's employment patterns: orientations to work revisited', *British Journal of Sociology*, 49: 118–36.

—— and Le Feuvre, N. (1996) 'Paid employment and the changing system of gender relations: a cross-national comparison', *Sociology*, 30: 427–45.

Cully, M., O'Reilly, A., Millward, N., Forth, J. (1998) *The 1998 Workplace Employee Relations Survey: First Findings*, London: Department of Trade and Industry.

—— Woodland, S., O'Reilly, A., Dix, J. (1999) *Britain at Work*, London: Routledge.

Cunnison, S. and Stageman, J. (1993) *Feminising the Unions*, Aldershot: Avebury Press.

Curtice, J. (1993) 'Satisfying work—if you can get it', pp 103–21 in R. Jowell *et al.* (eds) *International Social Attitudes: the 10th BSA Report*, Aldershot: Gower.

Dale, A. and Egerton, M. (1997) *Highly Educated Women: Evidence from the National Child Development Study*, RS25, London: Department for Education and Employment.

Dallos, S,. and Dallos, R. (1997) *Couples, Sex and Power: the Politics of Desire*, Buckingham: Open University Press.

Dally, A. (1982) *Inventing Motherhood: The Consequences of an Ideal*, London: Burnett Books.

Daniel, K. (1995) 'The marriage premium', pp 113–25 in M. Tommasi and K. Ierulli (eds) *The New Economics of Human Behaviour*, Cambridge: Cambridge University Press.

Date-Bah, E. (ed) (1997) *Promoting Gender Equality at Work: Turning Vision into Reality*, London and New York, NY: Zed Books.

Davies, H. and Joshi, H. (1998) 'Gender and income inequality in the UK 1968–1990: the feminization of earnings or of poverty?', *Journal of the Royal Statistical Society—A*, 161: 33–61.

—— —— and Peronaci, R. (1998) *Dual and Zero Earner Couples in Britain: Longitudinal Evidence on Polarization and Persistence*, Discussion Papers in Economics 8/98, London: Birkbeck College Department of Economics.

Davis, J. A. (1982) 'Achievement variables and class cultures: family, schooling, job, and forty-nine dependent variables in the cumulative GSS', *American Sociological Review*, 47: 569–86.

—— (1996) 'Patterns of attitude change in the USA: 1972–1994', pp 151–84 in B. Taylor and K. Thomson (eds) *Understanding Change in Social Attitudes*, Aldershot: Dartmouth.

Davis, K. (1984) 'Wives and work: the sex-role revolution and its consequences', *Population and Development Review*, 10: 397–417.

—— Bernstam, M. S., and Ricardo-Campbell, R. (eds) (1987) *Below-Replacement Fertility in Industrial Societies: Causes, Consequences, Policies*, Cambridge: Cambridge University Press.

Davis, N. J. and Robinson, R. V. (1991) 'Men's and women's consciousness of gender inequality: Austria, West Germany, Great Britain and the United States', *American Sociological Review*, 56: 72–84.

De Graaf, P. M. (1986) 'The impact of financial and cultural resources on educational attainment in the Netherlands', *Sociology of Education*, 59: 237–46.

—— and Vermeulen, H. (1997) 'Female labour-market participation in the Netherlands:

developments in the relationship between family cycle and employment', pp 191–209 in H-P. Blossfeld and C. Hakim (eds) *Between Equalization and Marginalization*, Oxford: Oxford University Press.

Delphy, C. and Leonard, D. (1992) *Familiar Exploitation: A New Analysis of Marriage in Contemporary Western Societies*, Cambridge: Polity Press.

Demeny, P. (1987) 'Pronatalist policies in low-fertility countries: patterns, performance and prospects', pp 335–58 in K. Davis, M. S. Bernstam, and R. Ricardo-Campbell (eds) *Below-Replacement Fertility in Industrial Society*, Cambridge: Cambridge University Press.

Dench, G. (1996) *The Place of Men in Changing Family Cultures*, London: Institute of Community Studies.

—— (ed) (1999) *Rewriting the Sexual Contract*, New Brunswick, NJ: Transaction Press.

de Neubourg, C. (1985) 'Part-time work: an international quantitative comparison', *International Labour Review*, 124: 559–76.

Dennis, N. (1997) *The Invention of Permanent Poverty*, London: Institute of Economic Affairs.

Denzin, N. K. (1978a) *The Research Act*, New York and London: McGraw-Hill.

—— (1978b) *Sociological Methods*, New York and London: McGraw-Hill.

Dex, S. (1988) *Women's Attitudes Towards Work*, London: Macmillan.

—— Joshi, H., and Macran, S. (1996) 'A widening gulf among Britain's mothers', *Oxford Review of Economic Policy*, 12: 65–75.

—— and Rowthorn, R. (1999) 'The case for a Ministry of the Family', pp 192–206 in G. Dench (ed) *Rewriting the Sexual Contract*, NY: New Brunswick, NJ: Transaction Press.

—— and Sewell, R. (1995) 'Equal opportunities policies and women's labour market status in industrialised countries', pp 367–92 in J. Humphries and J. Rubery (eds) *The Economics of Equal Opportunities*, Manchester: Equal Opportunities Commission.

DiMaggio, P. and Mohr, J. (1985) 'Cultural capital, educational attainment and marital selection', *American Journal of Sociology*, 90: 1231–61.

Dirven, H., Lammers, J., and Ultee, W. (1990) 'Werkend en toch Economisch Afhankelijk?' (Working but still economically dependent?), *Sociale Wetenschappen*, 33: 61–93.

Donovan, P. (1995) 'The family cap: a popular but unproven method of welfare reform', *Family Planning Perspectives*, 27/4: 166–71.

Drever, F. and Whitehead, M. (eds) (1997) *Health Inequalities: Decennial Supplement*, London: Stationery Office.

Dronkers, J. (1995) 'The effects of the occupations of working mothers on educational inequality', *Educational Research and Evaluation*, 1: 226–46.

Duggan, L. (1992) 'The impact of population policies on women in Eastern Europe: the German Democratic Republic', pp 250–64 in N. Folbre *et al.* (eds) *Women's Work in the World Economy*, London: Macmillan.

Dugger, K. (1988) 'Social location and gender-role attitudes: a comparison of black and white women', *Gender and Society*, 2: 425–48.

Duncan, A., Giles, C., and Webb, S. (1995) *The Impact of Subsidising Childcare*, Manchester: EOC.

Duncan, G. J. and Dunifon, R. (1998) 'Soft skills and long-run labor market success', *Research in Labor Economics*, 17: 123–49.

Dunnell, K. (1979) *Family Formation 1976*, London: HMSO.

Dunton, N. and Featherman, D. L. (1985) 'Social mobility through marriage and careers: achievement over the life course' in J. T. Spence (ed) *Achievement and Achievement Motives*, San Francisco, CA: W H Freeman.

Dykstra, P. (1999) 'Childless older adults: a group at risk?' in P. Dykstra and V. R. A. Call (eds) *A Cross-National Handbook on Parental Status in Late Life*, Westport CT: Greenwood.

—— and Call, V. R. A. (eds) (1999) *A Cross-National Handbook on Parental Status in Late Life*, Westport CT: Greenwood.

Edgell, S. (1980) *Middle Class Couples: A Study of Segregation, Domination and Inequality in Marriage*, London: Allen & Unwin.

Egidi, V. and Verdecchia, A. (1993) 'Sex inequalities in morbidity and mortality', pp 213–24 in N. Federici, K. O. Mason, and S. Sogner (eds) *Women's Position and Demographic Change*, Oxford: Clarendon.

Ehrenreich, B. (1983) *The Hearts of Men: American Dreams and the Flight from Commitment*, Garden City NY: Anchor Press.

Einhorn, B. (1993) *Cinderella Goes to Market: Citizenship, Gender and Women's Movements in East Central Europe*, London: Verso.

—— (1997) 'The impact of the transition from centrally planned to market-based economies on women's employment in East Central Europe', pp 59–84 in E. Date-Bah (ed) *Promoting Gender Equality at Work*, London: Zed Books.

Einstein, A. (1936) 'Physics and reality', *Franklin Institute Journal*, 221: 349–82.

Elder, G. H. (1969) 'Appearance and education in marriage mobility', *American Sociological Review*, 34: 519–33.

Engelstad, F. (1998) 'Changing family patterns and social stratification: new trends in the Scandinavian welfare states?', paper presented to the ESF conference, 'European Societies or European Society? Inequality and Social Exclusion in Europe', held in Castelvecchio di Pascoli, April 1998.

England, P. (1982) 'The failure of human capital theory to explain occupational sex segregation', *Journal of Human Resources*, 17: 358–70.

—— (1984) 'Wage appreciation and depreciation: a test of neoclassical economic explanations of occupational sex segregation', *Social Forces*, 62: 726–49.

—— (1992) *Comparable Worth: Theories and Evidence*, New York, NY: Aldine de Gruyter.

—— and McCreary, L. (1987) 'Integrating sociology and economics to study gender and work', pp 143–172 in A. H. Stromberg *et al.* (eds) *Women and Work: An Annual Review*, Beverly Hills and London: Sage.

English, J. (1989) *Childlessness Transformed*, Mount Shasta: Earth Heart.

EOC (1997) *Partnering Equality: Annual Report 1996*, Manchester: EOC.

EOC and OFSTED (1996) *The Gender Divide: Performance Differences Between Boys and Girls at School*, Manchester: EOC.

Erikson, R. and Goldthorpe, J. H. (1993) *The Constant Flux*, Oxford: Clarendon Press.

Ermisch, J. (1996) 'The economic environment for family formation', pp 144–62 in D. Coleman (ed) *Europe's Population in 1990*, Oxford: Oxford University Press.

—— and Di Salvo, P. (1997) 'Economic determinants of young people's household formation', *Economica*, 64: 627–44.

—— and Wright, R. E. (1992) 'Differential returns to human capital in full-time and part-time employment', pp 195–212 in N. Folbre *et al.* (eds) *Women's Work in the World Economy*, London: Macmillan.

Esping-Andersen, G. (1990) *The Three Worlds of Welfare Capitalism*, Cambridge: Polity Press/Princeton NJ: Princeton University Press.

Esser, H. (1996) 'What is wrong with variable sociology?' *European Sociological Review*, 12: 159–66.

Etzioni, A. (1993a) *The Parenting Deficit*, London: DEMOS.

—— (1993b) *The Spirit of Community*, New York, NY: Crown Publishers.

European Commission (1991a) *Lifestyles in the European Community: Family and Employment within the Twelve*, DGX special report on Eurobarometer No. 34, Brussels: European Commission.

—— (1991b) *Employment in Europe 1991*, Luxemburg: OOPEC.

—— (1992a) *Employment in Europe 1992*, Luxemburg: OOPEC.

—— (1992b) *Eurobarometer No. 38*, Brussels: European Commission.

—— (1993) *Europeans and the Family: Eurobarometer No. 39* by N. Malpas and P-Y. Lambert, Brussels: European Commission.

—— (1995) *The Demographic Situation in the European Union*, DG V-COM(94)595, Luxemburg: OOPEC.

—— (1996a) *Employment in Europe 1996*, Luxemburg: OOPEC.

—— (1996b) *The EC Childcare Network 1986–1996*, Brussels: European Commission.

—— (1997a) *Equal Opportunities for Women and Men in the European Union 1996*, Luxemburg: OOPEC.

—— (1997b) *The State of Women's Health in the European Community*, Employment and Social Affairs Unit V/F.1, Luxemburg: OOPEC.

—— (1997c) *Employment in Europe 1997*, Luxemburg: OOPEC.

—— (1997d) 'Interview with Allan Larsson' and 'Women and men in Europe: equality of opportunity?', *Equal Opportunities Magazine*, 2: 3–4 and i–viii.

—— (1999) *Employment in Europe 1998*, Luxemburg: OOPEC.

Eurostat (1998) *Education in the EU*, Report No. 9/98, Luxemburg: OOPEC.

Evans, G. (1996) 'Cross-national differences in support for welfare and redistribution: an evaluation of competing theories' pp 185–208 in B. Taylor and K. Thomson (eds) *Understanding Change in Social Attitudes*, Aldershot: Dartmouth.

Evans, J. (1995) *Feminist Theory Today*, London: Sage.

Fagan, C. and Rubery, J. (1996) 'The salience of the part-time divide in the European Union', *European Sociological Review*, 12: 227–50.

Farmer, H. S. and Associates (1997) *Diversity and Women's Career Development: From Adolescence to Adulthood*, Thousand Oaks, CA: Sage.

Faver, C. A. (1984) *Women in Transition: Career, Family and Life Satisfaction in Three Cohorts*, New York, NY: Praeger Special Studies.

Federici, N., Mason, K. O., and Sogner, S. (eds) (1993) *Women's Position and Demographic Change*, Oxford: Clarendon Press.

Fernandez, J. P. (1990) *The Politics and Reality of Family Care in Corporate America*, Lexington MA: Lexington Books.

Ferri, E. (ed) (1993) *Life at 33*, London: National Children's Bureau.

—— and Smith, K. (1996) *Parenting in the 1990s*, London: Family Policy Studies Centre.

Filer, R. A. (1981) 'The influence of affective human capital on the wage equation', in R. G. Ehrenberg (ed) *Research in Labor Economics*, vol 3, Greenwich, CN: JAI Press.

Finch, J. (1983) *Married to the Job: Wives' Incorporation in Men's Work*, London: Allen & Unwin.

Fine, B. (1992) *Women's Employment and the Capitalist Family*, London and New York, NY: Routledge.

Fiorentine, R. (1987) 'Men, women and the premed persistence gap: a normative alternatives approach', *American Journal of Sociology*, 92: 1118–39.

Firestone, S. (1974) *The Dialectic of Sex: The Case for Feminist Revolution*, New York, NY: Morrow.

Fogarty, M., Rapoport, R., and Rapoport, R. N. (1971) *Sex, Career and Family*, London: Allen & Unwin.

Forth, J., Lissenburgh, S., Callender, C., and Millward, N. (1997) *Family Friendly Working Arrangements in Britain*, Research Series No. 16, London: Department for Education and Employment.

Fowlkes, M. R. (1980) *Behind Every Successful Man: Wives of Medicine and Academe*, New York, NY: Columbia University Press.

Frank, O. (1983) 'Infertility in sub-Saharan Africa: estimates and implications', *Population and Development Review*, 9: 137–44.

Frank, R. H. (1997) 'The frame of reference as a public good', *Economic Journal*, 107: 1832–47.

Fredman, S. (1997) *Women and the Law*, Oxford: Clarendon Press.

Fried, M. (1998) *Taking Time: Parental Leave Policy and Corporate Culture*, Philadelphia, PA: Temple University Press.

Fry, V. C. (1984) 'Inequality in family earnings', *Fiscal Studies*, 5/3: 54–61.

Fujimura-Fanselow, K. and Kameda, A. (eds) (1995) *Japanese Women: New Feminist Perspectives on the Past, Present and Future*, New York, NY: City University of New York.

Galbraith, J. K. (1975) *Economics and the Public Purpose*, Harmondsworth: Penguin.

Gallie, D., White, M., Cheng, Y., and Tomlinson, M. (1998) *Restructuring the Employment Relationship*, Oxford: Clarendon Press.

Galtung, J. (1990) 'Theory formation in social research: a plea for pluralism', pp 96–112 in E. Oyen (ed) *Comparative Methodology: Theory and Practice in International Social Research*, London: Sage.

Garcia-Ramon, D. and Monk, J. (1996) *Women of the European Union: The Politics of Work and Daily Life*, London: Routledge.

Gauthier, A. H. (1996a) 'The measured and unmeasured effects of welfare benefits on families: implications for Europe's demographic trends', pp 295–331 in D. Coleman (ed) *Europe's Population in the 1990s*, Oxford: Oxford University Press.

—— (1996b) *The State and the Family*, Oxford: Clarendon Press.

Geerken, M. and Gove, W. R. (1983) *At Home and At Work: the Family's Allocation of Labour*, Beverly Hills, CA: Sage.

Genovese, M. A. (ed) (1993) *Women as National Leaders*, Sage Focus Editions No. 153, London: Sage.

Gerson, K. (1985) *Hard Choices: How Women Decide about Work, Career and Motherhood*, Berkeley and Los Angeles, CA: University of California Press.

—— (1986) 'Briefcase, baby or both?', *Psychology Today*, 20/11: 30–6. Reprinted in E. D. Salamon and B. W. Robinson (eds) *Gender Roles*, New York, NY: Methuen, 1987, pp 206–12.

—— (1987) 'Emerging social divisions among women: implications for welfare state policies', *Politics and Society*, 15: 213–21.

Gibson, C. (1980) 'Childlessness and marital instability: a re-examination of the evidence', *Journal of Biosocial Science*, 12: 121–132.

Giddens, A. (1984) *The Constitution of Society*, Cambridge: Polity Press.

—— (1991) *Modernity and Self-Identity: Self and Society in Late Modern Age*, Cambridge: Polity Press.

—— (1992) *The Transformation of Intimacy: Sexuality, Love and Eroticism in Modern Societies*, Cambridge: Polity Press.

Gilbert, N. (1997) 'Advocacy research and social policy', pp 101–48 in M. Tonry (ed) *Crime and Justice: A Review of Research*, vol 22, Chicago, IL and London: University of Chicago Press.

Gilligan, C. (1982, 1993) *In a Different Voice: Psychological Theory and Women's Development*, Cambridge, MA and London: Harvard University Press.

Ginn, J. and Arber, S. (1996) 'Patterns of employment, gender and pensions: the effect of work history on older women's non-state pensions', *Work, Employment and Society*, 10: 469–90.

Ginzberg, E. (1964) *Talent and Performance*, New York, NY and London: Colombia University Press.

—— (1966) *Life Styles of Educated Women*, New York, NY and London: Colombia University Press.

Girod, R. (1977) *Inégalité—Inégalités*, Paris: Presses Universitaires de France.

Glenn, N. D., Ross, A. A., and Tully, J. C. (1974) 'Patterns of intergenerational mobility of females through marriage', *American Sociological Review*, 39: 683–99.

Glezer, H. (1988) *Maternity Leave in Australia*, Melbourne: Australian Institute of Family Studies.

Godwin, J. (1973) *The Mating Trade*, New York, NY: Doubleday.

Goldberg, S. (1993) *Why Men Rule: A Theory of Male Dominance*, Chicago, IL: Open Court.

Goldin, C. (1990) *Understanding the Gender Gap*, New York, NY: Oxford University Press.

—— (1997) 'Career and family: college women look to the past', with discussion, pp 20–64 in F. D. Blau and R. G. Ehrenberg (eds) *Gender and Family Issues in the Workplace*, New York, NY: Russell Sage Foundation.

—— and Polachek, S. (1987) 'Residual differences by sex: perspectives on the gender gap in earnings', *American Economic Review*, 77: 143–51.

Goldthorpe, J. H. (1987) 'The class mobility of women', pp 277–301 in J. H. Goldthorpe, *Social Mobility and Class Structure in Modern Britain*, 2nd edition, Oxford: Clarendon Press.

Goodbody, S. T. (1977) 'The psychosocial implications of voluntary childlessness', *Social Casework*, 58: 426–34.

Goodman, N. (1999) 'Failure of the dream: notes for a research program on self-esteem and failed identity in adulthood', in T. Owens, S. Stryker, and N. Goodman (eds) *Extending Self-Esteem Theory and Research: Sociological and Psychological Currents*, New York, NY: Cambridge University Press.

Gordon, T. (1994) *Single Women: On the Margins?*, Basingstoke: Macmillan.

Greenhalgh, C. (1980) 'Male-female wage differentials in Great Britain: is marriage an equal opportunity?', *Economic Journal*, 90: 751–75.

Gregg, P. and Machin, S. (1999) 'Child development and success or failure in the youth labour market', pp 247–88 in D. Blanchflower and R. Freeman (eds) *Youth*

Employment and Joblessness in Advanced Countries, Chicago, IL: University of Chicago Press.

Grimshaw, D. and Rubery, J. (1997) *The Concentration of Women's Employment and Relative Occupational Pay: A Statistical Framework for Comparative Analysis*, Labour Market and Social Policy Occasional Papers No. 26, Paris: OECD.

Grint, K. (1988) 'Women and equality: the acquisition of equal pay in the Post Office 1870–1961', *Sociology*, 22: 87–108.

—— (1991) *The Sociology of Work: An Introduction*, Cambridge: Polity Press.

Guerin, G., St-Onge, S., Haines, V., Trottier, R., and Simard, M. (1997) 'Les pratiques d'aide à l'équilibre emploi-famille dans les organisations du Québec', *Relations Industrielles*, 52: 274–303.

Gustafsson, S. (1994) 'Childcare and types of welfare states', *Gendering Welfare States*, 35: 45–61.

—— (1995) 'Public policies and women's labor force participation: A comparison of Sweden, Germany, and the Netherlands', pp 91–112 in T. P. Schultz (ed) *Investment in Women's Human Capital*, Chicago, IL: University of Chicago Press.

—— and Stafford, F. P. (1994) 'Three regimes of childcare: the United States, the Netherlands, and Sweden', pp 333–61 in R. M. Blank (ed) *Social Protection versus Economic Flexibility*, Chicago, IL and London: University of Chicago Press.

Guthrie, D. and Roth, L. M. (1999) 'The state, courts, and maternity policies in US organizations: specifying institutional mechanisms', *American Sociological Review*, 64: 41–63.

Haas, L. (1992) *Equal Parenthood and Social Policy: A Study of Parental Leave in Sweden*, Albany, NY: State University of New York Press.

Hakim, C. (1979) *Occupational Segregation: A Study of the Separation of Men and Women's Work in Britain, the United States and Other Countries*, Research Paper No. 9, London: Department of Employment.

—— (1980) 'Census reports as documentary evidence: the census commentaries 1801–1951', *Sociological Review*, 28: 551–80.

—— (1982) 'The social consequences of high unemployment', *Journal of Social Policy*, 11: 433–67.

—— (1987a) *Research Design: Strategies and Choices in the Design of Social Research*, London: Allen & Unwin/Routledge.

—— (1987b) *Home-Based Work in Britain: A Report on the 1981 National Homeworking Survey and the DE Research Programme on Homework*, Research Paper No. 60, London: Department of Employment.

—— (1987c) 'Trends in the flexible workforce', *Employment Gazette*, 95: 549–60.

—— (1988) 'Homeworking in Britain' pp 609–32 in R. Pahl (ed) *On Work: Historical, Comparative and Theoretical Approaches*, Oxford: Blackwell.

—— (1989) 'Workforce restructuring, social insurance coverage and the black economy', *Journal of Social Policy*, 18: 471–503.

—— (1990a) 'Workforce restructuring in Europe in the 1980s', *International Journal of Comparative Labour Law and Industrial Relations*, 5/4: 167–203.

—— (1990b) 'Core and periphery in employers' workforce strategies: evidence from the 1987 ELUS survey', *Work, Employment and Society*, 4: 157–88.

—— (1991) 'Grateful slaves and self-made women: fact and fantasy in women's work orientations', *European Sociological Review*, 7: 101–21.

Hakim, C. (1992) 'Explaining trends in occupational segregation: the measurement, causes and consequences of the sexual division of labour', *European Sociological Review*, 8: 127–52.
—— (1993a) 'The myth of rising female employment', *Work, Employment and Society*, 7: 97–120.
—— (1993b) 'Segregated and integrated occupations: a new framework for analysing social change', *European Sociological Review*, 9: 289–314.
—— (1994) 'A century of change in occupational segregation 1891–1991', *Journal of Historical Sociology*, 7: 435–54.
—— (1995) 'Five feminist myths about women's employment', *British Journal of Sociology*, 46: 429–55.
—— (1996a) *Key Issues in Women's Work: Female Heterogeneity and the Polarization of Women's Employment*, London: Athlone.
—— (1996b) 'The sexual division of labour and women's heterogeneity', *British Journal of Sociology*, 47: 178–88.
—— (1996c) 'Labour mobility and employment stability: rhetoric and reality on the sex differential in labour market behaviour', *European Sociological Review*, 12: 45–69.
—— (1997) 'A sociological perspective on part-time work', pp 22–70 in H-P. Blossfeld and C. Hakim (eds) *Between Equalization and Marginalization: Women Part-time Workers in Europe and the USA*, Oxford: Oxford University Press.
—— (1998a) *Social Change and Innovation in the Labour Market: Evidence from the Census SARs on Occupational Segregation and Labour Mobility, Part-Time Work and Student Jobs, Homework and Self-Employment*, Oxford: Oxford University Press.
—— (1998b) 'Developing a sociology for the twenty-first century: Preference Theory', *British Journal of Sociology*, 49: 137–43.
—— (1999) 'Models of the family, women's role and social policy: a new perspective from Preference Theory', *European Societies*, 1: 33–58.
—— (2000) *Research Design: Successful Designs for Social and Economic Research*, London: Routledge.
—— (forthcoming) *Modern Work-Lifestyles in Britain and Spain: Ideals and Realities*.
—— and Jacobs, S. (1997) *Sex-Role Preferences and Work Histories*, Working Paper No. 12, London School of Economics, Department of Sociology.
Halford, S. and Savage, M. (1995) 'Restructuring organisations, changing people: gender and restructuring in banking and local government', *Work, Employment and Society*, 9: 97–122.
—— —— and Witz, A. (1997) *Gender, Careers and Organisations: Current Developments in Banking, Nursing and Local Government*, London: Macmillan.
Hall, R. and White, P. (eds) (1995) *Europe's Population: Towards the Next Century*, London: UCL Press.
Haller, M. and Höllinger, F. (1994) 'Female employment and the change of gender roles: the conflictual relationship between participation and attitudes in international comparison', *International Sociology*, 9: 87–112.
—— —— and Gomilschak, M. (1999) 'Family and gender roles in macrosocial constraints and cultural contradictions: A comparative analysis of attitudes and their recent changes in twenty countries', in R. Nave-Herz and R. Richter (eds) *New Qualities in the Life Course*, Wurzburg: Ergon Verlag.

Hantrais, L. (ed) (1990) *Managing Professional and Family Life: A Comparative Study of British and French Women*, Aldershot: Dartmouth.

—— (1992) 'La fécondité en France et au Royaume-Uni: les effets possibles de la politique familiale', *Population*, 4: 987–1016.

—— (1993) 'Women, work and welfare in France', pp 116–37 in J. Lewis (ed) *Women and Social Policies in Europe: Work, Family and the State*, Aldershot: Edward Elgar.

—— (1994) 'Comparing family policy in Britain, France and Germany', *Journal of Social Policy*, 23: 135–60.

—— (1997) 'Exploring relationships between social policy and changing family forms within the European Union', *European Journal of Population*, 13: 339–79.

—— and Letablier, M-T. (eds) (1996) *Families and Family Policies in Europe*, Harlow: Longman.

Hardill, I., Green, A. E., Dudleston, A. C., and Owen, D. W. (1997) 'Who decides what? Decision making in dual-career households', *Work, Employment and Society*, 11: 313–26.

Harkness, S. (1996) 'The gender earnings gap: evidence from the UK', *Fiscal Studies*, 17: 1–36.

—— and Machin, S. (1999) *Graduate Earnings in Britain, 1974–95*, Research Report No. 95, London: Department for Education and Employment.

—— —— and Waldfogel, J. (1995) *Evaluating the Pin Money Hypothesis: The relationship between women's labour market activity, family income and poverty in Britain*, STICERD Working Paper No. WSP/108, London: London School of Economics.

Harper, K. (1980) *The Childfree Alternative*, Battleboro, VT: Harper-Moretown.

Harrop, A. and Joshi, H. (1994) 'Death and the saleswomen: an investigation of mortality and occupational immobility of women in the Longitudinal Study of England and Wales', mimeo paper, University of London, Institute of Education.

Hartmann, H. (1976) 'Capitalism, patriarchy and job segregation by sex', pp 137–79 in M. Blaxall and B. Reagan (eds) *Women and the Workplace: The Implications of Occupational Segregation*, Chicago, IL: University of Chicago Press. Reprinted 1976, *Signs*, 1: 137–69. Reprinted in Z. R. Eisenstein (ed) *Capitalist Patriarchy and the Case for Socialist Feminism*, 1979, New York and London: Monthly Review Press.

Hassell, K., Noyce, P., and Jesson, J. (1998) 'White and ethnic minority self-employment in retail pharmacy in Britain: an historical and comparative analysis', *Work, Employment and Society*, 12: 245–71.

Heckman, J. J. (1976) 'The common structure of statistical models of truncation, sample selection and limited dependent variables and a simple estimator for such models', *Annals of Economic and Social Measurement*, 5: 475–92.

—— (1979a) 'Sample selection bias as a specification error', *Econometrica*, 45: 153–61.

—— (1979b) 'New evidence on the dynamics of female labour supply', pp 66–116 in C. B. Lloyd *et al.* (eds) *Women in the Labor Market*, New York, NY: Columbia University Press.

—— and Willis, R. J. (1977) 'A beta-logistic model for the analysis of sequential labor force participation by married women', *Journal of Political Economy*, 85: 27–58.

Hedström, P. and Swedberg, R. (1996) 'Rational choice, empirical research and the sociological tradition', *European Sociological Review*, 12: 127–46.

Hendrickx, J., Bernasco, W., and de Graaf, P. (2001) 'Couples' labour market participation in the Netherlands: the effects of economic and cultural characteristics of both

spouses', in H-P. Blossfeld and S. Drobnic (eds) *Careers of Couples in Contemporary Societies*, Oxford: Oxford University Press.
Hepple, B. and Szyszczak, M. (eds) (1992) *Discrimination: The Limits of Law*, London and New York, NY: Mansell.
Hill, M. and Fee, L. K. (1995) *The Politics of Nation Building and Citizenship in Singapore*, London: Routledge.
Hirdman, Y. (1988) 'Genussystemet—reflexioner kring kvinnors sociala underordning', *Kvinnovetenskapligtidskrift*, 3: 49–63.
Hoaglin, D. C., Light, R. J., McPeek, B., Mosteller, F., and Stoto, M. A. (1982) *Data for Decisions: Information Strategies for Policymakers*, Cambridge MA: Abt Books.
Hobson, B. (1990) 'No exit, no voice: women's economic dependency and the welfare state', *Acta Sociologica*, 33: 235–50.
Hock, E. *et al.* (1988) 'Maternal separation anxiety: its role in the balance of employment and motherhood in mothers of infants' in A. E. Gottfried *et al.* (ed) *Maternal Employment and Children's Development*, New York, NY: Plenum Press.
Hodgson, D. (1983) 'Demography as social science and policy science', *Population and Development Review*, 9: 1–34.
Hoem, B. (1995) 'The way to the gender-segregated Swedish labour market', pp 279–96 in K. O. Mason and A-M. Jensen (eds) *Gender and Family Change in Industrial Countries*, Oxford: Oxford University Press.
Hofstede, G. (1980) *Culture's Consequences: International Differences in Work-Related Values*, New York and London: Sage.
—— (1991) *Cultures and Organisations*, London: HarperCollins.
Hogarth, T., Elias, P., and Ford, J. (1996) *Mortgages, Families and Jobs: An Exploration of the Growth in Home Ownership in the 1980s*, Coventry: University of Warwick Institute for Employment Research.
Holcombe, L. (1973) *Victorian Ladies at Work: Middle Class Working Women in England and Wales 1850–1914*, Hamden, CT: Archon Books.
Hood-Williams, J. (1996) 'Goodbye to sex and gender', *Sociological Review*, 44: 1–17.
Hörning, K. H., Gerhard, A., and Michailow, M. (1995) *Time Pioneers: Flexible Working Time and New Lifestyles*, Cambridge: Polity Press.
Hoskyns, C. (1996) *Integrating Gender: Women, Law and Politics in the European Union*, London: Verso.
Houseknecht, S. (1979) 'Timing of the decision to remain voluntarily childless: evidence for continuous socialisation', *Psychology of Women Quarterly*, 4: 81–96.
—— (1982) 'Voluntary childlessness: toward a theoretical integration', *Journal of Social Issues*, 3: 459–71.
—— (1987) 'Voluntary childlessness', pp 369–95 in M. B. Sussman and S. K. Steinmetz (eds) *Handbook of Marriage and the Family*, New York, NY: Plenum Press.
Hout, M. (1982) 'The association between husbands and wives' occupations in two-earner families', *American Journal of Sociology*, 88: 397–409.
Humphries, J. (1998) 'Towards a family-friendly economics', *New Political Economy*, 3: 223–40.
—— and Rubery, J. (1992) 'The legacy for women's employment: integration, differentiation and polarization' pp 236–55 in J. Michie (ed) *The Economic Legacy of Thatcherism*, London: Academic Press.

Hunt, A. (1968a,b) *A Survey of Women's Employment: Report and Tables*, 2 vols, London: HMSO.

Huws, U., Podro, S., Gunnarsson, E., Weijers, T., Arvanitaki, K., and Trova, V. (1996) *Teleworking and Gender*, Brighton: Institute for Employment Studies.

Hyde, J. S. (1996) 'Where are the gender differences? Where are the gender similarities?', pp 107–18 in D. M. Buss and N. M. Malamuth (eds) *Sex, Power, Conflict*, New York, NY: Oxford University Press.

IER (Institute for Employment Research) (1995) *Review of the Economy and Employment: Occupational Assessment*, Coventry: University of Warwick Institute for Employment Research.

Ilmakunnas, S. (1997) 'Public policy and childcare choice', pp 178–93 in I. Persson and C. Jonung (eds) *The Economics of the Family and Family Policies*, London: Routledge.

ILO (International Labour Office) (1962) 'Discrimination in employment or occupations on the basis of marital status', *International Labour Review*, 85: 368–89.

Inglehart, R. (1977) *The Silent Revolution: Changing Values and Political Styles*, Princeton, NJ: Princeton University Press.

—— (1990) *Culture Shift in Advanced Industrial Society*, Princeton, NJ: Princeton University Press.

—— (1997) *Modernization and Postmodernization: Cultural, Economic, and Political Change in 43 Societies*, Princeton, NJ: Princeton University Press.

—— Basañez, M., and Moreno, A. (1998) *Human Values and Beliefs: A Cross-Cultural Sourcebook—Political, Religious, Sexual, and Economic Norms in 43 Societies: Findings from the 1990–1993 World Values Survey*, Ann Arbor, MI: University of Michigan Press.

Jacobs, J. A. and Furstenberg, F. F. (1986) 'Changing places: conjugal careers and women's marital mobility', *Social Forces*, 64: 714–32.

Jacobs, S. (1995) 'Changing patterns of sex segregated occupations throughout the life-course', *European Sociological Review*, 11: 157–71.

Jacobs, T., De Maeyer, S., and Beck, M. (1999) 'The division of labour within Belgian households: diversity, dynamics and emancipation', *Quality and Quantity*, 33: 291–303.

Jacobsen, J. P. (1994) *The Economics of Gender*, Cambridge, MA and Oxford: Blackwell.

James, O. (1997) *Britain on the Couch: Why We're Unhappier Compared with 1950 Despite Being Richer, A Treatment for the Low Serotonin Society*, London: Century.

Janssens, A. (ed) (1998) *The Rise and Decline of the Male Breadwinner Family?*, Cambridge: Cambridge University Press.

Jenson, J., Hagen, E., and Reddy, C. (eds) (1988) *Feminization of the Labour Force: Paradoxes and Promises*, New York, NY: Oxford University Press.

Jolivet, M. (1997) *Japan: the Childless Society?*, London and New York: Routledge.

Jones, C., Marsden, L., and Tepperman, L. (1990) *Lives of Their Own: the Individualisation of Women's Lives*, Toronto: Oxford University Press.

Jones, E. L. (1983) 'The courtesy bias in South-East Asian surveys', pp 253–60 in M. Bulmer and D. P. Warwick (eds) *Social Research in Developing Countries: Surveys and Censuses in the Third World*, Chichester and New York, NY: John Wiley & Sons.

Jones, G. W., Douglas, R. M., Caldwell, J. C., and D'Souza, R. M. (eds) (1997) *The Continuing Demographic Transition*, Oxford: Clarendon Press.

Jonung, C. and Persson, I. (1993) 'Women and market work: the misleading tale of participation rates in international comparisons', *Work, Employment and Society*, 7: 259–74.

Joshi, H. (1996) 'Combining employment and child-bearing: the study of British women's lives', pp 88–118 in A. Offer (ed) *In Pursuit of the Quality of Life*, Oxford: Oxford University Press.

—— and Davies, H. (1996) 'Financial dependency on men: have women born in 1958 broken free?', *Policy Studies*, 17: 35–54.

—— Macran, S., and Dex, S. (1996) 'Employment after child-bearing and women's subsequent labour force participation: evidence from the British 1958 birth cohort', *Journal of Population Economics*, 9: 325–48.

—— and Paci, P. (1998) *Unequal Pay for Women and Men*, Cambridge, MA: MIT Press.

Jowell, R. (1984) 'Introducing the survey', pp 1–10 in R. Jowell and C. Airey (eds) (1984) *British Social Attitudes—the 1984 report*, Aldershot: Gower.

—— and Airey, C. (eds) (1984) *British Social Attitudes—the 1984 report*, Aldershot: Gower.

—— and Witherspoon, S. (eds) (1985) *British Social Attitudes—the 1985 report*, Aldershot: Gower.

—— *et al.* (eds) (1993) *International Social Attitudes: The 10th BSA Report*, Aldershot: Dartmouth.

—— *et al.* (eds) (1998) *British and European Social Attitudes—the 15th Report: How Britain Differs*, Aldershot: Ashgate.

Julkunen, R. (1992) *Hyvinvointivaltio Käännekohdassa* (The welfare state at a turning point) Tampere: Vastapaino.

Kalmijn, M. (1991) 'Status homogamy in the United States', *American Journal of Sociology*, 97: 496–523.

—— (1994) 'Assortive mating by cultural and economic occupational status', *American Journal of Sociology*, 100: 422–52.

Kamerman, S. B. and Kahn, A. J. (eds) (1978) *Family Policy: Government and Families in Fourteen Countries*, New York, NY: Columbia University Press.

—— —— (eds) (1997) *Family Change and Family Policies in Great Britain, Canada, New Zealand and the United States*, Oxford: Clarendon Press.

Katona, G. (1975) *Psychological Economics*, New York, NY: Elsevier.

Kaufmann, F-X., Kuijsten, A., Schulze, H-J., and Strohmeier, K. P. (eds) (1997) *Family Life and Family Policies in Europe: Structure and Trends in the 1980s*, Vol 1, Oxford: Clarendon Press.

Kay, J. A. and King, M. A. (1978) *The British Tax System*, Oxford: Oxford University Press.

Keith, V. M. and Herring, C. (1991) 'Skin tone and stratification in the black community', *American Journal of Sociology*, 97: 760–78.

Kenrick, D. T. and Keefe, R. C. (1992) 'Age preferences in mates reflect sex differences in human reproductive strategies', *Behavioural and Brain Sciences*, 15: 75–133.

—— Trost, M. R., and Sheets, V. L. (1996) 'Power, harassment, and trophy mates: the feminist advantages of an evolutionary perspective', pp 29–53 in D. M. Buss and N. M. Malamuth (eds) *Sex, Power, Conflict*, New York, NY: Oxford University Press.

Kessler-Harris, A. (1990) *A Woman's Wage: Historical Meanings and Social Consequences*, Lexington, KY: University Press of Kentucky.

Keyfitz, N. (1987) 'The family that does not reproduce itself', pp 139–54 in K. Davis *et al.* (eds) (1987) *Below-Replacement Fertility in Industrial Societies: Causes, Consequences, Policies*, Cambridge: Cambridge University Press.

Kiernan, K. (1989) 'Who remains childless?', *Journal of Biosocial Science*, 21: 387–98.

—— (1992) 'Men and women at work and at home', pp 89–112 in R. Jowell *et al.* (eds) *British Social Attitudes: the 9th Report*, Aldershot: Dartmouth.

Killingsworth, M. (1983) *Labour Supply*, Cambridge: Cambridge University Press.

Kohn, M. L. (1989) 'Cross national research as an analytic strategy', in M. L. Kohn (ed) *Cross-National Research in Sociology*, London: Sage.

Komarovsky, M. (1982) 'Female freshmen view their future: career salience and its correlates', *Sex-Roles*, 8: 299–314.

Komter, A. (1989) 'Hidden power in marriage', *Gender and Society*, 3: 187–216

Kraus, S. J. (1995) 'Attitudes and the prediction of behaviour: a meta-analysis of the empirical literature', *Personality and Social Psychology Bulletin*, 21: 58–75.

Kreckel, R. and Schenk, S. (1998) *Full-Time or Part-Time? The Contradictory Integration of the East German Female Labour Force in Unified Germany*, Der Hallesche Graureiher 98–3, Martin-Luther-Universität Halle-Wittenberg.

Kuhn, T. (1962, 1970) *The Structure of Scientific Revolutions*, Chicago, IL: University of Chicago Press.

Kuiper, E. and Sap, J. (eds) (1995) *Out of the Margin: Feminist Perspectives on Economics*, London and New York, NY: Routledge.

Kurz, K. (1997) 'Einstellungen zur Rolle der Frau', pp 450–6 in Statistisches Bundesamt, *Datenreport 1997*, Berlin: Bundeszentrale für Politische Bildung.

Lam, D. (1988) 'Marriage markets and assortive mating with household public goods', *Journal of Human Resources*, 23: 462–87.

Lang, S. S. (1991) *Women Without Children: The Reasons, The Rewards, The Regrets*, New York, NY: Pharos Books.

Lapidus, G. W. (1988) 'The interaction of women's work and family roles in the USSR', pp 87–121 in B. A. Gutek, A. H. Stromberg, and L. Larwood (eds) *Women and Work: An Annual Review*, vol 3, Newbury Park and London: Sage.

Lawrence, E. (1994) *Gender and Trade Unions*, London: Taylor and Francis.

Lawson, T. (1997) *Economics and Reality*, London: Routledge.

Lazear, E. P. and Michael, R. T. (1980) 'Family size and distribution of real per capita income', *American Economic Review*, 70: 91–107.

Lerner, G. (1986) *The Creation of Patriarchy*, New York, NY and Oxford: Oxford University Press.

Lesthaeghe, R. (1995) 'The second demographic transition in Western countries: an interpretation', in K. O. Mason and A-M. Jensen (eds) *Gender and Family Change in Industrialised Countries*, Oxford: Clarendon Press.

—— and Meekers, D. (1986) 'Value changes and the dimensions of familism in the European Community', *European Journal of Population*, 2: 225–68.

—— and Van de Kaa, D. J. (1986) 'Twee demografische transities?', pp 9–24 in D. J. van de Kaa and R. Lesthaeghe (eds) *Bevolking: Groei en Krimp Van Loghum Slaterus*, Deventer.

Levinson, D. J. (1978) *The Seasons of a Man's Life*, New York, NY: Alfred Knopf.

—— (1996) *The Seasons of a Woman's Life*, New York, NY: Alfred Knopf.

Lewis, A. (1982) *The Psychology of Taxation*, Oxford: Martin Robertson.

Lewis, B. (1986) *No Children By Choice*, Ringwood, Victoria: Penguin Books.

Lewis, J. (1992) 'Gender and the development of welfare regimes', *Journal of European Social Policy*, 2: 159–73.

Lewis, J. (1993) *Women and Social Policies in Europe: Work, Family and the State*, Aldershot: Edward Elgar.
Lieberson, S, (1985) *Making it Count: The Improvement of Social Research and Theory*, Berkeley, CA and London: University of California Press.
Lightbourne, R. E. (1987) 'Reproductive preferences and behaviour', pp 838–61 in J. Cleland and C. Scott (eds) *The World Fertility Survey: An Assessment*, Oxford: Oxford University Press.
Lindblom, C. E. and Cohen, D. K. (1979) *Useable Knowledge: Social Science and Social Problem Solving*, New Haven, CT and London: Yale University Press.
Lipman-Blumen, J. (1984) *Gender Roles and Power*, Englewood Cliffs, NJ: Prentice-Hall.
Lipset, S. M., Trow, M. A., and Coleman, J. S. (1956) *Union Democracy: The Internal Politics of the International Typographical Union*, Garden City, NY: Anchor Books.
Lister, R. (1992) *Women's Economic Dependency and Social Security*, Research Discussion Series No. 2, Manchester: EOC.
—— (1999) 'Promoting women's economic independence', pp 180–91 in G. Dench (ed) *Rewriting the Sexual Contract*, N Y, New Brunswick, NJ: Transaction Press.
London Research Centre (1997) *Celebrating Diversity: Ethnic Minorities in European Cities*, London: London Research Centre.
Lovenduski, J. and Randall, V. (1993) *Contemporary Feminist Politics: Women and Power in Britain*, Oxford: Oxford University Press.
Lucas, R. E. (1976) 'Econometric policy evaluation: a critique', pp 19–46 in K. Brunner and A. H. Meltzer (eds) *The Phillips Curve and Labour Markets*, Amsterdam: North-Holland. Reprinted in R. Lucas, *Studies in Business-Cycle Theory*, Oxford: Basil Blackwell, 1981, pp 104–30.
Luckey, E. B. and Bain, J. K. (1970) 'Children: a factor in marital satisfaction', *Journal of Marriage and the Family*, 32: 43–51.
Luker, K. (1984) *Abortion and the Politics of Motherhood*, Berkeley, CA: University of California Press.
Luxton, M. (1987) 'Two hands for the clock: changing patterns in the gendered division of labor in the home', pp 213–26 in E. D. Salamon and B. W. Robinson (eds) *Gender Roles*, Toronto: Methuen.
Maccoby, E. E. and Jacklin, C. N. (1974) *The Psychology of Sex Differences*, Stanford, CA: Stanford University Press.
Machin, S. and Waldfogel, J. (1994) *The Decline of the Male Breadwinner: Changing shares of husbands' and wives' earnings in family income*, STICERD Working Paper No. WSP/103, London: London School of Economics.
Macpherson, D. A. and Hirsch, B. T. (1995) 'Wages and gender composition: why do women's jobs pay less?', *Journal of Labour Economics*, 13: 426–71.
Macran, S., Joshi, H., and Dex, S. (1996) 'Employment after child-bearing: A survival analysis', *Work, Employment and Society*, 10: 273–96.
Maddison, A. (1995) *Monitoring the World Economy*, Paris: OECD.
Main, B. (1988) 'The lifetime attachment of women to the labour market', pp 23–51 in A. Hunt (ed) *Women and Paid Work*, London: Macmillan.
Maital, S. (1982) *Minds, Markets, and Money*, New York, NY: Basic Books.
Mansfield, P. and Collard, J. (1988) *The Beginning of the Rest of Your Life: A Portrait of Newly-Wed Marriage*, London: Macmillan.
Markus, H. and Nurius, P. (1987) 'Possible selves: the interface between motivation and

the self-concept', pp 157–72 in K. Yardley and T. Honess (eds) *Self and Identity: Psychosocial Perspectives*, New York, NY: John Wiley and Sons.

Mare, R. D. (1981) 'Change and stability in educational stratification', *American Sociological Review*, 46: 72–87.

—— (1991) 'Five decades of educational assortive mating', *American Sociological Review*, 56: 15–32.

Maret, E. (1983) *Women's Career Patterns*, Lanham MD: University Press of America.

Marmot, M. G. (1996) 'The social pattern of health and disease' and 'Work and health', pp 42–67 and 235–54 in D. Blane, E. Brunner, and R. Wilkinson (eds) *Health and Social Organisation*, London: Routledge.

Marry, C., Kieffer, A., Brauns, H., and Steinmann, S. (1998) 'France-Allemagne: inégales avancées des femmes—évolutions comparées de l'éducation et de l'activité des femmes de 1971 à 1991', *Revue Française de Sociologie*, 39: 353–89.

Marshall, G. (1990) *In Praise of Sociology*, London: Unwin Hyman.

—— Rose, D., Newby, H., and Vogler, C. (1988, 1991) *Social Class in Modern Britain*, London: Hutchinson.

Marshall, H. (1993) *Not Having Children*, Melbourne: Oxford University Press Australia.

Marshall, S. E. (1987) 'Keep us on the pedestal: women against feminism in twentieth-century America', pp 347–55 in E. D. Salamon and B. W. Robinson (eds) *Gender Roles*, Toronto: Methuen.

Martin, J. and Roberts, C. (1984) *Women and Employment: A Lifetime Perspective*, London: HMSO for the Department of Employment.

Martin, J. K. and Hanson, S. L. (1985) 'Sex, family wage-earning status and satisfaction with work', *Work and Occupations*, 12: 91–109.

Marwell, G. and Ames, R. E. (1981) 'Economists free ride, does anyone else? Experiments on the provision of public goods, IV', *Journal of Public Economics*, 15: 295–310.

Marx, K. (1977) *The Eighteenth Brumaire of Louis Bonaparte*, in D. McLellan (ed) *Karl Marx: Selected Writings*, Oxford: Oxford University Press.

Mason, K. O. and Jensen, A-M. (eds) (1995) *Gender and Family Change in Industrialised Countries*, Oxford: Clarendon Press.

Mathews, E. and Tiedeman, D. V. (1964) 'Attitudes toward career and marriage and the development of lifestyle in young women', *Journal of Counselling Psychology*, 11: 374–83.

Matthaei, J. A. (1982) *An Economic History of Women in America: Women's work, the sexual division of labour and the development of capitalism*, New York, NY: Schocken/Brighton: Harvester.

May, E. T. (1995) *Barren in the Promised Land: Childless Americans and the Pursuit of Happiness*, Cambridge, MA: Harvard University Press.

McAllister, F. and Clarke, L. (1998) *Choosing Childlessness*, London: Family Policy Studies Centre.

McBroom, P. A. (1986) *The Third Sex: The New Professional Woman*, New York, NY: William Morrow.

McIntosh, C. A. (1983) *Population Policy in Western Europe: Responses to Low Fertility in France, Sweden and West Germany*, New York, NY and London: M E Sharpe.

—— (1987) 'Recent pronatalist policies in Western Europe', pp 318–34 in K. Davis *et al.* (eds) *Below-Replacement Fertility in Industrial Society*, Cambridge: Cambridge University Press.

McLaughlin, S. D., Melber, B. D., Billy, J. O G., Zimmerle, D. M., Winges, L. D., and Johnson, T. R. (1988) *The Changing Lives of American Women*, Chapel Hill, NC and London: University of North Carolina Press.

McMahon, M. (1995) *Engendering Motherhood: Identity and Self-Transformation in Women's Lives*, New York, NY: Guilford.

McRae, S. (1986) *Cross Class Families*, Oxford: Clarendon Press.

—— (1991) *Maternity Rights in Britain*, London: Policy Studies Institute.

—— (1993) 'Returning to work after childbirth: opportunities and inequalities', *European Sociological Review*, 9: 125–38.

—— (1997) 'Household and labour market change: implications for the growth of inequality in Britain', *British Journal of Sociology*, 48: 384–405.

Meadows, P. (2000) *Women at Work in Britain and Sweden*, London: National Institute of Economic and Social Research.

Melkas, H. and Anker, R. (1997) 'Occupational segregation by sex in Nordic countries: An empirical investigation', *International Labour Review*, 136: 341–63.

—— —— (1998) *Gender Equality and Occupational Segregation in Nordic Labour Markets*, Geneva: International Labour Office.

Menaghan, E. G. and Parcel, T. L. (1990) 'Parental employment and family life: research in the 1980s', *Journal of Marriage and the Family*, 52: 1079–98.

Menefee, S. P. (1981) *Wives for Sale: An Ethnographic Study of British Popular Divorce*, Oxford: Basil Blackwell.

Merrick, N. (1994) 'Benefits to suit all tastes and lifestyles', *Personnel Management*, December: 9–11.

Michielutte, R. (1972) 'Trends in educational homogamy', *Sociology of Education*, 45: 288–302.

Middleton, C. (1988) 'The familiar fate of the *Famulae*: Gender divisions in the history of wage labour' pp 21–47 in R. Pahl (ed) *On Work*, Oxford: Blackwell.

Milkman, R. (1987) *Gender at Work: The Dynamics of Job Segregation by Sex During World War II*, Urbana and Chicago, IL: University of Illinois Press.

Mills, C. (1996) 'Managerial and professional work histories', in T. Butler and M. Savage (eds) *Social Change and the Middle Classes*, London: UCL Press.

Mincer, J. (1985) 'Intercountry comparisons of labor force trends and of related developments: an overview', *Journal of Labor Economics*, supplement on *Trends in Women's Work, Education and Family Building*, 3: S1–S32.

Mirowsky, J. and Ross, C. (1995) 'Sex differences in distress: real or artefact?', *American Sociological Review*, 60: 449–68.

Mitchell, D. (1991) *Income Transfers in Ten Welfare States*, Aldershot: Avebury.

Moen, P. (1985) 'Continuities and discontinuities in women's labor force activity', pp 113–55 in G. H. Elder (ed) *Life Course Dynamics: Trajectories and Transitions*, Ithaca, NY: Cornell University Press.

—— (1989) *Working Parents: Transformation in Gender Roles and Public Policies in Sweden*, Madison, WI: University of Wisconsin Press and London: Adamantine.

Morell, C. M. (1994) *Unwomanly Conduct: The Challenges of Intentional Childlessness*, London and New York, NY: Routledge.

Morgan, S. P. (1991) 'Late nineteenth- and early twentieth-century childlessness', *American Journal of Sociology*, 97: 779–807.

MORI (1996) *Women, Setting New Priorities: A Study of Western European Women's Views on Work, Family and Society*, Benton Harbor, MI: Whirlpool Foundation.

Mósesdóttir, L. (1995) 'The state and the egalitarian, ecclesiastical and liberal regimes of gender relations', *British Journal of Sociology*, 46: 622–42.

Moss, P. (1996) *A Review of Services for Young Children in the EU, 1990–1995*, Brussels: European Commission Equal Opportunities Unit.

Mott, F. L. (ed) (1982) *The Employment Revolution: Young American Women of the 1970s*, Cambridge, MA: MIT Press.

Mouzelis, N. (1989) 'Restructuring structuration theory', *Sociological Review*, 37: 613–36.

—— (1995) *Sociological Theory: What Went Wrong? Diagnosis and Remedies*, London: Routledge.

—— (1999) 'Modernity: a non-European conceptualization', *British Journal of Sociology*, 50: 149–59.

Mullan, B. (1984) *The Mating Trade*, London: Routledge.

Murphy, M. (1993) 'The contraceptive pill and women's employment as factors in fertility change in Britain 1963–1980: A challenge to the conventional view', *Population Studies*, 47: 221–43.

Murphy, M. J. and Sullivan, O. (1985) 'Housing tenure and family formation in contemporary Britain', *European Sociological Review*, 1: 230–43.

Nave-Herz, R. (1989) 'Childless marriages', *Marriage and Family Review*, 14(1/2): 239–50.

Nazroo, J. Y., Edwards, A. C., and Brown, G. W. (1997) 'Gender differences in the onset of depression following a shared life event: a study of couples', *Psychological Medicine*, 27: 9–19.

Newell, S. (1992) 'The myth and destructiveness of equal opportunities: the continuing dominance of the mothering role', *Personnel Review*, 21/4: 37–47.

Ng, Y-K. (1997) 'A case for happiness, cardinalism and interpersonal comparability', *Economic Journal*, 107: 1848–58.

Nuttin, J. (1984) *Motivation, Planning and Action: A Relational Theory of Behaviour Dynamics*, translated from French by R. P. Lorion and J. E. Dumas, Leuven: Leuven University Press/Hillsdale, NJ: Lawrence Erlbaum Associates.

O'Brien, M. and Jones, D. (1999) 'Children, parental employment and educational attainment: an English case-study', *Cambridge Journal of Economics*, 23: 599–621.

O'Donnell, L. N. (1985) *The Unheralded Majority: Contemporary Women as Mothers*, Lexington, MA: Lexington Books.

O'Donoghue, C. and Sutherland, H. (1999) 'Accounting for the family in European income tax systems', *Cambridge Journal of Economics*, 23: 565–98.

OECD (Organization for Economic Co-operation and Development) (1995) *The Tax/Benefit Position of Production Workers 1991–1994*, Paris : OECD.

—— (1998) *Employment Outlook*, Paris: OECD.

—— (1999) *Employment Outlook*, Paris: OECD.

Oertzen, C. von and Rietzschel, A. (1998) 'Comparing the post-war Germanies: breadwinner ideology and women's employment in the divided nation, 1948–1970', pp 175–96 in A. Janssens (ed) *The Rise and Decline of the Male Breadwinner Family?*, Cambridge: Cambridge University Press. (Supplement to *International Review of Social History* vol 42, 1997)

O'Muircheartaigh, C. and Lynn, P. (1997) 'Editorial: the 1997 UK pre-election polls', *Journal of the Royal Statistical Society*, Series A, 160: 381–8.

ONS (1997) *Living in Britain: Results of the 1995 General Household Survey*, London: Stationery Office.

—— (1998a) *Social Trends*, No. 28, London: Stationery Office.

—— (1998b) *Living in Britain—Results of the 1996 General Household Survey*, London: Stationery Office.

—— (1999) *Social Focus on Older People*, London: Stationery Office.

Oppenheim, A. N. (1966, 1992) *Questionnaire Design, Interviewing and Attitude Measurement*, London and New York, NY: Pinter.

Oppenheimer, V. K. (1970) *The Female Labor Force in the United States*, Westport, CT: Greenwood Press.

O'Reilly, J. and Fagan, C. (eds) (1998) *Part-Time Prospects: An International Comparison of Part-Time Work in Europe, North America and the Pacific Rim*, London: Routledge.

Orloff, A. S. (1993) 'Gender and the social rights of citizenship: the comparative analysis of gender relations and welfare states', *American Sociological Review*, 58: 303–28.

Ormerod, P. (1998) *Butterfly Economics: A New General Theory of Social and Economic Behaviour*, London: Faber and Faber.

Oswald, A. J. (1997) 'Happiness and economic performance', *Economic Journal*, 107: 1815–31.

Paci, P. and Joshi, H. (1996) *Wage Differentials Between Men and Women: Evidence from Cohort Studies*, Research Series No. 71, London: Department for Education and Employment.

—— —— and Makepeace, G. (1996) 'Pay gaps facing men and women born in 1958: differences within the labour market', pp 87–111 in J. Humphries and J. Rubery (eds) *The Economics of Equal Opportunities*, Manchester: Equal Opportunities Commission.

Pahl, J. M. and Pahl, R. E. (1971) *Managers and their Wives: A study of career and family relationships in the middle class*, London: Allen Lane.

Papanek, H. (1973) 'Men, women and work: reflections on the two-person career', *American Journal of Sociology*, 78: 852–72. Reprinted in J. Huber (ed) *Changing Women in a Changing Society*, Chicago, IL and London: University of Chicago Press, pp 90–110.

—— (1979) 'Family status production: the work and non-work of women', *Signs*, 775–81.

Parasuraman, S. and Greenhaus, J. H. (eds) (1997) *Integrating Work and Family: Challenges and Choices for a Changing World*, Westport, CT: Quorum Books.

Parker, H. (1995) *Taxes, Benefits and Family Life*, Research Monograph No. 50, London: Institute of Economic Affairs.

Parsons, T. and Bales, R. F. (1955) *Family Socialization and Interaction Process*, Glencoe, IL: Free Press.

Pearlin, L. (1975) 'Status inequality and stress in marriage', *American Sociological Review*, 40: 344–57.

Pedersen, S. (1993) *Family, Dependence, and the Origins of the Welfare State: Britain and France, 1914–1945*, Cambridge: Cambridge University Press.

Peil, M. (1982) *Social Science Research Methods: An African Handbook*, London: Hodder and Stoughton.

Pencavel, J. (1998) 'The market work behaviour and wages of women 1975–94', *Journal of Human Resources*, 33: 771–804.

Petersen, T., Snartland, V., Becken, L-E., and Olsen, K. M. (1997) 'Within-job wage discrimination and the gender wage gap: the case of Norway', *European Sociological Review*, 13: 199–213.

Pfau-Effinger, B. (1993) 'Modernisation, culture and part-time employment: the example of Finland and West Germany', *Work, Employment and Society*, 7: 383–410.

—— (1998) 'Culture or structure as explanations for differences in part-time work in Germany, Finland and the Netherlands?', pp 177–98 in J. O'Reilly and C. Fagan (eds) *Part-Time Prospects: An International Comparison of Part-Time Work in Europe, North America and the Pacific Rim*, London: Routledge.

Phelps, E. S. (1972) 'The statistical theory of racism and sexism', *American Economic Review*, 62: 659–61.

Philliber, W. W. and Vannoy-Hiller, D. (1990) 'The effect of husband's occupational attainment on wife's achievement', *Journal of Marriage and the Family*, 52: 323–29.

Piliavin, J. A. and Charng, H-W. (1990) 'Altruism', *Annual Review of Sociology*, 16: 27–65.

Pilling, D. (1990) *Escape from Disadvantage*, London: Falmer.

Piper, N. (1997) 'Globalisation, gender and migration: the case of international marriage in Japan', paper presented to the 'Towards a Gendered Political Economy' Workshop, University of Sheffield, 17–18 September 1997.

Plaisance, E. (1986) *L'Enfant, la Maternelle, la Societé*, Paris: Presses Universitaires de France.

Plantenga, J. (1995) 'Part-time work and equal opportunities: the case of the Netherlands', pp 277–90 in J. Humphries and J. Rubery (eds) *The Economics of Equal Opportunities*, Manchester: Equal Opportunities Commission.

Pleck, J. H. (1985) *Working Wives/Working Husbands*, Beverly Hills, CA: Sage.

Polachek, S. W. (1975) 'Differences in expected post-school investment as a determinant of market wage differentials', *International Economic Review*, 16: 451–70.

—— (1979) 'Occupational segregation among women: theory, evidence and a prognosis', pp 137–70 in C. B. Lloyd, E. S. Andrews, and C. L. Gilroy (eds) *Women in the Labor Market*, New York, NY: Columbia University Press.

—— (1981) 'Occupational self-selection: A human capital approach to sex differences in occupational structure', *Review of Economics and Statistics*, 63: 60–9.

—— (1995) 'Human capital and the gender earnings gap: a response to feminist critiques', pp 61–79 in E. Kuiper and J. Sap (eds) *Out of the Margin*, London and New York, NY: Routledge.

Pollert, A. (1981) *Girls, Wives, Factory Lives*, London: Macmillan.

—— (1991) *Farewell to Flexibility?*, Oxford: Basil Blackwell.

Portocarero, L. (1985) 'Social mobility in France and Sweden: women, marriage and work', *Acta Sociologica*, 28: 151–70.

—— (1987) *Social Mobility in Industrial Societies: Women in France and Sweden*, Stockholm: University of Stockholm Swedish Institute for Social Research.

Pott-Buter, H. A. (1993) *Facts and Fairy Tales about Female Labor, Family and Fertility: A Seven-Country Comparison, 1850–1990*, Amsterdam: Amsterdam University Press.

Power, M. (1988) 'Women, the state and the family in the US: Reaganomics and the experience of women', pp 140–62 in J. Rubery (ed) *Women and Recession*, London: Routledge.

Procter, I. and Padfield, M. (1998) *Young Adult Women, Work and Family*, London: Mansell.

Procter, I. and Padfield, M (1999) 'Work orientations and women's work: a critique of Hakim's theory of the heterogeneity of women', *Gender, Work and Organisations*, 6: 152–62.

Pyke, K. D. (1996) 'Class-based masculinities: the interdependence of gender, class and interpersonal power', *Gender and Society*, 10: 527–49.

Quest, C. (ed) (1992) *Equal Opportunities: A Feminist Fallacy*, London: Institute for Economic Affairs.

Ragin, C. C. (1987) *The Comparative Method: Moving Beyond Qualitative and Quantitative Strategies*, Berkeley, CA: University of California Press.

Rainwater, L., Rein, M., and Schwartz, J. (1986) *Income Packaging in the Welfare State: A Comparative Study of Family Income*, Oxford: Clarendon Press.

Reskin, B. and Padavic, I. (1994) *Women and Men at Work*, Thousand Oaks, CA: Pine Forge Press.

—— and Roos, P. A. (1990) *Job Queues, Gender Queues: Explaining Women's Inroads into Male Occupations*, Philadelphia, PA: Temple University Press.

Rexroat, C. and Shehan, C. (1984) 'Expected versus actual work roles of women', *American Sociological Review*, 49: 349–58.

Riboud, M. (1985) 'An analysis of women's labour force participation in France: cross-section estimates and time series evidence', *Journal of Labor Economics*, supplement on *Trends in Women's Work, Education and Family Building*, 3: S177–S200.

Richards, J. R. (1994) *The Sceptical Feminist: A Philosophical Enquiry*, London: Penguin.

Richardson, J. G. (1979) 'Wife occupational superiority and marital troubles: an examination of the hypothesis', *Journal of Marriage and the Family*, 41: 63–72.

Robert, P. (1991) 'Educational transitions in Hungary from the post-war period to the end of the 1980s', *European Sociological Review*, 7: 213–36.

—— and Bukodi, E. (1998) 'Coupled careers: climbing up and falling down on the class ladder', paper presented to the European Science Foundation conference 'European Societies or European Society? Inequality and Social Exclusion in Europe', held in Castelvecchio Pascoli, April 1998.

Roberts, E. (1984) *A Woman's Place: An Oral History of Working Class Women 1890–1940*, Oxford: Blackwell.

Robinson, W. S. (1950) 'Ecological correlations and the behaviour of individuals', *American Sociological Review*, 15: 351–7.

Rockwell, R. C. (1976) 'Historical trends and variations in educational homogamy', *Journal of Marriage and the Family*, 38: 83–95.

Rodgers, G. and Rodgers, J. (eds) (1989) *Precarious Jobs in Labour Market Regulation*, International Institute for Labour Studies, Geneva: International Labour Office.

Rogers, B. (1981) *The Domestication of Women: Discrimination in Developing Societies*, London: Tavistock.

Rogler, L. H. and Procidano, M. E. (1989) 'Marital heterogamy and marital quality in Puerto Rican families', *Journal of Marriage and the Family*, 51: 363–72.

Rollins, B. C. and Feldman, H. (1970) 'Marital satisfaction over the family cycle', *Journal of Marriage and the Family*, 32: 20–8.

Rosen, B. C. and Aneshensel, C. S. (1976) 'The Chameleon Syndrome: a social psychological dimension of the female sex-role', *Journal of Marriage and the Family*, 38: 605–17.

Roseneil, S. (1995) 'The coming of age of feminist sociology: some issues of practice and theory for the next twenty years', *British Journal of Sociology*, 46: 191–205.

Rosenfeld, R. A. and Birkelund, G. E. (1995) 'Women's part-time employment: a cross-national comparison', *European Sociological Review*, 11: 111–34.

—— and Kalleberg, A. L. (1990) 'A cross-national comparison of the gender gap in income', *American Journal of Sociology*, 96: 69–106.

Ross, K. E. (1999) 'Labor pains: the effect of the Family and Medical Leave Act on the return to paid work after childbirth', *Focus*, 20: 34–6.

Routh, G. (1965, 1980) *Occupation and Pay in Great Britain 1906–79*, London: Macmillan.

—— (1987) *Occupations of the People of Great Britain, 1801–1981*, London: Macmillan.

Rovi, S. (1994) 'Taking No for an answer: using negative reproduction intentions to study the childless/childfree', *Population Research and Policy Review*, 13: 343–65.

Rowland, D. T. (1999) 'Cross-national trends in childlessness', in P. Dykstra and V. R. A. Call (eds) *A Cross-National Handbook on Parental Status in Late Life*, Westport, CT: Greenwood.

Rowland, R. (1982) 'An exploratory study of the childfree lifestyle', *Australian and New Zealand Journal of Sociology*, 18: 17–30.

Rubery, J. and Fagan, C. (1993) *Occupational Segregation of Women and Men in the European Community*, *Social Europe* Supplement 3/93, Luxembourg: OOPEC.

—— Horrell, S. and Burchell, B. (1994) 'Part-time work and gender inequality in the labour market', pp 205–34 in A. M. Scott (ed) *Gender Segregation and Social Change*, Oxford: Oxford University Press.

—— Smith, M., and Fagan, C. (1996) *Trends and Prospects for Women's Employment in the 1990s*, report to the European Commission.

—— —— —— and Grimshaw, D. (1998) *Women and European Employment*, London and New York, NY: Routledge.

Ruddick, S. (1989) *Maternal Thinking: Towards a Politics of Peace*, Boston, MA: Beacon Press.

Ruhm, C. (1998) 'The economic consequences of parental leave mandates: lessons from Europe', *Quarterly Journal of Economics*, 113: 285–318.

Russell, H. (1998) 'The rewards of work', pp 77–100 in R. Jowell *et al.* (ed) *British Social Attitudes—the 15th Report*, Aldershot: Ashgate.

—— and Barbieri, P. (1998) 'Gender and the experience of unemployment: a comparative analysis', paper presented to the 'Work, Employment and Society' Conference, Cambridge.

Rutter, M. (1979) *Fifteen Thousand Hours: Secondary Schools and Their Effects on Children*, London: Open Books.

Sainsbury, D. (1996) *Gender Equality and Welfare States*, Cambridge: Cambridge University Press.

Saunders, P. (1990) *A Nation of Homeowners*, London: Routledge.

—— (1997) 'Social mobility in Britain: an empirical evaluation of two competing explanations', *Sociology*, 31: 261–88.

Scanzoni, J. (1976) 'Gender roles and the process of fertility control', *Journal of Marriage and the Family*, 38: 677–91.

Sciama, L. (1984) 'Ambivalence and dedication: academic wives in Cambridge University, 1870–1970', pp 50–66 in H. Callan and S. Ardener (eds) *The Incorporated Wife*, London: Croom Helm.

Scott, J. (1990) 'Women and the family', pp 51–76 in R. Jowell *et al.* (eds) *British Social Attitudes: the 7th Report*, Aldershot: Gower.

Scott, J., Alwin, D. F., and Braun, M. (1996) 'Generational changes in gender-role attitudes: Britain in a cross-national perspective', *Sociology*, 30: 471–92.

—— Braun, M., and Alwin, D. (1993) 'The family way', pp 23–47 in R. Jowell *et al.* (eds) *International Social Attitudes: The 10th BSA Report*, Aldershot: Dartmouth.

—— —— —— (1998) 'Partner, parent, worker: family and gender roles', pp 19–37 in R. Jowell *et al.* (eds) *British and European Social Attitudes—the 15th Report: How Britain Differs*, Aldershot: Ashgate.

Scott, R. A. and Shore, A. R. (1979) *Why Sociology Does Not Apply: A Study of the Use of Sociology in Public Policy*, New York, NY: Elsevier.

Seccombe, W. (1993) *Weathering the Storm: Working Class Families from the Industrial Revolution to the Fertility Decline*, London: Verso.

Semin, G. R. and Manstead, A. S. R. (1983) *The Accountability of Conduct: A Social Psychological Analysis*, New York, NY: Academic Press.

Sexton, C. S. and Perlman, D. S. (1989) 'Couples' career orientation, gender role orientation, and perceived equity as determinants of marital power', *Journal of Marriage and the Family*, 51: 933–41.

Sexton, L. G. (1979) *Between Two Worlds*, New York: William Morrow.

Shavit, Y. and Blossfeld, H-P. (1993) *Persistent Inequality: Changing Educational Attainment in Thirteen Countries*, Boulder, CO: Westview Press.

Shaw, L. B. (ed) (1983) *Unplanned Careers: The Working Lives of Middle-Aged Women*, Lexington, MA: D C Heath.

—— and Shapiro, D. (1987) 'Women's work plans: contrasting expectations and actual work experience', *Monthly Labor Review*, 110/11: 7–13.

Shelton, B. A. and Firestone, J. (1989) 'Household labor time and the gender gap in earnings', *Gender and Society*, 3: 105–12.

Shepherd, G. (1987) 'Rank, gender, and homosexuality: Mombasa as a key to understanding sexual options', pp 240–70 in P. Caplan (ed) *The Cultural Construction of Sexuality*, London: Tavistock.

Shibata, A. (1992) 'The effects of Japanese income tax provisions on women's labour force participation', pp 169–79 in N. Folbre *et al.* (eds) *Women's Work in the World Economy*, London: Macmillan.

Shoen, R. and Weinick, R. M. (1993) 'Partner choice in marriages and cohabitations', *Journal of Marriage and the Family*, 55: 408–14.

—— and Wooldredge, J. (1989) 'Marriage choices in North Carolina and Virginia, 1969–71 and 1979–81', *Journal of Marriage and the Family*, 51: 465–81.

Siegers, J. J., de Jong-Gierveld, J., and van Imhoff, E. (eds) (1991) *Female Labour Market Behaviour and Fertility: A Rational Choice Approach*, Berlin: Springer-Verlag.

Siltanen, J. (1994) *Locating Gender: Occupational Segregation, Wages and Domestic Responsibilities*, London: UCL.

Simon, B. L. (1987) *Never Married Women*, Philadelphia, PA: Temple University Press.

Singly, F. de (1996) *Modern Marriage and Its Cost to Women: A Sociological Look at Marriage in France*, Newark, DE: University of Delaware Press and London: Associated University Presses.

Sixma, H. and Ultee, W. C. (1984) 'Marriage patterns and the openness of society: educational heterogamy in the Netherlands in 1959, 1971 and 1977' in B. Bakker, J. Dronkers, and H. B. G. Ganzeboom (eds) *Social Stratification and Mobility in the Netherlands*, Amsterdam: SISWO.

Skocpol, T. (1987) 'A social issue in American politics: reflections on Kristin Luker's *Abortion and the Politics of Motherhood*: Introduction', *Politics and Society*, 15: 189–96.

—— (1992) *Protecting Soldiers and Mothers: The Political Origins of Social Policy in the United States*, Cambridge, MA: Harvard University Press.

—— (1995) *Social Policy in the United States: Future Possibilities in Historical Perspective*, Princeton, NJ: Princeton University Press.

Smith, M. R. (1990) 'What is new in New-Structuralist analyses of earnings?', *American Sociological Review*, 55: 827–41.

Smits, J., Ultee, W., and Lammers, J. (1998) 'Educational homogamy in 65 countries: an explanation of differences in openness using country-level explanatory variables', *American Sociological Review*, 63: 264–85.

Social and Community Planning Research (1992) *British Social Attitudes: Cumulative Sourcebook for the First Six Surveys*, Aldershot: Gower.

Sokoloff, N. J. (1992) *Black Women and White Women in the Professions*, New York, NY and London: Routledge.

Somers, M. (1993) 'A comparison of voluntarily childfree adults and parents', *Journal of Marriage and the Family*, 55: 643–50.

Sorensen, A. (1994) 'Women's economic risk and the economic position of single mothers', *European Sociological Review*, 10: 173–88.

—— and McLanahan, S. (1987) 'Married women's economic dependency, 1940–1980', *American Journal of Sociology*, 93: 659–87.

—— and Trappe, H. (1995) 'The persistence of gender inequality in earnings in the German Democratic Republic', *American Sociological Review*, 60: 398–406.

Sorensen, A. B. (1990) 'Throwing the sociologists out? A reply to Smith', *American Sociological Review*, 55: 842–45.

Sorensen, J. B. (1990) 'Perceptions of women's opportunity in five industrialised nations', *European Sociological Review*, 6: 151–64.

Spain, D. and Bianchi, S. M. (1996) *Balancing Act: Motherhood, Marriage and Employment Among American Women*, New York, NY: Russell Sage Foundation.

Standing, G. (1997) 'Globalisation, labour flexibility and insecurity: the era of market regulation', *European Journal of Industrial Relations*, 3: 5–37.

Stephan, P. E. and Schroeder, L. D. (1979) 'Career decisions and labour force participation of married women' pp 119–35 in C. B. Lloyd *et al.* (eds) *Women in the Labor Market*, New York, NY: Columbia University Press.

Stevens, G., Owens, D., and Schaefer, E. C. (1990) 'Education and attractiveness in marriage choices', *Social Psychology Quarterly*, 53: 6–70.

Stockman, N., Bonney, N., and Sheng, X. (1995) *Women's Work in East and West: The Dual Burden of Employment and Family Life*, London: UCL.

Stolzenberg, R. M. and Relles, D. A. (1997) 'Tools for intuition about sample selection bias and its correction', *American Sociological Review*, 62: 494–507.

Storkey, M., Maguire, J., and Lewis, R. (1997) *Cosmopolitan London: Past, Present and Future*, London: London Research Centre.

Sunder Rajan, R. (1994) *Real and Imagined Women: Gender, Culture and Postcolonialism*, London: Routledge.

Szekelyi, M. and Tardos, R. (1993) 'Attitudes that make a difference: expectancies and economic progress', Discussion Papers of the Institute for Research on Poverty, University of Wisconsin, No. 1003–93.

Szreter, S. (1996) *Fertility, Class and Gender in Britain, 1860–1940*, Cambridge: Cambridge University Press.

Taeuber, C. M. (ed) (1996) *Statistical Handbook on Women in America*, Phoenix, AZ: Oryx Press.

Tam, M. (1997) *Part-Time Employment: A Bridge or a Trap?*, Aldershot: Avebury.

Tam, T. (1997) 'Sex segregation and occupational gender inequality in the United States: devaluation or specialised training?', *American Journal of Sociology*, 102: 1652–92.

Tanaka, S. (1998) 'Dynamics of occupational segregation and the sexual division of labor: a consequence of feminization of white-collar work', pp 85–122 in Y. Sato (ed) *1995 Social Stratification and Social Mobility (SSM) Research Series 3: Social Mobility and Career Analysis*, research report to the Ministry of Education, Science, Sports and Culture, Tokyo: University of Tokyo, Seiyama's Office.

Tanner, J., Cockerill, R., Barnsley, J., and Williams, A. P. (1999a) 'Gender and income in pharmacy: human capital and gender stratification theories revisited', *British Journal of Sociology*, 50: 97–117.

—— —— —— —— (1999b) 'Flight paths and revolving doors: a case-study of gender desegregation in pharmacy', *Work, Employment and Society*, 13: 275–93.

Taylor, B. and Thomson, K. (1996) (eds) *Understanding Change in Social Attitudes*, Aldershot: Dartmouth.

Taylor, M. G. and Hartley, S. F. (1975) 'The two-person career: a classic example', *Sociology of Work and Occupations*, 2: 354–72.

Taylor, P. A. and Glenn, N. D. (1976) 'The utility of education and attractiveness for females' status attainment through marriage', *American Sociological Review*, 41: 484–97.

Thair, T. and Risdon, A. (1999) 'Women in the labour market: results from the spring 1998 LFS', *Labour Market Trends*, 107: 103–29.

Thelot, C. (1982) *Tel Père, Tel Fils? Position Sociale et Origine Familiale*, Paris: Dunot.

Thompson, S. (1989) 'Search for tomorrow: or feminism and the reconstruction of teen romance', in C. S. Vance (ed) *Pleasure and Danger: Exploring Female Sexuality*, London: Pandora.

Thomson, K. (1995) 'Working mothers: choice or circumstance?', pp 61–91 in R. Jowell *et al.* (eds) *British Social Attitudes—the 12th Report*, Aldershot: Gower.

Tijdens, K. (1993) 'Women in business and management—the Netherlands', pp 79–92 in M. J. Davidson and C. L. Cooper (eds) *European Women in Business and Management*, London: Paul Chapman.

Tilly, L. A. and Scott, J. W. (1978, 1990) *Women, Work and Family*, London: Routledge.

Tokyo Metropolitan Government (1994) *International Comparative Survey of Issues Confronting Women*, Tokyo: Tokyo Metropolitan Government.

Townsend, J. M. (1987) 'Mate selection criteria: a pilot study', *Ethology and Sociobiology*, 10: 241–53.

Treadwell, P. (1987) 'Biologic influences on masculinity', pp 259–285 in Harry Brod (ed) *The Making of Masculinities*, Boston, MA and London: Allen & Unwin.

Treiman, D. J. (1985) 'The work histories of women and men: what we know and what we need to find out', pp 213–31 in A. S. Rossi (ed) *Gender and the Life Course*, New York, NY: Aldine.

Tsuya, N. O. and Mason, K. O. (1995) 'Changing gender roles and below-replacement fertility in Japan', pp 139–67 in K. O. Mason and A-M. Jensen (eds) *Gender and Family Change in Industrialised Countries*, Oxford: Clarendon.

Tyree, A. and Treas, J. (1974) 'The occupational and marital mobility of women', *American Sociological Review*, 39: 293–302.

Udry, J. R. (1977) The importance of being beautiful: a re-examination and racial comparison', *American Journal of Sociology*, 83: 154–60.

—— (1984) 'Benefits of being attractive: differential payoffs for men and women', *Psychological Reports*, 54: 47–56.

Ultee, W. C. and Luijkx, R. (1990) 'Educational heterogamy and father-to-son occupational mobility in 23 industrial nations—general societal openness or compensatory strategies of reproduction?', *European Sociological Review*, 6: 125–49.

Umansky, L. (1996) *Motherhood Reconceived: Feminism and the Legacies of the Sixties*, New York, NY: New York University Press.

Uunk, W. J. G. (1996) *Who Marries Whom? The Role of Social Origin, Education and High Culture in Mate Selection of Industrial Societies During the Twentieth Century*, PhD dissertation, Nijmegen: University of Nijmegen.

Vaessen, M. (1984) *Childlessness and Infecundity*, World Fertility Survey Comparative Studies No. 31, Voorburg: International Statistical Institute.

Van Berkel. M. and De Graaf, N. D. (1998) 'Married women's economic dependency in the Netherlands, 1979–1991', *British Journal of Sociology*, 49: 97–117.

Van de Kaa, D. J. (1987) 'Europe's second demographic transition', *Population Bulletin*, 42: 1, Washington, DC: Population Reference Bureau.

Van Deth, J. W. and Scarbrough, E. (eds) (1995) *The Impact of Values*, Oxford: Oxford University Press.

Van Doorne-Huiskes, A., van Hoof, J., and Roelofs, E. (1995) *Women and the European Labour Markets*, London: Paul Chapman.

Veblen, T. (1899/1953) *The Theory of the Leisure Class*, New York, NY: Mentor.

Veevers, J. E. (1972) 'Factors in the incidence of childlessness in Canada: an analysis of census data', *Social Biology*, 19: 266–74.

—— (1973) 'Voluntarily childless wives: an exploratory study', *Sociology and Social Research*, 57: 356–66.

—— (1974) 'Voluntary childlessness and social policy: an alternative view', *The Family Coordinator*, 23: 397–406.

—— (1979) 'Voluntary childlessness: a review of issues and evidence', *Marriage and Family Review*, 1–70.

—— (1980) *Childless by Choice*, Toronto: Butterworths.

Vogler, C. (1994) 'Money in the household', pp 225–66 in M. Anderson, F. Bechhofer, and J. Gershuny (eds) *The Social and Political Economy of the Household*, Oxford: Oxford University Press.

Walby, S. (1986) *Patriarchy at Work: Patriarchal and Capitalist Relations in Employment*, Cambridge: Polity Press.

—— (1990) *Theorising Patriarchy*, Oxford: Blackwell.

Waldfogel, J. (1993) *Women Working for Less: A Longitudinal Analysis of the Family Gap*, STICERD Working Paper No. WSP/93, London: London School of Economics.

—— (1997) 'Working mothers then and now: a cross-cohort analysis of the effects of maternity leave on women's pay', with discussion, pp 92–132 in F. D. Blau and

R. G Ehrenberg (eds) *Gender and Family Issues in the Workplace*, New York, NY: Russell Sage Foundation.

—— (1998) 'The family gap for young women in the United States and Britain: Can maternity leave make a difference?', *Journal of Labor Economics*, 16: 505–45.

—— (1999) 'The impact of the Family and Medical Leave Act', *Journal of Policy Analysis and Management*, 18: 281–302.

Walsh, J. (1999) 'Myths and counter-myths: an analysis of part-time female employees and their orientations to work and working hours', *Work, Employment and Society*, 13: 179–203.

Ward, C. and Dale, A. (1992) 'The impact of early life-course transitions on equality at work and home', *Sociological Review*, 8: 509–532.

—— —— and Joshi, H. (1996a) 'Income dependency within couples', pp 95–120 in L. Morris and E. S. Lyon (eds) *Gender Relations in Public and Private Lives*, London: Macmillan.

—— —— —— (1996b) 'Combining employment with childcare: an escape from dependence?', *Journal of Social Policy*, 25: 223–47.

Warr, P. (1982) 'A national study of non-financial employment commitment', *Journal of Occupational Psychology*, 55: 297–312.

—— and Yearta, S. (1995) 'Health and motivational factors in sickness absence', *Human Resource Management Journal*, 5/5: 33–48.

Webb, S. (1993) 'Women's incomes: past, present and prospects', *Fiscal Studies*, 14: 14–36.

Webster, M. and Driskell, J. E. (1983) 'Beauty as status', *American Journal of Sociology*, 89: 140–65.

Wellings, K., Wadsworth, J., Johnson, A., and Field, J. (1996) *Teenage Sexuality, Fertility and Life Chances: A Report Prepared for the Department of Health Using Data from The National Survey of Sexual Attitudes and Lifestyles*, London: London School of Hygiene and Tropical Medicine.

West, C. and Fenstermaker, S. (1995) 'Doing difference', *Gender and Society*, 9: 8–37.

Westoff, C. F. and Ryder, N. B. (1977) *The Contraceptive Revolution*, Princeton, NJ: Princeton University Press.

Wetzels, C. (1999) *Squeezing Birth into Working Life: Household Panel Data Analyses Comparing Germany, Great Britain, the Netherlands and Sweden*, Tinbergen Institute Research Series, Amsterdam: University of Amsterdam.

Whyte, M. K. (1978) *The Status of Women in Pre-industrial Societies*, Princeton, NJ: Princeton University Press.

—— (1990) *Dating, Mating and Marriage*, New York, NY: Aldine de Gruyter.

Wicker, A. (1969) 'Attitudes versus actions: the relationship of verbal and overt behavioral responses to attitude objects', *Journal of Social Issues*, 25: 41–78.

Wiggins, R. and Bynner, J. (1993) 'Social attitudes', pp 162–83 in E. Ferri (ed) *Life at 33*, London: National Children's Bureau.

Wilkinson, H. and Briscoe, I. (1996) *Parental Leave: The Price of Family Values?*, London: DEMOS.

Williams, S. and Calnan, M. (1997) *Modern Medicine: Lay Perspectives and Experiences*, London: UCL Press.

Willis, P. (1977) *Learning to Labour: How Working Class Kids Get Working Class Jobs*, Farnborough: Saxon House.

Willmott, R. (1996) 'Resisting sex/gender conflation: a rejoinder to John Hood-Williams', *Sociological Review*, 44: 728–45.

Winkler, A. E. (1998) 'Earnings of husbands and wives in dual-earner families', *Monthly Labor Review*, 121/4: 42–8.

Wolcott, I. and Glezer, H. (1995) *Work and Family Life: Achieving Integration*, Melbourne: Australian Institute of Family Studies.

Wright, E. O. (1997) *Class Counts: Comparative Studies in Class Analysis*, Cambridge: Cambridge University Press.

—— Baxter, J., and Birkelund, G. E. (1995) 'The gender gap in workplace authority: a cross-national study', *American Sociological Review*, 60: 407–35.

Wyatt, S. and Langridge, C. (1996) 'Getting to the top in the National Health Service', pp 212–44 in S. Ledwith and F. Colgan (eds) *Women in Organisations: Challenging Gender Politics*, London: Macmillan.

Young, M. and Willmott, P. (1973) *The Symmetrical Family*, London: Routledge.

Zetterberg, H. L. (1966) 'The secret ranking', *Journal of Marriage and the Family*, 28: 134–42. Reprinted in R. Swedberg and E. Uddhammar (eds) *Hans L Zetterberg: Sociological Endeavour—Selected Writings*, Stockholm: City University Press, 1997, pp 258–74.

—— (1997) 'The study of values', paper presented to the 87th Annual Meeting of the American Sociological Association, 1992, and reprinted in R. Swedberg and E. Uddhammar (eds) *Hans L. Zetterberg: Sociological Endeavor—Selected Writings*, Stockholm: City University Press, 1997, pp 191–219.

AUTHOR INDEX

Abramson, P. R. 2, 81
Adler, L. L. 185
Adnett, N. 30
Agassi, J. B. 77–8, 88, 146–7, 241
Airey, C. 76
Ajzen, I. 74
Albrow, M. 286
Allen, I. 98
Almquist, E. M. 96
Alwin, D. F. 23, 32, 53, 73, 77, 89, 91, 94, 125, 173, 176
Ames, R. E. 27
Aneshensel, C. S. 170
Anker, R. 5–6, 10, 31, 38, 65, 135, 138, 172, 237–41, 282
Antonides, G. 26, 37
Anttalainen, M-L. 240
Arber, S. 109, 205
Archer, J. 46, 180
Ashenfelter, O. 30
Atkinson, D. 111
Atkinson, M. 191, 218
Auerbach, J. D. 248
Axelrod, R. 27

Badcock, C. 198
Badinter, E. 55
Bain, J. K. 181
Baker, M. 257
Baker, P. 18
Baker, R. 21
Bakker, J. I. H. 257
Bales, R. F. 193
Barbieri, P. 121
Barnard, C. 61
Bartlett, J. 54
Baum, F. 54
Baxter, J. 118
Beck, U. 2, 12, 178
Becker, G. S. 31, 190–1, 193, 221
Beck-Gernsheim, E. 12
Beckmann, P. 98
Beere, C. A. 187
Benham, L. 205, 220
Benn, M. 235
Berent, J. 204, 207–8
Berger, P. A. 84, 104, 108
Bernard, J. 87, 268, 279
Bernasco, W. 24, 191, 205
Bernhardt, E. M. 51
Betz, N. E. 129, 149, 185–8
Beutel, A. M. 260
Bianchi, S. M. 116
Bielby, D. D. 77
Bielby, W. T. 77
Bifulco, A. 182–3
Birkelund, G. E. 171
Blackburn, M. L. 40, 117–18
Blake, J. 54–5
Blank, R. M. 106, 164
Blankenhorn, D. 236
Blanpain, R. 18, 68, 247
Blau, F. D. 22, 27, 30, 119, 123, 126, 240, 248
Blau, P. M. 204
Blaug, M. 22
Blitz, R. C. 60, 107
Bloom, D. 54
Bloom, D. E. 40, 117–18
Blossfeld, H.-P. 57–8, 68, 78, 99, 105, 120, 125, 171, 202, 204–5, 210–11, 228, 247, 282
Blundell, R. 132, 135, 137
Boh, K. 32
Boles, J. 191, 218
Boling, P. 229
Bonney, N. 84, 111
Borooah, V. 113–14
Bosch, G. 18, 68, 246–7
Boserup, E. 16, 266
Bottero, W. 39
Bouffartigue, P. 84, 101, 104, 108
Boulton, M. G. 53, 55, 181
Bourdieu, P. 13–14, 36, 162, 195–7, 268
Bradley, H. 59
Brass, W. 55
Braun, M. 23, 32, 53, 77, 89, 91, 94, 125, 173, 176

Breakwell, G. M. 170, 192
Breen, R. 132, 142
Brines, J. 119
Briscoe, I. 278
Brocas, A.-M. 125
Brown, G. W. 182–8
Browne, K. R. 198, 258
Bruyn-Hundt, M. 113
Bryson, A. 49, 71, 91
Buckingham, A. 132, 139
Bukodi, E. 191, 205
Bundesministerium für Familie, Senioren, Frauen und Jugend 89–90
Burchell, B. 84, 110, 152
Burke, R. J. 186–7
Burr, W. R. 181
Buss, D. M. 196–8, 201
Bynner, J. 132, 134, 141, 155, 180
Byrne, D. 279

Cain, G. G. 30
Cain, M. T. 196, 204
Caldwell, J. C. 24, 47
Caldwell, P. 47
Call, V. R. A. 55
Callan, V. J. 54, 182
Callender, C. 120–2, 130, 248
Calnan, M. 76
Cameron, J. 54–5
Campbell, E. 54
Cargan, L. 161
Carrier, S. 55
Cassidy, M. L. 102
CELADE 47, 76
CFSC 47, 76
Charles, M. 241
Charng, H.-W. 27
Chase, I. 160
Chesnais, J.-C. 55, 269
Chisolm, L. 91, 129
Clarke, L. 54
Cleland, J. 24, 45, 47, 51, 80
Coatham, V. 244
Cobble, D. S. 247, 249
Cockburn, C. 62, 66–7
Cohen, D. K. 25
Cohn, S. 59–60
Cole, S. 166
Coleman, D. 19, 24, 49–51, 54
Coleman, J. S. 199
Coleman, M. T. 84, 120
Coleman, S. 44–5
Collard, J. 144
Collins, P. H. 32
Connell, R. W. 22
Cook, A. 60
Cope, D. 54
Corcoran, M. 106
Cornwall, A. 45
Corti, L. 77, 101
Cousins, C. 18
Craib, I. 254
Cramer, J. C. 24
Creighton, C. 70, 87
Crispell, D. 54
Crompton, R. 15, 27, 98, 101
Cully, M. 248
Cunnison, S. 249
Curtice, J. 101, 147

Dale, A. 132–3, 135–40, 143–5, 208, 218
Dallos, R. 195
Dallos, S. 195
Dally, A. 55
Daniel, K. 277
Date-Bah, E. 125
Davies, H. 84, 111, 113–14, 132, 143–4, 189
Davis, J. A. 47, 73, 149
Davis, K. 24, 47, 80, 84, 268
Davis, N. J. 177
De Graaf, P. M. 24, 104, 112–13, 119, 218
Delphy, C. 22
Demeny, P. 225
Dench, G. 266, 268–9
de Neubourg, C. 69
Dennis, N. 236
Denzin, N. K. 36
Dex, S. 77, 126, 142–3, 154, 245
DiMaggio, P. 204
Dirven, H. 119
Di Salvo, P. 132
Donovan, P. 225
Drever, F. 21, 266
Driskell, J. E. 198–9
Dronkers, J. 219
DuBois-Raymond, G. 91, 129
Duggan, L. 225
Dugger, K. 77
Duncan, A. 121

Duncan, G. J. 17, 74
Duncan, O. D. 204
Dunifon, R. 17, 74
Dunnell, K. 48, 149
Dunton, N. 160
Dykstra, P. 53, 55

Edgell, S. 204, 217
Egerton, M. 132–3, 135–40, 208, 218
Egidi, V. 266–7
Ehrenberg, R. G. 123, 126, 248
Ehrenreich, B. 176, 266, 268
Einhorn, B. 31, 89, 225, 234–5, 243, 246, 266
Einstein, A. 28
Elder, G. H. 199–200
Elias, P. 111
Engelstad, F. 127, 191
England, P. 27, 38–9, 61, 139
English, J. 54
EOC 260, 271
Erikson, R. 2, 160, 205
Ermisch, J. F. 24, 40, 132
Esping-Andersen, G. 18, 34, 171–2, 237, 286
Esser, H. 34
Etzioni, A. 235–6, 277–8
European Commission 49–50, 54, 62, 64, 83, 86, 90–1, 115, 117, 120, 124–6, 171, 226, 238, 267
Eurostat 129
Evans, G. 172
Evans, J. 32
Eversley, J. 18

Fagan, C. 60, 68, 99, 101–2, 105, 155, 160, 171, 203
Farmer, H. S. 185–6
Faver, C. A. 185
Featherman, D. L. 160
Federici, N. 24, 196, 266
Fee, L. K. 163, 224, 226
Feldman, H. 181
Fenstermaker, S. 32
Ferber, M. A. 22, 27, 30
Fernandez, J. P. 248
Ferri, E. 111, 132, 146, 148, 154–5, 180, 219, 262
Filer, R. A. 80
Finch, J. 161
Fine, B. 282
Fiorentine, R. 166
Firestone, J. 111
Firestone, S. 15
Fishbein, M. 74
Fitzgerald, L. F. 129, 149, 185–8
Fogarty, M. 94, 96–7, 188, 191
Ford, J. 111
Forth, J. 248
Fowlkes, M. R. 161
Frank, O. 52
Frank, R. H. 80
Fredman, S. 56
Fried, M. 123, 242, 246
Fry, V. C. 111, 117
Fujimura-Fanselow, K. 57
Furstenberg, F. F. 220

Galbraith, J. K. 70, 162
Gallie, D. 71
Galtung, J. 20
Garcia-Ramon, D. 32
Gauthier, A. H. 125, 225, 227, 231–2, 234, 246
Geerken, M. 77
Genovese, M. A. 188
Gerson, K. 17, 51, 54, 79, 130, 149–54, 167, 175, 178, 185
Gibson, C. 181
Giddens, A. 2, 12, 80, 170, 261–2, 269
Gilbert, N. 126
Gilligan, C. 63
Ginn, J. 109, 205
Ginzberg, E. 79, 94–6, 164, 191
Girod, R. 160
Glenn, N. D. 160, 200
Glezer, H. 89, 120, 122–4, 248, 254
Godwin, J. 197
Goldberg, S. 2, 28, 141, 153, 185, 201, 221, 261, 282–3
Goldin, C. 8, 39, 59–60, 107
Goldthorpe, J. H. 2, 132, 142, 160, 205
Goodbody, S. T. 53–4, 181
Goodman, N. 192
Gordon, T. 161
Gove, W. R. 77
Greenhalgh, C. 203
Greenhaus, J. H. 248
Gregg, P. 132, 146, 262
Grimshaw, D. 240
Grint, K. 27, 59–60, 282
Guerin, G. 245, 248

Gustafsson, S. 113, 224, 226, 228, 234, 242
Guthrie, D. 248

Haas, L. 224, 238, 242–3, 261
Hakim, C. 2, 5, 8, 18–19, 28, 30–1, 36, 39, 42, 48, 56–7, 60–5, 68–72, 77–8, 84, 87, 93–4, 98–101, 103–5, 108, 110, 120–3, 126, 134–6, 138, 141, 153, 155, 160, 167, 174, 189, 193, 208, 228, 239, 244, 247–8, 256, 262, 270–1, 279, 282, 286
Hale, J. 244
Halford, S. 134
Hall, R. 50
Haller, M. 77, 92, 100, 179
Hanson, S. L. 71
Hantrais, L. 126, 226, 234
Hardill, I. 97
Harkness, S. 101, 113–14, 134–6
Harper, K. 54
Harris, F. 15, 98
Harris, T. 182
Harrop, A. 267
Hartley, S. F. 161
Hartmann, H. 281
Hassell, K. 39, 72
Hayashi, H. 60
Heckman, J. J. 105–6, 285
Hedström, P. 34
Hendrickx, J. 24
Hepple, B. 61, 269
Herring, C. 200–1
Hill, M. 163, 224, 226
Hirdman, Y. 32
Hirsch, B. T. 61
Hoaglin, D. C. 22
Hobcraft, J. 24, 51
Hobson, B. 241, 268, 274
Hock, E. 184
Hodgson, D. 24
Hoem, B. 5, 31, 238, 243, 261
Hofstede, G. 75, 283
Hogarth, T. 111
Holcombe, L. 59
Höllinger, F. 77, 92, 179
Hood-Williams, J. 279–80
Hörning, K. H. 18
Hoskyns, C. 56
Houseknecht, S. 54–5
Hout, M. 205
Humphries, J. 15, 27–8, 84, 102
Hunt, A. 108
Huws, U. 97–8
Hyde, J. S. 60, 260

IER 64
Ilmakunnas, S. 232–3
ILO 59
Inglehart, R. 2, 19, 56, 74–6, 81–2

Jacklin, C. N. 260
Jacobs, J. A. 220
Jacobs, S. 100–1
Jacobs, T. 217
Jacobsen, J. P. 27, 30
James, O. 180, 184, 198, 200–1
Janssens, A. 87
Jensen, A.-M. 24, 80
Jenson, J. 84
Jolivet, M. 44–5, 54, 60, 170, 265
Jones, C. 84
Jones, D. 118, 219–20
Jones, E. L. 16
Jones, G. W. 24, 80
Jonung, C. 5, 8, 31, 104, 120, 174
Joshi, H. 84, 111, 113–14, 130, 132, 135–7, 142–5, 154–5, 189, 267
Jowell, R. 75–6, 85, 224
Julkunen, R. 237

Kahn, A. J. 232
Kahn, L. M. 119, 240
Kalmijn, M. 195, 204–5, 207
Kalleberg, A. L. 5, 61
Kameda, A. 57
Kamerman, S. B. 232
Kane, E. W. 118
Katona, G. 17, 26, 37, 72
Kaufmann, F.-X. 126
Kay, J. A. 57, 70
Keefe, R. C. 197
Keith, V. M. 200–1
Kenrick, D. T. 197, 201
Kessler-Harris, A. 177
Keyfitz, N. 269
Kiernan, K. 54–5, 195
Killingsworth, M. 30
King, M. A. 57, 70
Kohn, M. L. 171
Komarovsky, M. 95
Komter, A. 217

Kraus, S. J. 74
Kreckel, R. 89
Kuhn, T. 13, 25
Kuiper, E. 27, 218
Kurz, K. 173

Lam, D. 194
Lang, S. S. 54
Langridge, C. 134, 164, 188, 244
Lapidus, G. W. 111, 226, 241
Lash, S. 2, 12
Lawrence, E. 250, 268
Lawson, T. 26, 28
Layard, R. 30
Lazear, E. P. 112
Le Feuvre, N. 101
Leonard, D. 22
Lerner, G. 10, 281–2
Lesthaeghe, R. 24, 80, 93
Levinson, D. J. 192, 256
Lewis, A. 26
Lewis, B. 54
Lewis, J. 126, 251
Lieberson, S. 22, 25, 34–5, 40, 107, 285
Lightbourne, R. E. 47, 52
Lindblom, C. E. 25
Lindisfarne, N. 45
Lipman-Blumen, J. 198
Lipset, S. M. 66
Lister, R. 268, 274
Lloyd, B. 46, 180
London Research Centre 18
Lovenduski, J. 32, 45, 175
Lucas, R. E. 26
Luckey, E. B. 181
Luijkx, R. 204, 213–15
Luker, K. 178
Luxton, M. 153–4
Lynn, P. 23

Maccoby, E. E. 260
Machin, S. 113–14, 132, 135, 146, 262
Macpherson, D. A. 61
Macran, S. 155
Maddison, A. 126
Main, B. 108–9
Maital, S. 37
Mansfield, P. 144
Manstead, A. S. R. 152
Mare, R. D. 204–5, 218, 220
Maret, E. 161
Marini, M. M. 260
Markus, H. 192
Marmot, M. G. 35
Marry, C. 164, 202
Marshall, G. 2, 182
Marshall, H. 54
Marshall, S. E. 176, 178
Martin, J. 77, 108
Martin, J. K. 71
Marwell, G. 27
Marx, K. 273
Mason, K. O. 24, 52, 75, 80
Mathews, E. 95
Matthaei, J. A. 103
May, E. T. 53–4
McAllister, F. 54
McBroom, P. A. 53
McCreary, L. 27
McIntosh, C. A. 50, 224, 226
McKay, S. 71, 91
McKee, P. 113–14
McLanahan, S. 112
McLaughlin, S. D. 47, 54, 92, 95–6, 112, 149, 202
McMahon, M. 48, 55, 63, 235
McRae, S. 50, 84, 120, 127, 130, 205, 218
Meadows, P. 240, 242, 246
Meekers, D. 24, 80, 93
Melkas, H. 5–6, 10, 31, 65, 135, 138, 171, 237–40, 282
Melko, M. 161
Menaghan, E. G. 217
Menefee, S. P. 18
Merrick, N. 250
Michael, R. T. 112
Michielutte, R. 204
Middleton, C. 63
Milkman, R. 282
Mills, C. 107
Mincer, J. 69
Mirowsky, J. 180
Mitchell, D. 227
Moen, P. 5, 238, 261
Mohr, J. 204
Monk, J. 32
Moran, P. M. 182
Morell, C. M. 53–4
Morgan, S. P. 54
MORI 92
Mósesdóttir, L. 18, 286

Moss, P. 126
Mott, F. L. 110
Mouzelis, N. 11–15, 170, 256, 287
Mullan, B. 196–7, 263–4
Murphy, M. 25, 44–5, 47, 80

Nave-Herz, R. 54
Nazroo, J. Y. 182–3
Newell, S. 76, 124
Ng, Y.-K. 80
Nurius, P. 192
Nuttin, J. 188–9

O'Brien, M. 118, 219–20
O'Donnell, L. N. 235
O'Donoghue, C. 227–8, 231
OECD 74–5, 117, 123, 125, 228–31, 233, 240, 262
Oertzen, C. von 89, 177
OFSTED 260
O'Muircheartaigh, C. 23
ONS 44, 47, 103, 115, 208–9, 262
Oppenheim, A. N. 74
Oppenheimer, V. K. 59
O'Reilly, J. 68, 99, 105, 171
Orloff, A. S. 274
Ormerod, P. 26, 28, 126, 279
Oswald, A. J. 38, 80

Paci, P. 132, 135–8, 155
Padavic, I. 27
Padfield, M. 2, 129, 155–6
Pahl, J. M. 204, 217
Pahl, R. E. 204, 217
Papanek, H. 161
Parasuraman, S. 248
Parcel, T. L. 217
Parker, H. 57, 227
Parsons, T. 193
Pearlin, L. 197
Pebley, A. R. 54
Pedersen, S. 87
Peil, M. 76
Pencavel, J. 84, 120
Perlman, D. S. 79, 217–18
Persson, I. 5, 8, 31, 104, 120, 174
Petersen, T. 240
Pfau-Effinger, B. 32, 171, 266
Phelps, E. S. 244
Philliber, W. W. 79, 191
Piliavin, J. A. 27
Pilling, D. 132, 138–9
Piper, N. 265
Plaisance, E. 125
Plantenga, J. 101
Pleck, J. H. 193
Polachek, S. W. 27, 31, 38–9
Pollert, A. 5 9, 68
Portocarero, L. 160
Pott-Buter, H. A. 5, 57, 59, 87, 104, 120, 174
Power, M. 84
Procidano, M. E. 217
Procter, I. 2, 129, 155–6
Pyke, K. D. 262, 265

Quest, C. 269

Ragin, C. C. 279
Rainwater, L. 40, 117, 127, 163–4, 185
Randall, V. 32, 45, 175
Rein, M. 40, 117, 127, 163–4, 185
Relles, D. A. 285
Reskin, B. F. 27–8, 39, 66–7
Rexroat, C. 110, 152
Riboud, M. 104
Richards, J. R. 269
Richardson, J. G. 205
Rietzschel, A. 89, 177
Risdon, A. 155
Robert, P. 191, 205, 212
Roberts, C. 77, 108
Roberts, E. 59
Robinson, R. V. 177
Robinson, W. S. 284
Rockwell, R. C. 204, 206–7
Rodgers, G. 68
Rodgers, J. 68
Rogers, B. 279
Rogler, L. H. 217
Rojot, J. 18, 68, 247
Rollins, B. C. 181
Roos, P. A. 28, 39, 66–7
Rosen, B. C. 170
Roseneil, S. 15
Rosenfeld, R. A. 5, 61, 171
Ross, C. 180
Ross, K. E. 120, 123, 130
Roth, L. M. 248
Routh, G. 64
Rovi, S. 55
Rowland, R. 52–4

Rowthorn, R. 126
Rubery, J. 60, 84, 101–2, 110–11, 115, 152, 155, 160, 171, 193, 203, 240
Ruddick, S. 55, 235
Ruhm, C. 120, 123
Russell, H. 91, 121
Rutter, M. 219
Ryder, N. B. 19, 44, 46–7

Sainsbury, D. 18, 33–4, 57, 228, 237, 251, 286
Sap, J. 27, 218
Saunders, P. 132, 141–2
Savage, M. 134
Scanzoni, J. 55, 78
Scarbrough, E. 74, 80
Schenk, S. 89
Schroeder, L. D. 105
Schwartz, J. 40, 117, 127, 163–4, 185
Sciama, L. 59, 177
Scott, C. 24, 51
Scott, J. 23, 32, 53, 77, 89, 91, 94, 125, 173, 176
Scott, J. W. 120
Scott, R. A. 80
Seccombe, W. 87
Semin, G. R. 152
Sewell, R. 245
Sexton, C. S. 79, 217–18
Sexton, L. G. 85
Shapiro, D. 109–10, 152
Shavit, Y. 202
Shaw, L. B. 109–10, 152
Shehan, C. 110, 152
Shelton, B. A. 111
Shepherd, G. 45
Shepherd, P. 132, 180
Shibata, A. 229
Shoen, R. 204
Shore, A. R. 80
Siegers, J. J. 50, 54, 76, 256
Siltanen, J. 266
Simon, B. L. 161
Singly, F. de 84, 141, 196, 200, 203, 217–18
Sixma, H. 204
Skocpol, T. 175, 178
Smith, M. R. 27, 134
Smits, J. 203–5, 215
Social and Community Planning Research 76
Sokoloff, N. J. 60
Somers, M. 54
Sorensen, A. 5, 31, 112, 138, 173
Sorensen, A. B. 27
Sorensen, J. B. 139
Spain, D. 116
Stafford, F. P. 226, 228, 242
Standing, G. 31
Stephan, P. E. 105
Stevens, G. 200
Stockman, N. 57
Stolzenberg, R. M. 285
Storkey, M. 18
Sullivan, O. 80
Sunder Rajan, R. 188
Sutherland, H. 227–8, 231
Swedberg, R. 34
Szekelyi, M. 74
Szreter, S. 45
Szyszczak, E. 269

Taeuber, C. M. 47, 51, 54
Tam, M. 282
Tam, T. 61, 135–7
Tanaka, S. 52, 87, 164
Tanner, J. 39, 72
Tardos, R. 74
Taylor, B. 85
Taylor, M. G. 161
Taylor, P. A. 200
Thair, T. 155
Thelot, C. 160
Thompson, S. 96
Thomson, K. 78, 85, 94, 101, 124
Tiedeman, D. V. 95
Tijdens, K. 59
Tilly, L. A. 120
Trappe, H. 5, 31, 138, 173
Treadwell, P. 185, 259–60
Treas, J. 160
Tokyo Metropolitan Government 139
Townsend, J. M. 200
Treiman, D. J. 106
Tsuya, N. O. 52, 75
Tyree, A. 160

Udry, J. R. 200
Ultee, W. C. 204, 213–15
Umansky, L. 235
Uunk, W. J. G. 195–6, 204, 215

Vaessen, M. 51
Van Berkel. M. 112–13, 119
Van de Kaa, D. J. 24, 50
Van Deth, J. W. 74, 80
Van Doorne-Huiskes, A. 27, 30
Vannoy-Hiller, D. 79, 191
Veblen, T. 162
Veevers, J. E. 54
Verdecchia, A. 266–7
Vermeulen, H. 104
Vogler, C. 195

Wacquant, L. J. D. 13–14, 36
Walby, S. 22, 30, 59–60, 198, 281
Waldfogel, J. 84, 113–14, 120–3, 130, 132, 134, 277
Walsh, J. 159, 167
Ward, C. 132, 143–5
Warr, P. 180, 256
Warren, B. O. 102
Webb, S. 113
Webster, M. 198–9
Weinick, R. M. 204
Weir, T. 186–7
Wellings, K. 48
West, C. 32
Westoff, C. F. 19, 44, 46–7
Wetzels, C. 122, 228
White, P. 50
Whitehead, M. 21, 266
Whyte, M. K. 10, 16, 88, 181, 196, 199–200, 218, 220, 282
Wicker, A. 73
Wiggins, R. 141
Wilkinson, H. 278
Williams, S. 76
Willis, P. 65
Willis, R. J. 105–6
Willmott, P. 191
Willmott, R. 280
Winkler, A. E. 111
Witherspoon, S. 76
Wolcott, I. 89, 248, 254
Wooldredge, J. 204
Wright, E. O. 6, 10, 61, 117, 238
Wright, R. E. 40
Wyatt, S. 134, 164, 188, 244

Yearta, S. 180
Young, M. 191

Zetterberg, H. L. 195, 199, 256

SUBJECT INDEX

abilities 9, 40, 91, 94, 138, 142, 164, 168, 173, 185–7, 200–1, 260, 276–7, 285
abortion 44–5, 48–9, 177–8, 289
absenteeism 180, 246, 248
achievement 4, 9, 16–17, 48, 60, 85, 95, 131, 138–9, 151, 164, 185–6, 199, 218, 255, 261, 275
acquiescence 45, 186
adaptive women/men 4–11, 15, 98, 150, 156–7, 165–8, 175, 191, 194, 226, 236–44, 248–50, 254, 257, 274–7, 280, 285
advocacy 15, 126, 239, 268–9, 288
Africa 1, 45, 52, 82, 224, 239, 266
age 86–8, 194, 197, 204, 258
agency 12, 14, 16, 26, 40, 188–9, 279
aggression 141, 185, 221, 259–60, 282–3
ambitions, *see* aspirations
anthropology 45, 196
Aquino, Corazon 188
Arabia 169
Argentina 47, 82
arts 2, 6, 36, 129, 158, 160, 165, 255–6, 277
Asia 1, 12, 16, 67, 204, 238–9, 266, 283
aspirations 16–17, 33, 40, 54, 60–1, 72, 79, 88, 129, 138–42, 151, 163, 168, 185, 192, 200, 218, 256, 260–1, 275
attitudes 3, 7, 13–17, 23, 37–8, 40, 43, 50–1, 53, 55–6, 60, 63, 72–82, 89–90, 95, 97, 102, 110, 127, 129–30, 141, 149, 172, 179, 188, 227, 257, 260, 265, 268, 275, 286, 288
Australia 1, 51–2, 54, 69, 89, 92, 116–19, 122–4, 167, 172, 181, 213–14, 223–4, 230–1, 240–1
Austria 49–50, 58, 89, 92, 119, 177, 202, 213, 215, 221, 230, 240, 283
authority 6, 10, 56, 187, 240, 282
autonomy 11–12, 44–5, 81, 92, 186
beauty 162, 195, 197–200, 222, 263–4, 267
Belgium 49, 51–2, 54, 58, 82, 86, 90, 104, 115–16, 125, 171, 174, 213–14, 217, 230–1, 241
Bhutto, Benazir 188
bias 1, 29–31, 36, 119, 131, 153, 196, 223, 249, 251, 269, 286
black community 200–1
black women 200
blue-collar occupations 3, 7, 63, 66, 82, 161, 218, 229–31, 240, 256, 276
bosses, *see* managers
Brazil 45, 264
breadwinner, *see* income-earning role
Britain 1, 3, 17–19, 23, 32–4, 39, 43–6, 48–54, 58–61, 67–9, 72, 82, 84, 86–7, 91–4, 102, 104, 108, 111, 113–15, 117–18, 120–1, 124–6, 130–49, 167, 169, 174, 177–8, 180, 184, 189, 202, 207–10, 219, 221, 223–4, 226, 230–1, 237, 240–1, 254, 264, 266, 269, 274–7, 281–3, 285, 287
British Household Panel Study (BHPS) 77–8, 122
British Social Attitudes Survey (BSAS) 75–8
Buddhist values 32
Bulgaria 92, 215
Canada 39, 48, 54, 72, 82, 92, 116–19, 153–4, 172, 186, 213, 223–4, 230–1, 240–1
Cameroon 52
capitalism 11, 168, 286
career 5–6, 28, 35, 38–9, 48, 60, 72–3, 79, 82, 85, 91, 94, 105–7, 109, 134, 139, 152, 160, 164–5, 194, 201, 243–7, 250–1, 256, 274
career planners 79, 97, 99, 105, 109–10, 139, 164–5, 260
Caribbean 224
caring work 57, 63

case studies 15, 17–19, 36, 38–9, 41–2, 50, 66–7, 144, 147, 190, 285
Central African Republic 52
Chamorro, Violetta 188
chaos theory 26, 40–1, 279
childbearing 4–5, 16, 21, 45–6, 48, 52–3, 120–3, 130, 162–3, 225, 228, 267, 274–5
childcare 4, 28, 35, 65, 73, 78, 91, 99, 101, 124–6, 136, 147, 164, 174, 176, 179, 192, 227–8, 232–6, 243–6, 256, 270, 274, 277
childlessness 4, 6, 16, 25, 31, 45, 50–6, 82, 92, 95, 126, 134, 149, 155–6, 164, 167, 175, 178, 181, 191, 231, 244, 256–7, 280
children 53–5, 73, 76, 82, 90, 92, 94, 105, 118, 121–4, 143–4, 148, 164, 167, 175, 180–4, 191, 228, 231–5, 256, 261, 269, 278
China 10, 12, 57, 135, 169, 173–4, 239, 241–2, 264
Christian values 11, 32, 49, 56, 59, 82, 204
cohort 4, 19, 23, 49, 51–5, 91, 95, 128–56, 206–11, 215
collective bargaining 122, 271
Commonwealth 224
companies 59, 69, 223, 229, 237, 242–51
competition 2, 63, 84, 141, 164, 177, 187, 193, 221, 255, 260–1, 271, 277, 282–3
complexity theory, *see* chaos theory
Confucian values 32, 204
Congo 52
consumption 70, 72–3, 117, 160, 162, 278
contraceptive revolution 3, 7, 19, 21, 43–56, 80, 82, 129, 149, 181–2, 256, 273–4, 280, 288–9
convenience factors in jobs 41, 70, 139–40, 260, 274
Costa Rica 283
crime 17, 76, 146, 259, 278
cross-national comparisons 18, 20, 29, 32–4, 49–51, 82, 86–91, 171–4, 177, 198, 204, 227, 237, 245, 273, 282–3, 286–7
cultural capital 36–7, 129, 195, 205, 222
Czechoslovakia 92, 119, 202, 213, 215, 221, 266
death 50, 210
defeminization of work 65
demasculinization of work 65
demographic transitions 24, 50
demography 23–4, 45, 50, 266–7, 269
Denmark 5, 50–1, 58, 82, 86–7, 90, 92, 104, 115, 121, 125, 171–2, 174, 203, 213, 215, 230–1, 238, 242, 266
dependence 110–17, 143–5, 175, 218, 227, 240–1, 268, 274–5, 281, 284
depression 146–9, 179–84
desegregated occupations, *see* integrated occupations
development 16, 241
diplomats 161–2
discontinuous employment, *see* employment breaks and employment continuity
dispositions 13–17, 40, 189
distress 146–9, 180
diversity 6, 32–3, 81, 84, 104, 150, 168–9, 175, 250–1, 256, 273, 276, 283, 286
divorce 18, 37, 50, 159, 166, 181–2, 229
Do-It-Yourself (DIY) 191
domestication of women 279
domestic break, *see* employment break
domestic work 35, 65, 70, 154, 173, 191, 228, 279
dowry 6, 59, 195
drifters 6, 37, 150–2, 165–8

earnings 20, 28–9, 35–9, 41, 59, 63, 70, 72, 74, 102, 105, 110, 114, 117, 119, 133–9, 144, 195, 200, 227–9, 235, 240, 242, 258, 260–1, 276
earnings differentials, *see* pay gap
economic capital 36, 195, 205, 222
economic theory 1, 22–42, 80, 138, 254, 278–9
economists 4, 36, 138, 185, 190, 195, 288
Ecuador 47
education 129, 131–8, 195–222, 279
educational qualifications 6, 16, 28, 36–7, 46, 48–9, 51, 55, 60, 63, 78–9, 84, 94–9, 129–35, 140, 142, 144, 146, 149, 155, 166, 185, 196, 201–17, 237, 255, 277, 279
Edwards case 61, 270
effort 139, 142, 276, 285

egalitarian attitudes 31, 102, 128, 172–3, 190, 200–1, 217, 239, 242, 254, 262
eldercare 246–7, 270
employers 59, 62, 68, 121, 179, 223, 236, 245–51, 270–1, 275–6, 282
employment 1–2, 5, 7–8, 19, 21, 24, 30, 41, 47, 55, 78, 159–60, 222, 273
employment breaks 5, 102–10, 120–3
employment continuity 28, 38–9, 70, 101–2, 104, 105–7, 136, 273
employment policy 36, 163, 176, 179, 223, 270
employment profiles 102–10, 274
endogamy 194, 201
equal opportunities 236, 241
Equal Opportunities Commission (EOC) 271, 278
equal opportunities revolution 3, 7, 19, 36, 43–5, 56–62, 82, 120, 131, 179, 268–9, 271, 273–4, 280, 283, 288–9
equal pay 28, 36, 56, 61, 63
equality 20, 56, 111, 128, 142, 220, 224–6, 238–9, 241–2, 278–9, 284
essentialism 82, 169, 258
ethnic minority groups 18, 32, 39, 72, 129, 131, 175, 177–8, 194, 196, 224, 252, 286
Eurobarometer surveys 53–4, 85–90, 115, 120, 157, 171, 226
Europe 1, 3–5, 11–12, 16, 18–19, 23, 32–3, 43–4, 47, 49, 53, 56–9, 61, 66, 68–9, 72, 80, 82–4, 88, 91, 105–7, 125, 130, 133, 142, 153, 157, 160, 166, 171–2, 177, 181, 190, 196, 200, 202, 214, 220, 223, 227, 230–1, 238, 240–2, 244, 246, 256, 258, 263–4, 269, 279, 286, 288
European Commission 125–6, 226, 237, 267, 274, 286
European Community, *see* European Union
European Court of Justice 269–70
European Union (EU) 49, 56, 62, 64, 86–7, 115, 120, 124, 157, 171, 203, 266, 269
evolutionary theory 189, 198, 222, 258, 287
exchange theory, *see* rational choice theory
exclusion 281
experiments, *see* social experiments

farm 53, 69, 87, 194, 264–5, 274
family 94, 163, 165, 178, 188, 192–3, 217–20, 227, 229, 231, 242, 247, 251, 261, 271, 278, 280
family business 53, 69, 194, 266, 274
family cap 225
family-centred men 254–7
Family Expenditure Survey (FES) 113–14
family-friendly policies 5, 20, 31, 51, 224, 236–7, 241, 245–51, 271, 276
family gap 134, 222, 277
family wage 70, 87
family work 1–2, 7–10, 19, 21, 30, 41, 126, 243, 256, 274
fathers 146–9, 181–4, 236, 242, 256–7, 268, 271–2
female-dominated occupations 39, 61, 239, 241, 245, 266
female organization 283
femininity 16, 65, 164, 283
feminism 12, 14–15, 27, 31–4, 45, 50, 73, 92, 119, 175, 177, 179, 222, 261, 265, 268, 275, 281–2, 287
feminization of work 67
fertility 6–7, 21, 24, 31, 44–56, 76, 80, 82, 95, 110, 126, 130, 149, 167, 198, 204, 225–7, 256, 269, 274, 289
Finland 5, 51–2, 58, 82, 89, 115–16, 129, 171–2, 213–15, 230–3, 238–43, 252
fiscal policy 56–7, 70, 113, 120, 223, 227–35, 238, 277
flexibility in work arrangements 226, 245–8, 260, 271
France 47, 49–52, 58, 69, 82, 86–7, 92, 104, 117, 123, 125, 132, 167, 169, 171, 174, 178, 200, 202–3, 213, 215, 217–18, 224, 226, 230–1, 233–4, 237, 241, 251–2, 266, 269, 277, 286
full-time work 18, 68, 70, 72, 99–101, 104, 106, 112, 124–6, 133, 135–6, 143–4, 195, 229

Gabon 52
Gandhi, Indira 188
gardening 35, 191–2
gender 32–4, 61, 64, 66–7, 82, 119, 129, 141, 164, 239, 243–4, 272, 276, 278–80, 282, 286–8
General Household Survey (GHS) 103, 113–14, 131, 134, 208–9
General Social Survey (GSS) 75–6

generational change 4, 88, 128–56, 201
German Socio-Economic Panel (SOEP) study 210–11
Germany 10, 31, 49–54, 58, 64, 69, 82, 86–7, 89–92, 94, 104, 110, 113, 115–16, 119, 124–6, 138, 171–4, 176–8, 184, 201–2, 210–11, 213–15, 218, 220–1, 224–5, 228, 230–1, 234, 237, 240–1, 246, 264, 266, 269, 283
Greece 49–50, 58, 64, 67, 86–7, 90, 104, 129, 230

half-time jobs 71, 99
harvest work 237
health/ill health 35, 52, 129, 168, 179–84, 244, 247, 266–8
heterogamy 191, 201
heterogeneity 7–11, 14–16, 31, 41, 55, 84, 104, 107, 125, 128, 157–92, 175, 179, 189, 206, 216, 252, 278, 283
heterosexual relationships 45, 129, 175, 222
hierarchy 5
Hinduism 32
history 1–4, 7–8, 18, 21, 25–6, 29, 45, 50, 59, 69–70, 87, 89, 174, 177, 241, 279, 285
Holland, *see* Netherlands
home-centred women 4, 6–11, 15, 21, 150, 156, 159–63, 175, 178, 226–36, 248, 274
homemaker 51, 71, 73, 84–5, 92, 97, 102, 104–6, 109, 124, 144, 147, 150, 159, 167, 188, 217, 223–4, 266–7
homogamy 79, 102–3, 118, 194–6, 201, 203–17, 284
homosexuals 45, 175, 195
Hong Kong 239
hours worked, *see* working hours
housewife 105–7, 159, 179
housework 99, 115, 190
housing 225–6
human capital 26–8, 37, 192
Hungary 52, 58, 82, 92, 119, 173, 202, 212–15, 221, 266

Iceland 5, 115, 230, 238, 242
identity 4, 32, 55, 71, 79–80, 116, 119, 129, 170, 184, 192, 244, 256, 275
ideology 56–7, 67, 70, 79–80, 138–42, 172–3, 178, 186, 279
immigration 82, 131, 168, 217, 223–4, 238, 269
income-earning role 30, 34, 70–1, 87, 99, 110–17, 141, 147, 176, 183–4, 193, 237, 262, 268
income tax 57, 113, 226–32, 252
India 224, 239
indirect discrimination 61
individualism 12, 50, 66, 81, 178, 236, 252, 278
Indonesia 283
industry 138, 173, 276
inequality 117–19, 127, 172
infertility 51–2
information technology 18, 21, 62, 67, 262
institutions 11, 27, 32, 34, 56–7, 129, 168, 172, 281, 286
integrated occupations 28, 67, 98
intention to return to work 120–1, 244
interests 8–10, 32, 71, 157, 175–9, 190, 223, 249–50, 255, 268–9, 282–3
intermittent employment, *see* employment breaks and employment continuity
International Labour Office (ILO) 8, 125, 138, 239–41, 245
International Social Survey Programme (ISSP) 75–7, 85, 92, 94
Iran 11
Ireland 49–51, 53, 58, 82, 86–7, 92, 94, 213, 230
Israel 57, 69, 202, 241–2
Italy 50–1, 58, 69, 82, 86–7, 92, 104, 115, 125, 129, 184, 202, 213, 215, 230, 240–1, 283

Japan 12, 44–5, 52, 54, 57, 60, 64, 69, 75, 82, 87, 170, 184, 202, 213–16, 219, 229–30, 234–6, 264–6, 283, 286–8
job satisfaction 37, 71, 101, 146–7
job segregation, *see* occupational segregation
job tenure 136
Judaism 32

kibbutz 241–2

Labour Force Survey (LFS) 40, 123, 180
labour law 61, 192, 233, 269

labour market segmentation 30
labour turnover 39, 59, 71, 101
language 4, 18, 263, 265
law 56, 60, 76, 233, 244, 269
legislation, *see* law
leisure 159, 162–3, 197, 264
lifecycle 88, 128, 156, 185, 227
life expectancy 21, 258, 265–8
lifestyle 72–82, 85–99, 127, 141, 168, 183, 222, 253, 256, 264, 266, 273, 280, 287
lone parents 49, 52, 163, 183
longitudinal studies 4, 8, 19, 38, 49, 105–7, 122, 128, 130–56, 184, 261, 275
lottery win questions 76
Luxembourg 58, 86–7, 115, 227, 230–1, 241

machismo 65
Malaysia 215, 239, 283
male dominance 9–10, 153, 173, 196–7, 201, 204, 221–2, 262, 269, 273, 281–3
male-dominated occupations 28–9, 39, 45, 61, 103, 110, 186, 188, 266
male organization 282–3, 289
managers 15, 38, 51, 55, 60–1, 79, 90, 102, 123, 134, 149, 217, 237, 240–6, 250, 256, 276
manual work, *see* blue-collar occupations
marginal jobs 8, 71, 99, 106, 120
market work, *see* employment
marriage 4, 18, 45, 52–3, 55, 73, 85, 94, 168, 181, 193, 197, 217–20, 268, 274–5, 284
marriage bar 59–60, 70, 107, 176
marriage career 91, 95, 99, 109, 159–63, 175, 274
marriage markets 16, 20, 37, 79, 119, 129, 159–63, 189, 193–222, 257, 262–5
masculinity 16, 65–6, 217, 283
mass media 33, 51, 73, 168
maternity leave 120–3, 243, 246, 248, 251
maternity rights 120–3, 130
Meir, Golda 188
Mexico 82, 230, 283
migration 168, 223–4
mixed occupations, *see* integrated occupations
modern society 1, 3, 7–13, 15, 17, 22, 41, 43, 56, 73, 81, 134, 194, 197, 214, 254, 263, 273, 283
Mombasa 45
mortality, *see* life expectancy
Moslem culture 11, 32, 204, 239
motherhood 5, 55, 76, 82, 90, 101, 124, 134, 156, 167, 170, 181–3, 185, 226, 235, 242, 249, 279
motivation 16–17, 37–8, 40, 47, 54, 103, 110, 138–9, 141–2, 185, 192, 234, 256, 275, 282–3, 285–6
multidisciplinary research 1, 36, 42, 73, 127, 196, 288

National Fertility Study 46
National Longitudinal Surveys (NLS) of Labour Market Behaviour 38–9, 105, 109–10, 128
natural experiments, *see* social experiments
NCDS 130–49, 219
Netherlands 8, 10, 19, 24, 33–4, 49, 52, 57–8, 64, 68–9, 81–2, 86–7, 91–2, 104, 112–13, 115–17, 119–20, 124–5, 167, 172, 174, 202–3, 213–15, 217–19, 221, 228, 230, 234, 237, 241, 262, 283, 287
New Zealand 54, 92, 172, 213, 223–4, 230–1
non-standard employment 69, 71–2
Nordic countries 5–6, 10, 32–3, 115–6, 126, 138, 226, 231, 237–43, 276, 282, 286–7; *see also* Scandinavia
North America 1, 3, 5, 43–4, 56, 69, 84, 153, 187, 238, 241, 264, 279
Norway 5, 49–51, 82, 92, 115, 118–19, 129–30, 213–15, 221, 230–1, 233, 238–43

occupations 62–8
occupational grade 61, 66, 79, 103, 115, 144, 250, 276
occupational segregation 5, 27, 40, 57, 63, 67, 101, 134, 137–8, 173, 239–40, 281–2
OECD 74, 104, 227, 229–31, 239–41, 245
official statistics 6, 8, 23, 31, 40, 172, 174
Oman 46

Panel Study of Income Dynamics (PSID) 38–9, 74, 105–7, 128
parental leave 90, 148, 172, 226, 238, 242, 246, 261
part-time work 5, 19, 30–1, 38–9, 58, 68, 70–1, 75, 83, 87, 89, 92, 99–101, 123–5, 136–7, 143–4, 147, 167, 171, 183, 228–9, 246–8, 258, 261–2, 273, 282
patriarchy 2, 7, 9–10, 14, 29, 31, 44, 60, 66, 90, 100, 105–6, 115, 153, 170, 196, 204, 221, 255, 269, 273, 276, 281–3, 288
pay, *see* earnings
pay gap 28, 36, 61, 70, 119, 133–8, 173, 195, 222, 240, 260, 284
pensions 234
Peron, Isabel 188
personality 45, 54, 186–7, 260
pharmacists 39, 72, 129, 153, 167
Philippines 264–5
physiology 63, 221, 259–61, 282
pill 44, 46–7
plastic surgery 46
Poland 58, 92, 202, 213, 221, 266
polarization 4, 8, 19, 83–156, 233, 251–2, 275, 277, 280, 283, 285, 288
policy 5–7, 10, 18, 20, 22–3, 32–3, 56, 148, 158, 163, 167, 175, 179, 192, 223–53, 256, 276–7, 280
political capital 36
political science 32, 74
politics 2, 6, 139, 158, 165, 255–6, 260, 276–7
polygamy 162
population census 23, 38, 131–4, 137, 208, 222
pornography 46
Portugal 49–52, 58, 64, 86–7, 90, 104, 129, 171–2, 230–1, 241
positive discrimination 177, 265, 269
power 9–10, 29, 36, 48, 56, 67, 195–7, 217–18, 255, 261
preferences 3, 7, 10, 13–17, 19–20, 37–8, 40, 47, 72–82, 95–8, 124, 141, 149–52, 157–92, 172, 184–9, 190, 222, 233–4, 238, 244, 251, 254–72, 275, 278, 280, 286, 288
pregnancy 48–9, 120–3, 149, 244, 274
primary earner 30–1, 41, 57, 69–70, 72, 88, 91, 229, 249, 274–5
printing 66–8
prisons of the mind 16–17
professionals/professions 15, 38–9, 51, 55, 60, 63, 65, 72, 79, 98, 102, 107, 123, 134, 148–9, 160–1, 167, 190–1, 217, 229, 241–5, 256, 276
promotion 134, 138–9, 167, 178, 243, 270, 274
pronatalist policies 11, 49, 82, 223–6
prostitution 45–6, 198
psychology 22–42, 60, 73, 170, 179–86, 192, 235, 279, 288
Puerto Rico 217

qualifications, *see* educational qualifications
queues for jobs 28–9

race 18, 32, 39, 56, 74
rape 44
rational choice theory 27, 31
recreational sex 45–6
religion 2, 32, 49, 165, 175, 194, 255–6, 277, 286
reproduction 162, 256, 281, 288–9
resegregation 39
retailing 72, 237
retirement 9, 30, 71, 164, 234, 262
Russia 11, 69, 92, 110, 215, 225–6, 241–2, 246, 264, 266, 286

sample selection bias 15, 138, 147, 285
Scandinavia 5, 33, 50, 119, 172, 237–43, 261, 271, 283; *see also* Nordic countries
school 49, 135, 188, 199, 218, 236–7
secondary earners 3, 7, 19, 30–1, 38–9, 41, 47, 57, 68–73, 79, 83, 87–8, 101, 111, 144–5, 167, 175, 232, 241, 249, 270, 274–5
secondary school 131–8, 199–200
secretary 161, 239–40
segmentation, *see* labour market segmentation
selection effects 102, 135, 179–80, 205, 273, 285
self-employment 61, 72, 98, 133, 262
serial monogamy 21, 162, 216
service sector 62–8
sex differentials 30–1, 60, 84, 104, 119,

133, 140–1, 180, 183, 190, 201–3, 256–62, 265–8, 275, 282–3
sex discrimination 2–3, 7, 29, 31, 39, 56, 138, 144, 169, 244, 270, 275–6, 282
sex ratio 129, 133, 138
sex roles 18, 27, 31–3, 47, 51, 55–6, 75, 77–80, 82, 85–7, 92–4, 99–100, 118, 127–9, 138–42, 147, 149, 153, 155, 161–2, 168, 173–4, 178, 183–4, 186, 192, 201, 217–20, 228–9, 242–3, 251, 257, 261–3, 267–9, 277
sexual activity 21, 44–5, 48, 52, 55, 260, 274, 289
sexual division of labour 29, 31, 47, 60, 73, 75, 80, 85–7, 92–4, 99–100, 118, 127–8, 142, 146, 148, 159, 173, 190, 193, 221, 228–9, 236, 238, 258, 262, 265, 268–9
sexual harassment 250
Seymour-Smith case 291
Shintoism 32
sickness 180, 234, 243, 246
Singapore 3, 163, 224, 283, 286
Slovenia 58, 92
social capital 36, 195, 285
social change 14, 18–21, 24, 31, 41, 43, 67, 273, 287–9
Social Change and Economic Life Initiative (SCELI) 100
social class 32, 72–3, 116, 118, 127, 129, 134, 141–2, 148, 175–6, 178, 194, 196–7, 200, 202, 264, 267, 286
social engineering 56–60, 227–43
social exclusion 226
social experiments 95, 279
socialism 31, 168, 172, 234, 242, 286–7
socialization 27–9, 119, 170, 185, 189, 221, 283
social policy 30, 32–4, 113, 223–53
social prestige 41
social psychology, *see* psychology
social status 29, 36–7, 41, 79, 133, 162, 197, 255, 261, 276
social stratification 2, 29, 204, 218
social welfare 48, 57, 70, 163, 225–6, 232–4, 262
sociological theory 1, 13–17, 22–42, 80, 254, 278–9
sociologists 227, 269, 288
South Africa 82
South America 1, 45, 47, 52, 266
South Korea 82
Spain 16, 49–51, 58, 69, 82, 86–7, 92, 115, 125, 129, 172, 230–1
sport 2, 6, 158, 165, 197, 255, 277
statistical averages 6, 8, 30, 127, 259, 278, 285
statistical discrimination 244
status, *see* social status
students 8, 30, 71, 120, 167, 177, 261
subordinates 261
Sudan 52
Sweden 5, 10, 31, 33–4, 49–51, 57–8, 69, 82, 89–92, 104, 113, 115–18, 129–30, 135, 169, 172, 174, 192, 202, 213, 215, 221, 224, 226–8, 230–1, 235, 238–43, 261, 266, 287
Switzerland 49–51, 202, 230–1, 241

Taiwan 202
tax, *see* income tax
teachers 166–7, 239
technological change 20–1, 44, 64–7, 289
tenure, *see* job tenure
testosterone 141, 185, 221, 259–60, 282
Thailand 264
Thatcher, Margaret 188
toyboys 201
translators 98
trade unions 31, 59, 62, 65–6, 68–71, 87, 223, 237, 245–51, 271, 275, 281–2
triangulation 36, 42, 127
Turkey 45, 224, 230
turnover rates, *see* labour turnover
two-person career 161–2, 166

United Kingdom, *see* Britain
United Nations 51
unplanned careers, *see* careers
USA 1, 3–4, 8, 17–19, 23, 32–4, 38–9, 43, 46–7, 49, 51–4, 58–62, 64, 66–9, 72, 77, 79, 82, 84–5, 87–8, 91–2, 94–6, 102, 104, 111–13, 116–18, 119–23, 126, 129–30, 149–56, 134–6, 138–9, 142, 149–56, 160, 166–7, 169, 172, 177–8, 181, 189, 196, 199–202, 206, 213–18, 220, 223–5, 228–31, 234, 239–43, 246, 254, 260, 264, 266–9, 274–7, 281–3, 285–7
utility 36

validity 11, 25, 288
values 3, 7, 11–17, 19, 31–2, 35, 37, 40, 43, 50–1, 72–82, 92, 110, 130, 163, 175, 229, 256, 260, 278, 280, 283, 286, 288
variable sociology 34–40, 188
vertical job segregation 5, 240
violence 259, 268
voluntary work 70, 92, 159

wage work, *see* employment
wars 52, 60, 64, 82, 95, 163, 167–8
wealth 52, 55, 81, 83, 115–16, 118, 156, 182, 198, 214, 255–6, 263, 266, 273, 284
welfare state 81, 171, 225, 227, 232, 237, 241, 251, 262, 286
West Indian culture 52, 266
white-collar occupations 3, 7, 43, 59, 62–8, 82, 229, 262
Women and Employment Survey 1980 (WES) 77
work-centred women/men 4, 6–11, 21, 89, 156, 164–5, 175, 178, 185, 223, 226, 237, 243–5, 249–50, 252, 254–6, 271, 274–7, 280
work commitment 6, 68, 72, 91, 125, 142, 164–5, 173, 242, 244
work experience 28, 143, 197, 284
work histories 4–6, 8, 30, 70, 103, 105–7, 127–8, 260, 273
working class 65–6
working hours 127, 135, 226, 229, 244–6, 260, 271
work orientations 32, 38, 70–1, 74, 77, 85–99, 101, 103, 138–9, 261, 282
workrates 24, 58, 68, 79, 95, 103, 112, 119–23, 227–8, 233, 238, 282, 284
World Fertility Survey (WFS) 47, 51–2, 204
World Values Survey (WVS) 55, 76, 81–2

Xaniths 46
xenophobia 33, 224

Yugoslavia 213, 221

Zaire 52